1976

be kept

Centennial

Also by William Peirce Randel

THE KU KLUX KLAN

EDWARD EGGLESTON

CENTENNIAL

American Life in 1876

by William Peirce Randel

CHILTON BOOK COMPANY

Philadelphia   New York   London

To the memory of my father
William Adonijah Randel, M.D.
1876–1960

Table of Contents

Preface *ix*

Chapter One *Not Just Another Year* *1*

Chapter Two *Centennial Ways of Life—A Sampling of Opinions* *14*

1 JOSIAH HOLLAND—DEAD CENTER *16*
2 OFFENBACH—ONCE OVER LIGHTLY *24*
3 JOHN LENG, FLYING SCOT *32*
4 NATHANIEL BISHOP AND HIS SNEAK-BOX *41*
5 ACROSS TEXAS ON HORSEBACK— COL. TAYLOR *45*
6 TWO CARPING FRENCHMEN *49*
7 MR. AND MRS. HUXLEY *59*
8 JOHN LEWIS, TRANSPLANTED ENGLISH-MAN *66*
9 EMILY IN SITKA AND LAPWAI *73*
10 JOSEPH HATTON'S FRIENDLY CHAT *77*

Chapter Three   *A Teeming Nation of Nations*   *87*
    1   CIVILIZED EAST   *94*
    2   FRONTIER   *111*
    3   WILDERNESS   *122*

Chapter Four   *The Age of Enterprise*   *157*

Chapter Five   *The Abuses of Power—A Tragedy in Three Acts*   *200*

    1   THE WHISKEY RING   *201*
    2   GRAFTERS IN THE CABINET   *207*
    3   THE DISPUTED ELECTION   *214*

Chapter Six   *The Southern Question*   *240*

Chapter Seven   *Good and Faithful Servants*   *260*

Chapter Eight   *The Exhibition*   *283*

Chapter Nine   *Quality of Life*   *307*

Chapter Ten   *The Arts, Fine and Otherwise*   *335*

    1   THE LIVELY ARTS   *335*
    2   THE VERBAL ARTS   *346*
    3   THE PLASTIC ARTS   *364*

Chapter Eleven   *A Great Year for Education*   *395*

Chapter Twelve   *A Mighty Fortress*   *434*

Bibliographical Note   *463*

Index   *465*

Preface

In 1880, after careers as, variously, preacher, editor, and novelists, Edward Eggleston turned to the pursuit that was to be his major concern until his death in 1902: the writing of history. With no formal training, he came to appreciate a point of view now common among historians, that "history is a bottomless pit." His own formulation, in a letter to his daughter, differed slightly: "New Eng. history & all colonial hist. is a horrible labyrinth." But he persevered, turning out ten solid articles in the early 1880's and two volumes shortly before his death that established his reputation as a social historian and hence as a pioneer of modern historiography.

The author's initial acknowledgment of gratitude, accordingly, must be to Eggleston, without whose example his biographer would have hesitated to venture into a discipline academically not his own. The author's second basic debt is to another kind of pioneer, the late Tremaine McDowell in particular, who has argued the feasibility and desirability of surveying all facets of American civilization. Something of the same idea may be found in Eggleston's preface to his third novel, in 1873: "I have wished to make my stories of value as a contribution to the history of civilization in America." This sentence, with only slight alteration, expresses my own desire, to add to the literature of American Studies by examining a single year in American life.

In ways both more general and more specific, the source citations reveal an enormous debt to the community of scholars, dead and living, whose special studies have cast light in the labyrinth. The libraries (and librarians) most often drawn upon have been those at Cornell, Harvard, Bowdoin, Florida State, and Maine; scores of other libraries have helped through our efficient national system of inter-library loans.

Students and colleagues over the years, especially my American Studies classes at Florida State University and the University of Wyoming, have been more helpful than they may realize. As for the one person who has helped the most, the author has consistently advised every aspiring academic to marry a librarian.

Waterboro Old Corner   W. P. R.

Centennial

Not Just
Another Year

"THE watch-night services at the depot church were attended to-night by an immense audience, every foot of space being occupied. Mr. Sankey sang several of his popular hymns, and Mr. Moody preached an interesting sermon. When the first service was over but few withdrew. As the hour of 12 arrived a prayer meeting was held."

This news item in the St. Paul, Minnesota, *Pioneer-Press*, reported an event that took place in Philadelphia, for everything that the evangelical team of Moody and Sankey did was automatically news everywhere. Their audience was probably the largest in the nation that night, New Year's Eve, 1875, but similar services were held in churches throughout the land.

The national exuberance as 1875 yielded to 1876 was genuine and unlimited. The popular mood was one of pride and confidence. America's independence had survived its first century, the nation's great progress was obvious, and the future seemed assured. It was a time to make merry as never before. Philadelphians who did not thrill to Sankey's saccharine hymns and

Moody's earthly eloquence sought less spiritual food and drink. A good many no doubt stepped out of doors into the balmy midnight to hear the incredible effect reported by John Lewis, a visiting New Yorker:

> At N Y eve at 12 o'clock we were all called out to listen to the most extraordinary noise ever heard. It had been arranged that at that hour every bell, whistle, or other instrument that would make a noise should be put into requisition &c. Phila is a *great* Railroad place and has many thousands of work-shops—also Churches. The effect was wonderfull, not loud, being scattered—rather melancholy, seeming as if some terrible disaster were occurring, such as the sacking of a city, and the sound of a vast multitude wailing & shrieking at a distance.[1]

Cincinnati put on a magnificent fireworks display, and Cleveland, the nation's oil capital, topped a mammoth bonfire with twenty barrels of crude petroleum. In New York, an ocean liner at its North River berth blasted its whistle for a solid half-hour, drowning out the bells that crowds had stood waiting to hear at downtown churches. Everywhere, if the newspapers reported correctly, bell ropes were pulled with unusual fervor, factory whistles blew louder and longer, public squares were packed as never before. The parades were the most colorful, the orations grandiloquent. For those Americans who saw in the century's progress the result of divine guidance and favor, deity itself could not have been unaware of the great show.

The New York *Herald* reported sumptuous feasting on New Year's Day, from the shanties of Mackerelville to the mansions of Fifth Avenue, and noted a good deal of promenading in the afternoon. A big dinner was given the boys at the Children's Aid Society on Rivington Street, four hundred old tars banqueted at Sailors' Snug Harbor on Staten Island, and the Barge Office was the setting for a Customs House party. In Washington, President and Mrs. Grant received in the Blue Room of the White House, and later the various cabinet officers held receptions of their own. On Sunday the common theme of sermons and editorials was the new dawn of hope and the meaning of the Centennial. As weekends go, it was a smashing success.

In St. Paul the *Pioneer-Press* exuded a local pride that was not an uncommon corollary of national pride. The state of Minnesota, the editor pointed out, though only seventeen years old, was already larger in population than any of the original colonies had been in 1776. At the current rate of growth, St. Paul would surely outstrip Philadelphia by 1976, when the nation's population would reach several hundred million. All that St. Paul needed was the completion of canals linking the Mississippi to Lake Superior and the Red River of the North. In New York the *Herald* made no such extravagant prophecies but did offer a sanguine lead editorial: "The last hundred years have been the most fruitful and the most glorious period of equal length in the history of the human race," as evidenced by the political progress of the cities, the many scientific advances, the abolition of slavery, and the growth of newspaper influence. "We are entering a year which will be ever memorable in our annals and which the nation has made fitting preparations to celebrate. . . . The HERALD of 1876 will furnish all the material needed by future historians for giving a lively picture of what the American people did on the first centennial of their independence."

Other editors were equally sanguine; so were preachers and orators and authors. So much had been done since 1776 that any friction that might exist in the land could be dismissed, for the moment, as illusory. The public exuberance was spontaneous, and it was real—the surface manifestation of a deeply felt and universally shared sense of national achievement, which yielded a rare degree of unity. Only an event of the first magnitude could have united the forty-odd million Centennial Americans in taking a backward look, could make them forget, however briefly, their inter-group conflicts and whatever in their recent past might be ugly and divisive. The hundredth anniversary of the signing of the Declaration of Independence was perhaps the *only* event that could have united so diverse a population.

The planning of local celebrations—parades, orations, fireworks, and the erection of liberty poles—involved a certain risk: any sudden worsening of the depression that had begun in 1873 could at any time destroy the patriotic impulse. The great Centennial Exhibition in Philadelphia, by far the largest of all the projects planned in celebration of the nation's first great birthday, ran the greatest risk of all, for it demanded detailed thinking well in advance and the accumulation and expenditure of large sums of money. There have been bigger, more spectacular, and more profitable world's fairs but none more indigenous, more *American,* than the Centennial Exhibition of 1876, which succeeded as well as it did partly because of its location at Philadelphia, where the Declaration had been signed, and partly because its promoters skillfully reiterated its purpose as the central focus of Centennial attention.

The Exhibition, apart from the foreign exhibits, was intended to put on proud display the manifold achievements of the American people in their first century of independence. Planned and carried to completion as an exhibit of what Centennial America viewed with greatest pride, it serves in retrospect as a peculiarly revealing portrait of the faults and the virtues, the triumphs and the failures, of the culture it sought to epitomize. Most critics have condemned it severely, and perhaps unfairly. It is not the intention here, however, either to support or oppose these critics. There is much more value in viewing the Exhibition as a mirror of the age, revealing better than any other single exhibit what America and Americans were like in 1876. If machinery was thought to need Greek and Roman decoration, the motive for decorating is more important than the actual designs that were used. And if, as was generally true, the costliest objects on display were the worst offenders against esthetic principles, if "art" was lavished alike on objects of daily practicality and those of no utility whatsoever, then this can be regarded simply as one more facet of Centennial thinking. The decision against architectural uniformity for the Exhibition's buildings produced a motley of styles that has often been condemned but, for our purposes, was fortunate in offering a variety of clues to contemporary taste.

Important as it was in its time, however, the Centennial Exhibition, as an aid to latter-day efforts to reconstruct Centennial realities, had severe limitations. It could contrast the crudities of 1776 with the marvels of 1876, but as a record of a century's progress it needed many complements. Popular and learned journals filled one of the gaps with their lengthy reviews of American achievements in literature and education, technology and speculative thought. All too often in these reviews can be detected a certain smugness, as if the present—1876—represented the very pinnacle of human progress. If more recent writers have held up to contempt the foibles of the 1870s, writers in 1876 showed a comparable contempt for their own remote past. One of the lengthiest reviews presented by any profession was a symposium that ran through several issues of the *American Journal of Medical Sciences,* which detailed the century's developments in surgery, medical methods, pharmaceuticals, and hospital methods. Pride in achievement was nowhere else more apparent. With few exceptions the contributors showed only scorn for medical practice in 1776 and the early nineteenth century. One man was modest enough to suggest that the methods of 1876 would one day be held up to equal scorn; but like other Americans considering the future, most members of the medical profession saw the future only as a limited extension of the wonderful present. By and large it was a year of astonishing complacency: contemplating the vast and rapid changes of the past century did not, for some reason, yield the notion of equally vast and rapid changes in the future. It is at least conceivable that the dominant group—the contemporary "Establishment"—sensed, however dimly, that continuing rapid change would diminish its dominance. But it seems more reasonable to link the complacency to the limited perspective that is one clearly discernible Centennial trait.

Without any reliable means for objective judgment of the past, or for the more difficult task of projecting beyond the present, Centennial Americans were probably more susceptible to a mystical view of past events than their great-grandchildren, and great-great grandchildren, are in an age when supernaturalism has been largely rejected. Nonogenarians in 1876 could recall the death of George Washington, on December 14, 1799—the only President to die in the eighteenth century. A much larger proportion of the population could remember July 4, 1826, exactly half a century after the signing of the Declaration, when America's second and third Presidents, John Adams and Thomas Jefferson, died a few hours apart. How could that be mere coincidence? In 1876 there were no living ex-Presidents to die at auspicious moments, a fact that confirmed, for the credulous, that later Presidents were not the demigods the origi-

nal trinity had been. Caught up as human beings are by the
number systems of their own devising, the rounding of a perfect
century itself took on a mystic significance, awesome enough
without another sign from heaven. A New York clergyman, the
Rev. Dr. Cummings, did predict the end of the world on the
Centennial Fourth, but this was going too far and prompted an
editorial suggestion that he belonged in an asylum.

The signs from heaven, for Americans of the dominant class,
at least, were ample enough in the growing national wealth, the
industrial advances, and all the other manifold measures of progress. Europe had held its breath in the early years of the republic,
dubious of the success of a nation so conceived and so dedicated,
or hoping for its failure. But now, at the hundred-year mark,
there could be little doubt that the experiment had succeeded,
and numerous foreign countries were happy to join in celebrating that success by sending both products and eminent representatives to the Exhibition. Dom Pedro, Emperor of Brazil, was
only the most impressive of the many visiting dignitaries; he was
also the most popular, often, on the fair grounds, becoming a
major attraction himself.

But Dom Pedro was there to enjoy, not to criticize; if he had
any doubts about the American system he kept them urbanely to
himself. Criticism of the Exhibition came instead from a few
plain-speaking Americans, like the prominent author and critic
William Dean Howells, who insisted on raising embarrassing
questions: why, for example, was there a Women's Pavilion but
not one for men? He joined other reporters, too, in sniping at
President Grant, whose spoken inanities at some ceremonial moments were bad enough, but whose conspicuous absence at
others was worse.

No other President, perhaps, has completed his tenure of
office in such ignominy, no other has had to serve as scapegoat
for so shameful a collapse of official morality, as Ulysses S.
Grant. It is questionable, however, whether judgments of the
Exhibition, and of the Centennial Year itself, should have been
colored as much as they were in 1876, and have been since, by
the harsh facts of what we call "Grantism." In a way, what we
may be confronted with is a pendulum shift from the vast
optimism of New Year's to the black despair produced by the

revelations of corruption in the Grant administration which came so early in the new year. The criminality within Grant's cabinet was serious, of course, but it was only one part of Centennial life, and it touched relatively few people. To judge the year by Grantism is no more justifiable than to suppose that the Centennial Exhibition gave a valid total picture of Centennial America.

The New Year's revelers were not unaware of unsavory conditions in the government; but these were not regarded as so unusual or difficult to live with that they could not be forgotten in the general holiday glow. Not for another two months would the worst be known, when the emerging facts were to cause a scandal so great that it easily exceeded what citizens could accept as normal in corruption. But in 1876 the government was far from being the force in everybody's lives that it has since become, and it could be ignored, much of the time, by most of the people. Dominant economic groups insisted that it remain weak, in the laissez-faire tradition; and relatively speaking, it *was* weak. But it must be understood that what Americans were celebrating in 1876 was the centennial not of the institution of the federal government, but of the nation's independence.

Who can recall, offhand, the month and day of the signing of the Constitution—or even the year? What American does not remember the Fourth of July, 1776? The Constitution is the document we all live by: every citizen entering military service must swear to obey and defend it; so must every alien in the process of being naturalized; so must every elected official assuming office, from President to rural postmaster; so must every applicant for a passport. Nobody ever has to swear support of the Declaration of Independence; it is actually a dead letter, a bill of particulars, drawn up to justify open resistance to established authority, which lost its practical relevance once the colonists won the Revolutionary War. Even so, it is the Declaration, and not the Constitution which remains forever vibrant for its defiance of arbitrary power and for its bold assertion of individual freedom. Its wording is less to us, far less, than the meaning we ascribe to it, the insistence, termed idealistic in political philosophy, that the real nation transcends its government and would survive even if the government should collapse. The key to that transcendence, reflected in our preferring "America" to "the United States," is our stubborn hope for the greatest possible individual freedom, a hope that brings us often into conflict with the government based on the Constitution. Until Americans become a breed quite different from what they always have been, their prime emotional commitment will be to the Declaration of Independence. Small wonder, then, that our great patriotic holiday is the Fourth of July.

As with the day, so with the year. Its very luster in the eighteenth century gave its recurrence in the nineteenth an almost mystical significance. A few people put logic ahead of sentiment to argue that 1889, when the Constitution became operative, was the proper centennial of the republic. And the *Quarterly Review* offered a British opinion that 1883, centennial of the restoration of peace, would be a better year for international celebrating. Reasonable suggestions, both of them, but they missed the point: just as the Fourth of July has always been *the day* for patriotic exuberance, 1876 was *the year* in its century that could have genuine popular appeal. At a time when American history was not being systematically taught, the one great electrifying event, undimmed by time, was the signing of the Declaration.

For Americans then living, it was this rounding out of a century that gave 1876 its initial great importance. For us in a later age, the interplay of this awareness with the actual events of the year makes it worth our examination. What happened in 1876 to justify the pride in a century of progress? And what if the actual events were such as to crush that pride, to replace it with shame, and to make a mockery of memories and dreams alike? In sober fact, it turned out to be a year of humiliating exposures, and it closed under the dark cloud of a disputed election. If the high hopes and confidence with which the year opened spell a kind of national innocence, their dispersal, under the hammer-blows of scandal, may mark the end of innocence —or, at least, of a particular kind of innocence, the Centennial variety.

One historian, writing in the 1890s, observed that in 1876 "the nation suddenly awakened to the fact that a hundred years had passed since the struggle for independence began, and throughout the land every citizen, rich and poor, every State, small and great, felt in lesser or greater degree a desire to commemorate the first century of existence as a united people." [2] A third of a century later, in 1927, Allan Nevins was much less neutral in his considered judgment of 1876: "It was a year," he wrote,

> to make Americans ashamed rather than proud; and the most hopeful fact of the time was that this sense of shame, this appreciation of the contrast between the pretentious national Exhibition and the seamy, shabby aspect of American life, was earnestly expressed. . . . The pulpit, the civic organizations, the professional leaders, the men of letters of the nation, all showed their mortification and resentment. The country was awakening, and the fact was itself a sign of convalescence from the long moral sickness which had followed the war. . . . An era of reform was about to open. [3]

Professor Nevins was right about the shame felt by many of the best people; if he was equally correct in pinpointing 1876 as the moment when the nation's conscience awoke and demanded reform, we have one of the best reasons for taking a close look at the year. It is possible, however, that the year and the period it belongs to have been magnified in their wickedness out of all proportion, and that Nevins in his scholarly way, was influenced by the debunking atmosphere of the 1920's that nurtured so many popular studies of the colorful entrepreneurs of fifty years before: books with such titles as *Diamond Jim, Incredible Carnegie, Morgan the Magnificent, Imperial Hearst, Lords of Creation, The Robber Barons,* and *The Dreadful Decade.* Harshest of all, though not confined to the post–Civil War period, was a slightly older book, *The History of the Great American Fortunes* by Gustavus Myers, who had not a single good word to say about anybody with money. The "compulsion to hate" that can be seen in the genre has given way to a milder, more rational treatment, as in Stewart Holbrook's *Age of the Moguls,* but the sheer number of the exposé biographies and period studies has yielded a general popular impression that the quarter-century following the Civil War was the low ebb of American history.

It *was* a time when political and business morality approached rock bottom, yet there were honest men, too. The managers of the Centennial Exhibition were not corrupt, and they probably represented a much larger fraction of the business community in 1876 than we have been led to suppose. The member of Congress who uncovered the gross corruption of Grant's cabinet members must have been honest, unless we adopt the cynical view, which Grant himself adopted, that the investigations were for partisan ends. And finally, the desire for reform, as Nevins remarked, was itself a good sign; a nation overwhelmingly corrupt would hardly have been ashamed enough to demand a higher level of political behavior.

Men did feel ashamed of their country in 1876, in proportion to the sensitivity of their characters. What produced a special bitterness was the lack of perspective, for the general awareness of history was almost wholly without precedent. In these latter years of the twentieth century, with another centennial just ahead, it may be hard to believe that Americans were ever so naïve or so unaware of having a history. The truth is that in 1876 the nation's schools and even the colleges paid scant attention, if any at all, to American history. Until the last decades of the nineteenth century, history was less a profession than an avocation of gentlemen scholars. Nor did patriotic organizations exist to campaign for history-consciousness: the Daughters of the American Revolution, to cite a conspicuous example, did not come into being until 1890. The American Historical Association is only six years older.

American history had been written before 1876, of course, but the representative author was George Bancroft, famed for his compulsion to prove divine guidance of American affairs, just as William Bradford and Cotton Mather had sought to do in colonial New England. The most gifted historians—Prescott, Parkman, and Motley—were pursuing what their group biographer, David Levin, aptly calls "history as romantic art": their concern was not the emergence of the American people but the colorful exploits of Spanish, Indian, and Dutch adventurers. Local history flourished, meanwhile, sponsored by private historical societies and perpetuating a kind of ancestor worship. Far from contributing to the panorama of a continental nation, it reflected a provincialism that still served in 1876—if not after 1900—to limit the outlook of most Americans.

The foregoing applies to Americans of older stock, chiefly English, whose forebears had made the history that was not being taught in 1876. Another sizable element of the population —soon to be, if not already, the statistical majority—were even less aware of American history. The past, for these millions of recent immigrants, was something to be forgotten as soon as possible: the poverty in Europe they had sought to escape; the miseries of steerage passage across the Atlantic; the cultural shock of the first landing in an alien, apparently indifferent, land; and the long slow struggle for something like security. For them, the precarious present was better than the remembered past, but it was the future that really mattered—not their own future but that of their children and their children's children. Whatever the Anglo-Americans took pride in, as achievements to be commemorated at the Centennial Exhibition, was likely as not part of a pattern that would have to be changed if the dreams of the newer Americans were to have any chance of coming true. To the older Americans, in contrast, their beloved cultural pattern was something to defend from subversion by these masses, whom they would never quite accept as "real" Americans.

Not all the older Americans enjoyed such towering advantage over the newcomers. Some had fallen sharply behind in the general economic progress. Every successful family had its poor relations, every community its sizable element known as "the poor." In the South they were identified as "poor whites" and were supposedly incapable of ever escaping the label. There was no great uneasiness about the widespread poverty, however, no sense that society had any responsibility for its less affluent members. In a land of unlimited opportunity, as Poor Richard had said and as the dominant class of Centennial Americans firmly believed, poverty was a man's own fault, prima facie evidence of depravity.

Centennial theory was also comfortable about the position in the nation of the Negroes who then comprised about a tenth of the population. God had intended them to be inferior just as he had intended the Anglo-Saxons to be the finest members of the human race. In their vast generosity the Anglo-Americans had given the Negroes their freedom; the idea of granting anything more than that, anything like social or economic equality, was as radical a notion as denying the divine right of property. The radicalism of the Abolitionists before the Civil War had spent its force, and so had the Radicalism of Reconstruction: by 1876 the nation had tired of trying to enforce racial equality in the South, and the federal government itself was on the verge of abandoning the effort.

In the spirit of objective inquiry, it is hard to imagine that the sense of national progress, so central to the concept of Centennial commemoration, was shared equally by all in the population. Poor whites, Negroes, Chinese railroad workers on the Pacific Coast, Mexicans in Texas, Indians, and recent immigrants were hardly in a position, economically or socially, to feel any deep gratification about the progress of a century. Such an attitude, had it been voiced, to the nation's spokesmen would have had a ready answer: such elements in the population were not real Americans, and what they might think did not count. The notion persists even today, of course, that some of us are more genuinely American than others. It is held especially by those who have never had their Americanism challenged, and who have never known, though their grandparents may have, what it means to face hostility and discrimination. But in 1876 the cleavage was much sharper: there were the "real" Americans, dominant in every compartment of national life, and the others, whose relative unsuccess, coupled with their inability to become assimilated, readily justified their exclusion. For these groups who lived beyond the pale of acceptance, 1876 *was* just another year, one of struggling to gain what the "real" Americans already had. And for the dominant group, in one respect, it was also just another year, one of assuming its own continued dominance.

But this is generalizing in advance of the evidence. What was the country really like in 1876? What were the people doing and thinking? What changes were at work, boldly or subtly, in reshaping the culture? What theories maintained their influence on behavior, and what myths? Did the arts play an important role? Was education geared to the past or to the future? Such questions could be multiplied; and it is easier to state them than to find good answers.

One thing seems certain: no single contemporary observer could capture the whole of Centennial America; the nation was simply too vast and too varied. Even the Centennial Exhibition, with all its multiform displays, could give only a partial picture. Our quest for comprehensiveness may begin, however, with some excerpts from published reports, by ten American and foreign observers of the day—if only to show how elusive Centennial America really was.

Footnotes for Chapter One
NOT JUST ANOTHER YEAR

1. John Lewis to his brother in England, January 20, 1876, in the Lewis Letters, Collection of Regional History, Cornell University.

2. A. Howard Clark, Assistant Secretary and Curator of the American Historical Association, in the A H A *Annual Report* for 1894, p. 549.

3. Allan Nevins, *The Emergence of Modern America, 1865–1878*, Vol. 8 of *History of American Life* (New York: Macmillan, 1927), p. 313.

Centennial
Ways of Life—
A Sampling
of Opinions

CENTENNIAL AMERICANS, preoccupied with their own affairs, were perhaps not fully aware of the deep and enduring interest of foreigners in the United States of America as an experiment in democracy. This interest was greatest in Europe, not only because most Americans were of European extraction, but also because of a general European sense that the New World, and the United States in particular, was an extension of Western civilization, its latest and geographically its greatest expansion. For many Europeans, the American experiment was exhilarating, a rare opportunity for renewal and redirection. For the less romantic-minded, it represented, at least, a postponement of inevitable decline—for a few more centuries, perhaps. No Arnold Toynbee existed in 1876 to formulate a cyclic theory, but Walt Whitman had expressed it, enthusiastically, in his "Passage to India." Thus, excitement about the progress of the United States in the century since independence was not felt by Americans alone. To countless people in the western world, here, on these shores, lay the hope of the future.

By 1876, many visitors to America had already collected their impressions of the States in volumes that sold readily in Europe. It is our misfortune, as students of Centennial America, that no foreign observer in that particular year produced so important a book as Alexis de Tocqueveile's *Democracy in America* (1835). There was not even so offensive a book as Mrs. Trollope's *Domestic Manners of the Americans* (1832) or the *American Notes* of Charles Dickens (1842). By 1876, it is true, the American attitude toward foreign criticism was one of extreme complacency coupled with indifference or even contempt for foreign ideas of whatever sort. But the interest abroad held constant, and the year produced its quota of books based on visits to America, some of which are excerpted and described in this chapter.

Certain Americans also traveled in 1876, visiting different parts of the nation and collecting their impressions. Again, they saw things in their own individual ways, whether in the wilds of Texas, or down the Mississippi, or at an army post in Idaho. Professional reporters, like Donald Grant Mitchell and William Dean Howells, chose to confine their impressions to the Centennial Exhibition; we may regret that no competent American author spent the year, or any part of it, trying to see the country as it was, in all its sections, with all its diversity.

The sampling of writings that follows can therefore hardly be deemed an adequate, inclusive portrait of the ways Americans lived in 1876. But neither could a much larger sampling; for the one fact that quickly emerges is the great diversity—in 1876 as today—of American life. Howells was perhaps the one American who might have come close to capturing that diversity in print; or perhaps Mark Twain. But Twain was busy completing *Tom Sawyer*, a novel set in just one of the nation's numerous sections.

Assuming, however, honest reporting without intention of deceit, these samples do reveal what a few people considered worth saying about America in its Centennial year—one hundred years after the Declaration that gave it birth.

I

JOSIAH GILBERT HOLLAND –
DEAD CENTER

The author and journalist Josiah Gilbert Holland (1819–1881) ably represented what was in his time the dominant element in American society. Hardly representative of the population as a whole but constituting what Holland considered its healthy core, this segment was conservative, religiously orthodox, moral, complacent, self-sufficient in their farm and village homes, reasonable comfortable, and uneasy about change. It is doubtful whether any other man in the intellectual circles of 1876 so closely reflected the thinking patterns and prejudices of this class, or reaped so fully the harvest of its approval, as Josiah Gilbert Holland. As a voice of the dominant group he was incomparable.

Holland was born the same year as Walt Whitman and Herman Melville, neither of whom ever tasted the sweets of success as he did, perhaps, because neither wrote what the nation's readers cared so much about. After several false starts towards a career, including the study of medicine and the superintending of schools in Vicksburg, Mississippi, Holland finally found his proper niche when, in 1870, he helped found *Scribner's Monthly*, which he edited with great competence until his death in 1881. In addition, he developed a considerable reputation as the author of volumes of poetry and essays, and several successful novels, often signed by his pen-name, Timothy Titcomb. Hardly anybody today reads of his own volition what is considered the best of Holland's novels, *Seven Oaks* (1875), or for that matter, anything else that Holland ever wrote. But his Centennial production, *Every-Day Topics*,[1] has a secure place among the unread masterworks of the self-satisfied and the didactic. No book, moreover, so eloquently betrays its period by not giving a true picture of it.

If on any issue an ambiguous position was possible, Holland could find it. In a section of *Every-Day Topics* titled "Amusements," for example, he began with a sprightly criticism of the churches for forbidding their members to attend the theatre. But he quickly shifted his ground: theatres had brought condemnation upon themselves by such things as "half nude dancing girls," "profanity and poorly disguised obscenity," and the like. Card playing, until recently banned in "every Christian household," was no longer considered dangerous in 1876; while billiards, also condemned in the recent past, was on the rebound: "Now a billiard-table is in nearly every house that can afford one."

Novels had also improved: "They have become the sources of moral, political, and social instruction." (Since Holland himself was writing novels, he presumably had to assume this stance.) "The novel has become, for good or evil, the daily food of the civilized world," and is social history; it is, in fact, "the only social history we have." Historians sometimes tell *lies*, novelists never do. True, there were many bad novels, but these were read only by bad people. Sooner or later, he was confident, the current flood of trash would come to an end.

Holland assigned a lofty purpose to writers; but readers had a role to play, too: "The golden age of American literature can never dawn until the world has learned to look upon the literary class as its helper, its inspirer, its leader in culture and thought; and it can never learn to look thus upon that class until it has been ministered to in all its wants by direct purpose, in simple things as well as in sublime." He was more explicit in his opinion of Walt Whitman, an opinion shared by Bayard Taylor and other stalwarts of decency and tradition. "We can imagine no good to come from 'attaining' a style by studying other men, except, perhaps, to cover up the coxcombry of such writers as Willis, the rhythmical follies of such men as Poe, or the affected barbarisms of—Mr. Emerson knows who, because he once did the world great mischief by praising him."

Writers, like other men, had to work at their craft: "He who becomes soured by toil shows that he is not fit for prosperity, and not to be trusted with it." Poe, presumably, had dissipated his genius by his poor work habits. "What," Holland asked, "could Poe not have done with Mr. Longfellow's habit?" He summed up this subject by remarking that the basis of all good style is formed by "simplicity, directness, perspicacity, and perspicuity."

Only by implication did Holland refer to Poe's notorious vices: he was zeroing in on that article of orthodox faith, now labeled the Puritan Ethic, that equated hard work with success and failure with inadequate piety. The principle had no exceptions: "No man now standing on an eminence of influence and power, and doing great work, has arrived at his position by going up an elevator. He took the stairway, step by step. He climbed the rocks, often with bleeding hands."

Just thirteen pages earlier, however, he had mourned the decline of the habit of play. "The great difficulty with us all," he observed, "is that we do not play enough." We work too hard, for too much of our lives, with the result that "it is all a man's life is worth to drop out of active employment." Holland's logic, however, takes another twist as he refers to famous men: the late Mr. Astor, he announced, "undoubtedly prolonged his life by his steady adherence to business, . . . while Commodore Vanderbilt, now more than eighty years old, is a notable example of healthy powers, prolonged by use."

Unless a man is named Astor or Vanderbilt, Holland seems to be saying, all work and no play makes him a dull boy. The quest for wealth also reduces the moral fiber of the public at large. "There is moral rottenness in every quarter" and "a low condition of public morality."

Corporations were everywhere considered fair game for plunder, by too large a number of the population. It took a really great crime, like the thievery of the Tweed Ring, to rouse public indignation. Much of the blame, he insisted, was assignable to widespread complacency: "Dishonesty in our Government and dishonesty in all our corporate concerns is based on the loose ideas of honesty entertained by our people." "Corrupt men are the offspring of a corrupt society."

Holland had a ready prescription for our ailing politics: "What we really want is gentlemen in politics." Congress had plenty of knowledge and culture but was lacking in principle. The most basic reason for the low state of official morality was that most men sought office for their personal advantage and not at all to promote the public good. "The bane of the republic is office-seeking." Gentlemen, presumably, would never actively seek an office. This problem perplexed Holland deeply, and forced him to consider progress itself, which has always been taken for granted, in the general American mythology, as a constant.

> Progress has doubtless been made in many things. We are richer, better clothed, better housed, better fed and better educated than we used to be . . . but during the past twenty-five years we judge that we have made no improvements in the typical American gentlemen. . . . The restless, greedy, grasping, time-serving spirit of our generation has vitiated and degraded this type. . . . Progress cannot be reckoned in railroads and steamboats, or counted in money, or decided in any way by the census tables. Are we producing better children and better men and women? This is the question which decides everything.

Holland did not, to his credit, follow the easy course of blaming everything on the wickedness of the city. After all, most men active in New York were, like himself, country-born; and if cities were corrupt, the transplants from the country shared some of the blame. At one point in his book, however, he did make a pronouncement about the urban-rural relationship: "No man is fit for the literary or the productively intellectual life of the city who has not had either a country training, or, for a considerable period of his life, direct and sympathetic association with nature." If anything he ever wrote would please his readers, this would.

Holland expressed himself (and his class) more confidently in regard to organized labor. "A laborer who will join a band of fellow-craftsmen in the attempt to extort an increase of wages from an employer who uses him well in adversity and fairly in prosperity, surrenders his manhood, either to his own selfishness, or to the despotism of his fellows." The word "extort" is crucial; men of Holland's mentality—and such men held the economic power—never saw any extortion in the prevailing exploitation of labor. Like others who addressed themselves to this question, including such liberals as Francis A. Walker and Washington

Gladden, Holland advised "the capitalist and the laborer to learn that they are brethren, and dependent in many ways upon one another." But he urged laborers to recognize and appreciate the heavy responsibilities assumed by capital—paying all the taxes, taking all the risks, organizing the industry, and supporting charities.

Holland was not a college man, but he had strong notions about coeducation. Men and women differed, that was all there was to it, and the idea of educating them in the same classroom was repugnant. "Now if any college is adapted just as well to the training of young women as of young men, it is well adapted to the training of neither. . . . The claiming of places for women in young men's colleges as a right, and the denunciation of their exclusion as a wrong to woman, are the special functions of fanatics and fools. . . . There are no wise fathers and mothers who would not prefer Vassar or Holyoke to Harvard or Yale as always will until that millennium comes, whose feet are con-

On the question of the vote for women, Holland was equally firm: "Woman cannot afford the ballot. It would tie her hands, weaken her influence, destroy her disinterestedness in the treatment of all public questions, and open into the beautiful realms of her moral power ten thousand streams of weakness and corruption."

Even greater earnestness attached to Holland's thinking about liquor. Sixty thousand men died each year of the effects of alcohol; or so he said. The drinking problem topped all other problems: "The question of American slavery was never anything but a baby by the side of this." No man alive, Holland was certain, could drink even a glass of wine without *some* bad effect. Certain people insisted that beer and wine were less harmful than whiskey, but he knew better: "They are all to be lumped together. They are all opposed to sobriety." The United States would rapidly become the world's richest nation if everybody stopped drinking altogether; "twenty-five years of total abstinence" would do the trick.

American women were the most beautiful in the world, for one reason alone—they did not drink. American males didn't need to, either: "There is not a country on the face of the earth where stimulants are needed so little, and where they are capable of doing so much mischief, as in our own. Our sparkling, sunny atmosphere, and the myriad incentives to hope and enterprise in our circumstances, are stimulants of God's own appointment for the American people." Holland was convinced that either Christianity would destroy drinking, or drinking would destroy Christianity; the two were totally incompatible and mutually destructive. Yet custom forced people to drink and to serve alcoholic beverages at social gatherings; people even joked about the matter, he noted. His greatest triumph in rhetoric, perhaps falls within this section on liquor: "The men who make a jest of water-drinking, all know perfectly well that wine and strong drink always have done more harm than good in the world, and always will until that millennium comes, whose feet are constantly tripped from under it by the drunkards that lie prone in its path."

A New Yorker by choice, Holland reported, no doubt accurately, a glaring contrast between the best and the worst things within the city. The Fulton Fish Market particularly repelled him; so did the rotting wharves, the unpaved streets, and the garbage and ashes dumped in the gutter and not carted off. Central Park, however, was the world's best, superior, in his judgment, to Berlin's Thiergarten, the Champs Elysées in Paris, or Hyde Park in London. And some of the city's churches were magnificent.

It was on the subject of churches that Holland expressed himself with the least deference to his middle-class concepts. The preacher he singled out for praise was not one of the fashionable pulpit orators but Dwight L. Moody, who, as an evangelist, was a transient with slight interest in fashion or wealth. But what a transient! "Mr. Tyndall and Mr. Huxley and Mr. Herbert Spencer," Holland wrote, "were not very much in men's minds, when Mr. Moody was around." Toward the established churches in the city, moreover, Holland was unusually critical. "There is one sad fact that stares the churches of this city, and of all other American cities in the face, viz., that Christianity is not preached to the poor. If we step into almost any church on Fifth and Madison Avenues, on any Sunday, we shall find there a well-dressed crowd, or a thinly scattered company of fashionable people, and almost no poor people at all."

Many of the rich churches maintained missions in the slums, he acknowledged, but these same rich churches would not have welcomed to their own services the poor who attended the missions. In general, America's poor were kept at a distance, and had little chance for the benefits of religion. "The poor have not come into the churches of the rich, and few of them, comparatively, have had the Gospel preached to them. . . . The high and the humble, who, if anywhere in the world, should come together in the churches, have kept themselves separate."

The next-to-last essay in *Every-Day Topics* is "The American Restaurant," and on no other subject did Holland express himself more indignantly. The essay is quoted here at some length because almost every Centennial observer had something to say about public eating in America.

> The typical American restaurant is an establishment quite as well individualized, and quite as characteristic, as anything of the kind to be found in the world. The French *café*, the German beer-garden, and the English chop-house, all have their characteristic habits, appearance, and manners; but the American restaurant is like neither of them. It can only be conducted by an American, and, we regret to say, it can only be frequented and enjoyed by Americans of the second and lower grades. The aim of the conductor seems to be to sell the greatest amount of good in the shortest possible time—an aim which the guests invariably second, by eating as rapidly as possible. We have seen, in a Broadway restaurant, a table surrounded by men, all eating with their hats on, while genuine ladies, elegantly dressed, occupied the next table, within three feet of them. In this restaurant there was as much din in the ordering of dishes and the clash of plates and knives and forks, as if a brass band had been in full blast. Every dish was placed before the guests with a bang. The noise, the bustle, the hurry, in such a place, at dinner time, can only be compared to that which occurs when the animals are fed in Barnum's caravan. We do not exaggerate when we say that the American restaurant is the worst-mannered place ever visited by decent people. No decent American ever goes into one when he can help it, and comparatively few decent people know how very indecent it is.
> Our best hotels have no equals in the world. . . . Our best

restaurants are mainly kept by foreigners, or, if not, are modeled upon the French type. Nowhere in the world can there be found better cooking, more quiet and leisurely manners, or better service, than in the restaurants of the hotels above alluded to, or the best class of eating-houses. These, however, are direct or indirect importations; while the American restaurant, pure and proper, serves the needs of the great multitude of business men—clerks, porters, and upper-class laborers generally. These do not eat—they feed. Thousands of them would regard it as an affectation of gentility to remove their hats while feeding; and they sit down, order their dinner, which,—pudding, pastry, vegetables, and meat, —is all placed before them in one batch, and then "pitch in." The lack of courtesy, of dignity, of ordinary tokens even of self-respect, would be amusing if it were not so humiliating. . . .

The average American, in the average American restaurant, eats his dinner in the average time of six minutes and forty-five seconds. He bolts into the door, bolts his dinner, and then bolts out. . . . A favorite method of devouring oysters is to stand, or to sit on a high stool, always with the hat on;—oysters on the half-shell and the eater under a half-shell.

So much for Josiah Gilbert Holland. Edward Eggleston, his close contemporary and possessor of many of the same conventional views, described Holland as a moralist, not an artist,[2] but added that readers seemed to like his moralizing even though the critics condemned it. Holland's most popular novel, *Sevenoaks* (1875), published under his pseudonym Timothy Titcomb, is, like his other fiction, a kind of prolonged sermon, or an *Every-Day Topics* in novel form. For a quick change of mood we turn to Jacques Offenbach, in 1876 one of the best-known of contemporary Frenchmen, who spent nine weeks in the United States during the hot Centennial summer, and found much to report, usually with gay Gallic humor but often enough in serious tone.

2

OFFENBACH —
ONCE OVER LIGHTLY

The managers of the Centennial Exhibition commissioned Richard Wagner to compose something suitable for the opening ceremonies on May 10. Titled "Festmarsch," it added nothing to his reputation and may even have retarded his American popularity. Jacques Offenbach, the popular and prolific composer of French operettas, was luckier: he was not asked to compose anything, but he did receive an ironclad offer of $30,000 for conducting thirty concerts in the Hippodrome, where Moody and Sankey had charmed the crowds earlier in the year.

Offenbach arrived in New York on May 6 and left on July 8. In that nine-week period he not only filled his Hippodrome contract but also conducted a week of his works in Booth's Theatre, another week of concerts at Philadelphia's Alhambra (called "Offenbach's Garden" while he was there), six nights of opera at Philadelphia, and, after a quick trip to Niagara Falls, a final New York concert for the benefit of the musicians' union the night before his departure. His profits, which considerably exceeded the expected $30,000, did much to lessen his perennial money problems.

During his American visit, Offenbach kept a journal, wrote numerous letters to his family in France, and clipped newspaper stories about his tour. Back home, he pieced these together as *Notes d'un musicien en voyage*, which he published in 1877. There were also simultaneous British and American editions.[3] The America he reported bears slight resemblance to Josiah Holland's America, partly no doubt because he was French, and partly because he was too busy conducting to do much observing, but also because he and Holland were worlds apart in their ways of reacting to what they saw around them.

Offenbach's impressions began, naturally enough for a visitor, with hotels and restaurants. In New York, he stopped at the Fifth Avenue Hotel, not quite realizing, perhaps, that for luxury and services it had few equals in the nation. "In Europe," he wrote, "people have no idea of this kind of establishment"—but neither did the great majority of Americans. He described the ground floor as an immense bazaar, complete with barbershop, hatter, tailor, pharmacist, and bootblack. His suite, costing twenty dollars a day, had a bedroom, a sitting room, a wash-stand, and a toilet. He was less pleased with the hotel dining room. The headwaiter chose the place for him to sit, often next to a stranger; a waiter brought him a glass of ice water and a tremendous bill of fare; then, more often than not, there was a long delay before the waiter came to take the order; and finally, to his consternation, everything he ordered was brought at once.

He thought that the best restaurants were foreign: in New York, the Brunswick (French), Delmonico's (Swiss), Hoff-man's (German), Morelli's (Italian), Frascati's (Spanish); in Philadelphia, Pétry's (French) and Pinelli's (Italian). There were, he insisted, "no American restaurants, properly speaking . . . and nothing is more difficult for a foreigner than to eat an American meal in America." But he did observe one peculiar American custom, the serving of free meals to customers buying drinks. He copied down the menu at one such place:

> A Ham
> An enormous piece of Roast Beef
> Bacon and Beans
> Potato Salad
> Olives, Pickles, etc.
> Cheese
> Crackers

Patrons could take as much as they wished, but some of them offended Offenbach by using only their fingers, even for the salad. When he expressed his horror, the headwaiter sought to soothe him: *"Time is money*, and these gentlemen are in such a hurry!"

The ice water brought first was no consolation to a well-bred visiting Frenchman, especially when the waiter hurried off be-fore he could order the drink or the glass of wine he'd been hoping for. Even worse was the law against drinking on Sunday.

After his concert one very hot night, Offenbach rushed to the bar and asked for a beer, only to be told that nothing could be sold on Sunday except soda water. Unable to believe this, he ran to the Hotel Brunswick and ordered a sherry cobbler, but with the same result. "What a strange kind of liberty!" But liberty, he noted, had other strange forms: Negroes had been emancipated, yet "cars, streetcars, and other public vehicles are forbidden to them; they are not admitted to theatres under any pretext; they are admitted to restaurants only if they are serving there." And at Niagara Falls he read a newspaper notice from the proprietor of the Cataract House: "Beginning today Jews are excluded from my hotel."

Sabbatarian restrictions endorsed by Josiah Holland particularly irritated Offenbach. On his first Sunday in Philadelphia he went to Fairmount Park only to find the Centennial Exhibition closed, and he remarked, "The only day in the week which belongs to the workman is Sunday. He might profit from these few hours of relaxation to educate himself or to amuse himself." Theatres and concert halls were also closed. "If he goes out with his family, he can't even quench his thirst with a bottle of beer. So what does he do? While his wife and children go to church or take a walk, he remains at home in tête-à-tête with a bottle of whiskey."

Among the puzzling facets of American liberty, one was profoundly shocking to Offenbach—the unfettered freedom to kill and maim on the Fourth of July by the senseless use of fireworks. He quoted several horrifying examples from New York's French-language newspaper, *Courrier des États-Unis:* one of a nineteen-year-old girl, her clothes afire from firecrackers thrown at her, running crazed with fear and pain until she finally died in the street; another of a bomb exploding in the crowd during a fireworks display in City Hall Park, wounding five persons, three very badly; and a reported total of forty-nine other injuries on New York's Centennial Fourth—eyes lost, hands severed, ribs broken, and bodies burned, nine-tenths of the casualties resulting from pistol shots fired, as the police put it, by "some unknown person". In Philadelphia, boys firing a cannon started a fire that gutted the section of the city between Laurel and Shackamaxon streets and cost a quarter of a million dollars for each shot fired. "As for me," Offenbach decided, "I admit that these disasters make me appreciate our detestable European governments that come right out and forbid such liberties as endanger the lives of citizens. . . ."

The only Americans who were really free, it seemed to Offenbach, were the women, nine out of ten of them ravishing— more beauty on the hoof, indeed, than in all of Paris, and all of them accomplished walkers. He was astonished to see them strolling casually about, entering restaurants as if they were men, engaging carriages for rides in Central Park, and apparently unafraid of pickpockets, to judge by the way they all carried pocketbooks loosely in their hands. They also seemed unafraid of men: "One strange thing for the depraved Paris male, who likes to follow women around, is that nobody in New York or any other city in the United States would take the liberty of following a young Yankee woman and still less of talking to her even to offer his umbrella." No contact was possible, he concluded, without a formal introduction; but if a relative or a mutual friend were not available for the purpose, "a want ad in the *Herald* will be sufficient."

Another social custom intrigued him: the differences in ways of greeting acquaintances—a deep bow for a millionaire, a slight bow to a man worth a mere hundred thousand, a tip of the hat to someone with no fortune at all. But this was understandable in America, "where work and the dollar determine the only aristocracy."

Much that Offenbach saw he admired. The numbering of streets, for example, instead of naming them for politicians and being forced to rename them when a different party won control. The little birdhouses built for the sparrows recently imported from Europe and protected by law. The iron tramcar rails crisscrossing most of the streets. And the cars themselves, not limited in occupancy as they were in Paris. The omnibuses in which passengers deposited their fares in small boxes. When Offenbach asked if the company lost money, the reply was prompt: "It would cost much more to hire a conductor." The money box served a double purpose, he observed, being lighted at night to become a lantern. The heavy traffic was hard on pedestrians, but at corners cobblestone crossings had been laid down, and policemen were assigned to help women and children cross in safety.

After a few days at the Fifth Avenue Hotel, Offenbach moved to a small house in Madison Square, one with particular advantages: central heating, gas in every room, hot and cold water at all hours, and three buttons—one to summon an errand boy, the next to call a policeman, the last to report a fire. He did not have in his room, but was awed by the chance of having, one of Edison's ticker-tape machines with stock quotations and an endless flow of news reports.

It is quickly obvious, from reading Offenbach's book, that what he saw, or chose to see, was only the top level of American life; most travelers could not afford the luxury hotels, or private houses in Madison Square, or the very best restaurants. There is no denying, however, that these were as much a part of Centennial America as the slums and factories that Offenbach never noticed, or the farms and small towns that he never visited.

Offenbach shared Josiah Holland's liking for Central Park, with its rocky meadows, carefully tended turf, clumps of fine trees, ponds, and magnificent drives; though hardly the Bois de Boulogne, it was already "the rendezvous of elegant society." If he noted the squatters' shanties lining its east border, facing the mansions of the *nouveaux riches* across Fifth Avenue, he was too polite to mention them. He did brand as ugly and clumsy the massive carriages that carried many passengers at a single time on circuits of the Park—something "from the Middle Ages." Nor did he like much better the other common vehicle used in the Park, especially by "girls of the highest society"—a buggy with a tiny box of a seat, a hood that could be raised, great wheels giving the impression of a monstrous daddy longlegs, a team of powerful horses, and flapping curtains suggestive of careless poverty.

To the north of Central Park, in those days, was Jerome Park, where Offenbach saw, or chose to see, American women at their fashionable best: "I cannot tell you how delightful was the sight of the race track embellished with the presence of these elegant ladies." The men were quite another story. Not only at the races, but at theatres and concerts, they wore "frightful suits" that Frenchmen would hardly have dared appear in at the seaside. Even men of distinction seemed indifferent to minimal sartorial standards as known in Europe. One male habit he found particularly disagreeable was winding a strip of batiste around the neck, the first thing in the morning, and wearing it all day, with no awareness of the incongruity of ceremonial white tie coupled with very informal clothing.

Holland never mentioned the race track, and what he said about theatres only exposed his Victorian prejudice. Offenbach, man-of-the-world that he was, attended the theatre as often as his crowded schedule permitted and became almost an instant authority. He liked the architecture: the long rows of rising seats, the balcony, the eight boxes, four on each side. But he noted that these boxes were unpopular; the best society preferred the orchestra or the front rows of the balcony.

The Academy of Music in New York was the place for grand opera, but he attended no performances because the Academy had been used only sixty days in the past eight months. Booth's Theatre offered opera, comedy, and tragedy. He saw there a production of *Henry V*, which he liked, and a Meyerbeer opera, *L'Étoile du Nord*, which suffered, in his expert opinion, from inadequate rehearsals: "The chorus and orchestra kept chasing each other around; a useless pursuit, they never got together." The orchestra pit was too small; some of the players had to sit outside, in front rows among the audience. At the Union Square Theatre he enjoyed two murder mysteries: Sardou's *Ferréol*, which ran for sixty performances in the spring of 1876, and *Conscience* by A. E. Lancaster and Julian Magnus. He liked even better *The Mighty Dollar*, at the Wallack; it was the kind of play that defied unanimous critical disapproval by running for more than two hundred New York performances in 1875–76 before going on tour. But he was quite critical of *Pique* at the Fifth Avenue Theatre, a melodrama "whose situations have been pillaged from nearly everywhere."

To his regret, Offenbach missed *La Dame aux Camélias*, the famous tear-jerker of Alexandre Dumas *fils* which had just completed its season at the Lyceum. But he criticized the theatre itself, the first to place the orchestra wholly out of sight, as Wagner was trying to do just then at Bayreuth. Few theatres, Offenbach thought, had the proper acoustics for such an innovation, or adequate space or ventilation. When the orchestra members had moments to relax, the only space was a cellar room too warm for comfort.

Theatre was theatre, in whatever country, and Offenbach was quite at home with it. He was entirely unprepared, by contrast, for American advertising—an aspect of American business that was equally novel and astonishing to Americans themselves. In Philadelphia, while observing a parade, he noticed that the big bass drum in the band advertised a drug store, "in fine black letters on the donkey's skin." It was not advertising as such that intrigued him, however. What constantly caught him by surprise was its many ingenious forms. In New York he saw two young men, arm in arm, each with a sign on his back announcing "Great Sale of Sewing Machines." Flags hanging from windows were commonly disfigured by advertisements attached; and triumphal arches over city streets publicized coming sales. A mustard firm carved its name and address in pavements. Broadsides and cards showered down on omnibuses and carriages. One trade name, SOZODONT, for a toothpaste that is still popular in England, annoyed him, but not enough to prompt him to ask what it meant. More effective, at least for Offenbach, was a gimmick he observed from a train. "ONLY CURE FOR RHEUMATISM" appeared on telegraph poles a kilometer apart, and only at the tenth was the mystery solved by the name and maker of the product. "I almost bought the medicine when I got out of the train!"

City nights were garish with advertisements lighted by gas, kerosene, or electricity; sometimes a magic lantern threw a series of pictures against a wall. "Men walk around the streets enclosed in sheds made of paper, illuminated on the inside and bearing inscriptions on their outsides." The impulse to advertise knew no limits; on one occasion, when a tramcar horse fell in the street from fatigue, Offenbach was astonished to see an urchin run up and stick a poster on its nose:

GARGLING OIL
GOOD FOR MAN AND BEAST

He saw the identical poster on an almost inaccessible spot at Niagara Falls.

Offenbach's final concert, in New York on July 7, was a great success in every way but one. He had earlier been annoyed by the adulation accorded Dom Pedro, perhaps because he thought he deserved as much attention himself. It was therefore galling to read in New York papers a notice of a farewell concert to be held two nights after his own, at the same place:

GREAT SACRED CONCERT IN HONOR OF
THE EMPEROR OF BRAZIL

And last appearance in public of his Majesty Dom Pedro
previous to his departure for Europe.

The words "Emperor of Brazil," Offenbach complained, stood out "as if he were a well-known singer or outstanding actor." And he took special joy in imagining the impresario announcing from the stage that "the Emperor of Brazil, having unexpected throat trouble, begs you to excuse him if he does not appear tonight for the last time."

A visit to Niagara Falls was virtually compulsory for all foreign visitors, but though Offenbach gave one paragraph, dutifully, to describing its majesty, he was more interested in his first chance to see some American Indians. Instead of the noble savages of expectation, however, he saw only shabby peddlers offering bamboo sticks, fans, cigar cases, and pocketbooks in dubious taste. They reminded him of the "Indians" selling penholders and paper knives in the Forest of Fontainebleau. He bought a few trinkets but suspected they came originally from the liquidation of a department store in Paris.

The Niagara trip was Offenbach's introduction to the marvels of American trains. He found the parlor car pleasant enough on his way to the Falls. There were comfortable armchairs, with copious leg room, and special compartments for smoking. And on the return he watched with admiration the swift conversion to a sleeping car. "What clever workmen! Or rather what clever gadgets!" He recalled hotels that provided flimsier walls and less privacy. But even in this paradise on wheels the serpent appeared, in the form of a man "accidentally" opening the wrong curtains and invading the privacy of a young lady until a chorus of "oh's" and "ah's" defeated his evil scheme.

Such were Offenbach's impressions of America—the America

that he saw. If anything is to be regretted, it must be that he saw no more. There were other visitors, however, without other commitments to interfere with the solid business of observation. Let us turn next to a Scot named John Leng, whose sole purpose in visiting Centennial America was to gather material for a book.

3

JOHN LENG, FLYING SCOT

Besides devoting enough time and energy to make his Dundee *Advertiser* an important newspaper, John Leng was an inveterate traveler; he had visited most of Europe, the Near East, Africa, and New Zealand before venturing to the United States. Nor was his 1876 visit to this country his only one; he was to return in 1905 when, after a sudden illness, he died in California. Well before that time his contributions to British public affairs would earn him a knighthood. But in 1876 he was plain John Leng, not yet Sir John.

John Leng planned his American tour carefully, allotted time enough for adequate inspection, and left most of his preconceptions at home. As a result, the book he wrote, *America in 1876*,[4] comes as close to being comprehensive as could be expected of a foreign visitor. True, there is an emphasis on American business and industry—so strong that the book sometimes takes on the character of a traveling salesman's handbook. But Leng was no dour Scot with narrowly materialistic interests. If he lacked Offenbach's Gallic wit he at least showed a genial humor, while his style at times exhibited a considerable degree of sparkle and grace.

Had Josiah Holland ever opened Leng's book, he would, no doubt, have just as quickly closed it, for Leng began by speaking of the "beer, brandy, and cigars *ad infinitum*" that made the ten-day Atlantic crossing endurable. Conditioned as he was by travel in European cities, Leng expected upon approaching New York, to see a skyline dominated by church steeples, but the two structures he supposed were steeples proved to be the twin towers of Brooklyn Bridge. It delighted him, as it later delighted Huxley, to learn that newspaper buildings, those of the *Tribune* and the *Herald*, were among the city's tallest structures.

Once arrived, Leng spent his first nights not, as Offenbach had, amid the luxury of the Fifth Avenue Hotel—he was, after all, a Scot—but at the Windsor, somewhat older but "very handsome." As his trip progressed, he pronounced judgment on hotels across the nation. In addition to the Windsor, he listed as the leading hotels in New York the Grand, the St. James, the Clarendon, the Westminster, the Astor House, and the Brevoort. But American hotel life reached its peak, he thought, at Saratoga, N. Y., the Spa where the "Big Four"—Congress Hall, Grand Union, Grand, and United States, where he stayed—each accommodated more than a thousand guests and exceeded in size and magnificence anything to be found in Europe. He insisted that "as a mere spectacle Saratoga ought to be seen by all who wish to enter into whatever is peculiar in American life."

Ornateness in hotel architecture was not confined to Saratoga, however. Chicago's Tremont, Sherman, Grand Pacific, and Palmer House greatly impressed him. In fact, he placed the Palmer House second, among city hotels, only to San Francisco's Palace, which he considered the largest and most complete hotel in the world. He was hardly alone in this opinion of the Palace; it was a view often voiced by San Franciscans, but coming from such a man as Leng it carried more weight. The Palace, with its 755 rooms was big enough to impress almost anybody. Great size, however, was not its only distinction. Each of its rooms had its own ventilating tubes, forerunners of air conditioning, and another set of tubes that provided communication by voice with the hotel office. The corridors were unusually wide—twelve feet. There were five hydraulic elevators, seven stairways, and an eighth, fireproof, that was a kind of interior fire-escape. The ground floor was twenty-five feet high and the upper floors fourteen or sixteen. A good deal of the interior space was allotted to glass-covered wells, the largest of these, the central court, measuring 144 by 84 feet; carriages entered this court to discharge or pick up patrons. The building had been built with earthquakes in mind, and was heavily beamed and pillared with iron. In almost every respect the Palace left other hotels so far behind that no comparison was possible.

Leng thought it an oddity that wealthy men so often built hotels. Prominent examples were the Sherman House and the Palmer House in Chicago, and the Lick House in San Francisco. It could not have been for greater income, he reasoned, because rates everywhere were surprisingly low. Single rooms, in the very best hotels, cost only five dollars a night, and the rate decreased with declining elegance to as little as a dollar a day, or five dollars a week, all meals included. With such modest costs, and considering the steep rents for houses and the high wages of servants, it was hardly surprising that people increasingly lived in hotels by choice. In most hotels, indeed, permanent boarders were the mainstay, far different than in Europe, where only travelers used the hotels. Leng liked the elaborate bills of fare no better than Offenbach did, but they at least assured the permanent guests of a welcome variety of menu.

New York seemed to Leng the least American of American cities by being the most Irish, Scottish, German, French, and Italian—and altogether the most foreign in its customs and manners. He called it "a youthful London" but hastened to show how it differed from London, which it did most strikingly in its mania for enormous office buildings, such as that of the Equitable Insurance Company. The thought of sheer size reminded him of American ferry boats; and, like other foreign observers, he marveled at their double-ended construction which obviated the turning about that was necessary for European ferries. New York most closely paralleled London in the mansions of its wealthy; which were, indeed, "as complete and as elegantly furnished as any in London." But New York was not nearly as big as London; beyond Fifty-seventh Street, Leng observed, Broadway ran into open country. Central Park was crowded in the afternoon with all sorts of horse-drawn vehicles; but Leng did not describe them as Offenbach did. On the other hand, Offenbach said nothing about the churches, which impressed Leng by their ability to thrive "without any aid from the state."

From New York, Leng began his swing around the nation by visiting the Centennial Exhibition in Philadelphia. He was unimpressed, finding there nothing to compare, either in grandeur of buildings or multitude and variety of exhibits with great fairs he had seen at London, Paris, and Vienna. He praised American barrels and buckets, boxes and cans, as "models of lightness, tightness, and strength combined"; and he particularly admired a patent reaper and binder. "Intelligent landed proprietors, farmers, or gardeners," he wrote, are "the men who will most enjoy this Exhibition." Machinery Hall left him cool, perhaps because its most striking objects, after the Corliss Engine, were "Krupp's enormous guns." In the art gallery, which he considered the finest building, what interested him most were photographs of the Yosemite and other Western regions.

Chicago provided Leng with a somewhat different perspective.

> Imagine a city of which all the principal public buildings—the Custom-House, Post-Office, Court-House, Exchange, railway stations, banks, hotels, newspaper offices, warehouses, and shops—were all burnt down in a conflagration that raged for three days and nights over four square miles of ground, and imagine all these replaced, in the course of five years, by much finer and more costly buildings, and you are enabled to form some idea of the wonderful activity that characterizes the Chicago people.

Elsewhere he had noted the prevalence of wooden buildings and the resulting American interest in fire engines and volunteer fire departments. In Chicago he noted the great advances in the waterworks, prompted by the fire of 1871. Lake Michigan was of course a magnificent reservoir, but Chicagoans had found it worth the effort and cost to bore a two-mile tunnel and amass a group of engines that could pump water to a height comparable to the tallest buildings in a volume of 120,000,000 gallons a day, or fifty-seven gallons per person per day for a population of one million. It was also fitting that Chicago had the world's largest and tallest grain elevators, with a mechanism like a dredge that could empty five hundred railroad cars a day. The stockyards provided comparable figures—eight hogs could be slaughtered in a minute, or five hundred in an hour. Then, after being hung and cured for two days, the hogs were cut up, salted, and packed at the rate of six thousand a day. The nerve center for these and other such activities was the Chicago Board of Trade, "a large room in which great and enormous transactions are carried on daily in a manner quite unintelligible to the uninitiated, who hear nothing but apparently frantic and delirious shouts, howls, and screams" of men who "seem to be maniacs, ejaculating and gesticulating. . . ."

But Chicago was not wholly devoted to business. The city had already a wonderful system of parks, and great churches. Leng, as a good Scot, attended the First and Second Presbyterian Churches. He also attended a Moody and Sankey midday meeting, in Farnell Hall, where the audience numbered three thousand.

Indianapolis, though hardly the size of Chicago, was attractive to Leng. For one thing, he learned that many of the "Belfast Hams" sold in Scotland were cured there. He visited the Republican headquarters and was awed by the vast campaign being organized for the Republican Presidential slate, Hayes and Wheeler. He also watched a great torchlight parade for the Democratic Presidential candidate, Samuel Tilden.

Passing through Springfield, Illinois, he was impressed with the trees planted along all the principal streets, and with the preponderance of brick dwellings, all neatly porticoed and balconied. The Illinois State House, would, when finished, be only ten feet lower than St. Paul's Cathedral, in London, and would cost five million dollars. Lincoln's house was modest, but the Lincoln Monument was spectacular—an obelisk set upon a pedestal which contained a marble sarcophagus. Its inscription pleased Leng: simply Lincoln's name and the words, "With malice toward none, with charity for all."

Leng noted the great rivalry between Chicago and St. Louis. Chicagoans had told him that their colder climate enabled them to do 15 percent more work than St. Louisans, but Leng saw the evidence of plentiful energy in St. Louis. The parks there particularly attracted him: Tower Grove Park, with three hundred acres and excellent drives; Lafayette Park, even larger, with more than two thousand acres; and Shaw's Gardens, privately owned by Henry Shaw, an Englishman, but open to the public and unequalled, in Leng's opinion, on the American continent. On the practical side, Leng described the great Vulcan Iron Works, the Eads bridge, (an engineering triumph of three steel arches completed in 1874 but reportedly operating at a loss), and the *Great Republic*, at twenty-six hundred tons the world's largest river steamship, with huge paddle wheels and two hundred berths, and able to navigate in five feet of water, even when fully loaded.

From St. Louis Leng went by train direct to California. It took a week, long enough to impress upon anyone, native or visitor, how truly vast the nation was. Leng thought there was a connection between national area and character: "The sense of greatness—the mere physical greatness of his country—is strong upon every American." He found good company in the Pullman cars but noted, as few other travelers thought of doing, the heat and the mosquitoes. Toward the end of his visit he generalized that the United States was too monotonously bright and warm; he may have been growing just a bit homesick for his Scottish mists.

Kansas evolved from a settled green east to a flat treeless west, where no plow had yet broken the sod. Stops along the way were at "mere rudiments of villages—future 'cities' perhaps in embryo." Buffalo Station, with ten inhabitants, Aroya with eleven; Monument, Monotony. "More dreary places to live in, either summer or winter, can scarcely be conceived." Higher land was most welcome: "After the hot vapour baths of Missouri, it is quite a luxury to enjoy the delicious cold of Colorado." In Denver he learned that antelope steak was as common as mutton or beefsteak elsewhere.

Leng's route turned north from Denver to Laramie, and then west again. He slept through most of Wyoming, but later he had the unusual privilege of riding for three hours on the platform above the train's cowcatcher. The sights he now saw could "only be described as indescribable in their wild and rugged grandeur." Here were the Exhibition photographs he had admired spread out before him in all their three-dimensional reality—the desolate canyons of Utah, the ravines of the Sierra Nevada, the serpentine descent into California, the snow sheds on steep slopes as protection against avalanches, and the sense of remoteness to match the overwhelming beauty of it all. Leng felt that the American West's natural beauty transcended the power of pen or paintbrush to communicate.

The long ride to California ended at Oakland, where a ferry took Leng to San Francisco. The city was in a state of transition from wooden frame buildings, and common brick, to cement and stone. Leng visited the Mining Board, comparable to Chicago's Board of Trade, and the mint, which had produced more than $31,000,000 worth of gold and silver coins from January through September. He learned that California had forty million grape vines, and that the 1876 crop, following abundant winter rains, was vast. He described San Francisco's carriages as the equal of those in Central Park, and he grew ecstatic over the Palace Hotel. But his observations about the Golden State are, in general disappointing. He had more of interest to report about Oregon.

It took three or four days by ship to reach Portland, Oregon, from San Francisco; Oregon did not yet have rail connections with the rest of the nation. Leng admired the numerous high headlands along the Oregon coast but noted the paucity of harbors. Portland, however, though set well back from the sea, was a thriving port, able to berth large ships. The city itself was very enterprising, though its public buildings were unimpressive. Roads in Oregon were poor, but the weather was excellent. Storms were rare, and no Oregon harvest had ever failed. Leng visited Ankeny Farm, of 4,680 acres, and admired the plows, much lighter than those in Scotland or New Zealand.

After a brief visit to Puget Sound, big and beautiful, with Mt. Rainier and other peaks visible, Leng returned to San Francisco to start his homeward journey. He stopped briefly at Virginia City and longer at Salt Lake. The wide streets with streams flowing down either side of the city, the fine stores, the Mormon Tabernacle, "which looks from the exterior like an enormous soup tureen wanting a handle," and lived up to its reputation of perfect acoustical qualities for an audience of twelve thousand —all these were things that no visitor could miss. A topical tidbit Leng passed along was that Ann Eliza's lawsuit for alimony from Brigham Young was hurting Mormonism and hastening the end of polygamy.

Of Nebraska he noted only that "the farmers here spend little on fences, which seem to be considered superfluous," and that they commonly planted shelter belts of trees around their homesteads. Iowa struck him as "a remarkably thriving state, . . . undulating, wooded, and abundantly watered, not at all unlike the West of England." Pittsburgh—he was now moving along very rapidly—reminded him so much of Newcastle, Sheffield, or Wolverhampton, that he did not stop there. Washington he thought comparatively mean in domestic architecture but laid out on a magnificent plan: "probably a half century hence, when its streets are properly built up, it will be one of the finest places in the world." Philadelphia was far more attractive, especially for its fine buildings. But the city he liked best was Boston, "unquestionably the most elegant as well as the most ancient and home-like of American cities. There is an aristocratic dignity . . . high culture and refinement," amply supporting Boston's right to the sobriquet "the Athens of America."

From Boston Leng went to see the Pacific Mills in Lawrence, Massachusetts, and found a good deal to admire. The buildings and facilities were impressive: the main building seven stories high, with 135,000 spindles for cotton and 25,000 for worsted, 4,500 looms, and a permanent work staff between five and six thousand. But of more interest was the evidence of paternalism. There were tenements and boarding houses built by the company; a library of seven thousand volumes open from 9:00 A.M. to 9:00 P.M.; a hospital; a Relief Society with compulsory dues of two cents a week; and reasonable working hours—in summer from 6:00 A.M. to 6:30 P.M. with an hour for lunch, and a half-day on Saturday, in winter from 6:45 A.M. to 6:00 P.M. (and 4:30 P.M. on Saturdays). A rough calculation yields a work week of 63½ hours in summer, and 60 in winter, substantially below the 72 hours prevailing in most American industries.

Leng did not, unfortunately, report the wage scale at Lawrence, but he generalized that American workmen were well paid—perhaps by Scottish standards. One evidence of the good pay was that many upper-class housewives felt they could not afford domestic help. As for the husbands, Leng was a little awed by how hard they drove themselves. "The average American," he noted, "has more enjoyments, but he has less leisure in his ordinary life than the average Englishman or Scotchman. He is always going at the very top of his speed." What Leng had discovered was an aspect of the Protestant Ethic that Holland had mentioned indirectly, specifically its tenet that hard work was a virtue and the enjoyment of leisure almost a sin. What he did not discover, on so brief and so hurried a journey, was the grim depression fact of widespread unemployment with all its attendant misery, not in Lawrence, perhaps, but in many American mill towns.

Some of Leng's judgments were obviously faulty and inadequate, but others, representing the opinions of an intelligent, conscientious visitor, have a high degree of validity. America was *not* Europe, and certain of its distinctive features come into particularly high relief when viewed through the eyes of one who was not a native. Where an American moralist like Josiah Holland might inveigh against drinking, the Scotsman Leng soberly reported that there was very little public drinking. Where historians have branded the Centennial era as a time of unusual dishonesty, Leng expressed astonishment that outbreaks of crime and violence were so few and far between. "Orderliness, not rowdyism, is the most conspicuous feature of American life." Leng was also glad to correct another widespread misconception: "Americans are quiet and reticent rather than noisy and intrusive. In the Far West you still come upon specimens of men who wish to know everything about you and your business, but generally you are as untroubled with inquisitiveness as in your own country." And he added, "The average American is not a bragging, boastful, blustering fellow, who exaggerates the praises of everything in his own country."

No visitor in 1876 could be unaware of the great public scandals of the year. They reminded Leng that the greatest flaw in American democracy was the political spoils system and the ever-present possibility of corruption that it engendered. But everywhere he went he found that thinking Americans agreed with him, and that the scandals that surrounded the Grant administration had intensified their opinions on the subject. It was reassuring to Leng that so many men he talked with hated the spoils system and hoped that one day "only men of proved competence and integrity should receive the appointments."

Somehow the impression has developed that Centennial Americans were scandalously permissive toward corruption. Leng for one did not find this true.

The final sentence of his book, directed at his Scottish readers, has a rather curious, perhaps even a bit condescending ring; yet it might serve as an appropriate epitaph for the Centennial generation: "Let us not grudge them their pride, for they [had] much to be proud of."

4

NATHANIEL BISHOP
AND HIS SNEAK-BOX

As a lad of seventeen Nathaniel Bishop walked, alone, across the continent of South America. In 1875 he completed a twenty-five-hundred-mile voyage by canoe from the St. Lawrence River to Fernandina in northeastern Florida. Almost at once, he began planning his next long voyage, and he decided upon a route that would take him down the Ohio and Mississippi Rivers. For this undertaking he looked about for a different sort of craft—sturdier and more weatherproof than a canoe. At Barnegat Bay, New Jersey, he found what he was seeking in a duck-hunting boat of a type built and used locally, twelve feet long, decked over like a kayak, well-suited for sleeping, with plenty of space for dry storage. It was called a "sneak-box." Bishop had one made for twenty-five dollars, named it "Centennial Republic," sent it by freight to Pittsburgh, and on December 2, 1875, he embarked on an American tour that was totally different from that of any undertaken by any other of our Centennial travelers.[5]

It was a time in our history when men were attempting, and the public was applauding, the achievement of unusual physical feats. One contemporary hero was Edward Weston, who earned instant fame in the early 1870s by walking from Portland, Maine, to Chicago, Illinois, covering 1,326 miles in twenty-six days. Even into his seventies, Weston continued to eclipse his own records. However, his major feat of the Centennial year—covering 110 miles in twenty-four hours—proved to be one of his lesser accomplishments.

At least as much fame accrued to a daredevil named Paul Boyton, who used a vulcanized rubber suit and a submersible thirty-inch iron boat, the "Baby Mine," for extended trips by water. Boyton achieved his first success in 1874, when, after being dropped into the sea from an ocean liner, he reached Ireland during a gale that wrecked fifty-six vessels. Both Weston and Boyton were saluted in popular sheet music of the time: "Weston's March to Chicago," a march, for piano and guitar, and "Captain Boyton on the Wave," a polka-galop.[6] Nathaniel Bishop, less famous, was not thus honored, but of the three he alone wrote a book that serves our purpose.

John Leng had dismissed Pittsburgh with a shudder; it reminded him altogether too much of the grimy factory towns of the English Midlands. Bishop, dependent on the current of the Allegheny River, from which he was starting out, couldn't be so selective. For the first few days of his voyage he knew the acrid taste and smell of Pittsburgh's soft coal smoke. He also encountered an oil slick that extended many miles and passed valley walls pock-marked with mines where farmers eked out their income by mining coal. In the cold December fog and rain the landscape was hardly attractive—it showed, Bishop felt, how efficiently men could violate nature. But he was not so indignant at human exploitation that he refused its benefits; he bought a coal oil stove, a Florence No. 0 with a single wick, and a supply of Pratt's Astral Oil. Cold food, day after day, could soon become monotonous.

After traversing the Ohio, which proved to be a crowded thoroughfare, Bishop reached the Mississippi, on New Year's Day, 1876. He quickly found that every town along the river had its rowdy element, who were prone to welcome the sneak-box with hilarity and, often enough, to seek to do it damage. Fortunately the decking had a rather steep pitch, and more than one drunken citizen, attempting to step on board, skidded instantly into the water.

The river traffic in 1876 was immense. If Bishop had read

Twain's *Life on the Mississippi* in its *Atlantic Monthly* installments, the year before, he did not allude to it, but his report, day
by day, complements and extends that account. Twain knew the
river from the vantage point of the pilot house of a steamboat;
Bishop knew it at water level. Both men feared the steamboats
with their strangely mixed cargo of humanity forever coursing
with the current toward New Orleans. Some of the passengers
were as rowdy and threatening as the roughs in the cities that
Bishop avoided, but most were not; instant friendliness was the
general rule.

There were college graduates as curious as Bishop himself
about life on the great river. There were families dispossessed by
hard times, trusting to an unknown future in a new part of the
country. There were perennial wanderers for whom the Mississippi was the easiest means of movement. There were also the
men who earned their living from the river. Some, living as
squatters along the banks, made a living by hunting and selling
meat to the river travelers, as a change in diet from the ubiquitous catfish. Others offered their services as floating cobblers,
tinsmiths, gunsmiths, tailors, midwives, sailmakers, and carpenters.

There were also families so utterly devoid of ambition that
they regarded three days marooned on a snag or sandbar, waiting for higher water, as total bliss. And there were great story
tellers, with their endless exchange of adventures. The world of
the Mississippi was an inner nation, existing separately from the
nation of hard times, public scandals, Centennial ceremonies,
social problems, slums and human exploitation, and even daily
newspapers. The news that counted was of droughts or freshets
upriver that would mean, a week later, slack water and slow
going or high water and rapid currents.

New Orleans, which Bishop had visited several times before,
severely taxed both his patience and his ingenuity. Every day,
gangs of rowdies badgered him, under a stubborn notion that he
was some kind of federal spy; by night it was hardly better. But
the French, Spanish, and German crews of a cluster of coastal
ships proved welcome allies. They too were "aliens," and only
too glad to watch over Bishop and his sneak-box.

For the second major phase of the voyage Bishop entered salt water, traveling eastward along the Gulf Coast. This was a region of almost total wilderness, desolate in the extreme. Much of the coast, especially the long curve marking the northeastern corner of the Gulf of Mexico, remains just as desolate today, with water too shallow for the majority of boats; vast swamps extending many miles back from the Gulf; virtually no beaches to encourage resorts; and generous supplies of alligators, mosquitoes, and water moccasins, not to mention occasional panthers. But before reaching the curve of the Gulf coast at the waist of Florida, Bishop passed through some of the most attractive regions he had ever seen. He was puzzled by the fact that the few coast resort areas were abandoned during the winter, "just the time of year when the climate is delightful" and sporting opportunities—hunting, fishing, yachting—at their very best. "I thought, while we rowed along this attractive coast in the balmy atmosphere, with everything brightened and beautified by the early moon, how many were suffering in our northern cities from various forms of pulmonary troubles induced by severe winter weather, while here, in a delightful climate, with everything to make man comfortable, private houses and hotels were closed." This of course was the opinion of a Northerner; Southerners knew better than to vacation in the winter time.

The very few individuals whom Bishop did meet were a mixed lot. One family, working a field, fled in panic at his approach; any stranger in that area was automatically regarded as a threat. One man, who alone had oxen to haul the boats over the longest portage, seven miles, was a notorious thief and murderer, J. D. Holly. Word came just a few weeks later that he had been shot dead, which gave Bishop a grim satisfaction because Holly had pilfered his best coil of rope. Another portage was made possible by two refugees from civilization, very shy, whom Bishop described as "woods philosophers." At Dauphine Island, a recluse named Robinson Cruse, paid to guard over a crumbling piece of federal property, proved a generous host during a two-day storm. At Appalachicola, Florida, Bishop was astonished to meet, among the residents, A. W. Chapman, the author of a book he greatly loved, *Flora of the United States*. He was less pleased at finding in Florida illiterate postmasters—former slaves who had been put into office by cynical white men who commonly cheated them of most of their collections. Emancipation, he observed, was almost meaningless unless accompanied by education. And, indeed, at Newport, Florida, the Reverend Charles Beecher, one of the famous Beecher family, was waging a herculean campaign to provide just such education for the local Negroes.

It is doubtful whether Bishop's book, when it appeared, stirred in Northern bosoms any wild desires to join the picturesque inner nation on the lower Mississippi, or to chuck civilization and its discontents for the idyllic independence of the Gulf coast, partly because the drawbacks he so honestly reported balanced the attractions. It is a region, much of it, still not popular for settlers or vacationists, who, when the great Florida boom began, found much more to their liking along the Atlantic coast and the part of the Gulf coast well south of Cedar Key. But in 1876, even if the wilderness Bishop skirted had been everywhere as attractive as the few parts that prompted his most rapturous passages, it was an area that hardly represented anybody's notion of the future. "America was west," as Archibald Macleish once put it, not south. Even the Southern people looked westward, and contributed a goodly share to the westward movement of the American population. Or, as in the North but to a lesser degree, they looked, and moved, to their own growing cities, most of them well inland and not accessible by sneak-box.

5

ACROSS TEXAS ON HORSE-BACK — COLONEL TAYLOR

The day after Nathaniel Bishop began his descent of the Mississippi, another Nathaniel—Colonel Nathaniel Alston Taylor—set out on quite a different sort of journey, intent on traversing by horseback the entire state of Texas, from Houston to El Paso. His subsequent account, *The Coming Empire or Two Thou-*

sand Miles in Texas on Horseback,[7] had something of a promotional quality, for Taylor was both an employee and a stockholder of the Texas Western Railroad and his primary purpose in undertaking the long ride was to explore a possible route for that railroad to follow. (The route he suggested is pretty much the present route of the Southern Pacific.) But discounting Taylor's special interest and his excess of enthusiasm, his book does give a detailed picture of the state of Texas in the year 1876. And although much of that vast and largely uninhabited land proved taxing both to the author's stamina and to his powers of description, his book must serve as our best and most complete Centennial portrayal of that large fraction of American territory which still lay in the condition of wilderness. The few towns and outposts that Taylor visited only accentuated the wildness that prevailed in most of Texas in the Centennial year.

Although already a city of twenty-six thousand in population, Houston was so small in area that by the time Colonel Taylor had ridden four miles he had passed its last habitation. Now cattle were everywhere, with room for many more on the billiard-table flatness—what he called the "Virgin heiress," the open Texas land. With just a little drainage and plowing, he predicted, the Houston prairie would become a great garden. The soil was rich, the climate perfect. All that was needed was settlers—farmers and a few hunters. But so far, the land, priced at fifty cents to two dollars an acre, was begging for buyers.

If the Houston prairie was virgin land, the Brazos Bottom was a kind of Big Woods in the Faulknerian sense—dark and gloomy, with tremendous trees and tangled undergrowth, "dense as an African jungle," neglected and mysterious. A start had been made toward clearing parts of it in order to tap its very rich soil, but the Civil War had forced abandonment of this project. Taylor was certain the trend would be reversed. "So noble a country cannot always remain desolate and a beggar. It will grow prosperous and rich again." No other river valley in the world, he supposed, with the possible exception of the Mississippi, was capable of producing so much wealth. The few scattered inhabitants he met there were former slaves, still exhibiting the politeness taught them by their old masters, now departed. Concerning Emancipation, one of them remarked:

"There's more freedom and less to eat; more privilege and lesser comfort."

Taylor turned next to San Felipe de Austin, one of the oldest towns in Texas, on the Texas Colorado River—a place famed for hard drinking and desperate living. But despite the rough character of its inhabitants, its location was superb, entirely suitable for the capital of a Texas destined for great wealth.

Continuing along, Taylor came to the upper valley of the Guadalupe River, which struck him as the finest region he had ever seen, the way he imagined Greece to be. But Texas was a state of many contrasts. Snake Prairie was a wind-swept desolation where nothing could grow. The country near Fredericksburg seemed like a primeval landscape, strewn as it was with gigantic boulders. Lost Rocks presented a cataclysmic landscape. But Loyal Valley was "a garden in the wilderness," and Fort McKavett, in an amphitheatre at the head of the San Saba River, could hardly be surpassed for the sheer beauty of its setting.

At one point Taylor met a herd of wild horses, handsome and frolicsome; he had to restrain his own horse from running off with them. The Indians he came across were a mixed lot—some noble and friendly, some skulking and treacherous, but all supporting this generalization: "I believe I never saw an Indian, even of the least exalted tribe, in whose countenance I could not detect a trace of melancholy." The Negro troops comprising most of the military at various Army outposts offered a strong contrast: all were tractable, competent, obedient, and hospitable, but those Taylor talked with complained of the deadly monotony of their lives.

What Taylor had not expected, and what may have astonished his non-Texan readers, was the large numbers of German settlers he found almost everywhere he went. Fredericksburg, for example, was four-fifths German; La Grange was half American, half German, and "the best of both"; while San Antonio, a great potpourri of ethnic and national types, was one-third German. As settlers, Taylor thought the Germans excelled all others, including native Americans, and he gave as the probable reason their solid education. One proof of their frugality was that they invariably accepted the dollar he offered for bed and breakfast; his American hosts, more open and casual, refused his money.

At Concho Springs, in an "embryonic" region, Taylor secured two soldiers as companions. The route ahead was uncertain, and hostile Indians were known to be near. Mesas and vast heaps of rocks drew from one of the soldiers the remark, "What *did* the Almighty make such a country as this for?" The Llano Estacado ("Staked Plain") was not only treeless but silent. Crossing its entire width was the Pecos, an extremely winding river with rapid current and vertical mud banks six feet high that made crossing extremely difficult. The taste of the water was vile, and coffee made with it was no better, it was all a matter of the chemicals in the soil.

Fort Stockton was a welcome change. Six hundred Negro cavalrymen occupied the fort, which stood on a magnificent hill about three thousand feet above sea level. Nearby were vineyards producing the excellent El Paso grape, and wheat farms. With fifteen to twenty inches of rain fall each year, mostly in August and September, the district earned Taylor's praise as "this magnificent garden in the desert." But the garden had its serpent: the post sutler charged Taylor four dollars for a bushel of corn and fifty cents a pound for ham and butter; he later learned that farmers' wives nearby would have charged much less.

Taylor had originally started out with no means of defense other than his pocketknife, perhaps wishing to demonstrate for his readers how completely safe it was to travel in Texas. There were times, however, when this little weapon was to prove woefully inadequate. In one forest clearing near Austin, wolves surrounded his camp, and when he climbed a tree to escape them, his horse bolted, and was caught only with the help of a pig-farmer who happened along. A herd of mustangs he encountered later also gave Taylor some uneasy moments. They seemed altogether too free with their hooves as they pranced about him. A pair of panthers, on the other hand, gave him no trouble; neither did the prairie dogs, antelope, or bison that he observed, nor the jaguar which he watched overtake and crush an antelope. He did, however, acquire a rifle at about this time, and realized his prudence in doing so when, as he neared the western limits of the state, a bear attacked him and he was forced to shoot it. At about the same time, he watched from higher ground as five mountain lions devoured the carcass of a deer he had killed. Parts of Texas undoubtedly deserved the description "gardens," but, like other unopened parts of the nation, Texas was still mostly a land of assorted dangers.

By 1876 virtually all the territory East of the Mississippi was amenable to civilized living: people could travel there with no worries about hostile Indians, dangerous animals, or waterless plains. But the land Taylor traveled belonged to the half of the national area which still lay in wilderness and was yet to be brought under human control. John Leng, traversing the continent by train, passed through more wilderness than Taylor could cover on horseback; but he could never know, as Taylor did, what wilderness really meant. What ought to astound us, as we think back to 1876, was the headlong rate at which the wilderness was subdued, a rate accelerating so fast that by 1890 the process, for all practical purposes, was completed. Yet Nathaniel Bishop, in his sneak-box, revealed something else about the process—that it left pockets of untouched wildness, even in sections that presumably had long since been "civilized."

6

TWO CARPING FRENCHMEN

Colonel Taylor's promotional Centennial prose finds a balance in the books of two visiting Frenchmen, Jules Leclercq and Paul Toutain. Leclercq, in *Un Ete en Amérique*,[8] warned readers at the outset that anyone expecting a panegyric should close the book and read no further. Toutain, in *Un Français en Amérique*,[9] issued an even stronger warning: readers should be prepared to be shocked. Both devices were almost certain to rouse reader interest. It should be noted, however, that once having stated their point of view, neither of these Frenchmen went on to find everything wrong; however reluctantly, indeed both were forced to compromise their initial statements by pointing to many good things in American civilization.

Leclercq, landing at Baltimore, was at once impressed by the American system of checking baggage—a system that took all foreign visitors by surprise. All he had to do was exchange his luggage for round, numbered disks. That done, he was free to ride a ferry to central Baltimore and walk the streets at his leisure until his train was scheduled to start for Philadelphia.

Baltimore's famous brick row houses reminded him of Holland, but the numerous Negroes in the passing parade made a marked difference in the scene. The Washington Monument provided him with an excellent view of the city. But although Baltimore proved to be, of all the cities he visited, most blessed with "monuments" (by which he meant great and beautiful structures), he missed the richness in this respect, of the cities of Europe. The Baltimore cathedral was a poor imitation of the Gothic, yet Baltimore people were very proud of it; as far as Leclercq was concerned, its only redeeming features were two paintings that had been gifts of European kings.

But if the American buildings were disappointing, American women were not: of every four, three were beautiful, and this first impression was confirmed for Leclercq in every city on his route. In an hour, he insisted, one saw more charming women in America than in an entire afternoon in Paris, London, or Madrid. Offenbach, too, had been delighted by American women: was there actually something special about Centennial women to impress the male foreigner? Or could it have been that Josiah Holland was actually correct in thinking that American women were beautiful because they did not drink?

Once aboard the express to Philadelphia, Leclercq found more to admire—the landscape, with its trees of a brighter green than those in Europe, and the train itself. The parlor car had swivel chairs with plenty of leg room, and every car had a W.C. and an iced water tap. *"Helas!"* he exclaimed, *"il n'y a qu'en Amérique qu'on ait songé à ce détail!"*

Philadelphia gave Leclercq his initiation to American hotels.

The bellhop ushered him to his room, No. 266, lighted the gas, and dusted him off with a whiskbroom. In the dining room he had two Negro waiters, one of whom stood just behind him and kept filling his water glass. Like Offenbach, he found this kind of service unsettling—there was simply too much of it.

Perhaps it was out of this uneasiness that Leclercq's dislike for the Quaker City developed. The gridiron pattern of the streets seemed monotonous; and there were very few "monuments." Independence Hall was of interest, and so were the houses nearby associated with Benjamin Franklin and Thomas Jefferson. Girard College he considered a good replica of La Madeleine; the Cherry Hill cellular prison was a model for all such structures; and the Masonic Temple, the world's largest, was striking for its massive towers, quite bellicose, and for its interior, which was reminiscent of the Thousand and One Nights. On the other hand, it seemed to him presumptuous that relatively modest dwellings, mostly of brick, had conspicuous white marble to dress up their entries.

The city had not a single café, music hall, or legitimate theatre for its population of eight hundred thousand. True, there was the Fox Theatre, but when he took his seat there, Leclercq was astonished to see an all-male audience. The production turned out to be a burlesque show, with "faux negres" and, for the finale, a licentious dance. He left the theatre revolted, convinced that Philadelphia's claim of being the nation's most religious city was a sham. What would William Penn say, he wondered, if he could leave his grave and see to what depths his city had sunk, *"la Jérusalem de la quaquerie et de l'amour fraternel!"*

If American women were modest, aristocratic, and well-groomed, the men, Leclercq observed, were taciturn in the extreme. Ten American men meeting together made less noise, he thought, than two Englishmen or a single Frenchman. The obvious reason was that every male in America was preoccupied with making money, and had no time for the true enjoyment of life. The inability to speak any language but English was only further proof of this mad worship of the dollar; so was the American indifference to music, art, or flowers. *"Pauvres Yankees!"*

New York, on first sight, seemed to Leclercq to be totally

lacking in distinction: it was a city of immense business activity, with great hotels, marble mansions, and numerous churches—but no true "monuments." Not until he took the Staten Island Ferry did Leclercq appreciate the massing of buildings near the Battery that even then gave Manhattan's skyline its distinctiveness. But more than architecture, Leclercq was aware of the great variety of the city's people. To prove the point he extracted from the 1870 Census the figures for twenty-three groupings by national origin, from the most numerous, the Irish, with 202,000, to the least, those from Turkey, with 38.

He concluded, as the dominant Anglo-Americans could hardly be conceived as concluding, that such mixing was the chief source of New York's great energy and progress. What he saw in New York was only confirmed by his observations in other cities; and we come upon a hypothesis, one that might have shocked most of the older inhabitants, that Anglo-Americans needed a very great capacity for assimilation, for fresh immigration alone was what kept them from degenerating. *"L'élément primitif anglo-américain est celui qui semble le plus dépourvu de vitalité."* That element, of course, thought exactly the opposite: that the recent immigrants were threatening the national character and putting progress in jeopardy. Leclercq's remark, had old-line Americans read it, might have seemed just one more example of dangerous foreign thinking—or perhaps of Gallic animus toward the English.

The very hot weather—the summer was the hottest in sixty years—limited Leclercq's energy and also his enthusiasm. He climbed the *Tribune* tower, for the view, but found tramping the streets to be quite another matter. Many heat prostrations were reported, and policemen's horses suffered! One day the temperature reached 110 degrees, and mail deliveries were suspended. Every day people lined up at stands for cold drinks of a dozen varieties, all costing three cents. Iced water with meals soon seemed no longer a mere eccentricity of the natives. New York consumed two hundred thousand tons of ice every summer, Leclercq learned, most of it from the upper Hudson River and New England, but he thought that the overuse of ice in drinks explained the thinness and paleness of American faces.

Sabbatarianism stunned him. New York streets, so crowded

six days a week, were deserted on the seventh. No beer or wine could be sold on Sundays, although he discovered a side door to the bar in his hotel, and promptly called it an example of *"pharasaisme américain."* Broadway, where all week men moved at a virtual run, was conspicuously forlorn, with no shops open and no carriages visible. The one thing to do on Sunday, he observed, as did other visitors, was to visit Central Park, the eighth wonder of the world. Europe had finer parks, but none so centrally located. It was a walker's paradise, Leclercq reported, with picturesque alleys, rustic bridges, ponds and cascades, and even small rocky mountains.

Fifth Avenue, the Park's eastern border, brought him abruptly back to thoughts about money: *"L'empereur de la ville impériale, c'est le dollar,"* and the city's religion was *"la culte au dieu Greenback."* (He evidently didn't know about the current Greenback dispute.) He tried to imagine a group biography of the wealthy men whose mansions lined the Avenue; it would be only proper, he suggested, if they adorned their marble doorways with round chips representing coins. He noted that money, however it had been amassed, won public respect for its owner. Yet failure was not held to be dishonorable. In fact, to fail several times and regain financial stature earned one a title of respect, since it was clearly a proof of the immense energy and ambition on which Americans prided themselves. Like John Leng, Leclercq saw Chicago's ability to rebuild within a year of its great fire as just one more striking proof of this great drive.

Because money was the measure of all things, American religion seemed rather tainted. The churches of New York, many of them on or near Fifth Avenue, and some looking more like concert halls, could all be classified: those of the aristocrats of wealth, those of the less successful, in descending order, and a few for the poor. Leclercq asserted that he had to pay a dollar to enter a wealthy church, half a dollar at a less aristocratic church, and five cents at a humble church. One expensive church he entered had a minister, several assistant ministers, and a fine robed choir, but a very sparse congregation. He decided that in America religion was generally considered a matter of form and expediency. But at one church, which he entered because he heard remarkable singing, he found an exception: it was a Negro

church, crowded and enthusiastic. He was welcomed cordially
and given a chair. What most struck him was the range of color,
from ebony to almost white, suggesting a range from the Congo
to Ethiopia.

The longer Leclercq stayed in New York, the more the city
grew on him but there was more of America he wished to see.
He left next for Washington, which he found to be *"la quintes-
sence d'ennui."* Philadelphia had been dull enough but at least it
had factories. Washington was not an intellectual center like
Boston or a business center like New York or an industrial
center like Pittsburgh or Cincinnati. The nation's capital was
glaringly unfinished, with yawning gaps between its buildings.
No other American city, moreover, was more unhealthful. After
a visit to the White House, where he was astonished to find that
even the President was monolingual, Leclercq set out toward
the Potomac. Within twenty paces he was in open, uncultivated
country—not a house, not a garden, not a wall or orchard. On
the river's bank, amid swarms of insects, he had the illusion of
being beside some river in central Africa.

Washington, which had been laid out on a grand plan by the
Frenchman, Pièrre L'Enfant, did, however, exhibit a few "monuments," but they all reflected the American mania for imitating
the Greeks and the Romans. Their classical façades outnumbered all the ruins of Attica. The Treasury resembled the Temple of Minerva, the Post Office the Temple of Theseus. The
Capitol alone was impressive, but its collected paintings were
mediocre, examples of art that would not be tolerated in any
museum in France. The only things to admire were the great
bronze door, reminiscent of the Florence baptistery, with eight
panels representing Columbus's discovery of America. But the
good things were cancelled out by the manners of the Congressmen, men skilled in the art of spitting into cuspidors. *"Je l'ai de
mes propres yeux vu."* ("I have seen it with my own eyes.")
Again, however, the great heat may have conditioned Leclercq's
judgments; Livingstone and Stanley in the heart of Africa could
not have suffered more, he supposed, than he did in Washington.

So much for the East. As he started for the interior, Leclercq
expressed in full measure the European excitement over the
Western movement, the opening of new regions, which was not

narrowly the concern of the United States but a focus of interest for Western man in general, as the present phase of a long continuing advance of civilization.

Et maintenant, en route pour l'Ouest. En route pour cette contrée lointain qui, il y a quatre-vingts ans à peine, était encore une région perdue, une sorte de terra incognita *de forêts où s'aventuraient seuls les Indiens, et qui aujourd'hui est cultivée, défrichée, sillonée des routes, de canaux et de chemins de fer, couverte de villes florissantes, au-dessus desquelles plane la fumée des usines.*

"And now, en route to the West. En route to that far-away land which, scarcely eighty years ago, was still a lost region, a sort of *terra incognita* of forests where Indians alone ventured, and which today is cultivated, cleared, furrowed with roads, canals, and railroads, covered with flourishing towns, above which hovers the smoke of factories."

Here, once again, as Colonel Taylor had expressed it in Texas, was the myth of the garden. The Eastern cities, which two centuries earlier had been the hope of the future, were already corrupt, as bad, Leclercq thought, as any in Europe. It was only in this newer region that something better could be imagined and hoped for, something closer to man's ancient dream of a paradise on earth. But the passage quoted above is romantic, written before the fact. Leclercq the realist did not let his dreams of the ideal obscure what he saw with his own eyes.

On a Chesapeake and Ohio train heading west from Washington, it was Leclercq's luck, good or bad, to strike up an acquaintance with a Southerner who passed along his views of lazy freedman (better treated as slaves) and carpetbaggers (*"cette vermine"*); the South, left to its own resources, would presumably have recovered promptly from the ravages of the Civil War —an hypothesis liked by all too many historians of the early twentieth century. Leclercq might have modified this notion had he gone to New Orleans, as he originally planned, but the heat persuaded him to cancel the visit, just as it persuaded Huxley not to visit his sister in her home in Montgomery, Alabama.

At Huntington, West Virginia, Leclercq and his fellow passengers boarded a packet for Cincinnati, which was then known as "Porcopolis" for its large industry of converting hogs to ham and bacon. Here the mingling of peoples was very evident—Italians and Swedes, Irish and Germans and Russians, Swiss and Norwegians, all well-assimilated in a single generation and yielding an admixture of skills and temperaments highly favorable to progress. Most American cities, east and west, seemed to Leclercq to have *"un air triste et sombre,"* ("a sad and somber air") but Cincinnati showed a livelier interest in the arts than most, indeed, one that even European cities might envy.

The train ride to St. Louis was broken by a fifteen-minute meal stop at Vincennes, Indiana. There, like Offenbach and Holland, Leclercq was horrified by the haste of American eating: *"l'Americain ne mange pas, il dévore"* ("The American doesn't eat, he devours.") What was more, American men ate in silence; they even drank in silence. They also drank *"beaucoup et souvent,"* ("Much and often") and usually with their hats on, as also in public libraries and courtrooms.

St. Louis, obviously, was not the West that Leclercq had dreamed of. Nor was Kansas City, where, in the Pacific Hotel, lacking all comfort, he was served *"ragout de prairie dog."* Kansas, where the train steamed along at a steady thirty miles per hour, was a marvel of wheat (thirty-two bushels per acre) and cattle (grazing where, only recently, the buffalo had swarmed). The air had a welcome transparency. Colorado was even better. Leclercq found Denver quite pleasing, perhaps because the Grand Central Hotel fulfilled his fondest hopes. So did the Manitou House at Colorado Springs, looking out upon Pike's Peak. Leclercq joined an expedition up that mountain, a two-day effort on horseback. He signed the guestbook at the summit and noted that the first date in the book was July 14, 1874. Later he inspected the Garden of the Gods, and Glen Eyrie, where he was shocked to see an advertisement for a Denver firm painted in large white letters on the rock wall of the gorge. Soon, he thought, there would have to be signs at all scenic spots reading "POST NO BILLS."

By rail and stage Leclercq ventured into the Rockies for glimpses of gold mines and mountain scenery. This time his train sported a diner, *"le plus sublime en Amérique";* there were magazines and a Bible in every car; there was even a traveling bookseller offering novels by Scott and Dickens, Thackeray and Bulwer.

He went next to Chicago. The city pleased him greatly. For one thing, he found numerous beer halls, which he had missed in Philadelphia. But despite Chicago's pre-eminence in the business of handling food, the meals there were very poor. The contrast of domestic opulence and repulsive industry was marked. The mansions of the wealthy rivaled the best in Paris, but the stock-yards——! Here, in 345 acres, was a disgusting massacre; naked men, their bodies covered with blood, their feet literally in a river of blood; and withal a disgusting odor. But Chicago also had its lovely Lincoln Park, with welcome shade, and its rail-road station, the nation's best, and fine hotels, where, as other visitors noted, not only travelers stopped but families lived, especially young couples still too restless to establish homes of their own. For, as Leclercq observed, *"Le Yankee est le plus nomade de tous les peuples."*

Leaving Chicago in a downpour, Leclercq rode the Michigan Central past Lake Michigan (a hundred times the size of Lac Leman, he noted), and on to Detroit, which he described as only a small provincial city. Here he crossed to Canada for the remainder of his American visit. Whether he felt that the Far West had fulfilled his dreams, he never quite said, although in general he liked the Western cities somewhat better than those in the East. Nothing proved to be quite without flaw—a poor meal, an outrageous advertisement. We should perhaps regret that he left the United States in mid-July and never saw the country when it wasn't hot. The cooler weather of August might have warmed his enthusiasm.

Leclercq's fellow Frenchman, Paul Toutain, noticed first of all that Americans paid scant attention to foreigners. Once a personal contact was made, however, the American could be expected to ask two questions—how the visitor liked this coun-try and whether he thought its political institutions excelled those in France. The American, however, never waited for an answer; instead, he characteristically launched into a detailed account of his own business affairs, his hopes and plans, and—to Toutain's embarrassment—a precise report of his financial status. But this same typical American was never as frank with his wife, who was neither her husband's confidant nor his friend, and knew nothing about his occupation. It disconcerted Toutain to discover that after just a few years of marriage the American husband paid little attention to his wife, respecting her about as much as he would the portrait of a venerated ancestress. Meanwhile the husband, as Toutain observed him at the Clifton House at Niagara Falls, at the Tremont in Chicago, and at other hotels, was a rather disgusting individual—careless in attire and manners, forever chewing tobacco and spitting into cuspidors. The younger men were less offensive, but they were so pale and thin as to seem lifeless. Only the girls were attractive—the lovely young brides at Niagara Falls, and the daughters whose grace and charm only accentuated their fathers' gaucherie.

The subtitle of Toutain's book is "Yankees, Indians, Mormons"; and he had much to say about them all. The first Indians he saw were at Omaha—a procession of chieftains on their solemn way to a conference with federal officials. This sight led Toutain to generalize about the unhappy lot of the red men in the United States. At Salt Lake he interviewed Brigham Young, "*le pape-empereur*" of Utah, and was gratified to learn how much he liked the theatre and dancing. But he was astonished by the degree of homage paid their leader by rank and file Mormons.

If Toutain had wanted his subtitle to be inclusive, it would have been longer, for he later visited two unusual communal settlements in upstate New York. The practice of eugenic mating at the Oneida colony filled him with scorn, while the rule of silence maintained by the Shakers at Mt. Lebanon struck him as contrary to nature, although he viewed the Shakers' ritualistic dancing as inoffensive.

Visiting the University of Notre Dame in Indiana and Oberlin College in Ohio, Toutain drew some conclusions about American higher education in general. The removal of nature study from the garden to the laboratory was, he thought, a serious mistake, and the study of modern foreign languages was so limited as to suggest indifference. The Board of Trustees which existed at every institution puzzled him; he could not see its function except, perhaps, as one kind of "*bureau d'education.*" But at least he looked at higher education, as most of our foreign observers did not.

All the French travelers were curious about the theatre. At

Chicago, where the citizens with their boldness, their energy, and their propensity to take chances, struck him as the quintessential Americans, Toutain attended a production of a play called *Civilization* at the Vickers Theatre. In Act II the hero, a Huron chieftain, visited Versailles and met Louis XV. It was a splendid vehicle for propagandizing about the superiority of American customs and institutions to those of France. Toutain did not exactly condemn the play, but he did observe that in France such a story line would make an amusing Offenbach operetta. He also saw fit to add that the writings of Mark Twain were a welcome antidote to American jingoism.

Toutain did not sustain his announced intention of shattering the favorable French image of the United States; just what it was that aroused his indignation is nowhere quite clear. That he arrived with high expectations and was forced to revise his opinions downward is about as much as can be said. At the close of the book he ventured a general prognosis for the American future. It was not an optimistic one. The sheer size of the country, its astonishing mixture of racial and national stocks, its great diversity of ways of life, and its divisions—political, social, religious, economic—that he considered far more dangerous than any in France, all suggested to Toutain serious trouble ahead. *"C'est le pays de Brobdingnag,"* he decided, referring to the land of the giants in *Gulliver's Travels,* peopled by little Gullivers.

7

MR. AND MRS. HUXLEY

By far the most famous of all the visitors to America in its Centennial year was the great English biologist, educator, agnostic, and exponent of Darwinism, Thomas Henry Huxley. The nation's militant orthodox would undoubtedly have preferred the term "infamous," for T. H. Huxley, the grandfather of Aldous and Julian Huxley, personified, perhaps more than any other man then living, the new scientific challenge to religious fundamentalism. For months before his arrival, conservative editors thundered their disapproval and advised the pious to shun the lectures on evolution that were a major purpose of his visit. At the opposite pole of opinion were the scientists, especially the teachers of science, who hoped that his influence would help them overcome the prevalent opposition to science education in the schools and strengthen their efforts to reduce the pre-eminence given to Greek and Latin. Somewhere in between were the people who bought and enjoyed a popular song issued in 1874, "Too Thin, or Darwin's Little Joke. A Humorous Song" with words by Grace Carlton and music by "O'Rangoutang." The following refrain ended each of its stanzas:

> It certainly is most absurd,
> The fact can never be
> My great grand daddy never was
> A "Monkey" up a tree.[10]

Grouping Huxley with other Centennial chroniclers is somewhat gratuitous, however, for his trip was not intended to help celebrate the nation's first great birthday, and, in fact, was not connected with the Centennial in any way. Huxley was persuaded to come to the United States by a group of American leaders in an educational revolution: Edward L. Youmans and W. H. Appleton, pioneers in scientific publishing; John Fiske, the foremost publicizer of the new science; and Daniel Coit Gilman, president of the new Johns Hopkins University, who felt that nobody was so well suited as Huxley to open the University's public lecture series. True, it was hardly possible for any visitor to America in 1876 to ignore the significance of the year; and in his address at Johns Hopkins Huxley did pointedly bring the Centennial into his electrifying peroration. But as far as Centennial records are concerned, it was only a happy accident that this, Huxley's single visit to the United States, occurred in 1876.[11]

Even though he carried two pocket diaries during his Centennial visit, Huxley recorded nothing more significant about his trip than a few temperatures, the names of some hotels, train departure times, and baggage check numbers,[12] and in after years never saw fit, even in a private manuscript, to record his impressions. But Huxley was so important a figure that journalists recorded everything he said within their hearing (and much that he never said). And, because he brought his wife Nellie along with him, and because they were separated for several days during their stay, we also have an exchange of letters between them to amplify the picture. There are, in addition, some letters that Nellie Huxley wrote to relatives back home.

George W. Smalley, the London correspondent of the New York *Tribune*, was a fellow passenger with the Huxleys aboard the west-bound *Germanic*, and he reported Huxley's first reactions to the United States on August 5:

> As we drew near the city . . . he asked what were the tall tower and tall building with a cupola, then the two most conspicuous objects. I told him the Tribune and the Western Union Telegraph buildings. "Ah," he said, "that is interesting; this is America. In the Old World the first things you see as you approach a city are steeples; here you see, first, centers of intelligence." Next to those the tugboats seemed to attract him as they tore fiercely up and down and across the bay. He looked long at them and finally said, "If I were not a man I think I should like to be a tug." [13]

William H. Appleton, one of the country's foremost book publishers, met the Huxleys and took them by his private yacht to his estate on the Hudson at Riverdale, where they stayed from Saturday until Wednesday. Nellie was glad to be there, in "this (comparatively) cool retreat instead of boiling at New York," and she expressed awe at the river scenery. The heat held on, however, so fiercely that she accepted an invitation to visit Saratoga while her husband went to New Haven to consult Othniel Marsh, the noted professor of paleontology at Yale.

Huxley almost missed the New Haven train; he reached the depot just as it was starting and the ticket seller waved him aboard. But once in his seat he marveled at the drawing car—"a new idea of the possibilities of railway traveling." At his destination he was met by Professor Marsh, who installed him in "apartments which were occupied by his uncle, the millionaire

Peabody and are as quiet as if I were in my own house." New
Haven delighted him: "This is the most charmingly picturesque
town with the streets lined by arching elm trees which meet
overhead—I have never seen anything like it and you must come
& see it." Marsh had more than enough fossils to keep him
occupied, but he had also seen to it that nobody would bother
them; only one person asked for an autograph.[14]

Two days later, after a side trip to inspect some fossilized
footprints beside the Connecticut River near Springfield, Huxley wrote again to Nellie: "We are hard at work still. Breakfast
at 8:30—go over with Marsh between 9 & 10—work until 1:30.
Dine, go back to museum and work till 6. Mr. Marsh takes me a
drive to see the view about the town and back to tea about half
past eight. He is a wonderful fellow full of fun and stories about
his western adventures." Huxley enclosed a clipped interview
sent from New York in which, to his amusement, he was called
"affable" and "of the commercial or mercantile type." "This is
something I did not know," he remarked, "& I am proud of it.
We may be rich yet."

The interview, which had appeared in the New York
World on August 8, was distinctive for being double-barreled:
"Professor Huxley / A Genuine and Apocryphal Interview." In
the actual interview, Huxley remarked to the reporter that it
was a novel experience "to be hunted to cover and subjected to
the tender mercies of an interviewer"; he had been industriously
dodging the press.

"By what instinct do you know my hiding-place?"

The reporter said that in America newspapermen had developed techniques not yet tried on the other side of the Atlantic;
he then asked Huxley's opinion of New York. He was not yet
ready, Huxley replied, to express an opinion. He did allude,
however, to the height of a newspaper office and a telegraph
building, and to the bustle and variety to be seen on Broadway;
it reminded him of Paris, he said, but the clear sky and atmosphere reminded him of Australia. Then, after outlining his proposed trip, he remarked that he was being "killed by kindness."
The apocryphal version merely reversed the roles, with Huxley
arriving to interview a reporter; one of the topical allusions was

to Mark Twain's "A Literary Nightmare," in the February *Atlantic Monthly*, with a rhyme.

> "Punch, brothers, punch with care,
> Punch in the presence of the passenjare,"

that somebody adapted to the year's most popular example of sheet-music.

From Saratoga, where she was now staying, Nellie Huxley described the elms there as being "like the groined roof of a cathedral." She was astonished by much that she saw—the gigantic hotels, each with its long piazza and its gas-lit drawing rooms, the springs which were "always under cover of some fanciful architecture," and the women's clothes. "Indeed I never saw so many extravagancies in dress." Saratoga's inflated economy shocked her: "What a price everything is—my laundry bill was 6½ dollars." She confessed to being a little heartsick at their separation, but it helped when the band, at her request, played some Welsh airs.

Soon she joined her husband in New Haven, and the couple proceeded to Newport for a visit with Alexander Agassiz, the noted naturalist and industrialist; to Boston for visits with Harvard's Asa Gray, the country's leading Darwinian; and then to Petersham for a reunion with the philosopher and historian John Fiske (who had visited them in London).

Petersham retained, as it still does, an eighteenth century atmosphere; and the house, actually the home of Fiske's brother-in-law, James W. Brooks, was bigger and more elaborate than the average in American villages. But village and house gave the Huxleys an intimate view of what was still, in 1876, the most typical kind of family living, an experience denied most other foreign visitors.

Fiske had assembled a blue-ribbon guest list—John Knowles Paine, Harvard professor of music and the first important American composer; the poet-painter Christopher Cranch; Rose Lathrop, Nathaniel Hawthorne's daughter, and Edith Longfellow. Gourmet that he was, Fiske had also engaged Professor Edward Everett's cook, while Everett was in Europe. The visit was idyllic, and before it ended, a guest-book was begun, with an original song by Paine, a picture by Cranch, a poem by Nellie Huxley, and a sketch by her husband of an ape-like Eve handing an apple to an ape-like Adam while a snake looks on.[15]

Now the public part of Huxley's tour began. The next day he and his wife left on a long train ride to Buffalo for the twenty-fifth meeting of the American Association for the Advancement of Science. Called upon to say a few words, Huxley spoke informally and briefly.

"I am not by nature a man of many words," he said, "and have thought the highest eloquence was in condensing what one has to say." He had discovered since his arrival that "the instinct of curiosity" was well developed in Americans; two reporters had put questions to him that could be answered only in a treatise. The States, from what he had seen so far, were not conspicuously different from England except in the great distances separating centers of population. Regarding national traits: "I have heard a great deal from your own writers about the degeneracy of the present American stock from the primitive English type. The late Nathaniel Hawthorne used an expression that rather rubbed us: he spoke of the distinction between English and American, and told us English women were rather too teethy. Now that was his expression, not mine." (Laughter reported.)

Huxley next alluded to someone's thesis that the climate was causing a reversion from the aboriginal North American type. He had no sign of this, however, except in the extreme hospitality that was said to be a savage trait. "I have visited your wigwams—and they are pretty good wigwams too. You entertain us with your best, and not only give us your best, but are not quite happy unless we take the spoons and plates away with us." It may be remarked, parenthetically, that some editors took him seriously and chided Huxley for what they considered a slur.

In a somewhat more serious vein, Huxley observed that Englishmen, when they became rich, bought estates and founded families, while successful Americans founded colleges. And he closed by saying that Americans did not need to cross the Atlantic to find antiquities. He had seen at New Haven much older things than Europe could exhibit. Professor Marsh's collected fossils, indeed, had changed the theory of evolution from a matter of speculation and argument to a matter of fact and history. The only remaining question, a subordinate one, was: How had it happened? [16]

These remarks, printed in the next day's papers, evoked predictable indignation in orthodox circles. More to the general liking was a "first impression" that a journalist-wit invented; "Huxley, at Niagara, according to Perkins of the Cincinnati *Times:* 'Oh, what a fall is here, my countrymen!' " [17]

More long hours on trains took the Huxleys to Nashville for a reunion with a sister, Lizzie Huxley Scott, and an impromptu but solid lecture "On the Geology of Tennessee," and then to Baltimore for Huxley's heralded discourse launching the Johns Hopkins lecture series. In his Hopkins speech, "Address on University Education," [18] Huxley spoke of many things; but what gave the address its enduring value was its conclusion, wherein Huxley exchanged his role of scientist and educational reformer for that of a social prophet, and challenged the nation of that time—and ours:

> I cannot say that I am in the slightest degree impressed by your bigness, or your material resources, as such. Size is not grandeur, and your territory does not make a nation. The great issue, about which hangs a true sublimity, and the terror of overhanging fate, is what are you going to do with all these things? What is to be the end to which these are the means? You are making a novel experiment in politics on the greatest scale which the world has yet seen. Forty millions at your first century, it is reasonably to be expected that, at the second, these states will be occupied by two hundred millions of English-speaking people, spread over an area as large as that of Europe, and with climates and interests as diverse as those of Spain and Scandinavia, England and Russia. You and your descendants have to ascertain whether this great mass will hold together under the forms of a republic, and the despotic reality of universal suffrage; whether state rights will hold out against centralisation, without separation; whether centralisation will get the better, without actual or disguised monarchy; whether shifting corruption is better than a permanent bureaucracy; and as population thickens in your great cities, and the pressure of want is felt, the gaunt spectre of pauperism will stalk among you, and communism and so-

cialism will claim to be heard. Truly America has a great future before her; great in toil, in care, and in responsibility; great in true glory if she be guided in wisdom and righteousness; great in shame if she fail. I cannot understand why other nations should envy you, or be blind to the fact that it is for the highest interest of mankind that you should succeed, but the one condition of success, your sole safeguard, is the moral worth and intellectual clearness of the individual citizen. Education cannot give these, but it may cherish them and bring them to the front in whatever station of society they are to be found; and the universities ought to be, and may be, the fortresses of the higher life of the nation.

The visit was nearly over: there remained only three New York lectures on the factual evidence for the theory of evolution, during the week of September 18, before the couple boarded the *Celtic* for home.[19]

8

JOHN LEWIS, TRANSPLANTED ENGLISHMAN

Thomas and Nellie Huxley's recorded views on America and Americans are, alas, too brief and few. The English view of Centennial America is more fully given by an immigrant named John Lewis. A permanent resident of New York, where he worked for a wholesale grocer, Lewis had not been so long in this country as to lose the sense of its differences from England. In letters to his brother back home he reported on many aspects and details about Centennial life that might otherwise have eluded us altogether.[20]

Lewis was, by and large, the most factual of reporters. Much of what he wrote was in answer to specific questions about the United States raised by his nephews.

Lewis spent Christmas, 1875, in Philadelphia with one of his sons. He enjoyed the city very much, he wrote, and was much struck by Philadelphia's enthusiasm in celebrating the holiday. Elsewhere in America the Christmas tree was disposed of immediately after the distribution of presents, but

> Not so in Phila. . . . There all the people seem to resolve themselves into Children for the occasion. I may say that the usual arrangement in this country is to have two parlours—be it a large or small house—opening to each other by sliding doors, the first being for state occasions. As *large* & fine a tree as can be accommodated being procured and set up, it is covered with every conceivable shape into which coloured & gilt paper & card can be cut, and . . . little pictures, glass balls, chains, garlands etc. anything to make a gay and imposing display. This being finished is placed mostly in the sliding door way, which allows it to be seen 2 ways. All the light possible is thrown upon it, often by reflectors, the lattice blinds being thrown open & it is thus open to inspection by passers by—which, as houses in Phila are only a little above the street, is an easy matter. Where the taste & industry of the owner prompts it, other attractions are added as fancy dictates—at one place I visited, an old doctor's, there was a very handsome river steamboat, perfect, 3 feet long with about 50 passengers (these last small pictures cut out) all of white, coloured & gilt card; also a beautiful fire hose carriage. When the show commences people go round with or without their children to see them & frequently knock at the door to be admitted to a closer inspection which is readily granted. I heard of one house where 75 were admitted in about 2 hours. Riding through the better class streets on the cars, the effect is novel & very fine as every 2nd or 3rd may be exhibitors. I believe some keep it up 2 or 3 weeks.

Lewis so much enjoyed Christmas in Philadelphia that he returned for New Year's Eve. At the house of the mayor's chief clerk he observed a mock trial that went on for three hours, with elaborate cross-examinations in which counsel quoted from such learned precedents as *Buckwheat Versus Muffins*. The group took time out only for the actual arrival of the new year. At midnight, after listening to a cacophony of whistles, bells, and other noises, it was time for refreshments—great molds of ice cream in different flavors, jellies, cakes, fruit. At about two o'clock the host donned his judge's costume again and went outside to mystify the neighbors.

The next day, Lewis attended a banquet, at four in the afternoon: two twenty-pound turkeys, "with all the trimmings," and then charades, "Nigger Minstrelsy," piano playing, dancing, and nobody waited to be asked to sing. Lewis thought the noise was astonishing; in New York people would have found it shocking.

In a letter on August 7, Lewis had much to say about the hot weather. From the last week in June, with a single cool interlude, the mercury had climbed daily into the nineties. Walls and pavements were extremely hot, and interiors were very like ovens. Ice and fans became necessities—however effeminate "foreigners" might consider the fans. Lewis admitted using both the Chinese variety, cut from a palm leaf and costing from one to three cents, and the superior Japanese article, of bamboo and paper, painted, costing a nickel. "Americans would not be bothered to make them at any price." He also admitted drinking plenty of iced water, "sometimes with a 'stick' in it."

The mild winter had limited the nearby supply of ice, but when the ice firms tried to take advantage of the scarcity by raising the price, companies in Maine sent all that was called for at $2.50 a ton. A ten-pound cake of ice left at one's door every day cost sixty cents a week. To prevent its melting, one needed to have an ice chest or water cooler, made of zinc for best results and insulated with powdered charcoal. Quite a different way of cooling off was to go to the seashore. Lewis tried "a place called Cony Island" two Sundays in July, and found about twenty thousand people there, on two miles of beach. But getting to sleep in the night heat was a major problem. Many New Yorkers slept on their doorsteps, or on flat roofs.

Lewis looked with favor upon American sweet corn. "Just now it is used in its green state, boiled, & the ears being taken in the fingers it is bitten from the 'Cob' after it is Butterd, pepperd, & salted. It is very nice, much of the taste of young wheat. Invention has hitherto failed to find a *good* substitute for the fingers even at fashionable tables."

He also spoke with obvious approval of tomatoes:

Tomatoes have always been favorites here. They generally require a person to be educated to them, but most people like them. They are great bearers, and are eaten in every possible way, mostly however cut up alone or with cucumber, or stewed & used as a sauce. They want *character*, but many like them raw to allay thirst. Next to potatoes, they are the most plentiful vegetable for a month or two, but of course dont keep. Large quantities of "ketchup" are made from them, that being indeed the national "Sass."

Americans, Lewis explained, managed on three meals a day—breakfast, dinner, and supper, all more-or-less substantial. They did not have afternon tea, as was customary in England. The breakfast staple was a steak or a chop, usually with fried potatoes but sometimes with fried hominy. In addition there were pancakes topped with molasses, and hot bread. Midday dinner, as in England, commonly consisted of a roast and vegetables, with a dessert of pie or pudding (and here he had to explain the American pie, very seldom in a deep dish as in England). Supper was a repetition of breakfast. At all three meals tea or coffee was served—and water, too, because of the relatively dry climate. Many Americans ate at restaurants or boarding houses; prices were so reasonable that it was hardly worth the trouble to prepare one's own meals. (Lewis was speaking, of course, for the city.) At his own favorite restaurant, he could count on a meat course and pie for twenty-five cents. Even in villages, he thought people ate often at taverns, leaving home when the bell rang and filling up for fifty cents. "Not much variety but good." And even ordinary country people commonly used napkins; indeed, "The use of table napkins is very general."

Baked beans and brown bread were not as nearly universal in New England as they had been earlier, when they were served first on Saturday night, kept warm in the oven for Sunday breakfast, and then eaten cold for Sunday dinner and supper—all in order to avoid cooking on the Sabbath. But although this Puritan practice had declined, the hot Sunday breakfast of beans was still popular in boarding houses and restaurants. Hash was also in demand, although to a lesser degree, and some establishments specialized in them, earning the title of "hashhouse."

Cheese and butter made at creameries were crowding out that produced by individual farmers; unseen, they brought half a cent or a cent more per pound. But oleomargarine, too, was beginning to attract buyers; made of suet in large city factories, it could be sold for much less than butter. The factory was also beginning to enter the scene in the production of yeast; factory-made yeast was of a consistent quality that yielded fine spongy bread. And bread itself was being made increasingly in bakeries instead of at home, especially after the Exhibition had popularized Dutch, French, and Vienna loaves. The Exhibition also catapulted lager beer into general favor; this beer of low alcoholic content had previously been known only among German immigrants.

If John Lewis had more to say about food than anything else, it was because he was, by occupation, concerned with the subject. But his letters touched on many other subjects as well. He reported the steady progress on the suspension bridge from Manhattan to Brooklyn, the preparations for blowing up Hell Gate, the bridge across the East River, and the work on a tunnel under the Hudson to Hoboken. He correctly predicted that Manhattan could not much longer depend on ferries; more and more people were commuting to work in Manhattan from Long Island and New Jersey. He also spoke of the decline in popularity of roller skating and the velocipede. What he called the "Rink," in actuality the Hippodrome, was ideal for skating but was being used in 1876 only for large meetings, such as those of Moody and Sankey, or for concerts.

Of life in remote parts of the nation Lewis knew nothing from personal experience; but his son, Ed, who was in charge of constructing a government telegraph line along the Rio Grande, told him some facts of frontier life. Mexicans were nuisances as cattle thieves, and they were now compounding their villainy by stealing poles and wire. On home leave in June, Ed told of having to ride fifty or sixty miles a day, of seeing frequent crude crosses marking graves along the way, "where some poor fellow met his death," and of one occasion when the reins he was holding were severed by a Mexican bullet, only inches from his hands. Elsewhere in the great West, Indians were causing trouble. But on this matter Lewis had his own views.

I suppose you have read in the papers . . . of the massacre of some of our troops by the Indians under "Sitting Bull." Thats what its called when our troops suffer. The fact is the Indians are systematically swindeld. Their lands are purchased, and pay & supplies promised, not one fourth of which reach them, and if Uncle Sam would only hang or shoot a few agents & Traders, the continual warfare with the Red Skins would be prevented. As it is, the same doctrine is applied to them, that used to apply to the "Nigger"—that "niggers have no rights that a white man is bound to respect." They are a lazy, worthless lot of rascals, yet they have rights, if only to be shot down, and they get *that* right whenever some of the border ruffians get a chance. A provocation is by no means essential, & by that means the animosity is kept alive. . . . One thing is certain, both the Indians & the Bison (Buffalo) are doomed to extinction, some day.

In a pattern familiar to travelers in unfamiliar countries, the more John Lewis wrote about America the less sure he seemed to be on particular points. It was one thing to talk about groceries, but quite another to assess, with confidence, such things as religion and politics. Lewis was shrewd enough to realize that Centennial Americans were more interested in politics than they were in religion. Republicans struck him as the more progressive major party, and Democrats as more concerned with "loaves and fishes," by which he meant the greatest possible benefits from government. He added that "the *body* of the great unwashed & the lower class generally [are] Democrats," but it may be that an ancient dislike of the Irish colored his thinking. "One thing is very marked," he wrote. "Our City seems to be at the marcy of the Irish to a great extent. No sooner does an Irishman land than he begins to look for an office, long before he is naturalized. . . . I say so much of the Irish because politics without the Irish would be like 'Hamlet' without the prince. Having said this much I place on record my opinion that *the man who is devoted to politics is seldom good for much else.*"

Lewis also commented in detail on religion in America. He knew that Methodists and Baptists were the largest Protestant groups, and he was also aware that denominational strength varied greatly from one section of the country to another. For

New York City he reported a total of 375 churches, 73 of them Protestant Episcopal, 54 Catholic, 50 Methodist, 41 Baptist, 25 Jewish, 21 Lutheran and 21 Dutch Reformed, and fewer than ten each for other sects. (He himself apparently belonged to no church.) But the city's assortment seemed to interest him less than the certain unusual groups elsewhere, especially the Shakers and the Oneida Community, albeit he had never seen them.

The Shakers he described as "a sort of Quaker, in dress at least, have everything in common, men & women live seperate & don't marry & keep up the organization by recruits from outside." A very moral and industrious people, they were known for the excellent quality of the products they offered for sale: "to say that it is of 'Shaker' make is to guarantee excellence." Regarding Oneida, Lewis was no doubt reflecting general popular opinion in saying that although its members were thrifty and orderly, "they live like brutes they do not marry or indeed select their partners, so the children & property are held in common. It is indeed a wise child that knows its own father."

As for higher education, Lewis was uneasy over the multiplicity of institutions granting degrees. There seemed to him to be as many "doctors" of this or that as there were "judges," "generals," and "colonels" in civilian life. No university in the land equalled Oxford or Cambridge, but Harvard, Yale, Princeton, and Columbia won his mild approval. Cornell, "founded by a gentleman of that name," was distinctive for permitting students to work their way through. It was even more distinctive for its famous crew. Nearly every state had "a University socalled which I suppose has the facilities & powers, in miniature, of the larger institutions—including rowing." Of special interest to Lewis, as to other observers, was the American practice of private endowment: "A favourite method with people here who have money to spare or wish to erect a memorial is to endow a new college or else to add a 'hall' or other buildings to one already in operation."

Regarding the lower schools, Lewis thought that "There is probably no country in the world where education is so well provided as in the U. S." He approved of the practice, when public lands were surveyed into townships of thirty-six square miles, of setting aside one square mile for the school. As the

township acquired a population, there was a more-or-less standard order in which institutions were established: gin-mill, school,
store, newspaper, jail, and gallows. But the New England model
of paying teachers very little and having them board around, a
week or a month with each family, seemed to Lewis "a miserable way, especially as the country people as a rule [are] of a
very stingy disposition." He also took a dim view of corporal
punishment, commonly outlawed in the cities but still practiced
in country schools—the shingle being used in the North, the
paddle in the South, especially for Negroes. The paddle he
described as a thin board with a handle, bored with large holes.
"This well applied," he wrote, "is said to produce pretty lively
sensations, as many a young darky could testify."

Lewis seldom resorted to the device of saying that something
"is said" to be or do this or that. Most of the time he reported
only what he had observed directly, and our purposes are well-
served by his honest, down-to-earth descriptions, and, indeed,
by his habit of trailing off into minutiae. After all, it is the
minutiae that matter; almost anybody could report such a generalization as the existence of corporal punishment in rural schools.
When the time comes to describe the Centennial Exhibition
itself, John Lewis will prove almost indispensable.

9

EMILY IN SITKA AND LAPWAI

Christmas in Sitka, Alaska, in 1875, in the home of Dr. Jenkins
FitzGerald, was a far cry from the elaborate festival that John
Lewis reported in Philadelphia. Dr. FitzGerald, the army post
surgeon, had selected the family tree and cut it himself, and had
also designed and made the candleholders. But it was Emily, his
young wife, who made the decorations: bits of ribbon, colored
cardboard in various shapes, flowers and stars made of paper, and

old neckties looped among the branches. Her one thought, she noted in a letter, was to please the children. On Christmas Eve the candles were lighted, and friends dropped in—the three other American couples at the post. Next night they all went to a party at the Major's, where the tree had real ornaments, and where everybody opened real bonbons and donned paper caps. It was something for Emily to write home about to her mother in Columbia, Pennsylvania—something less humdrum than the day-to-day news that usually filled her letters.[21]

Sitka was on Baranof Island in the Alexander Archipelago; nearby Chichagof and Kupreanof islands, the latter with a settlement named Petersburg, were other reminders that, only ten years before, Alaska had been Russian. Emily made little distinction between the "dirty little Russian town" on one side of the army post and the Indian village on the other side; but she wrote more about the Indians—"the most horrible, disgusting, dirty hideous set I ever saw," stealing everything they could lay their hands on. Indian wealth, she reported, was measured in blankets; Captain Jack, the richest man in his village, had four hundred of them. Rich Indians also had slaves. But their houses were wretched, with only one room for the entire family, and holes in the roof for chimneys.

Once a month the steamship arrived, from Portland, Oregon, bearing mail and whatever had been ordered by mail. Emily planned for weeks to brighten the bare army house with cretonne. It cost $1.10 a yard, but the pattern she ordered—water lilies and morning glories on a dark background—would be worth it. Then, when it arrived, it dismayed her by seeming too gay. By that time she and the other three wives had abandoned all pretense of fashion; they had even given up "store hair." Furs were a different matter. For about $75, Emily bought several fox skins, but decided against sables, for eight, ten, or twelve dollars a skin, because they were only fair in quality. In one letter to her mother, she enclosed a few Alaskan owl feathers.

Emily was astonished by the Easter ceremonies of the Russian Orthodox Church—the doleful Friday night service, the bier of Christ borne by candlelight into the church, the somber fasting on Saturday, the sudden relief at midnight and the loud rejoicing for the Resurrection; it was nothing an American Protestant like

Emily could possibly have been prepared for. But she could not give these festivities her undivided attention. She was busy packing for their return to Portland, two days later, and too anxious about the next assignment that General Howard would decide upon for her husband. She hoped it would be Fort Lapwai, in the Nez Perce Reservation in Idaho.

When they arrived in Portland she found that much as she liked the city, with its many shops, she was uneasy as the days of waiting there accumulated. Hotel life soon grew tiresome, and, what was worse, it cost from forty to sixty dollars a week—out of a monthly salary of $200.

Lapwai, where they arrived in mid-May, was all that Emily had hoped for: striking scenery, excellent climate, riotous wild flowers, a somewhat larger contingent of officers and wives, and mail three times a week. Jennie, the Russian maid acquired in Sitka, was wonderful with the children, but about as helpless in the kitchen as Emily herself. The doctor hunted up a Chinese cook, Mr. Sing, but he came high: "Just think of paying 35 dollars in greenbacks to a man who does not do nearly as much as a woman in the East does for 14." The greenbacks used for army pay had to be discounted by about ten percent. Gold was still the only currency that most Westerners considered real.

On July 16 Emily thanked her Aunt Annie for some pictures of the Centennial Exhibition, and asked, "Did you ever hear anything more terrible than the massacre of poor Custer and his command?" The news was certain to rouse terror in western army posts. Emily, for one, admitted constant worry about a possible uprising of the Nez Perce, and bluntly expressed her hope that "the Indians will be shown no quarter. War is dreadful anyway, but an Indian war is worst of all. They respect no code of warfare, flags of truce, wounded—nothing is respected! It is like fighting to exterminate wild animals, horrible beasts. Don't let anybody talk of peace until the Indians are taught a lesson and, if not exterminated, so weakened they will never molest and butcher again."

During September what she had feared happened: the Nez Perce attacked white settlers in the Wallowa Valley, where they had vowed no whites should ever live. But the trouble ended quickly "in a sort of compromise, and five Indian commissioners will be here next month. . . . I wish they would kill them all (the Indians—not the Commissioners)." The weather, she added, was fine—a lovely Fall.

A letter written on October 22 touched on a variety of concerns. The new thinking derived from science was upsetting old religious ideas, and Emily was confused. The Indians were quiet for the moment, but active not very far away, especially the Cheyennes. Readymade clothes, as in Altman's catalog, were so inexpensive it hardly paid to make one's own; for example, she was tempted to order a calico wrapper with pockets and "all the fixings," priced at just one dollar.

The Indian Commissioners arrived in November, together with thousands of Nez Perce. Very few of these Indians wore blankets, as in Sitka; the common attire was short pants, a shirt, and a coat or jacket. Their hair was cut short, for Indians—neck length. Their faces showed very little paint; they reminded Emily of Negroes. She and her husband stayed only briefly at the great formal opening meeting with them—she couldn't endure the smell of so many unbathed bodies. Later, she met the Commissioners at her home and described them as men of great culture, patience, and charm. But they left within a week without having come to an agreement with Joseph and the other Nez Perce leaders. It was no doubt the departure of the Commissioners that prompted Emily to write, in a rare show of disgruntlement, "Nothing ever happens at this post."

The year was nearing its close, and once again Emily was busy planning Christmas for her children. For Jennie, too; the shoes Emily got for her at the post store fit poorly and wore out quickly—would her mother send a pair, size five? Her mother had just sent something quite different but no less welcome—the best seller of 1876, *Helen's Babies* by John Habberton. "Those children," Emily wrote, "were the most wonderful I ever heard of."

The Centennial Year ended rather badly for Emily. Jennie, as fate would have it, had always liked an occasional nip, but on December 29, the date the FitzGeralds had invited the entire garrison for a party, Jennie had not had just a nip—she had gone on a bust. (Emily had to explain to her mother what this meant.) Mr. Sing had given way to Mrs. Perry, a fine cook, but even so, Emily had to work so hard preparing for her guests that minutes before they arrived she collapsed and went to bed. Her one solace was that she had left in a conspicuous place, for her guests to see and perhaps read, a little tract that she and her family had wept over, *The Little Captain*. Josiah Holland would have approved.

10

JOSEPH HATTON'S FRIENDLY CHAT

Joseph Hatton, a Londoner, introduced his two-volume *To-Day in America* [22] "not as an historical review, not as a book of travels, but as a friendly chat about 'our kin beyond the sea.'" He reverted to this idea in his closing pages, noting that he had tried "to promote the brotherhood of America and England." In his five hundred pages, however, he cited so many differences that his English readers may well have despaired of the kinship.

To-Day in America covers two visits, the first in 1876, the second in 1880; thus Hatton was able, as most visitors were not, to show something about the rapidity of American growth. New York, for example, which in 1876 had ended at Central Park, by 1880 had "marched steadily toward Harlem," while Chicago was annexing many miles of open prairie and laying out new streets. An even more striking example was Leadville, a mining town in the Colorado Rockies. A lonely gulch in 1876, and even in 1878, it was by 1880 a bustling city of thirty thousand, with five churches, four daily newspapers, three schools, a YMCA— and a hundred gambling houses. Reporting such marvels of growth, Hatton thought John Ruskin had missed the essence of America when he had said that he could not, "even for a couple of months, live in a country so miserable as to possess no castles."

Hatton never went to Leadville; as a matter of fact his direct observation was limited to New York and its environs, and

Chicago. The topics he discussed were also limited; his practice was to mention some facet of American life and then, in considerable detail, seek to explain how it had developed. Like other travelers, for instance, he noted that American women moved about more safely and freely than those in Europe. Then he offered as the reason the male respect, close to deference, paid to the sex, which made English rudeness seem shameful in contrast, but, more important, encouraged women to expect special courtesies as a right. If they only knew how much better off they were than women in other countries, he added, there would be much less agitation for even more rights for women. Their behavior reminded him sometimes of the childish whims described in *Helen's Babies*, the year's best-selling novel.

The freedom that women enjoyed, and expected, was only one example of the general American intolerance of restraint. To an Englishman, whose home was his castle, to be hidden, if possible, from other people's eyes, the absence of barriers in America was striking: "Nothing is fenced in." Nor were classes in the population segregated from one another. Clergymen were as accessible as anyone else, they were not, as abroad, protected from ordinary contact by an artificial facade of assumed dignity. Even the lowliest were permitted to express their ideas. An office boy's suggestion of how the firm could earn a dollar, or save an hour, was welcomed, considered, and perhaps adopted—a practice unimaginable in England. Hatton thought that such openness explained, in part, the headlong progress of business. He was somewhat less enthusiastic, however, about the endless bragging he heard in different cities, each insisting it was the finest and most progressive in the country. Editors were the chief offenders, especially when they wrote their lead articles in outrageous slang.

Sports were of great interest to Hatton. It was probably true, though few Americans would have happily admitted it, that most American sports were borrowings from England. It was also probable, as Hatton wrote, that American interest in outdoor sports was a fairly recent development. He wasn't interested enough in baseball to describe the game, saying only that it was played more widely, and with greater zest, than cricket. He did talk about the recently formed coaching clubs, in Boston and

New York, not as large as London's but remarkable for existing at all in a country that had no true coaches, only the old lumbering stages. He attributed the growth of boating to American eagerness to outdistance England, as the *America* had first done in international yacht racing, in 1851, and as the Yale and Harvard crews had done in defeating Oxford and Cambridge. Hunting was a less successful transplant, in the English sense of formal pattern; Americans were not yet ready for the traditional fox hunt. American women seldom rode horses; indeed, they took almost no exercise of any sort. Bicycles were not as popular as in England, perhaps because most roadways were rough. Walking, the easiest of all sports, was popular enough; and winners of walking races were public heroes.

One lack that Hatton noticed was the virtual absence of playing grounds—no village greens, no commons dedicated to sports, no local meadows, no old quoit-grounds or bowling greens or skittle-alleys. A few wealthy families had created their own game areas, but it would take time for the general interest in sports to develop to the point of demanding and getting public facilities.

The sport most popular in America, so far as Hatton could judge, was sulky racing. Like other sports, it called for no special costumes, as was the practice in England, and there was none of the formality or pageantry associated with Epsom Downs and other fashionable race tracks. One member of the Chicago Jockey Club spoke scornfully of what he and other Americans called the "running race," in which horses were ridden by jockeys, which he regarded as tame and contemptible compared with the American trotting race. Hatton thought the man might have talked otherwise if he'd ever seen a famous English horse race. He attributed the preference to American utilitarianism. A light two-wheeled carriage used for local business travel on weekdays could double as a racer on Sundays and holidays—and even after work, when its driver headed for the nearest open road in hopes of finding some competition. The road from New York, out to Jerome Park was a favorite place for this sport. The idea would simply not occur to the average Briton, Hatton thought.

Trotting, of course, was the most natural gait of the horse. But the mania for trotting races had prompted men in both Canada and the United States to breed trotters for speed, just as Europeans, for a much longer time, had been selectively breeding runners. Some trotters, especially those developed in Canada, were so ungainly that French visitors had derided them without mercy; but *The Spirit of the Times,* the best-known American sporting journal, retorted by citing the very graceful trotter developed in the South. Some of the trotters that Hatton watched, in Chicago and along the road to Jerome Park in New York, were far from beautiful, but upon reflection he acknowledged that beauty in horses was a European criterion. What counted in America was what the horse could *do* (the open-society concept, we might say, applied to horses as to men).

One peculiarity that Hatton reported was the timed race for only one horse. He was lucky enough to observe, at the Chicago Jockey Club, one such event, when the famous "Maud S" broke the previous record for the mile with a sparkling 2:10¾. (Modern records, in several classes, are under two minutes.) As the race ended, a Jockey Club member took Hatton by the hand and said, in all solemnity, "You have seen the biggest thing America can show you. I congratulate you."

The very next night, however, Hatton heard Robert Ingersoll, the orator and lawyer who was known as "the great agnostic," and thought him a worthy rival for the title of America's "biggest thing." It was a bright Sunday afternoon in Chicago. The streetcars were filled with churchgoers, but none of the churches were as crowded as McVicker's Theatre, despite the admission fee. The subject of the lecture was "What Shall We Do to be Saved?" When Ingersoll, a middle-aged man in evening clothes, with bright eyes and "intellectual forehead," stepped onto the stage, the applause was thunderous.

Ingersoll began by attacking fear as "the dungeon of the mind" and priests for inventing "a crime called 'blasphemy.'" Then he demolished the Eden story and the four Gospels, not as they stood but as the churches construed them. He accused the priesthood, indeed, with deliberately misreading the basic Christian message. Christ bade one wealthy sinner sell all he had and give it to the poor. But the church, in America at least, catered to the wealthy and ignored the poor. Ingersoll insisted, with his lawyer's logic, that Christ had never advised men to forsake their wives and families for His sake, and in a typical passage he dramatized the vicious interpretation given by the Church. An applicant for admission to eternal bliss is asked by the Recording Secretary,

> "What have you done to be saved?"
> "I deserted my wife and six children."
> "Go right in!"

Calvinism was Ingersoll's special target. He showed more hatred for the Presbyterians of his day than for the Catholics. But he denounced divine forgiveness as a fraud if the victim of the sinful act got no compensation. What he really advocated was true brotherhood on earth instead of cant, elaborate dogma, and hypocrisy. As for immortality, he closed his lecture by saying that he much preferred to think that those he loved had reverted to eternal nothingness than "that their naked souls had been clutched by an orthodox God."

Hatton was optimistic that Ingersoll was exerting a modifying influence on orthodox Protestantism. But he found in the United States widespread superstition, astonishing for a population so full of common sense and so utilitarian in behavior. Orthodox Christians accepted spiritualism and its revelations as a divine means of helping control infidelity; and mediums, though not uncommon in England, comprised an actual profession in America. One devout American told Hatton that God was "drawing the veil aside that the spirits of the departed may commune with the poor sinners and save their souls alive." And several Americans, though insisting they took no stock in the spirit world, testified that spiritualism had cured certain of their maladies.

Churchgoing in the major American cities reminded Hatton of the old-fashioned English churchgoing still to be seen in Worcester and Gloucester. He noted with approval the after-church strolling along Fifth Avenue, especially if the strollers were girls in their Sunday best. Philadelphia and Boston observed the sabbath more sternly than New York, and their people were shocked that Chicago permitted concerts and plays on Sunday. Sermons were less formal than in England, and more easily understood. One preacher in the West told Hatton that he thought well of Ingersoll, wishing only that he would stop denying the future of hell and heaven. He could reach, as clergymen never could, the sizable number of non-believers, with a message of Christian charity unfettered by the ecclesiastical threats of the churches. It was part of American freedom and diversity, Hatton decided, that orthodoxy, atheism, superstition, and Ingersoll could all co-exist in relative harmony.

The pictorial art that Hatton saw at the Salmagundi Club in New York, and in the pages of *Scribner's* and *Harper's*, he thought deserved recognition in England. An evening at the Salmagundi, as he described it, was a very pleasant occasion. The club met in Sarony's gallery, where at one end a table was loaded with lager beer, crackers and cheese, and cigars. Easels were scattered about, with a supply of chalk of different colors if members who happened to be magazine illustrators took a notion to sketch. Other members gathered around a piano to sing, or listen to a good pianist; there were also pauses in the music while members recited.

Social amenities apart, however, Hatton discovered that American artists fared less well, financially, than their English cousins. With no national standard of art, would-be artists had to establish a name abroad before their own countrymen would accept them. It was surely time, Hatton thought, for Americans, rich as they were, to develop a national standard and give up deferring to the past and the foreign. (Echoes of Emerson.) At the Centennial Exhibition, larger crowds gathered about the English and Dutch paintings than the American. There was surely no dearth of scenery of objects suitable for painting; but painters were in short supply and buyers in even shorter supply.

Hatton visited Bierstadt, one of the leaders of the Hudson River School, at his house, which looked out, appropriately, over the Hudson River, and he decided that within a few miles of New York were scenes enough, all worthy of painting, to keep a large group of artists busy. A voyage up the Hudson presented one wonderful view after another. Long Island Sound had its own wealth of scenes awaiting artists.

Americans might be indifferent to their painters, and lacking in self-confidence about art in general, but nothing could keep them away from the theatre except a really bad production.

Compared with audiences in England, they seemed to Hatton much less sophisticated, much easier to please and better behaved, never hissing a play however bad it might be. If they disliked a play, they simply left before the final curtain—which was message enough to the management. At the first night of one very poor comedy that Hatton attended, however, the audience stayed till the end and even listened to the author's curtain speech; but next night the theatre was empty.

It astonished Hatton that nobody dressed formally for plays. Men working downtown were often joined by their wives for dinner before going to the theatre. Many people arrived by streetcar; and it was not uncommon for people to drop in at a performance on the spur of the moment. Inside, there was a minimum of fuss. The programs were stacked in trays, free for the picking up; there were no attendants demanding hats and coats, for a fee, and no refreshment vendors. "You have come to see the play," Hatton summed up, "not to be annoyed by licensed plumbers who have bought from the manager the right to tax your patience and your pocket."

New York set the country's theatrical standard, and Edwin Booth set the New York standard, in his own acting, in his directing, and in Booth's Theatre itself, a "handsome and elegantly-proportioned house." But good actors and actresses abounded, and every city had its good theatres. The star system was a handicap, as in England. Because stars made the show, they had to travel a good deal, since their presence was what attracted audiences. The average American audience would sit absorbed in Ada Rehan, or Clara Morris, wondering, not about the development of the plot, but what she would do next. This narrow devotion to stars may have been explained, in part, by the poor quality of most plays written by Americans; conversely, it may have been the cause of inferior plays. Hatton wasn't thinking of the Negro minstrels or the burlesque shows that some of the visitors reported; he seemed unaware of them. He agreed with other visitors, rather, that the general moral tone of the American theatre was higher than in Europe.

Hatton's only venture West was to Chicago. What he wrote about western opportunities, chiefly in Kansas and Arizona, was drawn entirely from printed sources, especially pamphlets written to attract settlers. He said almost nothing about minority groups, perhaps because he saw only one, the Chinese, in New York; but his report fills a gap in our survey.

Of the Chinese in San Francisco, Hatton knew only such generalities as their monopoly on shoemaking and the prostitute status of virtually all the women—3,900 out of 4,000. In New York, however, with a detective as guide, he visited Chinese opium houses and gambling dens near the notorious Five Points; it reminded him of the London reality that Dickens put into *The Mystery of Edwin Drood*. A shriveled little Mongolian, whom the detective addressed as Captain John Chinaman, showed him a client cooking opium, much as a plumber soldered a gaspipe, and then inhaling the smoke until his face took on a look of total satisfaction. The fee for this privilege varied from eighteen cents to a quarter. The detective next showed Hatton a gambling den, where twenty-odd Chinese glanced up only briefly before resuming their intense and silent game of Tan, using dice and double dominoes.

After relating various anecdotes about the Chinese and their miserable way of living, Hatton concluded that the Anglo-Americans had as hard a nut to crack in assimilating this group as they did in absorbing the Indians. As a matter of sober fact, he thought it would be impossible; the only recourse was to exclude all Orientals from America as soon as possible. That many Americans agreed is obvious, although Congress passed the Chinese Exclusion Act only after 1900. That the American Chinese were unassimilable, however, proved in time to be completely false.

Footnotes for Chapter Two

CENTENNIAL WAYS OF LIFE—A SAMPLING OF OPINIONS

1. J. G. Holland, *Every-Day Topics: A Book of Briefs* (New York: Scribner, Armstrong and Co., 1876); subsequent editions were published in 1882 and 1904.
2. Edward Eggleston, "Dr. Holland the Moralist," *The Christian Union*, 12 (Oct. 13, 1875), pp. 297–298.

3. The contemporary American and British editions were titled respectively, *Offenbach in America* and *America and the Americans*. The present summary is based on *Orpheus in America; Offenbach's Diary of His Journey to the New World*, translated by Lander MacClintock with drawings by Alajalov (Bloomington: Indiana University Press, 1957).

4. John Leng, *America in 1876: Pencillings during a Tour in the Centennial Year: with a Chapter on the Aspects of American Life* (Dundee: Advertiser Office, 1877).

5. Nathaniel H. Bishop, *Four Months in a Sneak-Box. A Boat Voyage of 2600 Miles Down the Ohio and Mississippi Rivers, and along the Gulf of Mexico* (Boston: Lee and Shepard, 1879). Bishop's report of his earlier trip was *Voyage of the Paper Canoe: A Geographical Journey of 2500 Miles from Quebec to the Gulf of Mexico, during the Years 1874-5* (Boston: Lee and Shepard, 1878). Both the paper canoe, "Maria Theresa," and "Centennial Republic," the "sneak-box," were deposited in the Smithsonian exhibit in the U. S. Government Building at the Centennial Exhibition.

6. Lester S. Levy, *Grace Notes in American History: Popular Sheet Music from 1820 to 1900* (Norman: University of Oklahoma Press, 1967), pp. 14–22.

7. Revised edition (Dallas: Turner Company, 1936). Originally published in 1877 as the joint work of two authors, H. F. McDanield and N. A. Taylor, and catalogued under McDanield by the Library of Congress. The 1936 reprint, which nowhere gives McDanield's name, contains some added passages at the end and omits the final paragraph of the introduction of the original edition, which read: "This little volume is the joint work of two hands, but we have generally used the single pronoun, as one is less cumbersome than two." Whatever the actual facts of authorship, I have chosen to follow the "single pronoun" and to consider Colonel Taylor as the sole adventurer. The German settlements that Taylor visited are admirably reported in Terry G. Jordan, *German Seed in Texas Soil: Immigrant Farmers in Nineteenth-Century Texas* (Austin: University of Texas Press, 1966), while the work of one of the principal organizers of German settlers in Texas is fully covered in Irene Marschall King, *John O. Meusebach: German Colonizer in Texas* (Austin: University of Texas Press, 1967).

8. Jules Leclercq, *Un Été en Amérique de l'Atlantique aux Montagnes rocheux*, 2nd ed. (Paris: E. Plon, 1886).

9. Paul Toutain, *Un Francais en Amérique, Yankees, Indiens, Mormons* (Paris: E. Plon, 1876).

10. Levy, *Grace Notes in American History*, pp. 37–41.

11. Detailed study of Huxley's 1876 visit was made possible, in part, by

a grant-in-aid from the American Philosophical Society in the summer of 1966.

12. The two pocket diaries are among the Huxley material owned by the Imperial College of Science and Technology, London, and are cited here, together with extracts of personal letters in the Huxley Papers, by permission. The Huxley letters are catalogued in Warren R. Dawson, *The Huxley Papers* (London: Macmillan, 1949).

13. George W. Smalley, "Mr. Huxley," *Scribner's Monthly*, 28 (October, 1895), 516.

14. Huxley to Mrs. Huxley, August 9, 1876, Huxley Papers. Professorial salaries being as low as they commonly were in 1876, it was a distinct advantage to have a rich uncle; Othniel Marsh used some of his inheritance to finance the Western expeditions that yielded his famous fossils.

15. From "Guest Book kept by James W. Brooks in 'A. Brooks Office'" now owned by Miss Margaret Fiske, grand-daughter of John Fiske. The generous help of Miss Fiske, and her brother, the present John Fiske, both of whom live in Petersham, prove that the Fiske tradition of hospitality is still strong.

16. Buffalo *Express*, August 26, 1876.

17. Buffalo *Express*, September 4, 1876.

18. Included, together with his three New York lectures in *American Addresses* (New York: D. Appleton and Sons, 1877).

19. Mrs. Huxley to Mrs. Scott, October 8, 1876, Huxley Papers.

20. The John Lewis letters, twenty-one in number and dating from 1872 to 1881, are in the Collection of Regional History at Cornell University. Excerpts from the 1876 letters have earlier appeared in my article, "John Lewis Reports the Centennial," *Pennsylvania Magazine of History and Biography*, 39 (1955), 364–374. The punctuation in passages quoted herein has been somewhat modified.

21. *An Army Doctor's Wife on the Frontier: Letters from Alaska and the Far West, 1874–1878*, ed. Abe Laufe (Pittsburgh: University of Pittsburgh Press, 1962).

22. *To-Day in America, Studies for the Old World and the New*, 2 vols. (London: Chapman and Hall, 1881).

3

A Teeming
Nation
of Nations

CENTENNIAL AMERICA, quite clearly, was seldom the same for
any two observers. Philadelphia was one city for John Lewis,
quite another for a French visitor. Denver was a wretched place
for one traveler, most attractive for a second, because one hotel
was poor and another was excellent. Texas, for John Lewis's son,
was a cruel, hard place to work; for Colonel Taylor it was a land
of infinite promise. Foreign observers generally agreed about the
delights of Central Park, the pert beauty of American women,
the boorish manners of the men and their preoccupation with
making money, the breath-taking energy of Chicago, and the
bracing climate of the high plains and the western mountains.

For T. H. Huxley, America meant fossil horses at Yale, a
landscape like that of England, and universal hospitality; for
Nellie Huxley, it was extravagant feminine attire at Saratoga,
and an exorbitant laundry bill. For Nathaniel Bishop, it was
rowdies at landings, tramps in the country, the inner nation
along the Mississippi, the loneliness of the Gulf Coast. Emily
FitzGerald saw gay cretonne, a Russian maid too fond of liquor,

and Indians deserving of extermination. Josiah Holland's reality, contradictory as it may have been at times, may, nevertheless, have come closest to Centennial reality as the dominant American class in 1876 conceived it to be.

Centennial awareness of history, important though it was in giving the year a distinctive quality, was no more secure a base for understanding the present than contemporary experience and observation. It may even have obscured understanding. The most influential historian of the day, George Bancroft, had neatly punctured the Federalist myths of the early nineteenth century, replacing them with an interpretation favorable to the Jacksonian Democrats. One result, for him, was a series of important federal posts during Democratic administrations, and a lengthy career as Democratic boss of Massachusetts. His ten-volume *History of the United States,* begun in 1834 and completed in 1874, was very popular for its anti-British bias and its intense patriotism. In 1876 a six-volume revision extended the narrative to 1782; a later, "final" edition carried it to 1789. Such a work, however, though an excellent instrument for whipping up enthusiasm for the spirit of independence enunciated in 1776, left readers with no knowledge at all of the nineteenth century.

If Centennial awareness of history was hazy, the haze had a rosy tint, reflecting both Bancroft's nationalistic fervor and the shallow optimism of the McGuffey Eclectic Readers. Between 1836 and 1857, six editions of the Readers yielded the astonishing total of 122 million copies. Middle-aged citizens in 1876, if they had ever attended American schools, could hardly have missed exposure to the Readers, which they were likely to recall with nostalgia and gratitude but without realizing the extent to which McGuffey had shaped their thinking about things in general and their country in particular. We hear much at present about the inadequacies of public education in history; but no student today, reasonably capable of learning anything, has as feeble an acquaintance with the American past as had virtually all Americans, whatever their age, in 1876.

Americans living on the Eastern seaboard—a region so long inhabited as to give the illusion of permanence and with no direct memory of its pioneer beginnings—might have scoffed at any suggestion that they belonged, in 1876, to an unbroken

frontier culture still very much in flux. The frontier, in Easterners' general acceptance of the term, was the advancing westward
edge of civilization, a place of colorful adventure, interesting to
read about in Mark Twain's *Roughing It* and Bret Harte's striking stories, or of danger, as Custer's Last Stand clearly proved.
There was no scholar at that time to point out that the settled
East had itself been a frontier, the first frontier, or to propose
that the present remote frontier was not a new and separate
phenomenon but only the continuation of the first, the latest of
several stages, all of them related.

Settled Easterners might readily have visualized the frontier as
two-dimensional—the area where raw nature was being subdued
to human uses, and the period required for the transformation—
but would have had trouble grasping the third dimension—the
frontier as *process*, operating not only in a particular place at a
particular time but having its impact throughout the land. Casual
observation could not reveal the interaction. If anything, as our
Centennial observers testified, it could only confirm the great
contrasts and the general sense that the frontier was separate
from the rest of the country. But ties existed—political ones,
economic ones, and psychological ones. No matter how remote
the frontier seemed in 1876, it was the successor to older frontiers, each one becoming in turn an integral part of the growing
nation, sharing the growth and forcing on older sections some of
the new cultural patterns it had developed. It was a national
evolution that no amount of resistance, no clinging to older
patterns, could halt.

In the long view, then, the United States in 1876 was an
evolving national culture with an unbroken frontier history.
The original beachhead settlements along the East Coast, now
conveniently called the Atlantic Frontier, differed in only two
important respects from all subsequent frontiers: it required a
longer time to develop, and it was supported by countries an
ocean away. When at last, after more than a century, this frontier was secure enough to spare a few individuals, some of the
boldest and most restless moved beyond the area that was safe
and settled, to begin the frontier process all over again. If defeated, they could always return, and many did, but the frontier
kept moving westward, as a band of varying width—fifty miles,

perhaps, or two hundred. The migrants (or "pioneers") had the moral and financial support of friends and relatives back home, but "back home" was no longer in Europe, but in America. They also had the blessing of the few political leaders farsighted enough to see them as agents of expansion. The symbolic term for what they were doing was "Manifest Destiny."

The frontier process, very slow at the outset but steadily accelerating, was near its end by 1876. By 1890 the Census Bureau would declare the frontier officially closed, with only a few isolated pockets yet to be won from the wilderness. What this means is the astonishing fact that in 1876, with half the national area still in wilderness, the frontier process had barely a decade longer to operate. The Centennial Exhibition, in this context, was the last great spectacle of the frontier period.

In 1876 the continental United States comprised essentially three large areas. First was all the land east of the Mississippi River and that on its western bank. Demonstrably civilized, with permanent institutions and well-established patterns, this area contained the great majority of the American population. The second region included much of the area in the new states west of the river, where a smaller fraction of the population was busily at work subduing wilderness and creating fresh patterns that soon would coalesce into a civilized stage. In the third part of the nation, an even smaller number of people, a thin advance guard, were daring the unknown, seldom stopping long enough to build new social patterns, and creating more legends than traditions. These three great areas—secure civilization, transitional frontier, and wilderness—produced a diversity of human behavior that would end with the completion of the frontier process. After that, the three areas would merge into one, and the only valid question would be how old or how new was the local variety of civilization.

There were other kinds of diversity, too, and changes even within that diversity. Consider the great difference between the colonial and national periods in ethnic and religious distribution. Well into the eighteenth century each colony maintained its distinctiveness in this respect: Anglicans in Virginia, Catholics in Maryland, Swedish-Finn Lutherans in Delaware, French Huguenots in New Jersey, Reformed Dutch in New York, Calvinists and Dissenters in New England. British colonial policy did all it could to maintain the separation and to prevent intercolonial trade and exchange of ideas. But gradually increasing mobility, fresh immigration, and a dawning awareness of certain common interests weakened the early geographic-religious barriers.

In most of the country, by 1816 the colonial pattern was a thing of the remote past. The more recent arrivals from Europe replenished the loss of older stock to the West and destroyed or disrupted the homogeneity in most of the East. Local concentrations of newcomers, moreover, gave an interesting new diversity not only in older sections but in newer ones as well, for an appreciable number of immigrants escaped the limiting conditions of the port cities by moving directly to the West, lured by varied glowing inducements of new states, sometimes even having their fare paid in well-organized settlement campaigns.

On the newest frontier, where everyone was from somewhere else, immigrants were much less conspicuous than in older sections, and were spared the slow, often grim process of gaining acceptance that Oscar Handlin has so vividly described in such books as *The Uprooted* (1951). A generation or two was enough to create new social hierarchies with their own kinds of prejudice and resistance, but in 1876, at least, with a third of the national territory in the frontier stage, it was a good time to come to America—*if* the momentum carried one beyond the Mississippi. The impact of new mores, new cultural attitudes, differed widely from section to section. It was least felt in the South—the section most consciously desirous of resisting change and preserving its institutions, and having the fewest immigrants and the least mobility.

These facts, of a nation so much in flux, without a sense of its own history and with even its diversity in a continuous state of evolution, were of course reflected in the Centennial Exhibition itself. Whatever its magnitude, the Exhibition could do little more than sample the pattern of the moment. Its architecture was not that which had existed in the colonies, or in the early nation; nor would it be the architecture of times to come. A few displays, very popular with the crowds, did consciously evoke the past, especially the mementoes of George Washington and most of what the visitor saw related only to the immediate present. For this reason thoughtful observers, like the author and critic Howells, found the Centennial difficult to absorb; what it presented did not seem to add up to any sense of central unity. As a village youth who had gone to the big city, back-trailing like so many other literary hopefuls from the Middlewest to the East, Howells was somewhat more of a cosmopolite than people who had always lived in one section; his astonishment at the great variety of American types on the Exhibition grounds suggests a basic provincialism of the day.

But of all the reporters of the Exhibition, Howells was virtually alone in looking for meanings. Where others merely described and made critical judgments of specific things they saw, Howells expressed bewilderment: the underlying principle, if one existed, eluded him. Without quite realizing it, he was putting his finger on just the point where the Exhibition's managers had failed. There *was* no unifying principle; there could *be* none at just that moment of very rapid national change. The country was so diverse and so fluid that no exhibition erected in an area of less than a square mile could adequately represent the whole.

What the Exhibition displayed most clearly, perhaps, was the very disparity that existed between North and South, East and West. Massachusetts sent exhibits enough to occupy half the fine arts section, and more than half of the educational section. And in Main Hall the first six states in the order of amount of floor space used were all Northern: Pennsylvania, New York, Massachusetts, Ohio, New Jersey, and Connecticut. Most of the Southern states, for reasons to be discussed later in this narrative, had refused to be officially represented. Though this did not mean withdrawal of exhibits by Southern firms, still, the best the South could do in the way of exhibits was pitiable. The patriot might speak of one nation, indivisible, but it was a nation with glaring differences, section by section, that an Exhibition, far from concealing, could only emphasize.

The East-West differences were even more dramatic. Massachusetts displayed at the exhibition relics two-and-a-half centuries old; Colorado displayed Rocky Mountain flora, fauna, and minerals—not to mention Mrs. Maxwell of sharpshooting fame. Relative age could thus be displayed, but the psychological effect of being very old or very new could not be. In the East, the past impinged on the present. In a given village a brand-new mill might stand next to a frame house built in the 1630s. In the West, for the most part there *was* no past, and some western regions lacked even a present—especially in the Dakotas, Wyoming, Montana, Washington, Idaho, Utah, Arizona, New Mexico, and Oklahoma—the third of the national area still in Territorial status. In almost all that area, and also in parts of the newest states west of the Mississippi, the population density was less than two per square mile, a sparsity which on the Eastern seaboard was rare.

A frontier two centuries before, the Eastern seaboard now had the look of permanence: farms tilled for generations, well-fenced or walled, and villages as tidy and "finished" as any in Europe. The cities were another story. There was a degree of permanence in their street patterns, but change and growth were their normal condition. New York, the largest city, was approaching the two-million mark and swallowing thousands of new immigrants each year. Philadelphia, second largest with 800,000 and Boston with about 350,000, were regional capitals that shared a preference for solidity as opposed to the headlong growth of Chicago, already the nation's third city in population with half a million. Providence, New Orleans, Newark, Jersey City, Buffalo, Washington, Baltimore, Cleveland, Detroit, Pittsburgh, Cincinnati, Louisville, St. Louis, Milwaukee, and San Francisco complete the roll call of cities with more than one hundred thousand inhabitants in 1876. The fact that most of these were in the North and East is attributable less to these areas' greater population than to their pattern of more rapid migration from farm and village to city; and the fact has a close bearing on the preponderance of Northern and Eastern industrial exhibits at the Exhibition.

The South was almost as heavily populated, but the traditional agrarian economy had always kept the cities small, New Orleans with its two hundred thousand being the one exception. Atlanta was home for about thirty-five thousand, while Miami did not exist. West of the Mississippi the one metropolis (not counting St. Louis, on that river's west bank) was San Francisco, with two hundred thousand. Los Angeles had a paltry ten thousand,

Houston fewer than twenty thousand, Denver about twenty-five thousand, and Seattle three thousand. Oklahoma City, Phoenix and Spokane were not yet on the map.

Understanding one's own times is always difficult. It is most difficult of all at a time of rapid change and growth—and few societies have ever developed as rapidly as that of the United States after the Civil War. A firm sense of history would undoubtedly have helped, but it was not the only aid to self-knowledge that was missing. Few Americans, for example, had a clear idea of the nation's geography. Fewer yet were in a position to keep up to date on who was doing what where, or how the quality of life was being altered in all parts of the country, or what old problems, such as securing an initial foothold, were yielding to what new problems. Even with our current perspective we can hardly hope to recreate in detail the actualities of 1876 region by region and state by state. But as armchair travelers we can lay out an itinerary that includes parts of the country the Centennial travelers did not visit. For convenience we may divide the journey to emphasize the three great stages of the ongoing frontier process—the securely civilized East, the frontier transition between wilderness and civilization, and the remaining wilderness itself.

I

THE CIVILIZED EAST

New England in 1876 was an area old enough to have passed through several distinct stages, each leaving its ineradicable residue of tradition and forms. Apart from natural features, especially its heavy surface glaciation, the conditions existing in New England when it was part of the Atlantic frontier had radically altered, although there remained the prudent frugality which that frontier had demanded, and the high regard for the intellectual life which is Puritanism's most notable contribution to American civilization. Theocratic Calvinism had yielded to Congregationalism and, in time, to other religions, some of them as radical as Puritanism had been orthodox. But the meetinghouse pattern of church-town government survived, as it still does, in the famous New England town meeting. It is still the town and not the county or the villages within the town which is the focal center of New England's political life. Even when villages grew into cities they clung to their individuality and usually resisted the impulse, common in other parts of the nation, to merge with each other into super-cities.

The old agricultural-commercial economy of Massachusetts had begun early in the nineteenth century to yield to industrialism. Wherever flowing water could turn a wheel a mill was built. By 1876 the Merrimack was the most exploited river for its length in the nation: but an undeveloped river was regarded as something of a reproach. Capital for industrial development came from within the state, from old wealth painfully accumulated and carefully husbanded. Nature was not generous in New England, and both the stony fields and the rocky coast had been stern teachers. New wealth, however, could not shunt aside the Puritan heritage of regard for things of the mind; profits went more often into philanthropic institutions, the arts, and education than into conspicuous consumption.

This slow rise of economic wellbeing was paralleled by an increasing support of higher education: Massachusetts could boast in 1876 of Harvard and Amherst and Williams, Boston College and Holy Cross, Tufts and Boston University. There were four colleges for women—Wheaton, Mt. Holyoke, Wellesley, and Smith—and professional schools of fine arts and music, theology, pharmacy, and technology. Alongside the endowed institutions were six normal schools and a state agricultural college. On the lower level were private schools, the oldest, the Boston Latin School, dating back to 1634, and public schools almost as old, created by law in 1647.

No other state had come so far, and no other state, in 1876, could look back upon a major literary flowering like that of the Concord-Cambridge axis. One member of that axis, Oliver Wendell Holmes, had dubbed Boston "the hub of the universe," a term still printed in the prefatory section of the Boston City Directory. It cannot be denied that Massachusetts was the first state in the union to attain maturity. It led in humanitarian measures, for example, with methods of treating criminals, unemployables, and the mentally ill that other states used as models.

To be mature, however, was not to be static. Population lost by Massachusetts to the West was replenished by immigrants, with one result that by 1876 Boston, instead of the Brahmin citadel it once had been, was now almost an Irish-Catholic city. The factories which had once relied on girls from farm and village increasingly employed newcomers from Europe, and the Irish girl as "hired help" in middle-income households was a fixed institution. Despite what the Scotsman John Leng had said, help *was* cheap, in 1876, in the Atlantic port cities where immigrants debarked, and families approaching affluence had servants enough to stagger twentieth-century imaginations.

New England capital followed the New Englanders who ventured westward in search, not so much of adventure, as of the promise held by the rich Illinois or Iowa topsoil. But the West did not need to depend for very long entirely on Eastern capital. For the twenty years after 1874 an average of $85,000,000 a year flowed to the American West from Europe. And no new state, certainly, was ever the exclusive economic outpost of any older state. The capital outlays were private, not public, and the lenders as free as the borrowers to move from state to state. Regarding the pattern of movement in the civilized East, *Appleton's Annual Cyclopedia* for 1876 is a treasury of information.

These were depression days, but savings banks in Massachusetts were regularly paying six percent on deposits, and the 734 corporations in the state, with 1876 assets totalling $148,000,000, were by and large solvent. Of Maine's sixty-eight savings banks, four failed in 1876, no large number but unusual for New England, where most banks rode out the depression unscathed. New Hampshire, which also had sixty-eight savings banks, had no failures; and there was quiet pride in the number of depositors, nearly a third of the population. Connecticut did even better, with more than a third of its people owning accounts.

The railroads in Massachusetts were doing well, with an aver-

age net income of 5.6 percent on a total investment of
$110,000,000. The Hoosac Tunnel in the northwestern corner
of the state was nearly completed: 25,081 feet long, with
20,000,000 bricks used in the arching, it cost upwards of
$17,000,000 and was the pride of all the citizens. The state's
public debt stood at $33,500,000, a third of a million less than the
year before. Considering the depression still gripping the nation,
Massachusetts seemed very well off.

Prudence, caution, conservatism—whatever the name, the approach paid off in hard times. In Maine, the most perplexing
problem facing the state government was how to collect the
taxes that the Maine Central and certain other railroads refused
to pay; the sum involved $147,000, was not large, but officials
worried about the precedent and awaited with uneasiness the
decision of the state supreme court. The land-office, however,
sold twenty-two thousand acres to settlers for $46,399; another
twenty-six thousand acres of land in the state's public domain
remained to be sold. During the year the state also auctioned off
several islands. The most important act of the Maine legislature
in 1876 was the abolition of capital punishment. Opponents
argued that it would produce a rash of murders, but there was
not a single murder indictment in the state that year. Admirers
of the state's prohibition law, the first in the nation (1851), gave
it large credit for keeping the peace. But no other state felt
obliged to follow suit.

Everything considered, New England was eminently safe,
economically, in 1876, relatively untouched by the depression
that dislocated business in less conservative regions. Safety was
one of the satisfactions of maturity. An interesting barometer of
the times is to be found in the formation, in 1876, of the Appalachian Mountain Club, which pioneered a new "industry," wilderness recreation. The very fact that one region was well-
enough established to make a sport of what was still a grim
occupation on the edge of the frontier is part of Centennial
diversity.

T. H. Huxley was delighted with the elms of New Haven and
the rural landscape, which so much reminded him of parts of
England. John Leng reported with great approval the Pacific
Mills in Lawrence, and praised Boston as the best of American

cities. Perhaps more of the foreign observers should have visited New England to see for themselves what Americans had achieved in two-and-a-half centuries. The carping Frenchmen might have tempered their remarks about Americans' crudeness and narrow preoccupation with money. They might have noticed the region's commitment to culture in general—not only higher education but libraries and art galleries, and the old habit of serious reading. For the nation's book publishers and magazine editors, New Englanders were the salt of the earth. The creative impulse might have moved westward, but the *Atlantic Monthly* and other New England journals could at least maintain the illusion of literary supremacy. In the hundreds of trim villages, moreover, the Greek Revival, the classic architectural style which took hold in the United States in the late thirties and forties, was very much in evidence in gleaming white churches and dwellings, spaced along the village greens that a sound sense of beauty preserved from exploitation. The Romanesque, the one "revival" begun in America, was increasingly popular, for libraries, town halls, schools, and even fire stations. The mills, which had replaced agriculture and commerce as the chief source of wages and profits, and hence of the high cultural standards, were blemishes, of course, but some were architecturally sound and not yet the eyesores of a later age when so many firms moved South and abandoned them.

But Europeans were not much interested in America's finished products—if any region, even New England, could really be said to be finished. Europe was full of finished products. What excited Europeans, and Americans of older regions too, was the process by which form was being given to the dream of a new culture, as this process could be observed on a trip West, traveling from one stage to another of the developing nation. What New England might have provided was a basis for contrast and an example of the variety of forms that the process had actually led to.

If, as Huxley thought, New England's scenery resembled parts of England, and if Boston struck John Leng as similar to London, these were two good reasons for not bothering to visit the region. As for the New Englanders, it is hardly likely that they felt neglected. Most of them were quite contented with themselves and their region; they did not regard the headlong activity of other regions as anything to envy or wish for in place of their economic soundness, cautious conservatism, and beloved culture.

The middle States—New York, New Jersey, and Pennsylvania—were also a source of capital and people for the endless needs of new sections. New York was most fortunate in having the only water corridor by reason of the Erie Canal from the Atlantic to the Great Lakes. New England had more rivers but she did not have a network that could be easily canalized to carry products to market as New York had. Commodore Vanderbilt, when he turned from steamboats to railroads, shrewdly pieced together his New York Central along the same easy route, and the consequent combination of freight trains and canal boats not only served the industrial belt from Troy to Buffalo but made New York City the greatest port, and the largest, richest city, on the continent. By 1876 the port of New York was the chief gateway for newcomers to the nation.

The great diversity of New Yorkers in 1876 was only a modern phase of much earlier diversity in America. The First Families of Virginia and the scions of Puritanism were all Anglo-American—Byrds and Randolphs, Lowells and Cabots. But, especially after the English takeover in 1664, men of varied national origins competed in New York for position and appropriated each other's skills. The powerful old families in 1876 were a mixture of English and Dutch—Morrises, Clintons, and Livingstons, Brevoorts and Roosevelts and Schermerhorns—with an occasional Huguenot family like the Delanceys. Power was not a monopoly of these groups, however. Among the city's merchant princes were an Irish immigrant named Alexander Stewart, who died in 1876 leaving a fortune of about two hundred millions and the finest mansion on Fifth Avenue, and several Jewish families, most notably the Strauses and the Gimbels. Horace Greeley's advice, "Go West, young man," was sound enough. But Vanderbilt proved that staying at home was equally advisable, if home was New York, while other ambitious men, beginning elsewhere, often migrated to New York in pursuit of major financial ventures. The state stood first not only in population but also in per capita income despite the thousands of recent immigrants crowding the lower part of Manhattan Island —a phenomenon suggesting the economic advantage of social flux and ethnic heterogeneity. And New York had one more asset, which was its freedom, from the beginning, from preoccupation with such distractions as the Puritan dream of creating a New Jerusalem, or the New England determination to maintain culture on a high level, or the commitment, in the South, to agrarianism. New York was frankly concerned with wealth.

Fierce rivalry existed between New York City and upstate New York. In 1876 this was reflected in the political struggle between Senator Roscoe Conkling of Utica, the Republican state boss, and Governor Samuel Jones Tilden, who was the leading Democratic contender for the Presidency. But this rivalry did not mean geographic separation, as in Pennsylvania, where one long Appalachian ridge after another prevented a clear route for trade from the salt water of the Atlantic to the Great Lakes. Philadelphia, for many decades the nation's largest city, had fallen behind New York and was being challenged for second place by Chicago—chiefly because of this geographic disadvantage. Pittsburgh, almost at the Ohio state line, was developing on its own, from nearby coal and oil, with little direct aid from Philadelphia. The Susquehanna River, splitting the state, was unfortunately much too shallow to support a strong mid-state development; Harrisburg, on the east bank of that river, remained the capital only because of its central position; the citizens at neither end of the state wanted the state government moved to the other end.

New Jersey profited, as it still does, by its situation between New York City and Philadelphia, both of which it served by extensive truck farming. The hills in its northwest corner, and the vast pine barrens of the southeast, still a large wilderness area, were incapable of supporting any population to speak of. During 1876, the marked disparity in population distribution was posing a serious question: five counties with more than half the state's population and paying more than half the taxes had only one legislator each and could therefore be outvoted by the other sixteen counties. It was one of the earliest problems in reapportionment, much too early for hope of relief by Supreme Court action.

Delaware, wedged between New Jersey, Pennsylvania, and Maryland, was the only one of the thirteen original states without a large city or a substantial population. But the state was prosperous, and it was progressive enough to support a Delaware Association for the Improvement and Education of the Colored People (a kind of NAACP), which supported 1,197 young Negroes in twenty-nine private schools. Neighboring Maryland, which did have a major port city, Baltimore, was gratified in 1876 by the settlement of its boundary dispute with Virginia (although oystermen, even today, still quarrel about the line), and by the attention attracted by the opening of the Johns Hopkins University, where Daniel Coit Gilman was installed as president on Washington's Birthday.

Although the District of Columbia seemed very Southern to visiting Northerners, Virginia was where the South began. Spared the military occupation of Reconstruction, profiting by its location near the industrial North, Virginia had made a faster recovery than any other state in the former Confederacy.

West Virginia had become a state in 1863 after forty western counties seceded from Virginia. The state's finances were reported to be sound, but no payments had yet been made in its share of the old Virginia debt. On January 6 a new capitol building at Charleston was turned over to the state. Costing $100,000, it was paid for by the citizens of Wheeling, a prospering satellite of Pittsburgh.

The Carolinas were South beyond question. In North Carolina, schools for Negroes, a sore point further South, were well-established—1,372 of them, enrolling 153,000 pupils, alongside 2,702 schools for about 250,000 white pupils. The state was also experimenting with graded schools to replace the one-room schools of tradition. At the higher level, the state university at Chapel Hill seemed at last on its way after more than a decade of non-support; the state appropriation in 1876 was only $7,500, but this was $7,500 more than in the preceding year. South Carolina was hardly as fortunate. Far from having a legislature able to find funds for its university, it had two rival houses of representatives: the Mackey House (Republican) and the Wallace House (Democratic). Each certified a different Governor in the November, 1876, election—the incumbent Republican,

Chamberlain, and the Democratic challenger, Wade Hampton. The issue went unsettled until April 10, 1877, when President Rutherford B. Hayes, among his first official actions, gave the governorship to Hampton. Legislators throughout the Confederacy had problems hardly conceivable in the North. The military defeat of the Confederacy had of course rendered its currency worthless, but long-term obligations plus other financial necessities remained.

Throughout the South, in varying degrees, the traditional affection for agrarianism was a major barrier to economic recovery. Northerners, pointing to the results of their own conversion, earlier in the century, to an industrial economy, could easily insist that Southerners were their own worst enemies in opposing the spread of factories, in keeping their cities small, in rejecting social mobility, and in preserving ethnic homogeneity. But such talk annoyed most Southerners, who felt that the adoption of Northern patterns would be simply one more instance of surrender. Northern attempts to help the South during Reconstruction served only to exacerbate Southern sensitivity. However well-intended, the various aid programs, official and private, cemented conservative Southern resistance to all outside interference. The Northern novelist Albion Tourgée, after a decade in North Carolina, decided that the North's effort was no more than "A Fool's Errand;" and perhaps he was right.

Regionalism—or provincialism—perpetuated mutual misunderstanding. White Southerners tended to damn all Yankees as unprincipled opportunists and to discount their altruism because so much of it was directed toward the Freedmen, the former slaves. White Northerners, shocked by the reports of Klan violence against both the Freedmen and their Northern teachers, tended to think of all white Southerners as racists and reactionaries. The bitterness retarded, among other things, the perfect reconciliation and harmony that was one announced purpose of the Centennial Exhibition, and had significant effects on Congressional action and on the year's Presidential election.

What people could not or would not understand in 1876 was that long-familiar regional characteristics of thinking and acting defy all external pressures for change. New Englanders, for example, would have forgotten all their internal differences if the rest of the country had seemed intent, as the North did on the South, on demolishing the distinctive ways of life that they cherished. Sabbatarianism—no trains on Sunday, no retail trade, no theatres or public sports. City streets in total disregard of geometric logic, village commons, no two alike. Highways accommodating hill and valleys instead of following the shortest distances between points. Town meetings—decreasingly efficient, as population intensified, but so firmly based in tradition that replacing them seemed unthinkable. And the towns themselves, perpetuating the equal importance of all voters wherever they lived, and grass-roots democracy of particular strength. Almost total separation by sex in higher education. A quiet pride in the recent literary "renaissance," the nation's first. And a tolerance for deviant opinion, whether organized or individual, despite a general commitment to conservative stolidity.

If Southerners could not sympathize with New Englanders, they had their own ancient and beloved patterns that outsiders could never fully appreciate.

The habit of seeing only the major differences between regions led easily to the notion that every region except one's own was monolithic or homogeneous. The hill farmer in the Berkshires was well aware that his life was quite different from that of a lawyer in the Boston area, or a lobsterman out of Cape Porpoise, or a professor in New Haven. He would not have realized that even greater disparities existed in Virginia, where the upcountry farmers included many Scotch-Irish Presbyterians who had found their way down the Shenandoah Valley from Pennsylvania. Their numbers, and their almost total lack of sympathy with Tidewater Virginians, made it easy for them to secede and form the new state of West Virginia in 1863.

But throughout the South there were many more small farmers than plantation owners. Far from profiting from slavery, they competed with it, and for a sizable number of them the competition was so ruinous that they sank into the permanent status of poor whites, without hope of material success but proud of their self-sufficiency. In the North, they would have joined the growing numbers of factory hands, but the South had almost no factories to lure them. One may well wonder why they accepted Secession and formed the majority of the Confed erate army; but regionalism has a peculiar means of enlisting local loyalty. On the other hand, an appreciable number of the upcountry people, especially in eastern Tennessee, joined the Union forces.

Homogeneity of the population, however, did exist in parts of the South. This was particularly true in Mississippi where practically all the people, black and white, were, by 1876, native-born and had no more desire to leave the state than to welcome newcomers—a notable exception to the general American pattern of mobility. With no migrants sifting in from other states or from abroad, the state virtually isolated itself from fresh ideas. The intensity of its racial violence, its chaotic politics in 1876, and its bitter opposition to public education, may all reasonably be traced to its extreme repudiation of national trends, a distinction that boded little good for the future. Even so, the Mississippi Building, festooned with Spanish moss, was one of the minor successes at the Centennial Exhibition applauded by Howells and other reporters.

Howells also wrote, in the course of his *Atlantic* coverage of the Exhibition, that every region, every state, every city, was "only more unrepresentative than another." Going from one state's exhibition to another, he felt, was like traveling in different countries. The individuals who did move about, and reported what they observed, confirmed this statement.

Tennessee and Kentucky, like Maryland in the East and Missouri further West, were not "Southern" enough to join the Confederacy but at the same time were not quite Northern. Tennessee was proud of a twelve-hundred-page book just published, *The Resources of Tennessee*, a factual report that any state might have found useful. Nashville, itself, with its cluster of colleges, was congenial to T. H. Huxley. He would, however, have seen a different Tennessee if he had glimpsed the rugged uplands in the east, where Knoxville was becoming an important center, or Memphis on the Mississippi, a major cotton center and a prime example of white-Negro urbanism. Huxley saw Kentucky only from a train window in very hot weather; he might have enjoyed a brief stop at Lexington, the oldest settlement west of the Appalachians and a natural center of horse-breeding and tobacco. For one part of both Tennessee and Kentucky, the river boundary on the north and west, we have seen only the reports, not very complimentary, of Nathaniel Bishop. But as we cross the Ohio River, in our imaginary tour of the United States, we enter a region fairly well documented by our travelers.

Ohio, the first state carved out of the old Northwest Territory (in 1803), already had a population—almost three million —greater than that of all the states and territories in the entire western half of the nation. The only two states with more people than Ohio were New York and Pennsylvania.

Ohio was located on both of the great water routes of westward migration, the Great Lakes and the Ohio, and also on the first national road westward. Cleveland dominated the first of these routes, Cincinnati the second, and Columbus the third. The northeastern sector of Ohio, long known as the Western Reserve, had once been claimed by Connecticut, which had parceled out much of the land to Connecticut citizens who had lost their holdings during the Revolution. Akron, Ashtabula, Lorain, Sandusky, Youngstown, and Cleveland itself were thus first settled; some New England traditions still survived there in 1876. Cincinnati, known as the "Queen City," attracted settlers from the middle Atlantic states and from the upper South, but long before 1876 it was distinctive for its large German and Irish elements, who contributed a Continental flavor unique in the Western Reserve. Unlike most states on the Atlantic seaboard, Ohio had no large areas, still lying in a wilderness condition; the good earth made farming prosperous almost everywhere in the state, and there were coal and iron ore in plentiful supply, and natural gas and petroleum enough to create industries hardly known in the East.

Every traveler to Ohio, in 1876 or later, was struck by the large number of colleges there, some of them so old that only a few in the East were older. Ohio University in Athens and Miami University in Oxford, the two oldest, were established in 1804 and 1809 respectively, followed by Kenyon in 1824, Western Reserve in 1826, Denison in 1831, Oberlin in 1833, and Muskingum in 1837. In many important ways, Ohio gave observers the first glimpse of what the great heartland was to be. And in 1876 it was ready to provide its first President, in the person of its governor, Rutherford B. Hayes.

Michigan, geographically peculiar by virtue of its two peninsulas and its frontage on four of the five Great Lakes, was still largely undeveloped in 1876. Its southern counties, north of Ohio and Indiana, were occupied early; it even occupied for some years the northern area of both these states, an area known as the Toledo Strip, which it yielded only as a condition to statehood in 1837. By that time, however, it already had a state university twenty years old and two private colleges, Kalamazoo (1833) and Albion (1835). Some thirty-one thousand Michiganders registered at the Centennial Exhibition, where the state did very well with its displays of Michigan fruit.

Indiana, celebrating sixty years of statehood in 1876, was a younger Ohio, agrarian until the Civil War and increasingly industrial afterwards. Its capital, Indianapolis, was another Columbus but without the dubious benefit of larger cities near the state's borders. One oddity of Centennial Indiana was Governor Williams' nickname, "Blue Jeans," from his habit of wearing cotton twill clothing on all occasions, public and private.

Illinois, the nation's fourth largest state, was rapidly gaining on Ohio, chiefly because of Chicago. Chicago was the only city of consequence in Illinois, and no other state was so dominated by a single city. Springfield, the capital, on the same east-west route as Columbus and Indianapolis, seemed better suited to governing an agricultural empire, which Illinois certainly was. It was also the realm of the Patrons of Husbandry, better known as the Grange, organized in 1867 and strong enough in 1876 to force the "Granger Acts" through the legislature, requiring the state to set fees for storing grain. But farming was not the only basic occupation. Southern Illinois had almost as many miners as farmhands, tapping the nation's greatest coal reserves, estimated at well over one hundred billion tons. Most travelers never saw the mines, however, and relatively few of them saw the farms, though they may have seen the farm machinery made in Chicago. Some were glad they had visited Springfield to see the Lincoln tomb and relics, but most had eyes only for Chicago, the magic capital of the heartland, where everything seemed bigger, faster, bolder, and more optimistic than anywhere else.

The bold energy of Chicago radiated, like its railroads, outward in all directions, but the thrust carried further in some than in others. It carried northward into Wisconsin, where Milwaukee was not so much Chicago's rival as its satellite in the business mastery of the state's diary farms and northern mines and forests. St. Louis to the southwest firmly refused to be a satellite. It fought Chicago for trade in much of Illinois, especially in the flat south where the soil's black richness suggested the term "Little Egypt," and it was Chicago's major rival for the grain and cattle of northern Missouri and all of Iowa. Every growing city tried to extend its own trade area, but in 1876, in this vast central region—the corn belt, the corn-hog country, the nation's breadbasket, or whatever else it might be called—it was very much a tale of two cities, St. Louis and Chicago. There could be no truce [in their economic warfare,] as W. W. Belcher makes clear in *The Economic Rivalry Between St. Louis and Chicago 1850–1880* (1947).

Wisconsin, like Illinois, was engaged in 1876 in a struggle between the railroads and their customers. The so-called "Potter Law," providing state supervision over railroads, was the crucial subject of debate. But if the people of Wisconsin were progressive on this subject, they were not so on every issue. A Miss Goodell applied for admission to the bar but was rejected by the state supreme court: women's functions as set by nature, the justices decided, did not include the practice of law.

In Iowa, meanwhile, the lawmakers were deciding that women could not hold educational office; teaching was of course open to women (at lower pay than men, as was true everywhere in the nation) but not such grave responsibilities as superintendent of a community's schools. (The state Supreme Court subsequently reversed the legislature on the point.) A bill to outlaw capital punishment failed by a single vote in the Senate in 1876. Neither the legislature nor the Supreme Court could do much about the combination of wet weather, rust, and grasshoppers that limited the harvest that year; but in spite of nature Iowa maintained its position as the nation's leading agricultural state, with more than four million acres in corn and three million in wheat.

Iowa's acreage in corn and wheat covered, in fact, a larger area than the whole of New Hampshire, New Jersey, Maryland, or Vermont. The credulity of Easterners was strained to admit the size of the states in the newer regions. Except for Arkansas, Iowa was (and is) the smallest state west of the Mississippi but still larger than any state in the northeast and actually almost as large as all of New England (where Maine accounted for half the total size). Easterners also found it difficult to distinguish the several stages of civilization existing in the West. Certain of them were even reputed to mistake Ohio for Iowa, while everything west of the Hudson River was a total wilderness in their minds. The appropriate response on the part of such states as Iowa was that civilization began west of Chicago. It all depended on how the term was defined—and where one lived.

This Middlewest, this American heartland, sometimes considered the most typical of our regions, the most *American*, was an amalgam of all of the nation's older regions. The blurring of dialect lines, obscuring the distinctions quite clearly separating Northern, Midland, and Southern in the eastern United States, complemented the mingling, the further west one traveled, of people from every older region. The blurring was further affected by the large numbers of people from many parts of Europe, who were more diffused throughout the population in the West than they were in the East, where conditions tended to keep them in specific small areas—like lower Manhattan. If "American" implies the free and extensive mixture of peoples, the Middlewest *was* the most American of regions in 1876. As Joseph Hatton had observed, the question beyond the Appalachians was not, "Who was your father?" but, "What can you do?"

Consider Minnesota, the nation's northernmost state in 1876 by virtue of a small protrusion into Lake of the Woods, and, with its eighty-four thousand square miles, a good deal larger than *all* of New England. The Scandinavians, later so numerous, had hardly as yet begun to immigrate. The French explorers—Hennepin, Nicollet, Marquette—left little behind them except a few place names. The first permanent settlers were mostly from upper New England—Crosbys, Washburns, Pillsburys—and so were the lumberjacks and white-water rivermen who had subdued the stands of virgin white pine and opened the land to wheat. St. Paul and other villages in the southeastern corner of the state were founded in the 1830s. Not until the Treaty of

Traverse des Sioux, in 1851, was the great rich empire west of the Mississippi River opened to settlers.

A Territory in 1849, a state in 1858, Minnesota rapidly became a place of prosperity for small farmers—German and Irish as well as native-born migrants—and for men eager for fortune from river trade, timber, furs, and land. When Edward Eggleston, exhausted from circuit riding in Indiana, went to Minnesota in 1856 it was to regain his health, for the very air—the "ozone," as it was called—supposedly had therapeutic values. Henry David Thoreau ventured there too, in 1861, for the same reason but with less success. Duluth was originally a summer health resort popular with asthmatic Southerners. The panic of 1857 and the Great Sioux Outbreak of 1862 were two of the setbacks that Minnesotans were proud of their ability to overcome. Surviving the Minnesota winter was in itself a test and a proof of manhood; the great blizzard of 1873 was only an extreme form of the annual struggle. The grasshopper plague every summer from 1873 to 1877 was a different kind of ordeal, particularly worrisome in newly settled counties. The soil was rich beyond the imagining of New Englanders or New Yorkers, but it took a grim courage to plant seed year after year only to watch helplessly as the grasshoppers ate the young shoots.

But the firm foundation of sound economic growth in Minnesota was the New England concept of self-sufficiency, with as little help as possible from Chicago or anywhere else, coupled with skills brought from other countries. Transplanted New Englanders built the Minneapolis skyline of flour mills while German-born Frederick Weyerhaeuser organized in 1870 his Mississippi Boom and Logging Company to control the lumber industry, and Canada-born James Hill was planning his rail system to link St. Paul with Puget Sound. The Twin Cities would become a gateway to a vast empire spanning more than half the continent and extending into the undeveloped Canadian provinces. The typical Minnesotan, sharing the faith in the future expressed at New Year's by the editor of the *Pioneer-Press*, was apt to be amused by the loud boasting of people in other states, who simply did not know that living elsewhere than Minnesota was a misfortune.

The Minnesotan *knew*. His early sense of his own destiny is shown, in part, by the existence of a state historical society older than the state itself. He remembered the picturesque crudities of the frontier stage but commended himself on the fact that it had passed swiftly. At the height of the lumbering activity on the St. Croix, the red-shirted lumberjacks made Stillwater lively enough on Saturday nights, and Winona, some hundred miles down the Mississippi from St. Paul, was briefly notorious for its long street dedicated to assorted vice; but the impulse for law and order was too strong to be long evaded in Minnesota. Jesse James, the notorious outlaw, provided an object lesson in 1876. On September 7 with his full gang he tried to rob the bank in Northfield, but he had not allowed for what Minnesotans insisted on calling the Minnesota breed of men, who refused to be awed. The cashier, named Hayward, would not obey the order to open the vault, and was shot dead. Outside, citizens quickly went for guns. A young man named Wheeler, in a building across from the bank, calmly picked off one member of the gang; he or someone else killed another and wounded a third. Wheeler organized a posse of some four hundred men who by nightfall had killed one more of the gang and captured three, two of them the notorious Younger brothers. Jesse James escaped, but he was never again the menace he had once been.[1]

State pride, in fact, was everywhere in evidence throughout the nation, at one level of intensity or another. In Arkansas, one form it took in the 1870s was resentment at being made the butt of crude humor of the "Arkansas Traveler" sort; every rough back-country story, it sometimes seemed, was laid in Arkansas, perpetuating an image that was admittedly true in 1836, when statehood was granted, but had decreasing relevance, Arkansans thought, in 1876. A Little Rock firm, T. B. Mills and Company, set out to improve the state's image by issuing a weekly newspaper, *The Spirit of Arkansas*, systematically describing the state's scenic and physical resources, timber and minerals in particular, and encouraging migration from the upper Middlewest.

In September, 1875, seventy-six newspaper editors, most of them from Ohio, Indiana, Illinois, and Michigan, accepted an invitation to visit Arkansas. They assembled at St. Louis on September 28, boarded a special train of four Pullman Palace Cars donated for the occasion by the St. Louis, Iron Mountain,

and Southern Railroad, slept their way across two hundred miles
of Missouri, and woke to a sparkling Arkansas morning. For the
next four days they were shown everything of importance to be
seen and were entertained lavishly. Back home, they printed
their impressions in their own papers, and in 1876 Mills collected
these in a four-hundred-page book. This volume is something of
a bibliographical curiosity, being called *The Modern Arkansas
Travelers* on the cover and, on the title page, *A History of the
North-Western Editorial Excursion to Arkansas.* An inset map
shows the railroad land-grants, which crossed the state almost
like the bars of the Confederate flag; and a Hot Springs physician contributed a lengthy chapter on "Climatology, Etc., of
Arkansas." One of several full-page advertisements touted
Beard's Excelsior Round Door Burglar Proof Safes, made in St.
Louis—an unintended hint that burglars might exist in Arkansas.
Another advertised the Centennial Exhibition—Arkansas was
one Southern state that did not hold aloof. The back cover of
the book announced that T. B. Mills and Company not only
published *The Spirit of Arkansas* but were also prepared to
handle the sale of "Land for the Landless! Homes for the
Homeless! Prairie Lands! Timbered Lands! Mineral Lands!
Improved Farms!" That about summed up the entire westward
movement.

2

THE FRONTIER

Jesse James, like other famous outlaws of the period, was most
successful under frontier or wilderness conditions, where law
and order were not yet firmly established. His mistake in Minnesota lay in supposing that Northfield, about sixty miles south of
the Twin Cities, would be as easy a target as small frontier towns
where he had operated. Northfield was no longer a frontier

town but, rather part of the civilized East. It was, in fact, an instance of how rapidly the frontier was disappearing. The fact that eastern Minnesota was well past its frontier stage in 1876, hardly forty years after its first settlers had arrived, shows a marked advance over earlier frontiers. The process of converting total wilderness to frontier, and then to civilization, was accelerating.

If the degree of acceleration had been plotted on a chart, an extrapolation from the data might have indicated the end of the frontier by 1890; but nobody would have believed this in 1876. Some people refused to believe it even when it happened—or to be more precise, when the Census Bureau announced in 1890 that it had happened. Sizable areas still remained in total wilderness, for which we can be grateful, now that we have decided wilderness is worth preserving. The Bureau's official statement acknowledged these remaining wild pockets but insisted that, large as some of them were, they no longer constituted a significant barrier to the achievement of social order. The frontier in 1876—excluding the isolated frontiers in Colorado and Utah, Oregon and Nevada and California—ran almost due north and south across the waist of the nation. It included the western parts of Minnesota, Iowa, Missouri, Arkansas, and Louisiana—the column of states just west of the Mississippi—with protrusions into Nebraska, Kansas, and a considerable part of Texas. It is only a coincidence that almost the entire extent of this frontier also separated the green eastern half of the nation from the brown sagebrush west, a dramatic contrast that no traveler could fail to notice. In 1876, if frontier people turned their back on what Scott Fitzgerald was to call, in *The Great Gatsby*, "the green breast of America," they gazed out upon a wholly different landscape. The gaze was often one of dismay. What assurance could there be that such strange land was habitable?; it looked more like a desert than a potential garden, and Middlewest newspapers carried discouraging stories about it. The federal government, perhaps at the behest of railroads with land to sell, took the unusual step of issuing an official reassurance that settlement, plowing, and planting would indeed turn the area into a garden. It had taken courage and hardihood for the first migrants to cross the Appalachians. Now it took as much if not more for a new group of migrants to advance onto the high plains.

Ordinary prudence should perhaps have checked the advance at just that point; but such an attitude was outbalanced by typical migrant restlessness, coupled with the old familiar dream of fortune ahead. Kansas City, on the actual western boundary of Missouri and the major settlement of the 1876 frontier, was filled with people willing and eager to look westward. This city was a natural instate rival of St. Louis, but unlike St. Louis, which preoccupied itself with battling Chicago for commercial mastery of the Middlewest, Kansas City looked to the open west for its own best fulfillment.

Kansas, which lay most directly in this line of vision, and Nebraska, just to the north, had both become states in the 1860s, but statehood was no warranty that the frontier process had ended, or, indeed, had even begun. Only in the extreme eastern parts of this area was social order established. Omaha, on the western bank of the Missouri River, was the eastern terminus of the Union Pacific Railroad, whose route was the Platte River valley. Passengers could glimpse from the train windows only scattered hamlets, miniscule enough to cause mirth; beyond that valley there were not even hamlets; there was only land awaiting settlers. True, Nebraska had a state university, at Lincoln, the state capital, chartered in 1869, with 282 students in 1876, and farms and energy enough to convene a conference of the region's governors to discuss ways of fighting the grasshoppers, but essentially the state was still frontier and, mostly, wilderness.

The part of Nebraska being subdued in 1876 for human uses was only a minor fraction of the state's 77,227 square miles. Kansas was even larger, with 82,264 square miles, and again, civilization was confined to its easternmost section. Abilene, about 150 miles west of Kansas City, and Dodge City, 175 miles further west, were still wilderness communities in the best Hollywood-television tradition. As major stations on the route along which cattle were driven toward eventual slaughter, they existed apart from the major frontier process, which by and large was the gradual westward extension of agricultural holdings, with more and more enclosure by barbed wire, that epochal invention of 1873. The average assessed value of land in Kansas per acre was $4.18, a figure that might have awed Eastern property-owners even more than the state's enormous size.

Kansas had three institutions of higher education: Kansas State University at Manhattan and Kansas State Teachers College at Emporia, both dating from 1863; and the University of Kansas, established at Lawrence in 1865. During 1876 bills were introduced in the Centennial legislature to abolish capital punishment and to prohibit the sale of liquor. Both were defeated. There was also a brisk skirmish that year between two of the state's railroads and settlers who disliked the terms by which the railroads sold parcels of their land-grants. The action, known as the Osage Land Case, reached the United States Supreme Court, which ruled in favor of the settlers. A similar case in Nebraska, involving the Union Pacific, ended in a circuit court victory for the railroad.

State pride reached its peak in Texas, where perhaps it had a firmer historical basis than elsewhere. For one thing, from 1836 until 1845, Texas had actually been an independent republic. For another, a grim struggle was just ending in Texas to open the Cross Timbers-Prairie region to settlement. A rugged, bleak triangle of some twenty thousand square miles, lying between Waco, Abilene, and Wichita Falls, this region now has two million residents; prior to 1876, white men lived there only at their constant peril. The local Indians had resisted grimly; the land had always been their land, and they had not forgotten that during the 1860s the federal government had proposed the region to them as a great Indian reservation. But the Texans were not to be denied, and there were always more of them, migrants from older states, for whom the Indians were just one more barrier to the fulfillment of their dream. The Indians in Minnesota had expressed their own discontent in the Great Sioux Outbreak of 1862, bloody but brief. In Texas the war was a protracted one, with the white men building and maintaining a complex of forts and only gradually reducing the resistance of the natives. That they finally triumphed gave them, and their descendants, a peculiar sense of superiority; in no other region had the frontier been won with a greater struggle.[2]

The Cross Timbers-Prairie district in 1876 was not typical

frontier; but neither was it strictly wilderness. Indian Territory, between the states of Texas and Kansas, could more appropriately be called wilderness because white men were not supposed to settle there. In the system of federal courts the Indian Territory was assigned to the Western District of Arkansas.

The kind of justice being meted out in 1876, to miscreants for whom Indian Territory seemed like an ideal refuge, is a measure of just how rough the frontier could be. The judge for the Western District was Isaac Parker, a Congressman from 1871 to 1875, who was named Chief Justice of Utah by President Grant but was reassigned to Arkansas. Immediately upon taking office at Fort Smith on May 10, 1875, he appointed two hundred deputy marshals, and he obviously meant business. During his twenty-one years on the bench before death ended his career in 1896, he passed the sentence of death on 162 men; almost half, however, escaped the gallows. Among their victims has been sixty-five of the judge's own deputies. Political opponents tried to make a monster of Judge Parker after he died, but the record shows that he was not unduly harsh or cruel. It was the time and place, not the judge, that deserved condemnation; fortunately the frontier was very seldom like that.[3]

Apart from the main frontier, which was the western edge of American civilization, there were also other areas of frontier land, isolated from the main frontier and also from each other, like farflung islands in a vast sea of wilderness. Four of them—in Colorado, Utah, Nevada, and California—were tied together by the transcontinental railroad; the fifth, in Oregon, had no railway ties with the rest of the nation. Each of the five was a group of settlements with one major center, and with area enough to need its own internal transportation system—steamboats on Great Salt Lake, railroads in the other four regions. And each was old enough to have earned statehood by 1876—excepting Utah, which had to wait until national indignation over the Mormons' practice of plural marriage died down.

Colorado did not begin the Centennial year as a state, but by being admitted during that year acquired the nickname Centennial State. Territorial status had been granted in 1861, but a series of efforts to gain statehood had failed. In 1875, with an eye on the Presidential election of 1876, the House, with its Republican majority, passed an enabling act on the last hectic day of the session in March; it was apparent to all that Colorado would be Republican, and it was even more obvious that the next Congress, which would convene that December with a Democratic majority in the House, would not be interested in statehood for Colorado. The vote in March, 1875, was close; a companion effort on behalf of New Mexico was defeated.

A Constitutional Convention completed its work in March, 1876, and the voters ratified the constitution just in time for a celebration that also saluted the Centennial Fourth of July. A great parade in Denver featured a float with thirty-eight ladies, elaborately gowned, representing Colorado and her sister states. In fact, however, Colorado did not become a state until August 1, when President Grant made it official by proclamation. Had he not done so, Colorado would not have had three electoral votes to be counted for Hayes, and there would not have been the disputed election. Not until 1889, incidentally, were any more states admitted.

The fine high western edge of the great plains, under the front range of the Rocky Mountains, was a veritable Eden, which attracted and held a good many western migrants, who prospered quickly in agriculture and mining. By the time statehood was granted, Colorado already had three institutions of higher education: the University at Boulder; the Agricultural College at Fort Collins; and the School of Mines at Golden. These three communities, together with Denver, the capital, and Colorado Springs and Pueblo further south, comprised a slender corridor about 175 miles north and south, and about twenty miles wide. Apart from a few outlying hamlets, this was all that the state could really be said to be—a bit of incipient civilization surrounded by wilderness, a fragment of the frontier—three thousand square miles, more or less, in the center of a state with over a hundred thousand square miles. In 1876, some of those square miles were seen for the first time by white men, when the members of the Hayden Survey completed their mapping of the state.

To the railroad traveler, five hundred miles out of Omaha or Kansas City, Denver was a welcome sight, and Denver welcomed him. If he could not be induced to stay, he faced another

five-hundred-mile ride up through Cheyenne and across southern Wyoming, the route that earlier travelers, in covered wagons, had adopted to avoid the rugged Colorado mountains, in
order to reach the next garden in the wilderness: the Utah
Territory. Utah was quite different from Denver. The inhabitants, largely members of The Church of Jesus Christ of Latter
Day Saints—the Mormons, extended to travelers neither a welcome nor an invitation to stay—unless the traveler were a Mormon. Not even the railroad was welcome. The main line, instead
of passing through Utah's major settlement, Salt Lake City,
described a great arc to the north of the lake and across Promon-
tory Mountain, where the Union Pacific and the Central Pacific
joined.

Utah as nature had made it was anything but an earthly
paradise. The site had been chosen by the Mormons in 1847, just
because it *was* so unpromising, and so remote from the forces of
prejudice. American ingenuity and determination have never
been better exhibited than in the Mormon success of turning
desert into garden—through irrigation, careful planning, and
cooperation. Only a very small part of the Utah Territory—less
than one percent in 1876—was irrigable, but that small part was
maintaining a full, rich life.

As in the early New England towns, the church was the focus
of existence. Mormon preference for agriculture and prejudice
against mining somewhat limited the economic development, but
one steady source of income was the pilgrims whose transit of
their land the Mormons officially opposed but whose dollars
they did not refuse to accept. The beehive as a Mormon symbol
was expressive; what these zealots had done with so little was
a triumph, an inspiration, no matter how many wives the Mormon men supposedly had. Their leader, Brigham Young, had a
genius for organization, and by the time of his death in 1877 a
self-sustaining economy had been created for a large population.
He was survived by seventeen wives.

The People's Cyclopedia, issued by Phillips and Hunt of New
York in 1879, no doubt reflected the opinion of the vast majority
of Americans in stating that after the move to Utah the Mormon
practices "continued to outrage civilization." Had it not been for
their disapproval of the Mormon practice of plural marriage, the

rest of the nation might have studied with profit what the Mormons had done and were doing in Utah. Bostonians might have seen that history was repeating itself, for the zeal of their seventeenth century forebears in creating a tightly-knit theocratic community was equalled if not excelled by that of the Mormons. Just as Massachusetts Bay had resisted men and ideas opposed to its church-centered authoritarianism, so the Church of Jesus Christ of Latter Day Saints was now opposing all "gentile" forces including the United States government. Quakers and all other once-despised groups might have felt a certain kinship; but it was easy, even pleasant, to forget past woes—and polygamy was such an outrage.

Whether Salt Lake and the lesser Mormon communities comprised a remote outpost of civilization, as the Mormons might have insisted, or an isolated part of the frontier, need not concern us unduly. The Mormon settlement was certainly distinct from the vast wilderness on all sides, which stretched from the Canadian border to Mexico. Salt Lake commanded the largest potential trade area in the nation, and still does, if only because there is no comparable city anywhere near. In 1876 the lake settlement's geographic isolation, and its potential market, were even more apparent. For railroad passengers at that time, the dreariest part of the continental crossing was still ahead, five hundred miles of desert to be crossed before reaching the developed far corner of Nevada.

The Central Pacific railroad passed through Reno, the northernmost of the Nevada communities, before beginning its ascent of Donner Pass. From Reno, the Virginia and Truckee Railroad, at the time the richest short line in the nation, passed through nine hamlets before dividing at Carson City, one branch going south to Minden, the other winding and climbing eastward through more hamlets to Virginia City, which, at its elevation of 6,500 feet, was a fitting citadel for the "silver kings." The railroad provided sleeping car service to and from San Francisco.

Nevada had been rushed into statehood in 1864, eleven years before Carson City, its capital, was incorporated. Mark Twain had been in Virginia City in the early 1860s, when his brother was secretary to the territorial governor; he had contributed to the *Territorial Enterprise*, and his book *Roughing It* (1872) contained loving and mostly accurate pictures of the area. A fire had leveled much of Virginia City in October, 1875, but the people had rebuilt at once. The new International Hotel was now five stories high with a hydraulic elevator, Turkish carpets, mahogany furniture, a marble-floored dining room, and potted palms. The rich, and there were plenty of them in 1876, supported grand opera at Piper's Opera House, attending in evening dress, and staged expensive balls, replete with champagne and liveried servants, in their mansions on "Millionaire's Row." The city's population reached its height, twenty-five thousand, in 1876, but began to decline soon after, when the price of silver fell.[4] Reno, where most of the gambling houses were located, grew instead. Reno was on the main line west, as Virginia City was not, and, for travelers, this little corner of Nevada was a very welcome oasis after the long tedious crossing of the Great Basin, so arid that its few rivers dwindled and disappeared. Passers-through took Reno as something of a breather before attempting the formidable Sierra Nevada just to the west.

If outside the Mormon settlement Utah and most of Nevada were singularly unblessed by nature, the state that lay beyond the mountains, California, had almost more than its fair share of blessings. For transplanted farmers and fruit growers and cattlemen the vast fertile San Joaquin Valley was alone worth the long journey west. Truck farms, to supply food for the rapidly growing population, were in immediate demand. Cattlemen and sheep herders had their choice of ranch sites along other rivers —the Merced and the Salinas, the Russian and the American, and the Sacramento extending almost to Oregon. The great bonanza following the discovery, in 1848, of gold at Sutter's Mill, had slackened by 1854, but if miners could no longer hope for a killing, there was still a steady demand and the assurance of good wages for carpenters, masons, and others in the building trades; for teachers and draymen; lawyers and policemen; bank clerks and salesmen; cooks and waitresses; hotel maids and managers—all and any having the skills required by a booming new civilization. And there was plenty of room in the state, even with its immense tracts of rugged mountains and the arid deserts near the Mexican border for growth, far into the future. California had 158,693 square miles, the area of two Nebraskas, or of four Indianas with a Massachusetts and a Connecticut thrown in.

Texas had won its independence from Mexico by military means. California was a different kind of battleground, where Americans from elsewhere in the United States struggled long and hard for economic mastery against the Californios—people of Spanish origin who had been there much longer. By granting California statehood in 1850, hardly a year after the first great influx of Americans, Congress no doubt hoped to speed the victory and make California American beyond any doubt. But it wasn't that easy. The Californios resisted, as they might have been expected to, and even though their cause was lost by 1860, they held on grimly to their great tracts of land, intent on perpetuating what the 1876 legislature called the "land monopoly" and sought to destroy. The legislators did little more than talk, however; the 1876 session adjourned without having taken action on the land issue or on numerous other pressing problems. The Californios were not the only villains. Some Americans held deeds to large acreage, and the Southern Pacific Railroad controlled far more land than it needed.

California in 1876, though it had been a state for a quarter-century, still exhibited many of the characteristics of a frontier. Regularly authorized policing agencies, for example, were less effective than the extra-legal vigilantes. The state land office was shown in an 1876 investigation to be haphazard in the extreme, with more than $40,000 in receipts unaccounted for. The continuing economic boom depended much more on the steady growth of population, from immigration, than on a solid system of production within the state; almost every manufactured item used in California was imported from the East. San Francisco's Palace Hotel, one of the world's finest, and the mansions rising on Nob Hill, gave an illusion of stability, but the state was far from stable. The University at Berkeley, established in 1865, suffered from constant political interference, and Daniel Coit Gilman, its president from 1872 to 1875, concluded his presidency by quitting in disgust after accepting an offer from the new Johns Hopkins University in Baltimore.

Most Californians, perhaps, were less interested in the university than in San Francisco's waterfront, the fabled Barbary Coast (so-called after the pirate coast of North Africa), which was world-famous for its concentrated vice. All civilized cities had their vice, of course, but nowhere in the settled East was vice so openly tolerated, or spoken of with such pride, as in San Francisco. Everywhere on the frontier, before the forces of order and sobriety gained control, open vice was one of the attractions; San Francisco merely provided it on a larger scale. If recognition as a part of civilization in America depended on cleaning up the Barbary Coast, Californians seemed quite willing to wait.

Despite its instability, or perhaps because of it, California was truly the promised land, the ultimate as dreamed in restless dreams, the prime symbol of the western migration, and destined, even beyond the hopes of its editors and orators, for a primacy that Centennial Easterners could not have begun to imagine. Not all the western migrants chose California, however. Some preferred Oregon or Washington, which shared many of California's natural advantages—high mountains, fertile valleys along good rivers, an equable climate, and a magnificent coastline.

Oregon had become a state in 1859. With no good ocean harbor the settlers were fortunate in sharing a river, the Columbia, that was navigable for many miles. Where the north-flowing Willamette joined the Columbia, Portland grew, quite slowly compared with San Francisco, and deliberately more cautiously —a Western version of New England propriety and restraint. Other towns sprang up in the Willamette valley—Salem, the state capital; Albany; Corvallis, where Oregon State University was founded in 1868; and Eugene, where the University of Oregon opened four years later. Another and thinner line of settlement followed the Columbia River eastward. As in Colorado, only a very small area was developed in 1876, and while that area had one of the finest climates in the nation, the entire eastern half of the state was arid. One handicap to Oregon's development in 1876 was its lack of rail connections with the rest of the country. Another was the fact that a few cattle barons owned most of the grazing land and stubbornly opposed both sheepmen and homesteaders. In addition, Indian uprisings recurred sporadically throughout the 1870s.

Washington was even less advanced. Although designated a Territory in 1853, Washington enjoyed no significant growth in population until the 1880s, and statehood was achieved only in 1889, when four states were admitted on the hundredth anniversary of the Constitution. Settlement in 1876 was confined almost entirely to the shores of Puget Sound, the finest harbor waters on the Pacific coast. Seattle, the largest city, with about three-thousand inhabitants, served as the major port for Alaska, and was already the seat of the University of Washington, founded in 1861. Generally, however, the frontier process was in low gear in Washington in 1876; although nature had been profligate, this was the end of the line.

3

WILDERNESS

If most Easterners had hazy, romantic notions of the great western wilderness, and hardly more realistic ones about life on the frontier, a few men shared a vision that embraced both wilderness and frontier, and much more as well. To the extent that they were able to control that vision and direct it, we may call it a design—a grand design, in fact, for a future economic empire almost without limits.

An early form of this vision of economic empire must have prompted Thomas Jefferson, in 1803, to buy the Louisiana Territory. But it was much more grandiose, and more clearly defined, when Secretary of State William H. Seward negotiated the United States' purchase of Alaska from the Russians for $7,200,000 in 1867. Seward would have liked to acquire Mexico as well; at one time he envisioned it as a state and Mexico City as the future capital of the American nation. The western provinces of Canada were other quondam candidates for statehood. But although events pruned the dimensions of his vision Seward

did live to see both Mexico and Canada absorbed into the economic frontier of the United States, and Hawaii well along on
the road to annexation.

Seward, who believed that Manifest Destiny was ordained by
Providence, was the major political instrument of the businessmen and industrialists of the North and East who were able,
when the Civil War eliminated Southern representation in Congress, to dominate that body through their own representatives.
The power shifted irrevocably; agrarianism never regained its
control. One by one, in the early 1860s, Congress enacted laws
favoring the business community and the grand design: high
protective tariffs; centralized banking; the Homestead Act of
1862, to encourage the settlement of new land and thus extend
the market; vast land grants to railroads to hasten the extension
of lines further into the wilderness; and contract labor laws that
permitted the importation of low-paid foreign workers. There
was opposition, of course, from many groups in the country; but
once the business leaders had seized the initiative, the momentum
was irresistible.[5]

Our concern, in this chapter at least, is less with the vision of
economic expansion in its largest form than with the part of the
nation where, in 1876, the frontier had not yet begun or was in
its very earliest stage. Whatever level of probability attended
more distant areas included in the vision, the wilderness west was
already within the national territory, and nobody challenged our
right to it or questioned that it would eventually be tamed.
Horace Greeley supposed it might take another century. Other
men were more sanguine, though nobody dreamed that the
frontier process would run its course as fast as it did. Some
Eastern groups were uneasy about the developing new regions as
constituting threats to their own economic advantage, and the
uneasiness proved to be justified. But the men who read the
future most clearly, and had the power to guide the nation's
course, saw in westward expansion something much bigger than
parochial self-interest.

If the visionaries in and out of Congress agreed on the importance of completing the conquest of the West as quickly as
possible, what were the practical considerations they would be
likely to press? One, mentioned early, was to overcome, through

the reassuring words of a federal agency, the doubts of potential settlers concerning the habitability of the high plains. More significant was the legislation cited above. And one of the most immediate needs was policing the wilderness to make it safe for the pioneer process to begin. It was this need for policing that provided most of the action in 1876. But some of the action seems, in retrospect, a discordant element in the harmony of the grand design.

During 1867 the Union Pacific advanced through Indian hunting lands in Nebraska and Wyoming. The Sioux, primarily concerned about the depletion of the buffalo, staged a series of raids along the advancing line. At a peace conference presided over by General ("Uncle Billy") Sherman in 1868, a "Great Sioux Reservation" was established that was to include all of southern Dakota and eastern Wyoming. This Reservation was soon, however, whittled down to the Dakota part west of the Missouri, with hunting rights granted the Sioux in specified adjacent areas. The treaty forbade white hunting parties to seek buffalo within the Reservation, but the provision was poorly enforced. Between 1870 and 1875 an estimated five million of these animals that the Plains Indians relied on for food were killed, largely for sport, by white men. The railroads helped indirectly, for many of the hunters, including European nobility fascinated by this New World Grand Tour, would never have reached the buffalo range without benefit of the passenger trains. Buffalo on the tracks were a great nuisance, of course; the sooner the herds were reduced, the happier the train crews would be.

But if much of the slaughter was for sport, even more of it was for profit. Not all Indians worried about the possible depletion of their meat supply; many of them earned a tidy income by selling buffalo robes to traders who sent them East. The Kiowa Comanche Agency alone sold 70,400 robes to traders in 1876, while the Baker Company of Fort Benton, Montana, shipped 75,000 in the same year. White hunters, naturally, did not let the Indians enjoy a monopoly in the business. The demand for robes, beginning in 1871, first in California and later in the East, was apparently insatiable, but the supply was not unlimited. The Kiowa Agency sales dropped rapidly after 1876, to a mere 5,068 in 1879.[8] As with the passenger pigeon, the possibility of extermination was not considered, and the only thing that stopped the hunters was the growing scarcity of the hunted.

For the Indians in buffalo country, especially the Sioux in Dakota, Wyoming, and Montana, the depletion of the buffalo meant rapid sinking into impoverishment. Many of them took the easy way of subsisting on government doles, only to be cheated by federal agents. Othniel Marsh, the Yale fossil expert visited by T. H. Huxley, was so outraged by the cheating he observed on one of his field expeditions that he wrote a book about it in 1875, *A Statement of Affairs at the Red Cloud Agency, Made to the President of the United States.* Nothing came of it. The Indians who shared his opinions, or were too proud to go on relief, were branded as "hostiles."

The pace of history quickened in 1874 when gold was discovered in the Black Hills, just twenty years after the bonanza had ended in California. The Seventh Cavalry, based at Fort Abraham Lincoln, had kept reasonably busy with a variety of assignments: guarding the construction of the Northern Pacific, evicting an occasional white trespasser, hunting down recalcitrant Indians. It seemed only a slight variation of routine to accompany a scientific expedition to the Black Hills. But prospectors in the party confirmed the rumors of gold, and by taking the news back to civilization the officer in command, Lt.-Col. George Armstrong Custer, helped touch off the events that were to culminate in his "last stand" two years later.

A government without the power or the desire to keep buffalo hunters out of the Reservation could hardly prevent the wholesale migration of gold seekers, a breed of men indifferent to all deterrents. A village sprang up and was named, appropriately enough, Custer City. By 1876 it had forty houses built, sixty more under construction, a steam sawmill, numerous saloons, and a Methodist church. It also had inflation prices: flour at twelve dollars a barrel, bacon at thirty cents a pound.

Demand built up rapidly for cession of the Black Hills, and in 1875 the government made an offer of purchase. But even if the price had been attractive, the Sioux could hardly have been willing to give up the very heart of their Reservation, and its best hunting ground. The pressure was increased, to the point of withholding rations from any Sioux known to oppose cession.

Thousands of Indian families showed their resentment by joining Sitting Bull, Crazy Horse, Gall, and other "hostile" leaders in belligerent wanderings far outside the Reservation. How many joined in this effort is hard to determine, but a good guess puts the number between twelve and fifteen thousand, a third of them warriors. It was like old times for them, with no dictation from Washington, nothing to prevent them from fighting their old Crow enemies and roaming at will the far reaches of Wyoming and Montana. When they learned of a government edict dated December 1, 1875, ordering them back to the Reservation within two months, they saw no good reason to obey it. Indians had never liked to travel in winter.

January came and went. On February 7, 1876, a week after the deadline, the Interior Department and General Sherman authorized General Philip Sheridan to enforce the December edict by military measures. By armchair logic the defiant Indians were enemies, and it was not difficult to assemble plentiful evidence of overt hostility. By the end of February, Eastern newspapers could report that "the annual Indian war scare is upon us" and could describe the grand strategy which would bring three cavalry units together near Sitting Bull's camp. In the East it all seemed far away. One editor remarked on February 26, apparently unaware that it bore any relation to the Indian war, that "the new Eldorado, the Black Hills, is setting everybody in Chicago crazy."

It was clear enough to Custer, as to other officers acquainted with the facts at first hand, that responsibility for a major Indian war lay squarely at the feet of the graft-ridden, inefficient War Department. In *My Life on the Plains* (New York, 1874) Custer had expressed great indignation over a comment in a New York newspaper that two classes were always eager for an Indian war: the frontiersman and the Army; they were the very two groups, he knew, with the liveliest dread of such a war. He described the Plains Indians not as Noble Savages but as men "whose cruel and ferocious nature far exceeds that of any wild beast of the desert." The only group eager for a war, he added, were the Army contractors living far from the border. To the ordinary dangers of fighting the Indians, officialdom added others. In addition to his primitive weapons each Indian had "either a breech-loading rifle or revolver, sometimes . . . both —the latter obtained through the wise foresight and strong love of fair play which prevails in the Indian department, which, seeing that its wards are determined to fight, is equally determined that there shall be no advantage taken, but that the two sides shall be armed alike. . . . The only difference is, that the soldier, if he loses his weapon, is charged double for it. . . ." This continued to be true; Mrs. Custer, shortly after bidding her husband goodbye for the last time, watched a steamer pass Fort Lincoln with a cargo of Springfield rifles for the Indians, and she remembered, with sinking heart, that the Seventh Cavalry had only short-range carbines.

His writings caused Custer to be regarded as something of an authority and thereby a prime witness for a House committee probing the War Department in early 1876. Subpoenaed early in March, he dutifully traveled to Washington but was not called upon for several days. He was impatient to rejoin his regiment, now in hard training, and General Alfred H. Terry sent more than one telegram urging him to hurry back. When he finally gave his testimony, he told the truth as he knew it, bluntly, without thinking of consequences. "I would hate to testify," he said, "to the character of any post trader in these times. . . . The profits of the trader left the morals of the Indians far behind." He offered telling evidence about the War Department's present inefficiency: issue of obsolete guns to the troops, inadequate allocation of troops, frustrating delays. Sitting Bull had plenty of guns, ammunition, and men. It was to the credit of the Army, he told the Congressmen, that it was not completely demoralized. One of his statements declared that General Rice had accepted $5,000 for the post tradership at Fort Lincoln. Rice branded this assertion a lie in a "card" printed in the Washington *Republican* on March 30; the next day the two men met on a Washington street, and it was reported that Custer "gave him a tremendous caning." Exciting times.

Asked why he had not volunteered his information sooner, Custer cited a general order issued on March 15, 1873, which forbade officers to communicate directly with members of Congress and required all petitions to be channeled through the General of the Army and the War Department. To disobey was to risk the loss of one's commission. The order thus effectively sealed the mouths of men best qualified to report irregularities, and smoothed the way for grafters.

Custer might have known there would be repercussions. When the Clymer committee let him go at last, he hurried West to join his regiment. But at Chicago an order from Sheridan detained him: he had reportedly failed to pay the obligatory calls on Sherman, the General of the Army, and on Grant, the Commander in Chief. He was able to refute both charges: Sherman had been out twice when he called, and Grant had refused to see him. He was allowed to proceed, but at St. Paul even worse news awaited him: General Terry had been given full command and he was not even to join the expedition. On May 6 he telegraphed a plea to the President: "I appeal to you as a soldier to spare me the humiliation of seeing my regiment march to meet the enemy and I not to share its dangers." Grant relented, probably because of pressure from Terry and Sheridan.

Custer was well enough known, because of his daring exploits in the Civil War, for the incident to rouse considerable interest. It was charged, and denied, that he had been relieved of his command for testifying about the post traderships. Grant explained that he had wanted Custer to stay in Washington until he could testify, but that the Seventh Cavalry was soon to march and could wait no longer for a commanding officer. Sherman denied a rumor that he had protested against the shift in commander; the Army, he insisted, "had hundreds equally competent for such an expedition." The Radical Republican press had a field day excoriating Custer. The New York *Commercial Advertiser* asserted that "any humiliation that could ought to be put upon this place-seeking soldier . . . eternally in search of notoriety." Custer was "designed for a circus rider, not a soldier, but by some unhappy chance he got to West Point, and now the country has to support him." To this the Elmira *Daily Advertiser* replied that the Indians feared Custer as much as they did the Great Spirit: "Custer is foolish, but brave, although not very veracious." Heroes must not expect unanimous approval.

Custer was back at Fort Lincoln only a few days before the expedition was to set out. As a place to live, half-way across Dakota and well beyond the forested eastern half of the country, it was barren and treeless, but bracing. Fire had partially destroyed his house two winters before but had spared his trophy room, packed with mementoes. Staring from the walls were the heads of animals he had shot: a buffalo, his first grizzly bear, an antelope, a black-tailed deer. Stuffed specimens—jackrabbits, a great white owl, a sandhill crane, a mountain eagle—competed for space with his fine collection of sabres, and an assortment of guns. Scattered on the floor, and over chairs, were beaver and mountain-lion skins. It was not much like a room in any mansion built by a newly-rich merchant in New York or Chicago, but it was genuinely American. Two Rogers pieces, "Letter Day" and "Wounded to the Rear," were his concession to popular taste. Signed photographs of the actor Lawrence Barrett and Generals Sheridan and McClellan stood on the piano, near the harp. Most of the furniture was somewhat battered, for Custer had a habit, upon receiving orders for action, of throwing chairs about in his elation.

When the column started from Fort Lincoln, on May 17, Custer was more exhilarated than apprehensive; he was always at his best with danger just ahead. In the dull fog that did not lift all day, the troopers rode out to the tune of "The Girl I Left Behind Me." Custer's wife Elizabeth went along for the first day's ride of fourteen miles, returning with the paymaster the next morning. She actually expected her husband to send for her soon. Under his tutelage she had hardened to campaign conditions and could drop from her horse and go to sleep at once on the hard ground.

Few military displays could equal the color of a cavalry regiment, each company mounted on horses of the same type—bays or grays, blood bays or sorrels. There were also several infantry companies and over a hundred supply wagons, some of them horse-drawn but most with six-mule teams. Other supplies were to follow by water, aboard the "Far West," up the great curve of the Missouri and Yellowstone rivers while the column was marching due west across country.

Custer was in one of three columns setting out from widely separated forts; the other two were in southern Wyoming and western Montana. Without modern means of communication, the men had to rely on the ability of all three columns to reach the designated rendezvous at the agreed-upon time. Eastern editors, learning the strategy as announced from Washington, were optimistic that the campaign would be short. The "hostiles" were increasing their activity, picking off whites whenever they could; it was reported on June 19 that over a hundred white men had been killed within the past week. The House Committee on Indian Affairs, meanwhile, was recommending the passage of a bill opening to exploration and settlement all the area north of the Platte River and east of the Big Horn summits; the 1868 treaty, the committee insisted (without seeking the opinion of the Indians), did not actually exclude whites. People in the East might wonder how the pincers campaign was progressing, but they knew they would have to wait a long time for news.

By June 9 the column was at Powder River, but the next twenty miles looked so rough that Terry doubted whether the wagons could get through. Custer, whose beard was growing fast, auburn in hue, found a route for them. On June 21 the column divided, Custer leading his cavalry up the Rosebud while Terry, reinforced by the Montana troops under Gibbons, proceeded to and up the Bighorn, a few miles further west. Custer was nettled because a scouting party that found a fresh Indian trail had turned back: "Think of the time lost!" But the adventure intoxicated him. He used only mules for supplies; he liked them better than wagons. "We take no tents," he wrote, "and desire none." This was life at its best, reduced to elementals, with the highest test of manhood almost at hand.

The regiment proceeded cautiously up the Rosebud, June 22 to 24. At the twenty-mile point the Indian trail turned right, ascending the ridge between the Rosebud and Little Bighorn valleys. At the crest, as day broke on June 25, scouts saw the smoke of distant campfires, but by the time Custer arrived, the brilliant sun striking the valley haze obscured the exact location. The attack had been set for the next day, but the scouts were sure the "hostiles" knew of their presence, and Custer decided to press closer lest the Indians withdraw. At noon Custer divided his forces. Captain Benteen was sent with three companies on a flanking maneuver to the left of the trail. The main body aimed as straight as they could at the encampment, Major Reno with three companies following the left bank of a small stream, Custer and the remaining five companies keeping to its right. About two miles above the camp Custer ordered Reno to cross the Little Bighorn and attack, while he himself kept to the east bank, intent upon a surprise frontal assault across the river.

Reno soon learned that the Indians' strength was much greater than had been supposed; bluffs and cottonwoods gave excellent cover to their tepees. Indians swarmed toward him in such numbers that he dismounted his men to form a skirmish line, ordered a retreat almost at once, tried a second stand in a thicket, and finally let the men fend for themselves in an utter rout. Benteen soon came up, and the loss of nerve in Reno's troops spread to his by contagion. The six companies dug in as best they could before a renewed onslaught from the Indians which kept on till sundown, halted overnight, and resumed at dawn. Volunteers braved Indian fire to go down to the river for water. Relief came only on the second evening when the Indians, learning of Terry's approach from the north, withdrew, taking their tepees with them and firing the valley grass. The battle was over.

What happened to Custer was not learned until June 27, when Terry's column stumbled upon the bodies. Custer apparently had not realized his danger until the very end. One messenger, sent back to move up the supplies, had shouted to Benteen as he galloped past, "We've got 'em, boys!" And a second messenger, urging Benteen to hurry along, had cried in elation that the Indians were "skedaddling." But Company D, sent by Benteen along Custer's route, had to turn back under sharp enemy fire, and it was shortly after this that the Benteen-Reno troops were surrounded. The rough ground may have misled Custer into a fatal underestimate of the odds, but he had never been known to count the odds. Lieutenant Calhoun, his brother-in-law, had been able to keep his own company in an orderly skirmish line. The rest were scattered in death, some on the open hillside, others in ravines. Terry, reaching the scene, wept openly. The only living thing on the battlefield was Comanche, Lieutenant Keogh's horse. Many scalps had been taken, and most of the clothing, but body mutilation was relatively slight. Custer was untouched. The dead were buried where they fell, 206 men and officers. Fourteen, missing, were never found.

Terry withdrew the entire command. Not until July 5, when

the steamboat bearing the wounded arrived at Fort Lincoln, did the world learn of the incident; then the local telegraph operator was kept at his key for twenty-four hours. The Army, redeploying its forces, resumed the campaign and systematically broke down Indian resistance. By the end of August it was possible to send a Peace Commission to the disputed area: on September 12 Buffalo Bill was on his way home, his services as a scout no longer needed. Various survivors of the Battle of the Little Bighorn gained momentary fame by telling what they knew; the legend was beginning to take form. In 1877 Custer's body was removed to the post cemetery at West Point. The warhorse Comanche, retired with honors at Fort Riley, was saddled and paraded at every regimental ceremony but was never ridden again, and dying at the age of thirty-two, was stuffed and put on display in the Dyche Museum at the University of Kansas. The site of the battle has become a national monument in clear view of U. S. Highway 87 and the lines of the Chicago, Burlington, and Quincy Railroad. An unending flow of books has debated the relative blame for the debacle, but the need for heroes has preserved the popular memory of "the Boy General with the Golden Locks." [7]

For a good many Easterners in 1876, Custer was what they wanted in the untamed West—a hero. Eulogistic poems appeared overnight. One of them prompted an editor to remark, "It is not enough that Custer should have had a death so cruel, but Walt Whitman has composed a sonnet in his memory." Three days later the same editor printed a tribute by Edmund Clarence Stedman that he praised as "worth a thousand effusions of Walt Whitman," [8] which begins:

> Young lion of the plain,
> Thou of the tawny mane!

But it is more appropriate, in a discussion of the western wilderness, to mention Captain Jack Crawford, chief of scouts for the Black Hills Rangers, a co-founder and member of the Board of Trustees of Custer City. Immediately after receiving a telegram from Buffalo Bill, "Have you heard of the death of our brave Custer?" he dashed off a poem, "The Death of Custer." Its opening is typical of his style:

> Did I hear news from CUSTER?
> Well, I reckon I did, old pard;
> It came like a streak of lightnin',
> And, you bet, it hit me hard.

He could turn out verse for any occasion, enough of it to fill a volume of 208 pages, entitled *The Poet Scout.*[9]

In his preface Crawford disclaimed any thought of literary fame. If anybody remembered him in later years, he hoped it would be for his fight against the evils of drink. In a way that may shake our image of the hard-drinking pioneers, he described the scene at his dying mother's side:

> That day was perhaps the greatest epoch of my life. Kneeling by her bed-side, with one hand clasped in mine, the other resting upon my head, she whispered: "My boy, you know your mother loves you. Will you give me a promise, that I may take it up to heaven?" "Yes, yes, mother; I will promise you anything." "Johnny, my son, I am dying," said she; "promise you will never drink intoxicants, and then it will not be so hard to leave this world." Dear reader, need I tell you that I promised "Yes;" and whenever I am asked to drink, that scene comes up before me, and I am safe.

Captain Jack also reported that he had "never figured as a hero of fiction or dime novels," but perhaps he should have. He was the Oliver Wendell Holmes of the wilderness West, ready at a moment's notice to turn an event into poetry. His typical opening is shown again in "The Ruined Virginia," after the fire that almost totally destroyed Virginia City, Nevada, in October, 1875:

> Did I hear the news from Virginny—
> The news of that terrible fire?

But perhaps his greatest service was to provide rhymed tributes to departed friends: Wild Bill Hickok, for example, who was killed in 1876; Charlie Reynolds, one of Custer's scouts, and Muggins Taylor, Custer's courier; Buffalo Chips, another scout; and of course Custer himself. Captain Jack was living proof that the West could produce its own poets; what could civilization offer of greater interest?

But wilderness America had to share its heroes with the effete

East, where Custer's death caused a sensation. Within weeks, there was a somber sheet-music "Requiem to the Memory of Gen. George A. Custer," by Charles Glover, whose title page bore a likeness of Custer and facsimile of his signature. And in 1879 A. R. Milner brought out "General Custer's Last March," with a sketch of an Indian tomahawking an army officer.[10] Painters took somewhat longer to record the event. John Mulvany's "Custer's Last Rally," completed in 1881 circulated from one gallery to another throughout the country for about a decade, but "Custer's Last Fight" by Cassily Adams, painted later in the 1880s, or rather a modified version of it lithographed by Otto Becker and distributed by the brewers of Budweiser beer, still serves to keep Custer's fame alive, as the prime popular symbol of 1876, and has possibly been seen by more Americans than any other painting.[11]

On August 5, not long after Custer's death, *Harper's Weekly* offered a comment that Custer would have endorsed: "We make treaties . . . and then leave swindlers and knaves to enforce them." Custer deserved a monument. "But a truer monument, more enduring than brass or marble, would be an Indian policy intelligent, moral, and efficient." Earlier in the year, on March 4, the same editor had cited a remark by Congressman Seelye, former president of Amherst College, that it cost a million dollars to kill an Indian but only $2,000 to keep him alive. "Yet General Sheridan persists in the axiom that 'The only *good* Indian is a *dead* Indian.' " Whether or not they used the same words, a great many Centennial Americans agreed with General Sheridan, including the Centennial observer Emily FitzGerald, the army doctor's wife.

The historical record of our dealings with the Indians contains little that white Americans can be proud of, as Loring Priest makes very clear in his book *Uncle Sam's Stepchildren*.[12] It could be argued that anything like true justice for the Indians, who never numbered more than a million, was impossible if the needs of the other Americans, more than forty million strong in 1876, were to be accommodated. In terms of the grand design, moreover, if Indians resisted the subjugation of the wilderness they would have to be brought into submission; not to use available force would be an abject denial of what Providence had ordained. In any case, most Americans were too impatient for results to listen to anything that intellectuals might say in defense of the Indians' cause.

One intellectual giant of 1876, Lewis Henry Morgan, a lawyer, whose *Ancient Society* (1877) was to become a classic for its theory of social evolution, had something to say about the Indian wars. Writing for the *Nation* in July, 1876,[13] he asked who could blame the Sioux for defending themselves. He maintained that the lack of intelligence in federal handling of the Indians was a disgrace; the only solution was the creation of a Department of Indian Affairs, headed by a man of cabinet rank. Morgan had long been sympathetic to the Indians' plight; he had become interested, early in life, in the condition of Indian life near Lake Cayuga, New York, and in 1837 had become an adopted member of the Seneca tribe.

A young lawyer who had graduated from the Columbia Law School in the spring of 1876, Perry Belmont, shared Morgan's thinking. He had dined one evening with a family friend, Secretary of War Don Cameron, in the company of General Sherman. "I shall never forget," Belmont wrote years later, "the general's use of the only too familiar phrase, 'The only good Indian is a dead Indian.' " He also recalled that President Grant, in his second inaugural address in 1873, had said that the advantages and strengths of the whites should "make us lenient toward the Indian. The wrong inflicted upon him should be taken into account and the balance placed to his credit. . . . Cannot the Indian be made a useful and productive member of society by proper teaching and treatment?"

But such sentiments were lost on the nation's top military officers. In Chicago, en route to Canada with a friend, Count Louis de Turenne, Belmont saw General Sheridan, who echoed Sherman's axiom. Belmont and Count Louis also learned that travel through Indian territory in Canada would be quite safe, in contrast to the United States, where federal agents never met for discussion with Indians without a large accompanying force of soldiers. At one border meeting the Canadian officials arrived with just two of their mounted police. In a letter to his father from Canada Belmont wrote, "The fact is our people are very wrong about this Indian question. What I heard from Cameron and Sherman in Washington and Sheridan in Chicago leaves me with little hope for any more rational way of dealing with this matter on the part of the present administration." In Canada, he had learned, the government never regarded Indians—even the same Sioux tribesmen that Custer faced—as necessarily hostile: "Above all, they are treated honestly." Bargains once made were kept, and the prohibition against selling liquor to the Indians was strictly enforced. In the course of traveling about six hundred miles on foot and by canoe, Belmont learned an Indian maxim: once false always false. This applied all too obviously, he thought, to the whites' treatment of Indians in the United States. He returned to his Long Island home just in time to vote the Democratic ticket in the November election.[14]

But Congressman Seelye, Lewis Henry Morgan, and Perry Belmont were prophets whom nobody heeded. Indians, docile or hostile, were regarded, and treated, as encumbrances that had to be pushed aside. Policing, not teaching or retraining, was the American way. The Civil War had left an ample legacy of manpower proficient in policing. Most of the regular army in 1876, which numbered some twenty-three thousand, officers and troops alike, were veterans of either the Union or the Confederate army.

It has already been noted that Colonel Taylor, the Centennial observer who covered Texas on horseback, had been impressed by the number of Negro troops he encountered. If many white soldiers found regular army life attractive enough to continue in the service during peacetime, this life was particularly advantageous to Negro veterans, who had less chance of civilian employment after the war. Enough of them remained in the Army to form two cavalry regiments, the Ninth and Tenth, and for two decades they helped police the great plains, under white officers who appreciated their capacity for learning, their docility, and their excellent behavior under fire. Some higher officers in the War Department, however, felt it was quite all right to give them inferior equipment and the hardest assignments, and there was considerable prejudice among settlers near their posts. Various derogatory appellations were common, such as "Africans" or "Brunettes"; their own favorite was a term the Indians called them, "Buffalo Soldiers." The Tenth Cavalry even devised a crest with a buffalo.

The part these Negro soldiers played in civilizing the western wilderness has seldom been reported. The Army was not large in 1876, only about 28,000 men altogether.

Some of the Negro troops were in the South, where sensitive whites charged that their presence was just one more evidence of the Yankees' vindictiveness and wish to humiliate. Yet the simple fact was that the Army had a great many Negro troops, some of which would inevitably be found among the forces policing the South. More of them, however, were in the West, where they were busy building roads and forts, helping settlers organize towns, and protecting farmers and ranchers from wild animals, bandits, and Indians. It is high time America acknowledged how very much these black men in blue did in settling the West.[15]

Acknowledgment of a different sort should be given the British investors who, despite the risks involved, poured millions of pounds into Western enterprise, especially mining and cattle. One estimate for the twenty years after 1874 places the amount at almost two billion dollars. Some groups of British investors were able to send representatives to make sure they were not being defrauded. British shares in American firms were safer, of course, because the American shareholders developed their own means of observation. But the British seemed to prefer joint stock companies of their own. Between 1860 and 1900 more than five hundred of these companies were registered, operating chiefly in Colorado, Nevada, and Utah. The development began about 1870. Before that time, the absence of transcontinental railroad and telegraph facilities had been an insuperable barrier.

British-born residents in the West numbered thirty-two thousand in 1870, fifty-three thousand ten years later. Their home attachments were apparent to all in both the cricket clubs they organized in farflung communities and such social groups as the Sons of Malta, the Sons of St. George, and the Albion Society. A Cornish concentration in the Lake Superior region produced such nicknames as "Cousin Jacks" and "Saffron cake eaters."

When at all possible, the mining companies shipped their ore to Liverpool or Swansea for refining. Labor was cheaper there and the processing machinery better than in the United States. Promotional articles in British periodicals sustained investor interest, and a generous use of "big names" on boards of directors helped overcome hesitation. The Emma Mine, for example, listed on its board the American minister to England, a United States Senator, three members of Parliament, and a Commander of the Order of the Bath. The situation was a bonanza for lawyers, whose services were required to give the authority of legal language to leases, land sales, and company prospectuses. They were also helpful in securing some of the free land available under the generous federal terms for public lands. But although the British mining firms, together with a few Dutch ones, did almost as much as American firms to move people into the wilderness, thus abetting the hopes of settling the region, the drain of profits to foreign investors was a continual source of worry. It may even have been comforting to American visionaries that lawyers and brokers involved in the operations proved clever enough to keep a good fraction of the proceeds at home. During the 1870s, on the frontier, lawyers were regarded with almost as much suspicion as Indians.[16]

The very isolation of most mines made it expedient, and sometimes necessary, for some firms to build company towns. Morley, Colorado, created in 1875 by the Colorado Fuel and Iron Company was one such town. It was a good deal better than most, eventually having neat concrete houses, each with a garden, for six hundred people. Carbon, Wyoming, another coal town, organized by the Union Pacific in 1868 for its own fuel needs, had a company store and a company doctor, but the miners owned their own houses. Lumber company towns were older. Port Gamble in Washington was probably the oldest of all, begun by Pope & Talbot in 1853, when the entire firm moved from Machias, Maine. It had—and still has—picturesque New England architecture. Almost as old was Seabeck, also in Washington, established by the Washington Mill Company in 1856 but collapsing in 1886 when the mill burned.[17]

Coal mining, at best, has never been a glamorous occupation. The firms had to provide living quarters and could not depend on the eager rush to this or that valley that followed word of a strike in gold or silver. The raw new gold towns in the Black Hills, Deadwood and Custer City, sprang into existence even before mining firms could be organized. Not even their isolation, hundreds of miles beyond the advancing frontier, and not even the barrier of badlands that had to be crossed, could deter once the siren call had been heard. It was a replay, as any new gold strike could be expected to be, of Sutter's Mill in California, with actual miners outnumbered by hunters, tradesmen, gamblers, mill operators, horse traders, lively ladies, money-lenders, saloon-keepers, and land speculators, not to mention men with no visible means of support.

If one thing could be identified as clearly distinguishing the wilderness from the rest of the country, it was the open gambling found there. The East had laws to suppress or control gambling. The frontier, in its effort to emulate the East and achieve social order, sooner or later organized against it. But the wilderness was different. For a good many people there, gambling was symbolic of their freedom, something to cherish in whatever time was left before the frontier process engulfed them. And it was also symbolic in another way. Gambling at tables, with chips or dice, was a microcosm of the gamble of life itself. It was seldom possible to be sure that the new community would survive and the numerous ghost towns throughout the West are proof that many did not.

The historian Frederick Jackson Turner, in his controversial address "The Significance of the Frontier in American History," delivered to the American Historical Association in 1893, oversimplified the sequence by which the wilderness was subdued. Turner visualized a chronological succession of stages: first the fur-trader, then the hunter, the cattle-raiser, the farmer, and finally the city-builder. The overnight creation of mining towns, in Nevada, in Colorado, in Dakota, and elsewhere, was not mentioned. Entire large areas of the West never did have cattlemen or farmers, although in other areas cattle were the only interest.[18]

An acute meat shortage in the North and East during the Civil War prompted butchering firms to seek new sources for beef, and the one reliable source proved to be Texas. But as Colonel Taylor reported, even as late as 1876 the railroad network did not extend to the prime cattle-producing regions. What did develop on a large scale after the war's end was the practice of driving cattle from Texas across Indian Territory to the existing railheads, mostly in Kansas. The Shawnee and the Chisholm Trails both started at San Antonio. The Shawnee, the most easterly, split in Indian Territory into the East Trail to Kansas City and the West Trail to Junction City. The Chisholm ended at Abilene. These three cities were all on the Kansas Pacific Railroad. The third major trail, called the Western, originated at Bandera, somewhat west of San Antonio, and carried through Dodge City to Ogallala on the Union Pacific in western Nebraska. The last trail, longest of them all, went from Fort Concho west to the Pecos River, along that river half way up through New Mexico Territory, and then on north to Pueblo, Colorado.

The trail-drivers, many of them Confederate veterans, were a hardy, self-reliant lot. They had to be, for the drives took several weeks, the terrain was often very rough, and there was always danger of Indian attack. When they reached the railheads and turned over the cattle, the men were in no mood for refined relaxation, and the towns, by providing all the gaudy vice that could be wished for, earned the reputation for wickedness that westerns keep alive for them. In 1876, after years of cattle-driving, the railroad cattle towns, like mining towns and other isolated communities, were still creatures of the wilderness. But their days were numbered; the frontier was moving steadily toward them, and besides, the long drives from Texas were so uneconomical that cattle ranches were being established near the railroads—in Nebraska and Kansas, Colorado and Wyoming, and eventually as far as the Canadian border.

One product of civilization, barbed wire, which was invented in 1873, was a peculiarly efficient enemy of the wilderness. In 1874, factories in Illinois and Iowa produced and sold about ten thousand pounds of barbed wire, the next year six hundred thousand pounds, and nearly three million pounds in 1876. Whether barbed wire was used to keep cattle *in* or trespassers *out*, it was particularly offensive to cattlemen, who regarded wholly open land as their birthright. Some men were so indignant that they cut the wire, and fence-cutters' wars raged, especially in Texas and Wyoming. But gradually their opposition dwindled as they accepted the invention as a necessity in a region with too little rain to grow hedges, too little wood to build fences, and too few stones for stone walls.[19]

Just two years after the discovery of gold in the Black Hills, another government survey party reported that the region had excellent potential for cattle-raising—and cattlemen promptly moved in. Until then, no cattle had been raised west of the Missouri River. But the reports of abundant grass, clear spring water, and natural protection from storms[20] could not alone have brought the cattlemen. A more practical consideration was the growing population around the mines and the certainty of a steady market for fresh meat and dairy products. By August, 1876, the Park Ranch Company was able to advertise in a Black Hills newspaper that its ranch, about seven miles from Deadwood, was ready to herd livestock,[21] and by October, John and Erasmus Defferbach established a herd large enough to supply at least some of the demand.

It was easier to make a success with cattle where a railroad was close by, as in southern Wyoming. Once the Union Pacific was built, indeed, men discovered that cattle could thrive as well in high northern country as on lower land in Texas, and what came to be known as "cow country" began to spread wherever there was a combination of grass, water, and an accessible railroad. Cheyenne, Wyoming, where the main Union Pacific line joined with the line up from Denver, quickly became a cattle transfer point; it was also a center for rough characters, as were Laramie and Rawlins further to the west. Wyoming also attracted a number of Englishmen with more money than knowledge of cattle. Some of them went home soon, wiped out, but others learned the business and stayed.

Cattle rustling was a perennial problem, producing, in 1890, the famous "Johnson War" that is still a controversial subject in Wyoming. As in other regions not yet brought under effective legal controls, the ranchers protected their interests by organizing vigilante groups to run the worst elements out of the area or, when this failed, to apply "purification by hemp" (a colorful euphemism for hanging).[22] In theory, the frontier sequence followed ranchers with farmers, thus accelerating the advance of civilized control. But, in fact, in some of the high country, especially in Wyoming, farming never was very practical, and the ranchers' problems continued. A law passed by the Territorial legislature in 1875, requiring a bill of sale for the exchange of cattle as a means of thwarting rustlers, was almost impossible to enforce.

The high grasslands were as good for sheep as for cattle. During the 1870s, large numbers of Merinos and other kinds of sheep were moved from places as far away as California, Oregon, and New Mexico to Wyoming, Montana, and the Black Hills of Dakota. Costly though the transfer was, the results were excellent. In April, 1876, one sheep outfit in Smith's River Valley in southern Montana reported such gratification at the way their sheep had wintered that they planned to drive fifteen thousand more from California to Montana later in the season.[23] That same fall, the Montana Wool Growers Association was organized in Helena, and a herd of fourteen hundred sheep was located on the future site of Miles City on the Yellowstone River. In most parts of the West—in Oregon, California, Arizona, and New Mexico—cattlemen and sheep men were rivals for grazing lands, and sometimes the rivalry led to open enmity. But the two groups sometimes merged their interests, as in southeastern Wyoming where, in 1873, the Laramie County Stock Growers Association was formed to advance the interests of all stock growers and dealers.

The year 1873 was also the peak year of the cattle driving from Texas, when 405,000 head were moved. The northward spread of the grazing area did not, however, reduce the Texas drives substantially; 322,000 head of cattle were driven north to the railheads in 1876, the fourth largest year, and in 1880 the figure was almost 395,000—a lot of cattle in anybody's language. What was happening, no doubt, was an increasing demand for meat in the East.

The cattle driven from Texas were Longhorns, a breed now almost extinct because selective breeding of other kinds of cattle produced faster-growing animals with more and better meat. One experimenter was John D. Gillett of Illinois, who developed a hardy strain that needed no shelter at any time of year. When in 1876 he sent to England a hundred head, weighing an average of 2,100 pounds, there was a flurry of consternation among cattle growers there. But the most extensive experimentation in the 1870s, in both breeding and feeding, took place in Oregon. When Oregon cattle, despite the greater distance, brought higher prices than Longhorns, it was a signal that cattlemen did not fail to read, and ranchers on the high plains were soon bidding for any available surplus of the Oregon herds.[24]

Thus, by 1876 cattle production was becoming big business, whereas in the early days, it had been more of an adventure. Some modern men look back on those days with real nostalgia, and none more lovingly than the late Frank Dobie of Texas, whose book *The Longhorns* is a classic on the subject. On the question of just how large the Longhorns' horns were, he tells about one boy's discovery of a skull with horns intact that measured eight and a half feet from tip to tip. Unfortunately, however, the lad left the amazing skull in the place where he stumbled across it.

Better authenticated are the stories about Charles Goodnight's famous lead steer, Old Blue. In the summer of 1876, Goodnight decided to close his ranch in Colorado and return to Texas. With Old Blue leading a herd of about sixteen hundred, they filed down through the thousand-foot bluffs into Palo Duro Canyon. There the men saw a herd of about ten thousand buffalo; in the course of routing the buffalo Goodnight decided that the canyon would be an excellent wintering place, and went no further. (The canyon became in time the heart of the JA Ranch of about a million acres.) Late that October, a thousand steers were selected for a drive to Dodge City, 250 miles away. In the lead was Old Blue, proud of a brand new bell, and at the flooded Cimarron River, he plunged right in and the others followed. At the Arkansas River, which they reached in early December, they waited overnight, enduring a pounding sleet storm; the next morning Old Blue led the herd through the river and took them at a gallop straight into the Dodge City pens, where by noon all were in cars on their way to Chicago—except Old Blue, who went back with the men and horses. He held his rank as "lead ox" for many years, dying at the age of twenty; his horns are in the Panhandle-Plains Historical Society at Canyon.[25]

Such, with infinite minor variations, was the way of the cattle drives. Unexpected catastrophe always lay in wait. Electrical storms made the cattle nervous, sometimes to the point of stampeding, and when that happened, the cowboys tried to ride ahead of the herd to slow the front runners or to divide the herd if it was approaching a gully. Stampede Gully west of the Brazos Bottom owes its name to the death of twenty-seven hundred stampeding cattle owned by Wilson Brothers of Kansas City. A shot fired by an excited Mexican was said to have caused the stampede.[26]

The sheep drives were somewhat different. The peak years of sheep driving were in the 1870s, when the exhaustion of the grass in one place forced a move to another grazing area, often in Kansas or Nebraska, as a prelude to the final drive to a railhead. Later, increased use of alfalfa reduced the need for such mobility. Shepherds learned that the most economical numbers for a drive were from twenty-five hundred to five thousand breeding sheep, or up to seven thousand wethers (castrated rams). Two bands were commonly driven at once and could be managed by five men—the foreman, the cook, and three hands. The ideal schedule was a cool early start, eight or ten miles before the heat of the day, a siesta beside a stream, and more mileage in the cool late afternoon. But the ideal was seldom possible because the streams did not cooperate. There was also danger from predators —wolves, lynx, bobcat, which cattle drivers did not have to worry about, but one advantage of sheep was that they could go longer without water. One astonishing yarn, apparently authentic, concerns two boys, Israel and David Bennion, fifteen and eleven years old, who in the fall of 1875 took five thousand sheep into the Utah desert and returned the next May with the flock intact. Both sheep and Bennions must have been hardy— and the latter precocious. The Bennion family had arrived in Utah in 1847 with just seven sheep and by 1875 had about seven thousand, along with eighteen hundred cattle and a hundred horses.[27]

Edward F. Beale owned what may have been the nation's largest sheep ranch, the Rancho Tejon near Bakersfield, established in the 1850s with some thought of making it an Indian reservation, and gradually enlarged until it approximated

200,000 acres in 1876. Beale, in and out of political favor (at one time the Superintendent of Indian Affairs, and under Lincoln the surveyor-general of California), began raising sheep on a large scale; he and a partner owned 13,900 in 1866, 37,000 in 1871, and 58,000 in 1876. When the drought that summer destroyed the Rancho Tejon feed, he turned the entire flock loose to fend for themselves, and when he rounded them up in the rains of October, 53,000 had survived.[28]

Sheep were raised in all parts of the United States, but the greater space available in the Far West produced very rapid increases between 1870 and 1880—from less than five to more than eighteen million. Even after the national total began to decline, about 1890, the number of sheep in the Far West continued to increase. All during the 1870s, the national ratio of sheep to human beings held fairly constant, just under eighty sheep to one hundred people. After 1880 the percentage of sheep fell rapidly, to less than half the human total by World War I.[29]

Just as great as the occupational diversity of the wilderness West were the differences in geography—high level plains with little rainfall; vast forests with heavy rainfall; forbidding mountain ranges; great rolling hills; deserts; fine, well-watered valleys; deep canyons; buttes and mesas; lakes; long treacherous coastlines and a few magnificent harbors. Because it was wilderness, however, an underpopulated area without social control, it was an area where "badmen" flourished, and no summary account, whatever else it might omit, could fail to take note of the outlaws and famous gunmen, the notorious women, and the places they helped make famous in the old wild west.

Judge Parker was perhaps justified in his harshness by the very number of desperadoes in the Western District of Arkansas. In more remote regions the law was less competent, leaving a vacuum filled by extra-legal vigilantes. For no occupation in the wilderness was without constant danger from men as indifferent to civilized order as the cougar, the rattlesnake, and the grasshopper.

The wilderness was a place where myths easily developed. A legend has grown up about William H. Bonney, alias Billy the Kid, who in 1872 at the age of thirteen is supposed to have killed his first man for uttering disparaging remarks about his mother. He was still in his teens when he and a crony killed three Indians to get their horses; a little later he killed a soldier at Fort Bowie. Thereafter his career in homicide continued to be erratic, and marked by a total absence of qualms. His youth, his slight build —not quite five foot eight and only 135 pounds—his innocent smile, and his habitual politeness earned him his immortal nickname.[30] In any state east of the Mississippi, no boy could have killed so often without being committed to a reformatory. The wilderness had no such institutions—only rope to hang with, and bullets to kill with. Billy the Kid died when he was barely twenty-two, shot by a sheriff, and disproving the adage that only the good die young. But in the line of work he engaged in, the West disproved the adage with monotonous frequency; few bad men lived very long. One who outlived the average was James Butler Hickok, alias Wild Bill Hickok, who was thirty-nine when he died in 1876. A drifter, trying one occupation after another, he had grown in notoriety through the years. On occasion he acted as a scout for the military; and he served well enough to earn Custer's admiration: Hickok, Custer wrote in *My Life on the Plains* (page 69) was ". . . one of the most perfect types of physical manhood I ever saw . . . entirely free of all bluster and bravado." He became a United States Marshal after the Civil War and was renowned as a marksman against outlaws. But a good many of his exploits are questionable. Whatever the legend of his killings, however, his own death tops them all.

On August 1, 1876, in Deadwood, he joined a draw poker game in which one player was Jack McCall, a saloon bum and a typical moocher of free drinks and lunches. The next afternoon, Hickok sat in on another poker game; but being the last to arrive, he couldn't sit, as he liked to, for the sake of safety, with his back to the wall. McCall entered and shot him in the back of the head. The word spread fast along Main Street—"Wild Bill has been killed!" McCall was tried by a miners' court and set free. Some time later a regular court in Yankton sentenced him to hang. Hickok's hillside grave in Mt. Moriah Cemetery was graced with a slab erected by a friend. It is typical of many graves in the old West:

WILD BILL
J. B. HICKOK
KILLED BY THE ASSASSIN
JACK MCCALL
DEADWOOD CITY
BLACK HILLS
August 2nd, 1876
Pard we will meet again in the happy
hunting ground to part no more.
GOOD BYE
Colorado Charlie
C. B. Utter

The cards Hickok held when he was shot are still remembered in the West, if not wherever poker is played, as the "Dead Man's Hand"—ace of spades, ace of clubs, eight of spades, eight of clubs, and queen—or as some insist the jack—of diamonds.[31]

Hickok's own queen of hearts, if she is to be believed, was Calamity Jane. At her death in 1903 she was buried beside him in Mt. Moriah Cemetery, as she had requested. The book she brought out in 1896, *Life and Adventures of Calamity Jane*, departed considerably from the truth, yet the truth hardly needed embroidery. She was born in 1852, Martha Jane Canary, the daughter of an easygoing farmer who had met her mother in a brothel and married her as a kind of rescue. When Jane was big enough to carry it off, she adopted the practice, not uncommon in the West at that time, of passing as a man—wearing men's clothes and doing men's work. One job she liked and did well was serving as a scout in Custer's command. If she hadn't been ill in a hospital in June, 1876, she might have died with Custer in Montana. Earlier in the year she had been a guide, like Hickok, for miners headed for Deadwood; it's likely that they met. It is far less likely that after Hickok was shot Jane chased McCall into a butcher shop and cornered him with a meat cleaver, but she said she did, in her book, and may even have come to believe it.[32]

A contemporary sketch of Jane has survived from an 1876 journal kept by one John G. Bourke: "It was whispered that one of our teamsters was a woman, and no other than 'Calamity Jane,' a character famed in border story; she had donned the raiment of the alleged rougher sex, and was skinning mules with the best of them. She was eccentric and wayward rather than bad . . . as rough and burly as any of her messmates." [33]

Other wayward ladies are remembered, some of them with nicknames that betrayed their calling. One was Cattle Kate Weston of Wyoming who was willing to accept cattle in payment for her favors, without demanding a bill of sale. But this proved a mistake, for one day a landowner group took Kate and her lover out and hanged them both. Other women of dubious morality were Poker Alice Ives; Hattie and Hester Benton, who sold illicit liquor in Arkansas; Madame Vestal in Denver; Minnie the Gambler, who hailed from Paris and whose real name was Eleanor Dumont; and Madame Moustache, another gambler, who was well known in Utah, Nevada, and California before taking her own life, by prussic acid, in the wicked town of Bodie, just across the state line from Reno. [34]

One historian of the Northwest, Harold Briggs, insists that the vice of its early days has been all too prominently reported and that even in the roughest communities virtue and culture had their earnest supporters. One example Briggs offers is of a dancing club organized in Deadwood in 1876 by a group of respectable bachelors who set exacting standards for membership. And he quite properly points to the courage and persistence of the clergymen who carried the gospel to the roughest communities. In the Centennial summer a new preacher named Smith arrived in Deadwood from Connecticut, and at once showed ability in his sermons; but on August 20 he was killed by Indians. In November a replacement came to carry on, the Rev. L. P. Norcross. Miners, irreligious though many of them were, treated their "sky pilots," as clergymen were affectionately dubbed in Western slang, with exaggerated respect. They were also courteous to the girls brave enough to enter the saloons and sing hymns. The church, in the person of the clergyman and his parishioners, had to be aggressive if religion was to make any headway whatsoever. The preacher was often the one man in an entire town with any interest in culture and the only man who organized theatricals or charitable drives. [35]

All this is no doubt true, but a major reason for labeling Deadwood and similar towns "wilderness" instead of "civilization" or transitional "frontier" is the demonstrable scarcity of churches, clergymen, dedicated church members, and other symbols of respectability. There *was* a church in Deadwood, in 1876, but there were also reputed to be a hundred saloons.

If the vice-loving majorities of such towns could have had their way, the wilderness conditions might have endured in fact as they have in the nostalgic imaginings of the great audience for American westerns. To that audience, the names of Wyatt Earp and Bat Masterson are thoroughly familiar and Dodge City the best-known town in the entire Old West.

Earp and Masterson were professional gamblers and also deacons in the local church, not surprisingly, for leading gamblers were sometimes held in more respect than bankers. The classical sequence for such men began with a killing in self-defense, an excellent credential for a job as gunman-bouncer in a saloon or gambling house. It was a step upward to the rank of house gambler earning a percentage of the profits, and at the top was ownership or partnership in a saloon, dance hall, or gambling establishment. If a man behaved prudently and made no enemies who might at any time return to gun him down, he could hope for acceptance at the Long Branch Saloon, the gathering place of the local men of distinction. Other leading saloons were the Alhambra, the Alamo, the Old House, the Green Front, and the Opera. But the safest course of all, once a man had accumulated a respectable sum of money, was to leave town and enter some other business in another state; for money bred envy, and robberies were common. Masterson had his own methods of protection. When he first arrived in Dodge, in 1876, he was still limping from a Texas gunfight, and he used a cane that doubled, in times of trouble, as a bat to knock assailants down—hence his nickname, "Bat." A more common technique was to "buffalo" a man, meaning to strike his skull with a pistol held flat.

Dodge City, at the crossing of the westward-bound Santa Fe trail and the most popular of the four great cattle trails, the Western, leading from Texas to Nebraska, had in any given week an unusual variety of visitors. There were bullwhackers, with their wagons drawn by oxen, usually six, in three double yokes; mule skinners driving a variable number of big Missouri mules, those masterpieces of animal breeding; the Texas cattle drivers; horse traders; soldiers from the nearby fort; celebrities, including generals—Sherman, Sheridan, Custer, Miles—and such others as Cody, Hickok, and Calamity Jane. The Texans were the liveliest, but the bullwhackers were the most profane; people respected their proficiency with the bullwhip, with its two-foot hickory handle, its twelve-foot lash, and its buckskin popper a foot long, which produced the sharp cracking sound. Although everybody rode horses, the first livery stable in Dodge was not built until 1875; a block long, it was called the Elephant Barn. But while it was a busy place it had nothing to do with one of the most famous of all the Western terms, "going to see the elephant"—another typical euphemism, like "Died of lead poisoning" or "Dead from lightning" on wooden grave markers in the original Boot Hill Cemetery. Whatever its origin, the term was associated with such well-known Dodge citizens as Little Dot, Emporia Belle, Miss One Fin, Hop Fiend Nel, and Scarfaced Lillie. In Dodge, incidentally, as generally in the wilderness West, these ladies were treated in public with total politeness.[36]

Dodge City was typical of wilderness towns in being without the effective majesty of established law, even though Kansas was already a state. On various occasions, the mayor of Dodge telegraphed the governor for help or advice, but the replies offered only moral support.

In the Territories the legal authority was even weaker. The national area still in Territorial status in 1876 included Colorado (until August 1), Dakota, Wyoming, Montana, Idaho, Washington, Utah, Arizona, and New Mexico. Indian Territory, now Oklahoma, had its own special status. Congress had ultimate authority over the Territories, but delegated responsibility to different executive departments. In 1876, Zachariah Chandler, as Secretary of the Interior, used the Territories as he used anything else he could get his hands on, for political patronage. Governors of Territories were usually appointed by preferment —Easterners for whom such appointment would be a step to better jobs later. Each governor had one secretary. The Justice Department assigned federal judges, three or more to each territory. Military policing was the responsibility of the War Department, which also, in 1876, selected the post traders.

Considering the recognized future importance of the Territories, it might astonish us that they were administered so laxly, and with such divided responsibility. Salaries and supporting funds were very meagre. In 1876 the contingent fund allotted each governor, formerly $1,000 a year, was reduced to $500. From 1873 to 1878, Territorial legislators were paid six dollars a day for a forty-day session (with ten dollars for the officers presiding in the two houses); travel allowances for each session were three or four dollars for every twenty miles. A limit of $4,000 a session was set on official printing. Each Territorial legislature could select a nonvoting delegate to Congress, as a kind of one-man lobby, but no delegate, in 1876, was very successful in securing federal funds; an economy-minded Congress doled out sums for public improvements with pained reluctance. An estimate for 1876 shows that the federal government met only a tenth of the Territorial costs, although it held much of the control. The tight money policy did, however, reduce the opportunities for graft, a solace of sorts.[37]

In only one of the Territories, Utah, was there an area large enough and developed enough to be labeled frontier. Of the wilderness communities discussed in the present chapter, some were in states and some in territories. This should make it clear that in 1876 frontier and wilderness did not divide neatly between states and territories, but the issue is confused by the tendency of writers to speak of the "mining frontier," the "cattle frontier," or the "military frontier" as though an isolated mine, a trail used for driving cattle, or the scene of a military exercise could qualify as frontier. Lest any question exist about the usage of terms here, the Census Bureau definitions are followed: sizable areas with a population density of less than two per square mile are considered wilderness, and those with more than two being civilization. While it might simplify the discussion to speak of these two only, and eliminate the term "frontier," the frontier process is considered too important, and the areas transitional between wilderness and civilization too significant, to warrant abandonment of the threefold distinction.

The Territories in 1876, considered as geographical units, were all wilderness by the Census Bureau definition. So were all the states west of the major frontier except California. In contrast, no state east of the Mississippi, or in the north-south band recognized as frontier, qualified as wilderness. But major *parts* of those frontier states, especially Texas, Kansas, and Nebraska, together with California, were still clearly wilderness, as were a very few parts of some eastern states.

Population was increasing in every state and territory. In all the West beyond the major frontier, the rate of increase greatly exceeded that in older parts of the nation. But even in the 1880 census only California showed more than two people per square mile. At this point, with so many political units involved, a tabulation should he helpful.

POPULATION DENSITY PER SQUARE MILE
1870–1967

A. Territories and Young States

Political Unit	1870	1880	1876 (estimate)	1967
Arizona	.1	.4	.25	11.5
Colorado	.4	1.9	1.2	16.9
Idaho	.2	.4	.3	8.1
Montana	.1	.3	.2	4.6
Nevada	.4	.6	.5	2.6
New Mexico	.7	1.0	.85	7.8
North Dakota [1]	.1	.9	.5	9.1
Oregon	1.0	1.8	1.5	18.4
South Dakota [1]	.1	.9	.5	9.0
Utah	1.1	1.8	1.5	10.8
Washington	.4	1.8	1.2	42.8
Wyoming	.1	.2	.15	3.4

B. Representative Older States

	1870	1880	1876 (estimate)	1967
New Hampshire	35.2	38.2	37.	67.2
Connecticut	111.5	129.2	121.	520.6
Pennsylvania	78.6	95.5	87.	251.4
Maryland	78.6	94.0	86.	313.5
Florida	3.4	4.9	4.	91.5
Ohio	65.4	78.5	72.	236.7
Iowa	21.5	29.2	25.	49.2
Kansas	4.5	12.2	9.	26.6
California	3.6	5.5	4.5	100.4

[1] The two Dakotas were the single Dakota Territory in 1876.

Population totals and densities are two quite different things, but the sheer size of the western units, while greatly reducing the density figure, is itself a significant fact. Collectively, the western units, beyond the frontier, together with Indian Territory and the wilderness parts of the frontier states, made up almost exactly half of the national territory of three million square miles.[38] The people in this wilderness, advance agents of the frontier and of civilization, were there because even the frontier could not provide the quality of life they wanted. Many of them, perhaps, far from acknowledging their role in the frontier process, hoped the wilderness could remain, with all its freedoms from civilizing restraints—cattlemen who hated barbed wire, Civil War veterans driving cattle from Texas to the Kansas railheads, mining firms with no love for taxation or legislative controls, hunters slaughtering buffalo for fun or profit, soldiers who liked to fight the Indians, and the Indians themselves, homesteaders who moved on if they could see the smoke from a neighbor's chimney, bad men who gloried in the lack of policemen, wagoneers whose prosperity would decline as railroads multiplied, whiskey sellers and gamblers and gaudy women and all the other adventurers who made life exciting in the roaring wilderness towns.

Their days of wilderness freedom, though they could not know it, were numbered; the wilderness was doomed. But who in 1876, in Boston or Chicago, in Denver or Kansas City, in Deadwood, Fort Concho, or Dodge—who anywhere in Centennial America could have foreseen the completion of the frontier process within the next two decades? The sheer impossibility of such foresight was one more distinctive fact of the Centennial Year: history was advancing far faster than anyone could realize.

Footnotes for Chapter Three
A TEEMING NATION OF NATIONS

1 Jesse James's Northfield fiasco is well told by Stewart Holbrook in *Little Annie Oakley and Other Rugged People* (New York: Macmillan, 1948); it was given ample newspaper coverage in 1876. Dur-

ing the trial of the Younger brothers, late in November, Minnesota's no-capital-punishment law was sharply criticized.

2. A good account of the Cross Timbers-Prairie struggle is found in Rupert Norval Richardson, *The Frontier of Northwest Texas, 1846 to 1876* (Glendale, Calif.: A. H. Clark Co., 1963).

3. S. W. Harman, *Hell on the Border: He Hanged Eighty-eight Men* (Fort Smith: Phoenix Publishing Co., 1898) is less reliable about Judge Parker than Glenn Shirley, *Law West of Fort Smith* (New York: Henry Holt, 1957).

4. Oscar Lewis, *Silver Kings* (New York: Alfred A. Knopf, 1947); and Lewis Beebe and Charles Clegg, *Virginia & Truckee: A Story of Virginia City and Comstock Times* (Stanford: Stanford University Press, 1949).

5. This concept of a grand design is adapted from Walter LeFeber, *The New Empire: An Interpretation of American Expansion 1860–1898* (Ithaca: Cornell University Press, 1963).

6. From Harold E. Briggs, *Frontiers of the Northwest: A History of the Upper Missouri Valley* (New York: D. Appleton-Century, 1940).

7. The specifics of the Custer story are pieced together from several of the very large number of books about Custer, among them Col. W. A. Graham, *The Custer Myth: A Source Book of Custeriana* (Harrisburg: Stackpole Co., 1953); Fred Dustin, *The Custer Tragedy* (Saginaw: privately printed, 1939); Frederick Whittaker, *A Complete Life of Gen. George A. Custer* (New York: Sheldon & Co., 1876), the most laudatory account; Frederick F. Van de Water, *Glory-Hunter—A Life of General Custer* (Indianapolis: Bobbs, Merrill, 1939), the most hostile; Paul Wellman, *Death on the Plains* (New York: Macmillan, 1934); Elizabeth B. Custer, *"Boots and Saddles": or Life in Dakota with General Custer* (New York: Harper, 1885) and *The Custer Story: the Life and Intimate Letters of General George A. Custer, and His Wife Elizabeth,* ed. Marguerite Merington (New York: Devin-Adair, 1950); Edward and Evelyn Luce, *Custer Battlefield National Monument,* National Park Service, Historical Handbook No. 1 (Washington: Government Printing Office, 1952); Milo Quaife, "Historical Introduction" to Custer's *My Life on the Plains,* reissued in Lakeside Classics (Chicago: Lakeside Press, 1952); Edgar I. Stewart, *Custer's Luck* (Norman: University of Oklahoma Press, 1955); Mari Sandoz, *The Battle of the Little Bighorn* (Philadelphia: J. B. Lippincott, 1966). Comanche's air-conditioned glass case in the Dyche Museum stirred the author's envy one extremely hot August afternoon.

8. Elmira *Daily Advertiser,* July 12 and 15, 1876.

9. *The Poet Scout: Being a Selection of Incidental and Illustrative*

Verses and Songs by Captain Jack Crawford (San Francisco: H. Keller & Co., 1879).

10. Levy, *Grace Notes in American History*, pp. 290–92.

11. Robert Taft, *Artists and Illustrators of the Old West, 1850–1900* (New York: Charles Scribner's Sons, 1953), pp. 129–48.

12. Loring Benson Priest, *Uncle Sam's Stepchildren: The Reformation of United States Indian Policy 1865–1887* (New Brunswick: Rutgers University Press, 1942).

13. Lewis Henry Morgan, "The Hue and Cry Against the Indians," *The Nation*, July 20, 1876; and "The Factory System for Indian Reservations," *ibid.*, July 27, 1876.

14. Perry Belmont, *An American Democrat: The Recollections of Perry Belmont*, 2nd ed. (New York: Columbia University Press, 1941), pp. 157–81.

15. William H. Leckie, *The Buffalo Soldiers: A Narrative of the Negro Cavalry in the West* (Norman: University of Oklahoma Press, 1967).

16. Clark C. Spence, *British Investments and the American Mining Frontier 1860–1901* (Ithaca: Cornell University Press, 1958).

17. James B. Allen, *The Company Town in the American West* (Norman: University of Oklahoma Press, 1966).

18. For an evaluation and bibliography of Turner's thesis, see Ray Allen Billington, *The American Frontier* (Washington: Service Center for Teachers of History, 1958) and *America's Frontier Heritage* (New York: Holt, Rinehart, and Winston, 1966).

19. Henry D. McCallum and Frances T. McCallum, *The Wire that Fenced the West* (Norman: University of Oklahoma Press, 1965).

20. W. P. Jenney, *Official Geological Report Submitted to the Secretary of the Interior* (Washington: 1875).

21. Advertisement in *Black Hills Tribune*, Aug. 31, 1876.

22. Harold E. Briggs, *The Frontiers of the Northwest*, pp. 212–213.

23. Editor's note in *Rocky Mountain Husbandman*, Apr. 6, 1876, recorded in Briggs, *Frontiers of the Northwest*, pp. 314–15.

24. Charles Wayland Towne and Edward Norris Wentworth, *Cattle & Men* (Norman: University of Oklahoma Press, 1955).

25. J. Frank Dobie, *The Longhorns* (Boston: Little, Brown and Co., 1941), pp. 208, 267 ff.

    J. Evetts Haley, *Charles Goodnight: Cowman & Plainsman*, New edition, (Norman: University of Oklahoma Press, 1949), p. 433, assigns Old Blue's first trip as lead-ox to 1877, not 1876.

26. Dobie, *The Longhorns*, pp. 124–25.

27. Charles Wayland Towne and Edward N. Wentworth, *Shepherd's*

Empire (Norman: University of Oklahoma Press, 1945), pp. 271–272.

28. Mary Austin, *The Flock,* cited in *Shepherd's Empire;* and Paul W. Gates, *California Ranchos and Farms 1846–1862* (Madison: State Historical Society of Wisconsin, 1962), p. 47.

29. L. G. Connor, "A Brief History of the Sheep Industry in the United States," *Annual Report of the American Historical Association for the Year 1918* (Washington: 1921), Vol. I, pp. 91–197.

30. *Pat Garrett's Authentic Life of Billy the Kid,* ed. Maurice Garland Fulton (New York: 1927); the first edition of Garrett's book was published in Santa Fe in 1882. In *Burs Under the Saddle; A Second Look at Books and Histories of the West* by Ramon F. Adams (Norman: University of Oklahoma Press, 1964), many of the books on the old West are severely criticized for perpetuating errors. Pat Garrett's book, for instance, created a false legend that is still believed. For a thorough discussion of the Garrett book see *Burs Under the Saddle,* pp. 197–212.

31. Joseph G. Rosa, *They Called Him Wild Bill: The Life and Adventures of James Butler Hickok* (Norman: University of Oklahoma Press, 1964), pp. 214–220.

32. Briggs, *Frontiers of the Northwest,* pp. 75–82, "The Calamity Jane Myth"; Roberta Beed Sollid, *Calamity Jane* (Helena: The Western Press, 1958).

33. John G. Bourke, *On the Border with Crook* (New York, 1902), p. 343, cited in Mark H. Brown and W. R. Felton, *The Frontier Years: L. A. Huffman, Photographer of the Plains* (New York: Holt, 1955), p. 147.

34. Lucius Beebe and Charles Clegg, *The American West: The Pictorial Epic of a Continent* (New York: E. P. Dutton, 1955), in the section titled "Pistol-Packing Madames."

35. Briggs, *Frontiers of the Northwest,* pp. 94–95, 104–107.

36. Stanley Vestal, *Queen of Cow Towns: Dodge City "The Wickedest Little City in America" 1872–1886* (New York: Harper, 1952). In *Burs Under the Saddle,* pp. 514–15, Adams criticizes Vestal's use of Stuart Lake's *Wyatt Earp, Frontier Marshal* (Boston: Houghton, Mifflin, 1931) as source material; Lake's account falsely glorifies Earp, who liked to give credit to himself which should have gone to others. Dodge City is chronicled briefly, but with authority, in Paul J. Wellman, *The Trampling Herd* (New York: Carrick & Evans, 1939), pp. 193–202.

37. Earl S. Pomeroy, *The Territories and the United States, 1861–1890: Studies in Colonial Administration* (Philadelphia: University of Pennsylvania Press, 1947).

38. Alaska was not admitted as a territory until 1912.

4

The Age of Enterprise

ON THE AFTERNOON of August 24, 1876, the ship "City of San Francisco" eased its way toward its berth at Honolulu, bearing good news. The Senate had passed the reciprocity treaty with Hawaii on August 14, and President Grant had signed it the next day. It also bore a passenger with a particular interest in the treaty, the sugar magnate Claus Spreckels. He stayed three weeks, long enough to buy up more than half of the 1877 sugar futures of the islands.

Anybody with money enough could have done what Spreckels did, for it was obvious that once the treaty took effect, removing the duty on sugar sent from Hawaii to the States, the profit would be substantial. Spreckels had more than money enough from his successful sugar refineries in California. But that was no reason why he shouldn't increase his fortune. Wasn't this what opportunity meant, and what God wanted men to do, in America, to implement his divine favor? Nobody put it quite that boldly, but some of the preachers said almost as much, in the millionaires' churches. In somewhat different terms the leading defender of laissez-faire, Herbert Spencer in England, lent his support: in the materialistic jungle, the fit survived, the unfit failed, and the fittest reached the top, where they stayed as long as they were able. Not to seize the big chance when it came along, not to use power to gain more power, and money to make more money, was simply a sign of weakness.

For all his subsequent reputation as a high-handed capitalist, Claus Spreckels did much for Hawaii. One specific result of the brief 1876 visit was learning that increased production would require extensive irrigation; it needed a ton of water to produce a pound of sugar. On his next trip Spreckels took along an engineer.[1]

In his desire for empire Spreckels was typical of his time, but in one sense he was an exception. For few entrepreneurs were now building empires in agriculture. Industry, burgeoning during the Civil War and accelerating rapidly in the post-war years, had long since outstripped agriculture as the major arena for profitable activity. The fortunes that were still to be made in wheat and hogs and cattle, and a little later in citrus, were not what we remember as the really great American fortunes. They came instead from steel and oil and railroads.

The interest that Spreckels showed in Hawaii, while it was primarily related to sugar, was part of an awareness, only dimly shared in 1876, that economic growth would of necessity, sooner or later, require foreign sources of raw materials. For the moment, the potential of growth within the nation's borders was still very great. But a few businessmen, and legislators eager to serve their interests, were already dreaming, and sometimes talking, about political expansion—the grand design, the New Empire, alluded to earlier. Canada and Mexico no longer seemed attainable, in 1876, but a few men were still looking covetously southward, to the Caribbean and to Central and South America. Someday, it seemed logical, Hawaii itself would be gathered in, distant though it was; but annexation was not essential for business expansion. Existing sea trade showed what might be done.

Documented American vessels in 1876 numbered 25,934, with a total gross tonnage of 4,279,000. The Middle Atlantic states, the Gulf region, and New England, in that order, had the most ships. The Pacific coast could boast only 250,000 gross tons, less than half the tonnage available on the Great Lakes, less even than on the Western rivers. Dreams of a vast Pacific trade under American control were for a future quite remote. But even on the East Coast the prospect was not altogether reassuring: the cost of building ocean-worthy ships was increasing faster in the United States than abroad. With Pennsylvania and Maine, through their combined strength in Congress, blocking the purchase of foreign-made ships, American owners either resorted to operating under foreign flags or abandoned international business altogether.[2] Either choice hurt our foreign trade, or prestige, or both. In this area of activity, free enterprise wasn't as free in fact as it was in theory.

But the most logical reason for the American decline in ocean shipping after the Civil War seems to have been the intense preoccupation with internal development. Even the United States Navy suffered; as one author sadly remarks, the fifteen years from 1870 to 1885 were "one of the most humiliating periods in the history of the United States Navy . . . the Navy was allowed to go practically to decay."[3] But the merchant marine suffered even more. Allan Nevins speaks of "our drooping merchant marine" in a chapter titled "The Half-Century of Neglect," and another author, writing about the mercantile importance of New York harbor, devotes more than four hundred pages to the years before 1861 and closes with an abrupt five-page "Aftermath" deploring the nation's loss of first place upon the sea.[4] While such extreme pessimism may be unjustified, there is little to temper it for the Centennial period. American shipbuilders were slow to accept the shift from sail and wood to steam and iron. When the coal trade, growing rapidly after 1870, produced a demand for large vessels, New England shipyards merely increased the capacity of existing wooden three-masted schooners. The four-masters, sixty-eight of them in all, were built after 1880; the few five-masters, capable of carrying about twenty-five hundred tons, were built after 1890.[5] In 1876, vitrually all the steam boats were of wood, both sidewheelers and sternwheelers, plying the coastal water, the rivers, and the lakes by the thousands, still competitive with railroads for both passengers and freight, and often, in the West, spared even the threat of railroad competition. The more firmly established the railroads became, the less attention was paid to steamboats. In St. Paul, for example, for many years, the arrival of the first river-boat each spring, after the frozen Mississippi melted, was the occasion for a general celebration. But this historic tradition ended abruptly when St. Paul was connected by rail with the rest of the country.[6]

On the West Coast, where no railroad as yet connected California and Oregon, coastal shipping still had an importance almost forgotten in the East. Shipping was particularly important to San Francisco, located as it was at the point of a peninsula and relying on ferryboats for visitors arriving by train from the East and on all sorts of freight-carrying craft for ordinary business transactions.[7] Ferryboats, indeed, were indispensable in almost all parts of the country, crossing streams and rivers, bays and harbors, most of which have since been bridged. Americans took for granted the efficiency of the double-ended construction that so astonished and pleased foreign visitors.

Even a cursory review of American shipping in 1876 reveals that it was decentralized and that no one man or even a small group of men dominated the industry as they did railroads and meat-packing and petroleum. The Pennsylvania Railroad, however, made an effort to restore something of the supremacy on the Atlantic that had been lost to foreign countries. The railroad bought up bonds of the American Steamship Company, totaling about $1,500,000, and Philadelphia citizens contributed another $2,000,000. The *Pennsylvania* was launched on August 15, 1872, in the presence of at least fifty thousand people, and, along with the *Ohio*, the *Indiana*, and the *Illinois*, gave Philadelphia by 1876 a fleet of steamers, flying the American flag, that the city could be proud of. True, the railroad undertook the venture for its own greater profits: goods and passengers brought from the west by rail were transferred on the company's wharves to the company's ships bound for foreign ports. But no other railroad did so.[8]

Ocean travel was far more hazardous in 1876 than it is today since the advent of radio, radar, and legislated safeguards. Centennial Americans were unduly apprehensive about railroad accidents, but disasters at sea were actually frequent and deadly. Free enterprise (by which is here meant freedom from governmental regulation) pretty much ignored such things as the safety of clients. Passengers assumed whatever risks there were, in the knowledge, for what it was worth, that crews shared in the wish to survive, while the owners were interested in keeping their property intact.

Navigation was also hazardous on inland waterways—canals, rivers, and lakes. The Mississippi was still as dangerous and unpredictable as it had been when Mark Twain, before the Civil War, took lessons in piloting. One stretch of the river below St. Louis was still notorious as the "Graveyard," with wrecks averaging one a mile and with fifty or sixty steamboats sunk at the worst bend of all. Canals, in which the flow of water was closely regulated, were of course much safer. But though the Erie and other canals stoutly resisted the competition of railroads, they were fast losing ground as a major means of transportation.

The further west one travelled, the more important the rivers became. But in some regions there were neither railroads nor rivers large enough for navigation, and where this was the case, wagon-freighting reached boom proportions. It was particularly useful where mining was developing, as in the Black Hills (gold) and New Mexico (silver). The wagonmasters were resourceful, adapting readily to change, and they were everywhere welcome. Before a big freighting outfit was organized in Deadwood Gulch in Dakota, flour cost sixty dollars for a hundred pounds; in the fall of 1876, when the wagons arrived on regular schedule, the price was down to nine dollars [9]—still expensive, of course, by Eastern standards. Most of the wagonmasters were independents, sharing with the established express companies a major responsibility for the opening of new sections, especially where the railroads had not yet probed. With the West developing so fast, horses were in greater demand than ever before.

The express companies with their familiar wagon colors— green for Adams, red for Wells Fargo, and dark blue and red for American Express—were all prosperous in 1876, and would continue to be for many more years, despite the competition from the railroads. Wells Fargo was somewhat caught off balance by the speedy construction of the first railroad line crossing the continent; one immediate result was the loss of its federal mail contract, valued at $1,750,000 a year. But shrewd agreements with railroads were mutually profitable, and Wells Fargo kept on paying annual dividends to its stockholders of from 8 to 10 percent. By 1876, the danger from Indian attacks had all but ended, but holdups were on the increase, reaching a peak at the close of the decade. The most troublesome, persistent, and evasive highwayman, known as Black Bart, held up Wells Fargo stages twenty-eight times in eight years in Calaveras County, California, beginning in 1875. He always dressed in a long linen duster, concealed his head in a flour sack with holes cut out for his eyes, and brandished a sawed-off shotgun; he also carried a hatchet to open the strong-box.[10]

Black Bart had no monopoly, however, in the robbery business. Wells Fargo reported a total of 313 stage robberies between 1870 and 1884. But the company could also point to a high number of arrests and convictions, in large part the result of its standard reward: $300 in cash and a fifth of the money recovered. The most successful robbers operated in gangs, moving from one region to another. These gangs preferred stages to railroad trains; but the Jesse James gang was not chary of trains —in 1876 it held up a Missouri Pacific train at Otterville, Missouri, and made off with $17,000.[11] The one mode of transportation almost never attacked was the river steamboat, perhaps because the ubiquitous riverboat gamblers were in league with holdup men.

The Adams Express Company, which operated chiefly in the settled East, was not much bothered by bandits. The Civil War imposed a regional split, with the branch in Confederate territory becoming the Southern Express Company. The third major express company, American Express, dramatized the prosperity of all express firms by taking over, in 1875, a large New York sugar warehouse, at Sixty-Five Broadway, for its central office. Partitions were ripped out, one side was lined with financial cages, and the opposite wall had stalls for packages received. At Christmas each year long tables were set up with wrapping paper, cord, and address labels for the free use of the public. On the ground floor, wagons drove inside the building, and the whole place smelled like a livery stable. But people liked the convenience, and the company's willingness to be of service. As a special favor, there were numerous spittoons. In other words, the place had everything anybody could desire in 1876.[12]

The express companies, none of them very old, and the independent wagonmasters, were genuine entrepreneurs, seizing the opportunities at hand, adjusting easily to changing circumstance, and contemptuous of government regulation. Some of the drivers were picturesque rascals, as were smalltime operators of riverboats or coastal vessels. But none of them approached the notoriety of the big railroad men, like Cornelius Vanderbilt, Tom Scott of the Pennsylvania, Daniel Drew, Jay Cooke, Jim Fisk, or the Big Four in California, for the simple reason that by 1876 no other form of transportation came even close to the railroads as sources of great wealth, power, and corruption.

In the United States the period of most rapid growth happened to coincide with the development of the railroad. In the public imagination this development was the prime symbol of material progress, and in every statistical measure the facts supported the image. In 1840 there were only 2,818 miles of track in the nation; by 1860 the figure reached 30,626, and by 1876, 76,808. Freight was already dominant, with 384,903 cars compared with 14,621 for passengers, mail, baggage, and express. Freight revenues in 1876 topped $361,000,000; passenger revenue was about $136,000,000. Bonded debt and stock obligations stood at four and a half billion. Interest paid on the funded debt amounted to $93,560,000; dividends on the stock totalled $68,040,000—astronomical figures, compared with any other major business in the country.[13] When Cornelius Vanderbilt died early in 1877, his estate, almost entirely in railroads, amounted to $105,000,000; he was easily the richest American to that date. But large as his fortune was, it was less than a fortieth of the total value of railroads in Centennial America.

In the first decades of the railroad, it cost relatively little to form a modest company, buy rights-of-way, lay tracks, acquire equipment, hire employees, and open for business. Many of the original short lines connected with no other, but by 1860 many of the lines were connected, in an intricate pattern that reached many more communities than are served today.

Indeed, the great number of independent short lines was a

national phenomenon, reflecting a more open competitive economy in the first half-century of railroading than later, when most small railroads were combined or absorbed into big systems. Consider the companies serving the people of Elmira, New York, and competing for their patronage: the Erie; the Delaware, Lackawanna, and Western; the Utica and Chenango Valley; the Northern Central; the Lehigh Valley; the Utica, Ithaca, and Elmira; the Syracuse, Binghampton, and New York; the Southern Central; the Albany and Susquehanna; the Bath and Hammondsport; the Corning, Cowanesque, and Antrim; and the Tioga. Not all of these had tracks within the city limits, but all advertised daily in the Elmira papers.

On the national scale, several lines were already advancing beyond the Mississippi, with one reaching to California—a combination of the Union Pacific from Omaha to Ogden, Utah, and the Central Pacific from Ogden to Oakland. In the northern tier of states and Territories, the Northern Pacific existed as two ends without a middle, while further south the Southern Pacific had not yet gotten out of California. The Kansas Pacific was somewhat more successful, reaching as far west as Denver and Cheyenne. The most important Eastern railroads were the Grand Trunk line from Portland to Detroit via Montreal, the Vanderbilt lines (alternately known as the New York Central), the Pennsylvania (to Chicago and St. Louis), the Erie (to Buffalo), and the Baltimore and Ohio. Although Bostonians might view Boston as "the hub of the universe," the natural hub of the rail complex, by 1876, was increasingly Chicago. Uniquely situated at the foot of Lake Michigan, the only Great Lake entirely within the United States, Chicago radiated lines that went out in all directions like spokes but with no perimeter except, eventually, the continent's saltwater boundaries.

It is only stating the obvious to observe that there was hardly any facet of the nation's economic development in 1876 that was not related to the railroad or dependent upon it in one degree or another. Its capacity for moving heavy loads of raw materials to factories stimulated both the extraction and the manufacturing processes. The return trips, bearing finished products, favored the urbanizing of all sections and the growth of retail business. The passenger services accelerated the flow of rural and village youth to urban centers with their increasing economic opportunities, and the lesser (but better known) movement of individuals to the frontier. The railroad, perhaps more than anything else, hastened the advance of the frontier itself. Never before had a single invention so stimulated growth, or served it so well. Never again would a single industry so dominate the nation's economy.

The multiplicity of railroads, and their total freedom, were phenomena that had to yield, in time, to various pressures—both private and public. Regulation and mergers were inevitable. Consumer demands for safety would one day lead to government standards, and owners saw that uncontrolled rivalry could end only in financial disaster. Mergers were being considered before 1860—in 1853, for example, Vanderbilt consolidated ten independent lines into the New York Central, and the tendency to merge was increasing in the 1870s—partly from a general American impulse toward fewer and bigger concerns, but also from the ambitions of entrepreneurs to amass as much wealth and power as possible. It was a golden age for energetic, capable men, and the greatest arena for their energy was the railroad. Apart from John D. Rockefeller, all the most important entrepreneurs of the Centennial period were in the railroads. It was, as it would not be after 1900, the Railroad Age.

When, in the decade prior to 1876, men began to plan a great national exposition as the central focus for celebrating the centennial of independence, the railroad network was taken for granted as the means of making it feasible. In Europe, where population was dense, huge fairs were less dependent on railroads; in the United States, the railroads were crucial in assembling both the displays and the audience from all over the vast country.

From a railroader's point of view, the Exhibition occupied a tract of land northwest of Philadelphia, between the Pennsylvania and the Philadelphia and Reading, and promised revenue enough to warrant the construction of special trackage and depot facilities. The Pennsylvania was in the most advantageous position; its approach was on the same level as the site, and there was ample space for an elaborate pattern of circles and sidings. Spurs were laid into the grounds and even into the largest buildings. The Philadelphia and Reading, however, skirting the west bank of the Schuylkill, delivered more passengers to the Exhibition—3,295,120 compared with the Pennsylvania's 2,612,213. On its busiest day, the Pennsylvania ran 250 trains to the grounds, with a total of 58,247 passengers; the Philadelphia and Reading, on *its* busiest day, carried 185,000 people on 370 trains. But in this comparison, the Pennsylvania far surpassed its rival, in profits, by its monopoly on freight. The passenger totals would no doubt have been much greater, incidentally, if the fair had been open on Sunday. The general prejudice against running trains on the Sabbath played a part in the decision to close the Exhibition on the one day of the week when working people could most easily attend.[14]

Although only two of America's railroads served the Exhibition directly, every line in the country stood to profit from the traffic. Early in February, some hundred general ticket agents from most of the major lines met in Louisville to consider special fares. They agreed on a 25 percent reduction in round-trip rates, with a dollar added if the traveler included New York in his itinerary. Special trains were added to the New York-Philadelphia run for the duration of the Exhibition, and the fares on these added trains were so low that New Yorkers could hardly afford not to attend: four dollars round trip by first class, three dollars for second class, and two for third class, which meant wooden benches in box cars. While it seems quite an ordeal, people could leave New York at 5:30 A.M., be at the Exhibition gates by 9:30, spend nine hours on the grounds, and be back in New York shortly after midnight.

In mid-February, shortly after the Louisville meeting of ticket agents, special twelve-hour express runs were announced from Boston to Philadelphia. The routing from Boston illustrates the multiplicity of short lines and the complexity of arrangements: the New York and New England as far as Willimantic, Connecticut; the Providence, Hartford, and Fishkill to Hartford; the New York, New Haven, and Hartford to New Rochelle; the Harlem Branch of the New Haven to the Harlem River; tracked steamer (the "Maryland") around Manhattan Island to Jersey City; and the rest of the way by the Pennsylvania.[15]

In addition to such trips planned by the railroads, a great many excursions were arranged by individuals and local groups from communities in various parts of the country.

The railroads cooperated with each other, most of the time, on the operating level, in such matters as moving and transferring freight and passengers, connecting their lines, and agreeing on excursion rates. Joint terminals, however, were very rare; Toledo's union station, serving six lines, was a notable exception. The warfare that sprang up sporadically was waged by the managers and owners, whose power was something the employees could do nothing to limit until the unions grew stronger. Occasionally, however, open conflict occurred on the actual tracks. During the summer and fall of 1875 the Pennsylvania Central kept a locomotive on its track at Hopewell, New Jersey, at just the place where the Delaware and Bound Brook wanted to put in a crossing, and moved it only when one of its own trains needed to pass. On January 5, 1876, the rival company, running out of patience and hoping to force the issue, sent a gang of two hundred men who seized possession when the locomotive was moved, tore up the track, and chained one of their own engines to the spot. A large crowd quickly gathered, eager for more excitement, but the governor of New Jersey ordered to the site five companies of the Seventh Regiment to prevent disorder.[16] This incident, however, was nothing compared with the widespread disorders of the nation-wide railroad strike in 1877.

It took from thirty-six to thirty-nine hours to travel from New York to Chicago, about twice the time of the fastest trains of today, but in view of the state of the equipment perhaps it was just as well. Roadbeds were excellent, and to the great credit of American engineering and workmanship few railroads have ever needed major rebuilding, despite the rapidity of their construction. But ties and rails were generally poor. Steel rails were obviously much stronger and safer than the older iron rails, and metal cars were better than the wooden ones of Civil War days, but replacement was slow. Westinghouse automatic brakes were available as early as 1872, but by 1876 only about two-thirds of all cars had them. Coal had replaced wood as the common fuel, but the smoke it produced was thicker and smellier—and few cars were airtight. The trains were noisy, too. Visiting Europeans complained about the incessant whistling at crossings, which were not barred or guarded as they commonly were in Europe.

By later standards, train travel in 1876 was far from pleasant, but passengers were less disturbed by the actual conditions of riding than by the fear of accidents. Early in 1876 the *American Journal of Medical Sciences* offered some figures that should have been reassuring on this point: "An item of interest to passengers may be worth stating, viz., that the average number of miles of travel necessary to consummate the maiming or slaughter of each passenger was, in 1868, 2,621,826." Thus, train-riders actually had equal chances with stay-at-homes.[17] But even if these calming remarks had been printed in a magazine of much wider general circulation, it is doubtful whether they could have allayed the deeply felt fears, one that each new fatal accident aggravated. Visitors from abroad were spared this fear of accidents; they were more aware of whatever differed from their railroads at home—the larger dimensions of American passenger cars, the comfort of the parlor cars, and above all the wizardry of the Pullman sleeping cars. They were much less happy over the meal stops along the way, with poor food badly served, and too little time to eat it. Corrective measures were being taken, however. One line out of Chicago already had dining cars, and in the station at Topeka Fred Harvey opened, in 1876, the first of the famous Harvey Restaurants, with a stress on good food well cooked and pretty waitresses to serve it.

The Pullman sleepers were fairly new but were in general use by 1876, making George Mortimer Pullman one of the nation's richest men. Unlike most of the other rich men, he had not had to elbow his way to the top or crowd rivals to the wall; he enjoyed a monopoly of his own devising. Trained as a cabinet-maker, he began, in 1859, to convert old railroad coaches into sleeping cars fit for long trips. About 1864 he built the *Pioneer*, the first of his sleeping cars, and in 1867 he formed the Pullman Palace Car Company. In 1870 the first through train went from Boston to San Francisco—"Faneuil Hall to the Golden Gate"—bearing 129 members of the Boston Board of Trade and attracting crowds everywhere along the route. The "Pullman Hotel Express" took ten days for the trip. In 1875 the firm began making day coaches and extra-fare parlor cars with swivel seats made luxurious by pillows and hassocks. But the supreme achievement came in 1876—a private car that cost $38,000. Pullman sometimes let others use it—people like President Grant and Emperor Dom Pedro—but most of the time he used it himself for business travel. When his family went along for summer vacations at the seashore or for trips west, three other cars were added: two for baggage and the twelve servants, the other for the family's five riding horses. The Pullman mansion on Prairie Avenue was a Chicago showplace. For his frequent visits to New York, Pullman had a permanent suite in the Windsor Hotel on Forty-Sixth Street.[18]

Despite their great success, however, the railroads were not without their problems. It was no lack of skill or devotion among the workers that hurt the railroads in Centennial America. The blame for what was wrong can be ascribed to the handful of men who set policies, fought each other in the jungle of business warfare, and enriched themselves at the expense of both their employees and the public.

During 1876 in the *Atlantic Monthly*, Charles Francis Adams, Jr., was enhancing his reputation as the foremost authority on railroad matters with a series of impressive articles: two separate pieces on accidents, and a three-installment essay on the government and the railroads.[19] In the United States, competition was the tradition, and any degree of government ownership was unthinkable. But the fact was that although all lines prospered in good times, weaker lines failed when times were bad. The one alternative to bankruptcy, Adams contended, and the logical successor to competition, was combination. "The law is invariable. It knows no exception." The public might condemn Commodore Vanderbilt's famous conference at Saratoga in August, 1873, but Adams considered it wholesome: the Pennsylvania, the Erie, and the Vanderbilt lines had merely agreed on rates and had substituted arbitration for warfare. They had not gone so far as to agree to pool their profits. The Baltimore and Ohio had chosen to stay out of the combination, and had suffered heavily before it finally capitulated—which, to the chagrin of the Johns Hopkins University board of trustees, it did too late to prevent a severe decline in the value of its shares. The city of Chicago held aloof from also and suffered by losing ground to more co-operative cities such as Milwaukee and Peoria.

The major point in the Adams argument was that bankruptcy was a greater evil than the surrender of total autonomy through combination. A bankrupt railroad, or any other company that did not have to pay dividends, could set rates so low that solvent competitors could not possibly match them. Most cities had learned that a single gas or water company was better in every way than several operating in competition with each other. Adams was well aware that railroad management was often corrupt, but in his realistic frame of values, Centennial vintage, efficiency and continuing dividends were preferable to insolvency and collapse. The pooling of interests by merger, even if done for cynical reasons, struck him as less offensive than a competitive anarchy that profited nobody except perhaps the lone eventual survivor of the ruthless struggle. If business could not maintain itself, whatever course it adopted, there was the bogey-man threat of government interference—and nothing could be worse than that.

Adams was no apologist for the railroads; if anything, he was their severest critic, and in being so incurred the hatred of the men whose conniving he understood and exposed. These men were ruthless, cunning, and powerful enough not to be afraid of what he might say in print; and besides, his basic premises were theirs. Business and industry were expanding so fast that the railroads assumed each year a greater importance. So essential were they, indeed, that even the grossest violations of ethical principle went unchecked. Like any other example of finance capitalism, the railroads existed to yield profits to their owners, and anything that endangered the flow of profits—whether poor service or operating inefficiency, government interference or disastrous competition—was a threat to the services the railroads could provide and hence to the nation's economic health.

Adams rather expected the Vanderbilt combination to fail—and it did during 1876, partly because the Commodore fell ill on May 10 and was no longer able to exert his forceful will.[20] But failure of one combination, Adams insisted, did not invalidate the principle. He could have cited a Southern example that seemed to promise enduring results: the Southern Railroad and

Steamship Company, which began to operate in 1875 from a central office in Atlanta. Albert Fink, longtime superintendent of the Louisville and Nashville, served as a kind of umpire, assigning through traffic to competing lines.

The Southern combination (or pool) was born of desperation: the economy of the entire region could not improve unless something were done to pull the railroads out of their doldrums. There never had been enough of them in the South. Federal troops had destroyed much of their tangible property, and the war left little capital to rebuild the lines, let alone extend them or to convert to the standard gauge. As late as 1880, 77 percent of Southern trackage was still nonstandard, mostly five feet. The paucity of traffic, moreover, meant higher freight rates than elsewhere in the nation, while passengers paid a staggering five cents a mile. Highways were at their worst in the South, and though many Southern rivers were navigable, their development was negligible. The South was not only behind other sections in both transport and economic activity but was falling further behind each year. It helped not at all that tradition-minded Southerners, who viewed railroads and business as parts of a Northern plot to subvert their agrarian way of life, were smugly pleased by the state of affairs.

The enormous literature concerning the "robber barons" of the post-Civil War period invites the conclusion that in that era business honesty, as we now measure it, was nonexistent. It is probable that most business men of the era were reasonably honest but that the very humdrum, methodical nature of their transactions rules them out as the subjects of popular best-sellers. But even if we were all agreed that most Centennial business was honest, or at least not grossly dishonest, the fact remains that in that period conditions permitted some men to abuse every concept of ethics in their desire for wealth and power. And, further, that the very flagrancy of the abuses hastened the imposition of social controls through governmental regulation.

One fact of life in Centennial America was that men almost totally ignorant of particular industries could seize control of them through financial trickery. Jay Gould, who turned forty in 1876, had the uncanny ability to read a corporation charter, find in an obscure clause a single vulnerable point, and apply his peculiar genius to exploiting the weakness. He was also devoid of respect for the laws. In his successful struggle against both Daniel Drew and Commodore Vanderbilt for control of the Erie Railroad, he ignored court injunctions, bribed members of the New York state legislature, some of whom had already been bribed (or bought) by Vanderbilt, double-crossed Drew in stock manipulations, and issued new stock that Vanderbilt had no choice but to buy until he abandoned the contest by accepting a compromise. By 1868 Gould had won full control of the Erie, and, early in 1875, acting on a tip that the railroad was about to drop into receivership after defaulting on bonds, he sold out just before the stock fell from thirty to eighteen. It was not until later that the extent of the damage he had done was fully known. In 1876, the Erie's clients put the blame on Daniel Drew, who had begun the process that Gould, through his habitual secretive methods, completed. In 1876 Gould's attention was focused on the Union Pacific and the Pacific Mail Company, both of which were to profit by his manipulations. By 1881 he had acquired twelve railroads, with 15 percent of the nation's total trackage. But the one time he tried the actual management of a railroad, he quickly realized it was beyond his abilities, and he reverted to doing what he *could* do, which was to acquire lines and divert most of the profits to his own pocket. Railroads just happened to be the major source of profit during the period when he was active.[21]

Cornelius Vanderbilt, Gould's principal rival in the East, was more than twice Gould's age—eighty-two years old in 1876, and nearing the end of his career. He had been slowing down since 1874, plagued by an assortment of ailments that would have killed an average man, and during his final illness until he died on January 4, 1877, a battery of attending physicians could only ask each other what was keeping him alive. The answer seemed to be sheer willpower. He remained the blasphemous curmudgeon he had always been, and rewrote his will to concentrate power in the only one of his many children who had shown capacity for continuing the dynasty, his son William Henry. He was deaf to the entreaties and cajolings of his daughters and his weaker sons. Yet he revealed the sentimental religious piety that many of the "robber barons" either shared or pretended to share by insisting that the women of his household gather frequently and sing his favorite hymns. He also showed a weakness for Spiritualism, with some hope, apparently, that it could extend his life.[22] After his death, Henry Ward Beecher expressed strong doubts as to Vanderbilt's greatness, adding that he was suspicious of men who are religious "only at the fag end," a remark that drew a quick retort from Vanderbilt's minister, the Rev. Dr. Deems: "I confess that I do not like the tone of Mr. Beecher's talk." [23] Deems, it should be noted, had been handsomely subsidized by Vanderbilt, and received a legacy befitting his willingness to pray at the dying man's bedside whenever asked.

Vanderbilt differed from Daniel Drew, Jay Gould, and others of their kind in his knowledge of the operational side of his enterprises. He had been in the transportation business from boyhood, most of the time in shipping, and he enjoyed the respect and confidence, even the personal loyalty, of his employees. In a way, he represented an older type of magnate, and an older tradition, which was being replaced by what we now know as financial entrepreneurship, a style in business affairs which may or may not involve direct knowledge of particular operations. Vanderbilt was already a millionaire by 1850, and thus he had the money reserves to expand from ships to railroads during the later period when capital became the most pressing need, and when pioneers in particular ventures usually lost out to men virtually ignorant of managing those ventures who had the cash that was increasingly essential.

Lobbying became a vital element in American business only after 1870. Like almost every other new facet of enterprise, it reflected the rapid growth of business as the central force in American economic life.

William Chandler, a Republican politician who served later as Secretary of the Navy and as a U. S. Senator, was a pioneer lobbyist, typical of the profession before it reached its maturity. As a part-time one-man lobbying firm after the Civil War, he sold his services to various railroads. It was not easy work, he learned, nor did it pay very well. In 1869, for example, the Union Pacific paid him a paltry $5,000 for several years' work, and in 1870 he had to settle for stock in the company in lieu of payment. The railroads were not yet convinced of the value of lobbying.[24]

It was not long, however, before they changed their views. The intensifying struggle between the Southern Pacific and the Texas and Pacific for Congressional handouts overcame the initial reluctance. There was danger in not having agents in Washington to counteract the work of rival agents. Collis Huntington seemed over-cautious to his partners; but he realized the importance of winning Congressional support in the fight against strong rivals. He divided Congressmen into three categories: "clean," "commercial," and "communist." Clean men, by his definition, did not expect rewards. Commercial men could be bought. Communists resisted both persuasion and cash.

By 1876 an ex–Civil War general named David Colton, was entrenched in Washington as lobbyist for the Southern Pacific. Huntington had reason to think that Tom Scott, president of the Pennsylvania railroad system, had two hundred lobbyists advancing the interests of the Texas and Pacific, working mostly with the "commercial" breed of Congressmen. Scott was offering large sums, Huntington wrote to Colton on January 29, "but you know I keep on high ground." He assumed the same pious tone in a letter on February 19: "You know our rule is never to buy a vote." He had grave doubts, however, about the dependability of Senators. In another note, dated February 12, he remarked that Scott "switched Senator Spencer of Alabama and Walker of Virginia this week, but you know they can be switched back with the 'proper arguments' when they are wanted." But all too many Congressmen, after accepting favors ranging from free passes to substantial tracts of land, had a disturbing habit of voting out of loyalty to principles or constituents.[25]

After Colton's death, his widow sued the Southern Pacific for a settlement she could live on. The letters she produced were widely printed in newspapers; but Huntington was not a bit embarrassed. "Where's the evidence of corruption in these?" he asked a reporter. "I've been in business fifty years and practiced the usual methods known among business men to accomplish certain objects, but I've never bought votes or bribed men directly or indirectly." [26] Whether or not his disclaimer was justified in fact, Huntington seems to have had no sense that exerting influence through professional lobbyists was in any degree unscrupulous; it was something that had to be done in self-defense. It might be concluded that the chief difference in lobbying between 1876 and any year after 1900 is that it was only in its infancy in Centennial America, and that experience since then has rounded off the rough edges, making an art of it.

Numerous sensational biographies, at their peak in the 1920s, have singled out a very few colorful rascals of the early days of American big business, most of them in just one business—railroads. The enormity of their crimes against employees, competitors, consumers, and stockholders can hardly be exaggerated; yet we are surely in error when we blanket all Centennial business with the censure these few so richly deserve.

One of the authors of the 1920s states his thesis neatly: "That which seemed all right in the 1870's, provided one could get away with it, was distinctly off color in 1908; the things which were condoned in 1908 simply are not done in 1926." [27] By extension, presumably, the American businessman has steadily come closer to saintliness in the decades since. But is it the individual who has changed, or his moral and legal environment? Again, current "conglomerates" should not be overlooked.

Businessmen, whether cynical crooks or pillars of virtue, could completely ignore their employees' welfare in 1876, since labor had no collective power or recourse to protective laws. The extremely rapid expansion of business, moreover, had outstripped society's power to create effective controls; business operated, if not in a legal vacuum, at least in a field with only a few low hurdles. It also operated with the blessing of the dominant Protestant orthodoxy, a formidable force. In a sense, nothing that business might do could be altogether bad, in the way that labor unions were assumed to be bad, or foreigners, or non-Protestant religions, or cities, or government interference. What a heavenly time it was for business! And what an open invitation to abandon probity!

Albert S. Bolles, writing his *Industrial History of the United States* in 1877, viewed with admirable objectivity all facets of the nation's economic life. His comparison of life and fire insurance is particularly revealing. Great fires took a terrible toll in the five years from 1871 to 1876. The loss in the Chicago fire alone was about $150,000,000, of which only about $49,000,000, half the insurance in force, was recovered. Of two hundred insurance firms involved, sixty-four were forced out of business. Other major fires occurred in New York and Pittsburgh; in Boston, with two, in 1872 and 1873; and again in Chicago. "This is an extraordinary record," Bolles wrote, "and, should the history of the next twenty years present a similar picture of destruction, it will become a problem, whether fire-insurance can continue to prosper." [28] In earlier decades, fire insurance had been marked by wholesale fraud and incompetence, but after 1860 state laws were strengthened to protect the public and especially the policy-holder. No laws, however, could prevent the great fires that had recently been hurting the business. Yet the hurt was not *too* serious, for fire insurance companies operating in the United States numbered 851 (34 of them foreign) in 1876.

Life insurance was much younger than fire insurance, but instead of profiting from experience it seemed forced to suffer the same growing pains. The depression of 1857 began, Bolles suggested, with the failure of one life-insurance firm—the Ohio Life and Trust Company of Cincinnati. He did not attribute the depression of 1873 entirely to frauds or flaws in life insurance, but he intimated at least a partial responsibility. In 1870 the Great Western Mutual of New York failed, and after that

> the companies came toppling down like a row of trees in the woods. . . . One company would be closed by the attorney-general, and its affairs put in the hands of a receiver. Its policy-holders would be re-insured in some other brand-new and equally weak company, which would go down in turn, often in the very same year. Each failure was worse than the preceding; and when 1876 and 1877 were reached, and the Continental, the Security, the American Popular, and the Atlantic Mutual went down, an examination of their affairs revealed a shamelessness of corruption, in the management of the first three, which shocked the moral sense of the American people, and led every man to ask the question of his neighbor, "Well, who is there in the community that we can trust now?" [29]

Bolles answered the question at once, by listing the nine life insurance companies he considered the most reliable. By far the largest was Mutual of New York, founded in 1847, which subsequently changed its name to New York Insurance Company. The solid companies survived largely by prudent, conservative practices, careful adherence to sound actuarial tables, and a reputation for sobriety. The more numerous companies that quickly failed, as Bolles described them, "came up like mushrooms year after year," with gaudy office fronts, gilded signs, frescoes and bronze statuary, and uniformed porters.[30] Instruction booklets issued to agents encouraged every conceivable high-pressure device, and made it crystal-clear that profit, as much of it as possible, and fast, was the one great goal. The typical companies, however, were the failures.

Businesses vary so much that conclusions drawn from the history of one can hardly be taken as valid for all. But the history of insurance does suggest that any kind of business, in its early stages, shows a greater range of moral standards than later, after consumers learn to distinguish the reliable from the dubious, and after legislators, responding to public pressure, revise and tighten the means of control. The first laws passed are seldom altogether effective; successive laws are often needed to plug the loopholes that companies (or lone wolves of the Jay Gould stripe) quickly discover and exploit. New forms of business, moreover, have to develop their own most effective methods; and a good many firms, organized with high hopes, fail before the methods are developed, or because their personnel prove unsuited for the company's particular kind of work. Given a period of tremendous business expansion, with many new kinds of enterprise, a condition close to chaos is hardly avoidable. The dozen years after the end of the Civil War witnessed the greatest business acceleration in American history, and near-chaos might have been predicted. But equating this condition to a low in morality seems very dubious.

The insurance business was mature enough in 1864, at least in Hartford, Connecticut, where four of the nine leading life insurance companies on Bolles's list had their home offices, to get a new kind of insurance off to a firm start. On a trip to Europe, one James Batterson noticed the success there of accident insurance, and on his return home he organized the Travellers' Insurance Company, chartered in June, 1863. His first customer was a man named James Bolter, who, meeting him in front of the Hartford Post Office, asked what it would cost to insure his life for $5,000 on the way to his home on Buckingham Street. "Two cents," Batterson told him. Bolter paid the two cents which, after his safe arrival home, were framed for preservation in the Travellers' office.[31] The company was sound from the beginning and for several years had no serious competition.

The post-Civil War era also saw the advent of exciting innovations and inventions that affected American business life. Inventors as we normally picture them—men with newly-devised instruments or tools or methods—seldom try to market their products themselves, chiefly because it takes more cash than they have. One exception, the best-known of all American inventors, was Thomas Alva Edison. In 1869 he had penetrated to the very heart of capitalism by marketing, for $40,000, his stock-ticker. His electric vote-recorder went begging; Congress seemed less interested than the stock market in streamlining its activities. The only important Edison invention in 1876 was the mimeograph, patented on August 5. He was busy all year in his new laboratory at Menlo Park, New Jersey, with a much more significant project: the incandescent electric lamp. It became commercially feasible in 1879.

Meanwhile, on January 14, 1876, Edison filed at the Patent Office a caveat (meaning a description of an invention not yet perfected) for an apparatus that would analyze waves produced by different sounds. He was not aware at this point, of the device's potential. But if Edison didn't know a telephone when he saw one, two other inventors did. By a coincidence almost too remarkable to believe, Elisha Gray and Alexander Graham Bell, a few hours apart on February 14, both filed caveats for telephones. Gray, of the Western Electric Company in Chicago, described a device with a liquid transmitter, while Bell, whose interest in the subject began when he was a teacher of the deaf and dumb, submitted a device like Gray's and also one in which vibration of a diaphragm produced transmittable waves. Bell's caveat was nearer the top of the pile than Gray's and was therefore the first seen by the Patent Office staff, who gave it priority and dated the patent March 7. Three days later Bell produced, inadvertently, the first distinguishable telephone message—the famous "Come here, Watson, I want you." The first outdoor trial was on October 9 over a two-mile line between Boston and Cambridge. Gray sought relief through the courts but without success, and he remains a symbol of the worst kind of luck.

Some cultural anthropologists insist that inventions occur when society is ready for them, but the Centennial public showed a remarkable ability to conceal its readiness for the telephone. It took Bell several years to persuade men with money to support his little gadget, which was one of the great curiosities, but nothing more, at the Centennial Exhibition. This fact seems the more remarkable when we think of the parallel with the telegraph, which by 1876 was familiar everywhere, with 7,072 telegraph offices, 184,000 miles of wire, and almost 19,000,000 telegrams sent in the year ending June 30, 1876. Western Union was capitalized at $55,000,000, with annual revenues of $9,000,000 and dividends of $2,500,000. A real mystery of 1876, a year when almost everybody was searching for ways to make profits, was that nobody except Bell—and Elisha Gray, but not Edison—foresaw that the telephone, as a business, was potentially at least as big as the telegraph.

Bell did have backers, Gardiner Hubbard of Cambridge and Thomas Sanders of Haverhill. But Bell worried them. He had too many different ideas and wouldn't concentrate enough on any one of them, they feared, to make a success of it. In October, after Bell proved the practicability of his gadget over the two-mile circuit, Hubbard offered the rights to Western Union for $100,000 but was turned down. In order to finance further work, Bell had to resort to lecturing about his invention. The public liked his lectures, and gladly paid the admission fees. The first order for a telephone line was given in April, 1877, by a Boston businessman, and the next January the first commercial exchange was opened in New Haven. During 1878, licenses to local companies gradually increased. By this time Western Union was interested: it tried to buy out Bell's backers, and failing that, set up a rival telephone company. Litigation ended in 1879 with the Bell group victorious. From the outset, the telephone system proved the advantage of a single system over several in competition.[32]

The story of the typewriter is somewhat the same. The idea was an old one. It took a rare kind of mind to conceive of conversations over a wire, but almost anybody could imagine a machine that would put letters, one after another, on a sheet of paper. Besides, the utility of such a machine was obvious in reducing the time and effort required for the growing paper-work of business. But when such a machine reached the practical stage, the instant reception that might have been expected in the business world was nowhere evident. Christopher Scholes of Milwaukee built the first practical model in 1873; it had no shift key, only capital letters. His associate James Densmore per-suaded E. Remington and Sons, of Ilion, New York, to buy the rights for $12,000, and early in 1874 the "Remington No. 1" was put on the market. But sales were very slow. Even in 1876, at the Exhibition, the machine on display was, like the telephone, just another novelty to be gawked at. Sometime during the year Mark Twain, after seeing an exhibit in Boston, bought a type-writer, but few other writers, and few business firms, were ready to risk their good money.[33] We have here, it seems, two prime examples of the "man from Missouri" attitude, which, before being willing to try the new, says, "Show me."

Not every aspect of Centennial life, perhaps, would reveal such hesitation. And, indeed, comparison might show that Americans were less wary of the new than people in other countries. An anonymous English observer, writing about the iron industry, warned his countrymen that they might fall be-hind if their iron-making plants were not modernized as had been done in the United States. The American desire for labor-saving devices was unalloyed by other emotions; English manu-facturers worried unduly about the men who would be thrown out of work. "The Americans have been quicker than ourselves to apprehend the period of transition" from iron to steel, "and have gained a good start in saving labor and in improving proc-esses and machinery. Among a people desirous of new things, a new suggestion is immediately inquired into; if it is practical, it is tried; and, if successful, applied."[34] This echoes the comment noted earlier, from the book by Joseph Hatton, also an Englishman, that American businessmen heeded even the suggestions of their office boys.

Abram S. Hewitt, Peter Cooper's son-in-law and partner, and the national Democratic chairman in 1876, was among the nation's leaders in iron and steel. The Cooper and Hewitt steel furnaces in Phillipsburg, New Jersey, were as modern as any. In his Centennial address as president-elect of the American Institute of Mining Engineers, Hewitt reviewed the progress made in mining since 1776, but departed from the dominant capitalist formula in suggesting, as befitting the Centennial Year, the creation by each coal company of a department "for the moral, mental, social, and physical improvement of the workingmen and their families, and by the appropriation of a fixed charge on coal for this purpose." From coal the idea might spread to other industries, producing at last "that Christian commonwealth which has been the dream of the patriot, the philanthropist, and the statesman, of all ages." He quoted from Thomas More's *Utopia* on the equitable distribution of wealth—nobody in abject poverty, nor too rich—and he described corporations as "mere machines until they are inspired by the associated conscience of society." [35]

Hewitt had been sent to the Paris Exposition of 1867 to study the various industrial methods shown there, especially the applications of the Bessemer process that converted iron to steel. In reporting what he had learned he had helped significantly in the modernization of the industry in America. Where he had learned compassion for the workingman is not clear, unless it was from *Utopia;* but with such notions he was obviously not interested in doing what a man had to do to consolidate a monopoly. Iron-making, however, had always been decentralized, and so had mining, which varied greatly from ore to ore and from region to region—coal, bituminous and anthracite, some of it mined by farmers on their own land, as Nathaniel Bishop had observed from his sneak-box below Pittsburgh; copper, mostly in open pits; quicksilver in California; gold and silver, dug out of lodes with pick and shovel, or panned in streams, or produced by hydraulic machines of great capacity. A steel firm would be more likely to absorb a soft coal mine, as a source fuel for its blast furnaces than to acquire a gold or copper mine. Fortunes could be and were being made in both mining and processing, but neither seemed to attract high-powered financiers. The Guggenheim interest in copper did not begin until after 1880.

Other industries were equally decentralized, like lumbering, then at its peak in upper Michigan, or underdeveloped, like rubber and shoes. Charles Goodyear had patented in 1844 a process for vulcanizing rubber. It had been discovered accidentally, and only later was its scientific basis understood. The patent expired in 1865, opening the way for the creation of rival firms. In 1876, six of the nine members of the Associated Rubber Shoe Companies bought out and closed the factory of a troublesome rival, the Newark India Rubber Company, as an early step toward the formation, in 1892, of the United States Rubber Company.[36] As for leather footwear, the sudden demand caused by the Civil War and the shortage of shoemakers took production out of the home into the factory, especially in New England, where the industry was consolidated by 1875.

Rubber was not yet a major industry, in terms of the dollar value of production. Clothing and textiles, widely dispersed throughout the nation, stood easily first, and the top dozen included also lumber, iron and steel, leather, boots and shoes, sugar, paper, flour and meal, printing and publishing, horse-drawn vehicles, foundries and machineshops, and liquors, both malt and distilled.[37] The evolution since 1876 has created an entirely different industrial elite—such categories as chemicals, utilities, telephone and telegraph, gasoline-propelled vehicles, electrical gadgets, aviation, and petroleum. This last was just beginning to move up on the scale of value and importance in 1876. It was also on the verge of creating the one great monopoly in our business history.

Rock oil (which is what *petroleum* means) had been known far back in history in one form or another. In the early nineteenth century, oil taken from a few surface wells competed with candles, spirit lamps, and whale-oil to provide illumination. By mid-century enough oil was extracted from bituminous coal to keep several refineries busy turning out kerosene; and by the late 1850s kerosene lamps were quite good, producing the best light available. All that was needed was the discovery of a source of petroleum copious enough to meet the growing demand.

The first major effort in this direction was launched by a newly-formed corporation, the Pennsylvania Rock Oil Company, to explore for petroleum in the Titusville area, where surface wells were common. On August 28, 1859, a one-time railroad conductor, Colonel E. L. Drake, sank a shaft and hit an oil pocket at 69½ feet. The oil rose at once to within five inches of the surface, and the well subsequently proved its ability to yield four hundred gallons a day. The news spread fast, and the region quickly became a congested scene of rigs and derricks, tanks, and burning gushers—for deeper wells soon released pressure that drove the oil above ground. All during the Civil War, in Bradford, Oil City, Franklin, and other communities northeast of Pittsburgh, the oil boom flourished, stimulating business of every sort almost as if there were no war. At first the crude oil was taken out of the region in barrels, seven or eight to a wagon, and the traffic was highly profitable to the wagoneers even though the wagons seldom held together for more than three or four trips. Later, barges took most of the oil down Oil Creek and the Allegheny River to Pittsburgh, the nation's first great oil distribution center. By 1867, when tracks could be extended into the producing center, railroads had become the prime mover. The best and final method, wherever gravity could be utilized, was the pipeline, using iron pipes two inches in diameter. By 1870, some thirty million dollars had been spent on the transportation alone. Oil was the youngest major industry of the Centennial period, and it was rapidly becoming one of the most important.[38]

In later years, "monopoly" was to become a bad word in the United States, but in the Centennial era, though few could have had any real hopes of achieving it, it was still the implicit goal of all men engaged in business. The record shows, however, that in only one major industry, petroleum, did one man actually achieve the great ambition. To offer any single reason may seem naive, but it is possible that the very youth of the petroleum industry and its extremely rapid growth produced a continuous confusion behind which a man of indomitable will, great foresight, and the mastery of various potent weapons could operate almost without its being known until he had gained a control that no combination of opposing forces could destroy.

John Davidson Rockefeller was born in Richford, New York, in 1839, the son of a "pitchman" who called himself a cancer-specialist and seldom stayed anywhere for more than one day. The self-styled "doctor" did well enough to send his son to Oswego Academy, where his schoolmates included Tom Platt, subsequently a Senator and the Republican boss of New York State, Ben Tracy, who became Secretary of the Navy under President Hayes, and Frederick Hewitt, who in time left two and a half million dollars to the New York Post Graduate Hospital. Just what Rockefeller owed to this threesome is matter for conjecture, but by 1870, when he was barely thirty, he was able to organize the Standard Oil Company of Ohio, with a refinery capacity of fifteen hundred barrels of oil a day. By guaranteeing to ship sixty tank cars daily to New York, he secured a shipping rate lower than his thirty-odd Cleveland competitors, four of whom dropped out of competition almost at once. In 1872 he organized the South Improvement Company, which was designed to let the biggest refinery in each city buy out the competition and to require special railroad rebates to the survivors.

By 1876 Rockefeller had won to his side most holdouts, and was ready for expansion into the New York area. There the independents still resisted him. Tom Scott, overlord of the Pennsylvania Railroad, and Col. Joseph Potts, of the Empire Transportation Company, combined forces to stop him. In reply, Rockefeller declared war by reducing kerosene prices in every city where Potts had a refinery, and by forcing the Erie and the New York Central to give special reduced rates for Standard Oil shipments. In April, 1876, a Congressman from Pittsburgh introduced a bill "to regulate commerce and prohibit unjust discrimination by Common Carriers"—a measure aimed directly at Rockefeller. But with just such developments in mind he had bought up certain key Congressmen, who saw to it that the bill did not come up for a vote. The year closed with the struggle growing in intensity. The railroad strike in 1877 helped Rockefeller. Pennsylvania Railroad stock fell to twenty-seven, Tom

Scott had to capitulate, and so in turn did Colonel Potts. By 1878 Rockefeller had his monopoly, the nation's first. In April, 1879, the law almost caught up with him, in the form of a grand jury indictment for criminal conspiracy, but he was now too rich and powerful to be stopped. Only much later did society decide that monopolies were immoral and that Standard Oil had to be broken up.[39]

Rockefeller's chief biographer, Allan Nevins, seems to have undergone a change of heart in the course of his writings. His first book left a pretty clear impression of Rockefeller as a public enemy; his second, thirteen years later, substantially softened his opinion.[40] Whether or not readers of the two books can follow the author's lead in shelving the early quick condemnation after sober reflection, certain conclusions remain. Rockefeller made nothing and invented nothing, not even the monopoly, although he was the first to prove its possibility. He certainly resorted to devices that would be quite uniformly censured today, but in his time these devices—even the manipulation of Congress—were not unanimously regarded as immoral. Nobody ever questioned Rockefeller's personal piety; he was no swaggering buccaneer, sneering at the public, nor was he coldly cynical in his behavior. He was entirely confident, in fact, that what he was doing was God's will, and that the money rolling in was God's reward. If he had had any doubts about this, the dominant Centennial orthodoxy would have silenced them: he was doing what the great Protestant middle class seriously supposed that God meant men to do. It did no harm to his reputation that, year after year, he taught a Sunday school class. Not until almost the end of the century did he consider the value of a public relations expert. His Centennial image—except among his competitors—could hardly have been better.

A major phase of Rockefeller's eventual philanthropy was the endowing of higher education. It is just possible that he regretted his own limited schooling, although it made him eligible for the myth of humble beginnings that the Horatio Alger dime novels did not invent but did much to confirm. Walt Whitman, earlier, had subscribed to this view, remarking once in a conversation, "Everything comes out of the dirt—everything: everything comes out of the people, the people as you find them: not university people, not FFV people." It was an idea common among the Romantics, who were suspicious of hyperculture, but Whitman carried it further than most, even proposing a religion of the common people with himself as high priest.[41] The myth of lowly origins had a variant in the Log Cabin Myth, although precious few Presidents were born in log cabins. Migration from Europe in early childhood was also supposed to favor a man. Enough conspicuously successful men did arrive as penniless immigrants, or rise from lowly origins, to confirm the notion in popular thinking; and it seems a pity, almost, to insist that it was not the case in the latter nineteenth century. An authoritative study of the industrial elite in the 1870s, based on three major industries—textiles, railroads, and steel—concludes with this composite picture of:

> American by birth, of a New England father, English in national origin, Congregational, Presbyterian, or Episcopal in religion, urban in early environment, he was rather born and bred in an atmosphere in which business and a relatively high social standing were ultimately associated with his family life. Only at about eighteen did he take his first regular job, prepared to rise from it, moreover, not by a rigorous apprenticeship begun when he was virtually a child, but by an academic education well above the average for the times.[42]

Most of the men named so far in this chapter, however, conformed more to the myth than to the scholars' composite. Pullman began as a cabinetmaker, Daniel Drew as a cattle dealer, Gould as a country store clerk, Huntington as a storekeeper, Rockefeller as an office clerk. Edison had only three months of schooling. But Bell was educated at the universities of Edinburgh and London and Hewitt graduated from Columbia in 1842. The composite portrait would gradually fill in if we studied one industry or business after another, the kind that made up the bulk of the nation's economic life without being in the Centennial limelight. We would also recognize the composite in the managers of one venture very much in the limelight in 1876—the Centennial Exhibition.

In certain basic ways the Exhibition was a business venture that differed from all other business ventures. It enjoyed from the outset a monopolistic status. Its managers never had to worry about possible bankruptcy, or even survival, for it was planned to have an official existence of only six months. Yet its officials talked about it exactly as they would have talked about a purely private business, and the more they talked, the more clearly they exhibited the Centennial attitudes toward business and government. In regard to the Centennial Exhibition, the profit motive, basic to all free enterprise, was so minor as to be virtually nonexistent, yet the official statements sounded very much like explanations—or apologies—to stockholders.[43]

General Joseph Hawley, an honor graduate of Hamilton College and a successful financier, was president of the Centennial Commission. He referred in his statement to Charles Sumner's objection, expressed several years earlier during a Senate debate on the Centennial Appropriation Bill, that monarchial countries would not take part in a celebration of republican success. This at least had not proved true, he noted, for thirty-nine foreign countries, monarchial as well as republican, had sent exhibits and spent upwards of two million dollars. Recalcitrance was found rather in the several states, mostly Southern, which were represented in limited fashion or not at all. "The masses of the American people," Hawley observed, "desired to make long strides in the Centennial year toward perfect reconciliation. Divine Providence gave us a splendid opportunity to shake hands . . . The jealousy of states and localities has been very discouraging."

On the opening day of the Exhibition there were 76,172 paid admissions; the next day drew fewer than 15,000 and the third day about 10,000. The daily average for May was 19,146. June proved only a little better—26,756. The Fourth of July festivities accounted for a small peak in attendance figures from the third through the sixth, but the intense heat pushed the July daily average down to 24,281. The buildings were often like ovens, the asphalt streets and pathways like lava flows. Every day a large number of visitors suffered heat prostration. It was no cooler in August, but growing interest boosted the daily average for the month to 33,655. The long-hoped-for boom began in September. State days helped: Connecticut Day, the seventh, drew 64,000; Massachusetts Day, the fourteenth, 79,000; New York Day, the twenty-first, 118,000; and Pennsylvania Day, the twenty-eighth, set the record with no fewer than 257,169 paid admissions. The daily average for September was an encouraging 81,961; in October, it reached 89,789, and for the final nine days, in November, 102,106. Just a few more weeks at the final rate would have spared the officials all reason to assign blame, offer excuses, and reaffirm the credo of free enterprise.

The figure for the total of paid admissions was 8,004,325; what the visitors paid, some at half price, totalled $3,813,749.75, enough to meet all running expenses. If each visitor paid to enter four separate times, it would mean two million different people; but no method was devised for counting separate persons. There were 1,785,067 free admissions—officials, complimentary guests, workmen, policemen and firemen, concessionaires, and judges; but since many of these entered every day, and some more than once a day, again it is impossible to estimate with any assurance the number of different individuals who attended. A reasonable guess would be that one out of every fifteen Americans living in 1876 visited the Centennial Exhibition.

Director-General Goshorn, a graduate of Marietta College, was less dissatisfied than Hawley with the attendance. He had made a cautious pre-opening prediction of a 40,000 daily average, and with the late rush it reached 52,859. He was gratified, too, that visitors and exhibitors alike had complied with the regulations which he had spent six months preparing and which needed no subsequent modification, probably because they were both liberal and clear. The various foreign commissioners were pleased by the freedom they had been granted to arrange their exhibits in their own way. They were far from pleased—and at this point all the sweetness and light went out of Goshorn's report—by the behavior of the federal government. "The administration of the customs laws gave them a good deal of annoyance which I could not obviate. The customs officials never comprehended the Exhibition. Instead of regarding it as exceptional and peculiar, they treated it like a retail shop, and tied it up with all the red tape they could apply." What was worse, various branches of the customs service worked at cross purposes. This was one of the occasions, as Thoreau might have

observed, when the government did not help by the alacrity
with which it got out of the way.

Could he have started over, Goshorn would have chosen a
different system of judging and giving awards. Instead of competitive evaluation, the judges—125 American and 125 foreign
—considered each exhibit on its own merits. If sixteen exhibits
were entered in any given category, all sixteen might be judged
worthy of the round bronze medals, four inches in diameter.
Conversely, all sixteen might go unrewarded. The plan made it
easy for the judges, who never had to decide between two
objects of comparable excellence and could therefore be very
generous. The exhibits were divided into twenty-eight groups,
each with various subdivisions. In Group I, mineral ores and
combustibles, 616 awards were given; in Group II, chemicals
and pharmaceuticals, 785; and so it went. The result was a
minimum of hard feelings, even though, in the long run, the
multiplication of awards robbed each one of any special value.
Harper's Weekly on October 14 reported three advertisements,
each in a different New York paper, and all three identical: in
the *Post*, the statement that the Weber was the world's best
piano; in the *Tribune*, the statement that the Steinway was the
world's best piano; in the *Times*, the statement that the Decker
was the world's best piano. Each company could prove it by
showing the medal its piano had won at the Exhibition. To the
super-patriot, certain of American superiority in all things, it
may have seemed reassuring that so many American products
won top honors; the fact was that almost as many foreign articles
were equally accredited.

The system made everybody feel good and no doubt contributed to the general opinion that the Exhibition was a success.
Amherst graduate Francis A. Walker, Chief of the Bureau of
Awards, pointed out that the system had never been tried before; its faults, he thought, were largely due to its novelty. A
medal given for "a can of maple sugar or two or three bottles of
wine, or a piece of hand-worked embroidery," on the established
basis of intrinsic merit, diminished the value of an identical
medal given to an exhibit of great commercial importance.
Walker praised the judges for their "astonishing zeal and en-

ergy" but, along with Goshorn, he regretted the excess of awards. Actually, the medal was supposed to be only a token that an award had been made; the official award was embodied in the written report of the judges, who were instructed to answer the Socratic question of "good for *what?*" It is likely that the strictures of both Goshorn and Walker reflected the fact that all the written reports, totalling twelve thousand, were left for the Commission to sort and examine after the judges had received their pay ($1,000 apiece) and scattered to the four winds. Many of the reports, it was discovered, were not in proper order, but by then it was too late to ask for correction.

By far the most critical of the Centennial officials was John Welsh, president of its board of finance. He had hoped for ten million paid admissions, and he blamed the deficit on the railroads for their tardy fixing of excursion rates and on the newspapers for insisting that the Exhibition could not open on time. But he was particularly bitter toward the government. The Senate, he thought, understood that the stockholders were to be paid first; it was the House, or rather a few members of the House, that insisted on immediate repayment of the federally appropriated $1,500,000. As Welsh was writing his report, there was talk of a Congressional resolution *forcing* prior payment to the government, and this got his dander up: "Congress ought, instead of adopting such a resolution, to pass one thanking the managers of the Exhibition, and exempting us from all demands on the part of the government. We have been celebrating the birthday of the nation. The government refused to appropriate anything for the purpose until the success of the movement was assured. I cannot believe it will now step in and grab all the assets, and thus throw the whole expense upon its citizens who were patriotic enough to subscribe to the great enterprise."

Setting aside the opinions of the officials, we might examine the Exhibition as an example of the Centennial capacity for efficient management. No private business ever had to operate in such a glare of public scrutiny. Reporters were constantly on hand, sending to their editors every fact and impression they could assemble. And when it was over, every detail of the operation was recorded in the multi-volume official report. At every stage and in every part, the Exhibition was a model of efficiency. It was proof by itself, if no other evidence had been available, that American business methodology was able to plan and execute on a large scale and without a hitch.

Commentators on the Centennial era, including reputable historians, have taken a grim pleasure in branding it the worst in our history. The statistics on business failure are often introduced as evidence that the American world of business was a kind of jungle where the stronger destroyed the weaker in a ruthless struggle for survival. In 1872, with depression just ahead, there were 4,069 business failures, and the number increased to 5,183 in 1873, 5,830 in 1874, and 7,740 in 1875. But if we resort to statistics, we should present them objectively: the *rate* of business failures means more than the actual number, and in 1876, when the depression was nearing its worst, the rate was 142 in 10,000. This means that of every 10,000 firms or individuals engaged in business, 9,858 did not go under. If business operated in what really was a "jungle" of lawless competition, those precursors of modern businessmen must have been a sturdy lot, indeed, to resist the pressures.

Most Centennial businessmen were not ruthless competitors; they didn't have to be in order to be successful. Nor were most of them in danger of being wiped out; the few real predators had specialized appetites—for railroads, mostly. If any group had reason to feel victimized or to liken the world of business to a jungle, it was the employees, whose welfare the generality of employers did not consider to be their concern. There were exceptions, of course, like the paternalism John Leng admired at the Pacific Mills in Lawrence. But advocates of an eight-hour work day were labeled radical. As for such modern phenomena as sick leave with pay, workmen's compensation, and retirement plans, nobody in 1876 went *that* far.

A few men did speak out in defense of labor, but the defense was rather feeble. Francis A. Walker, the Exhibition official who was also a professor of political economy and history at Yale, brought out in 1876 a book, *The Wages Question: A Treatise on Wages and the Wages Class*, in which he mildly challenged the notion that labor always realizes the highest wages available. But he saw no possible improvement until the workers owned the factories, and even if and when they did it would be very hard, he supposed, to find a competent managerial class. Another 1876 contribution was *The Conflict Between Labor and Capital* by Albert S. Bolles, whose major work, cited earlier, appeared in 1877. Labor and capital, Bolles asserted, were not really foes but were, instead, co-workers with identical interests and mutual dependence, and any overt friction could be remedied by patience, calm discussion, and education. As long as labor's dependence on capital was crucial, as a result of the current oversupply of workers, such statements as those of Walker and Bolles were hardly worth the paper they were printed on. No employer in 1876, not even one as liberal as Abram Hewitt, would have had the slightest doubt about his right, and his alone, to decide what wages to pay. Even so, conservative businessmen were uneasy about the ideas of Walker and Bolles.

Walker was a professor and Bolles an editor. A third author on the subject, Washington Gladden, was a clergyman. His book, *Working People and their Employers*, was more widely read in 1876 than those of the others, probably because Gladden was known for his work in slum missions and knew the workers and their problems at first hand. Disturbed by the dislocation caused by industrialization—the old story of villagers deserting their balanced way of life for the dubious benefits of factory wages—he advised the workingmen to try a little farming on the side, especially when the factories were closed. He cited the Biblical injunction that idleness is sin, but he offered no distinction, perhaps because he saw none, between the Old Testament concept of dignified self-sufficiency and the often dehumanizing conditions of factory work. Machines, indeed, he viewed not as the enemy of labor but as part of God's plan: "Mind steadily gains on muscle." Machines produce cheaper commodities for workers to buy, increase the demand for those commodities, lighten labor, and eventually raise wages.

Gladden admitted that the gains to labor lagged far behind the increase in owner wealth and, like Walker, saw no final solution "until the machines are owned, as well as operated, by the workmen." Just as slavery had been outmoded by the wage system, the wage system, he thought, would someday be replaced by worker ownership. For the present, Gladden advocated more education, improvements in the moral and mental qualities of workingmen, and a general spirit of mutual trust and brotherly cooperation. Gladden belonged to the majority of spokesmen in opposing socialism and in deploring the Working-men's Party, which was organized in 1876 and was the precursor to the Socialist Party, because its founders were mostly German immigrants who leaned heavily on the ideas of Marx and Engels and hence were considered un-American and dangerous.

Gladden later disowned *Working People and Their Employers* for the support it unintentionally gave to the conservatives. In conservative laissez-faire thinking, better wages would encourage the production of more children, and the increase in family size would lead to demands for even larger wages. Furthermore, only so much money was thought to be available for labor; any increase would upset the balance and perhaps force companies to close down. The best people rose to the top; the dregs sank to the bottom. A workman's position at the bottom was proof of his inferiority and the best reason not to raise his wages.

Men who reasoned in this way, and most businessmen did in 1876, could be expected to oppose any and every effort workingmen made to improve their economic status. The union movement was one source of alarm, but it was actually very weak. Late in 1869, in Philadelphia, nine members of a garment cutters' association organized as Assembly No. 1 of the Knights of Labor; but not until 1872 was a second assembly formed, and a power struggle between Philadelphia and Pittsburgh hurt subsequent growth. A convention held in Philadelphia on July 3, 1876, adopted an official name: National Labor League of America. The group's journal, the *National Labor Tribune*, founded in 1873, took firm positions on various subjects, but arguing for federal ownership of railroads, and for the issuance of more greenbacks to employ idle men, won little approval from the public at large. Although the *Tribune* encouraged labor support of the Greenback Party in the 1876 election, that party ignored labor—a pretty good sign of labor's weakness at the time. Only in Pennsylvania did labor give many votes to Peter Cooper, the Greenback candidate for President.[44]

The violence of a group called the Mollie Maguires in the Pennsylvania hard coal region, and their abrupt suppression in

1876, gave labor a serious setback in general public opinion. The "Mollies" were not a labor union, but people thought they were. In actuality, the "Mollies" dated back to the 1850s when recent migrants from Ireland had begun using against mine operators the same clandestine violence that had been used against landlords in Ireland. During the early 1860s, they earned growing notoriety in their resistance to the Civil War draft. Later, the violence, including numerous killings, reflected no principle except the avenging of slights to members. Arrests were almost impossible because the Mollies used a procedure that worked well for the Ku Klux Klan in the South; importing members from distant places to do the actual killings. When the anthracite miners' union finally came into being and called a strike, known as the "long strike" from December, 1874, to June, 1875, the "Mollies" turned it into a crime wave. They did not know they had been infiltrated by a detective, James McParlan, in a careful scheme worked out by the Pinkerton Agency and the Philadelphia and Reading Railroad. Using the alias McKenna, he rose within the organization to the rank of district secretary and was able to collect evidence enough for wholesale arrests in the fall of 1875, after the "long strike" failed and the union collapsed. The trials occupied several months in 1876, and the convicted leaders were hanged the next year. The Mollie Maguires were smashed, but the union movement suffered, in general thinking, from guilt by association.[45]

Thus, in 1876, labor was not even a major topic of owner-class discussion. One burning question that preoccupied all businessmen in 1876—and many other people too—had almost nothing to do with the essential nature of capitalism: what to do about the "Greenbacks?" During the Civil War both governments, federal and Confederate, printed paper money to finance their operations. After Lee's surrender the Confederate paper was totally valueless. But the federal greenbacks, with a total face value of $430,000,000, remained in circulation and were the subject of fierce debate. They were backed by the guarantee of the United States of America, but Centennial Americans, large numbers of them, could not believe that a rectangular piece of paper was real money the way silver coins were real, or copper pennies. In the West, as Emily FitzGerald reported, greenbacks were actually discounted; the prejudice was strong. The situation in general was like a game of musical chairs: nobody wanted to be the one caught with greenbacks when the music stopped.

Some groups urged immediate resumption of specie payment, while other groups, notably the Pennsylvania coal and iron interests, argued that redeemable paper money was needed to keep business expanding. Ohio Congressman James A. Garfield, writing in the *Atlantic Monthly* for February 1876, stated the solid, conservative, hard-money position; so long as paper money continued in circulation, the country's economy was artificial. In April, President Andrew D. White of Cornell read an essay, "Paper Money Influence in France," before a joint session of Congress and again at the influential Union Club in New York. It was an impressive object lesson from history but hardly parallel because the United States had not recently thrown off the incubus of an *ancien régime* which for two centuries had been systematically impoverishing the people. The *Atlantic* in March printed an answer to Garfield by Henry C. Baird, who made what should have been the obvious point that money is whatever performs the function of money and cited the British success with very little specie and large sums in credits, checks, and drafts. Opposition to paper money, Baird insisted, was sheer stupidity—as if the actual *money* itself were master instead of its users. Baird spoke for a large and strong element of the public; but when Peter Cooper, the respected New York industrialist, ran for President on the Greenback ticket in 1876, he polled only 1 percent of the vote—which may only prove that one-issue candidates get nowhere in our national elections.

It is of course not uncommon that issues seemingly crucial at the time prove, later on, to have been only tangential to the matters that really counted. If any schemer had hoped to distract the Centennial public from really important issues, or from activities that needed secrecy in order to succeed, the paper money argument would have been a masterful stroke. But a world's fair would have served about as well. Neither really touched the essence of free enterprise, Centennial vintage, but both were engrossing in their very different ways. The people had no way of knowing how much their economy would

196

change in the decades just ahead, nor could they have realized
that free enterprise as they knew it was nearing its end. The very
next year brought the system's first real challenge by labor, and
federal regulation was not much further in the future.

The vocabulary of free enterprise is still heard on many
tongues, but it is a very different kind of freedom that operates
today. Private initiative has not been destroyed: the "private
sector" is still the heart of our economy, and every year the
young face a greater range of opportunity than ever before.
What has vanished is pure laissez-faire, gone now as surely as
rural self-sufficiency. It was in its golden hour in 1876, but the
gold light comes when the sun is at the western horizon, ready to
drop from sight; and after the dark of night comes another day.

Footnotes for Chapter Four
THE AGE OF ENTERPRISE

1. Jacob Adler, *Claus Spreckels; The Sugar King of Hawaii* (Honolulu: University of Hawaii Press, 1966).

2. *Historical Statistics of the United States;* Robert G. Albion, *Sea-
   ports South of Sahara* (New York: Appleton-Century-Crofts,
   1959).

3. Francis J. Reynolds, *The United States Navy from the Revolution
   to Date* (New York: P. F. Collier & Son, 1915).

4. Allan Nevins, *Sail On: The Story of the American Merchant Ma-
   rine* (United States Lines Co., 1946) Chapter 3; Richard C. McKay,
   South Street: A Maritime History of New York (New York: G. P.
   Putnam, 1934), pp. 427–31.

5. W. J. Lewis Parker, *The Great Coal Schooners of New England
   1870–1909* (Mystic: Marine Historical Association, 1948). One
   four-master, the *Weybosset,* was originally built in 1863 but was
   rebuilt in 1879.

6. William J. Petersen, *Steamboating on the Upper Mississippi* (Iowa
   City: State Historical Society of Iowa, 1937), p. 463.

7. Jack McNairn and Jerry MacMullen, *Ships of the Redwood Coast*
   (Stanford: Stanford University Press, 1945).

8. *A Century After: Picturesque Glimpses of Philadelphia and Pennsylvania,* ed. Edward Strahan (Philadelphia: Allen, Lane & Scott,
   and J. W. Lauderbach, 1875).

9. Henry Pickering Walker, *The Wagonmasters: High Plains Freighting from the Earliest Days of the Santa Fe Trail to 1880* (Norman: University of Oklahoma Press, 1966), pp. 283–90.

10. Edward Hungerford, *Wells Fargo: Advancing the American Frontier* (New York: Random House, 1949), pp. 140 ff.

11. Oscar Osburn Winther, *The Transportation Frontier: Trans-Mississippi West, 1865–1890* (New York: Holt, Rinehart, and Winston, 1964), p. 144.

12. Alden Hatch, *American Express: A Century of Service* (Garden City, N. Y.: Doubleday, 1950).

13. *Historical Statistics of the United States.* An authoritative study of American railroad development in the period is George Rogers Taylor and Irene D. Neu, *The American Railroad Network 1861–1890* (Cambridge: Harvard University Press, 1956).

14. Facts and figures for the Centennial Exhibition are found in U. S. Centennial Commission, *International Exhibition, 1876, Reports,* 11 vols. (Washington: Government Printing Office, 1880–1884): hereafter referred to as *Exhibition Reports.* Vol. 1, "Report of the Director General," and Vol. 2, "Reports of the President, Secretary, and Executive Committee," contain most of the "housekeeping details." Vols. 3–8 are concerned with the awards; Vol. 9 is on "Grounds and Buildings;" Vols. 10–11 contain "Report of the Board on behalf of the U. S. Executive Departments."

15. Announcements about special rates and excursions, together with a great variety of incidental information about the Exhibition, appeared in all newspapers as news items or fillers; the Exhibition publicity department was clearly very efficient, and the editors were cooperative.

16. *Elmira Daily Advertiser,* Jan. 7, 1876.

17. Edward Holden, "Relative Mortality of Mariners, Railroad Men, and Travelers," *American Journal of Medical Sciences,* 71 (January, 1876), pp. 102–13.

18. Stanley Buder, *Pullman: An Experiment in Industrial Order and Community Planning 1880–1930* (New York: Oxford University Press, 1967).

19. "The Revere Tragedy," 37 (January, 1876), 92–103; "The Railroad Death Rate," 37 (Feb., 1876), 207–214; "The State and the Railroads," 37 (March, 1876), 360 ff; 37 (June, 1876), 691–699; 38 (July, 1876), pp. 72–85.

20. Edwin Palmer Hoyt, *The Vanderbilts and Their Fortunes* (Garden City: Doubleday, 1962).

21. Julius Grodinsky, *Jay Gould: His Business Career 1867–1892* (Philadelphia: University of Pennsylvania Press, 1957).

22. Hoyt, *The Vanderbilts and their Fortunes*.

23. Wayne Andrews, *The Vanderbilt Legend: The Story of the Vanderbilt Family 1794–1940* (New York: Harcourt, Brace, 1941).

24. David J. Rothman, *Politics and Power: the United States Senate 1869–1901* (Cambridge: Harvard University Press, 1966), pp. 193–94.

25. The Huntington letters to Colton and Hopkins are quoted in Rothman, *Politics and Power*, pp. 195–97.

26. San Francisco *Morning Call*, Dec. 27, 1883, quoted by Rothman, p. 197. The Senate subsequently investigated the Southern Pacific, in the 50th and 53rd Congresses.

27. Charles Frederick Carter, *When Railroads Were New* (New York: Simmons-Boardman Pub. Co., 1926); the first edition appeared in 1908.

28. Albert S. Bolles, *Industrial History of the United States*, Third edition (1881), reissued in Reprints of Economic Classics (New York: Augustus M. Kelley, 1966), p. 835.

29. *Ibid.*, pp. 847–48.

30. *Ibid.*, p. 841.

31. *Ibid.*, pp. 848–49.

32. James Blaine Walker, *The Epic of American Industry* (New York: Harper, 1949), Chapter XXX, "The Telephone."

33. *Ibid.*, Chap. XXXI, "Business Machines."

34. "American Ironmaking," *Van Nostrand's Engineering Magazine*, XV (Sept., 1876), 276.

35. Abram S. Hewitt, "A Century of Mining and Metallurgy in the United States," *Van Nostrand's Engineering Magazine*, XV (October, 1876), pp. 315–32. For Hewitt's life see Allan Nevins, *Abram S. Hewitt* (New York: Harper, 1935). Hewitt's expressed attitudes toward the "conscience of society" were rare in 1876; it would be hard to imagine such words from Andrew Carnegie, who in 1876 was becoming the nation's greatest steel maker. But as Louis M. Hacker observes in *The World of Andrew Carnegie, 1865–1901* (Philadelphia: Lippincott, 1968), Centennial business men operated in a climate of approval of the capitalistic process; and what is more, they created in one generation the greatest industrial nation the world has yet known. Edward C. Kirkland, in his *Industry Comes of Age . . . 1860–1897* (New York: Holt, Rinehart and Winston, 1961) confirms the major achievement of this generation so often (and so easily) branded as wicked and anti-social; in the preface to his *Dream and Thought in the Business Community 1860–1900* (Ithaca: Cornell University, 1956) Kirkland alludes to what is, after all, still a controversial question: whether the so-called "robber barons" deserved censure or credit.

36. Glenn D. Babcock, *History of the United States Rubber Company* (Bloomington: Bureau of Business Research, Indiana University, 1966).

37. Carroll D. Wright, *The Industrial Evolution of the United States* (Meadville: Flood and Vincent, 1895).

38. Bolles, *Industrial History*, pp. 768–80; Harold F. Williamson and Arnold R. Daum, *The Age of Illumination 1859–1899* (Evanston: Northwestern University Press, 1959).

39. John T. Flynn, *God's Gold: The Story of Rockefeller and His Times* (New York: Harcourt, Brace, 1932).

40. Allan Nevins, *John D. Rockefeller: the Heroic Age of American Enterprise*, 2 vols. (New York: Scribner's, 1940) and *Study in Power: John D. Rockefeller, Industrialist and Philanthropist*, 2 vols. (New York: Scribner's, 1953).

41. William Randel, "Walt Whitman and American Myths," *The South Atlantic Quarterly*, 59 (Winter, 1960), pp. 103–13.

42. Frances W. Gregory and Irene D. New, "The American Industrial Elite in the 1870's: Their Social Origins," in *Men in Business: Essays in the History of Entrepreneurship*, ed. William Miller (Cambridge: Harvard University Press, 1952), p. 204.

43. *Exhibition Reports*, Vol. 1.

44. Norman Ware, *The Labor Movement in the United States 1860–1895: A Study in Democracy* (New York: D. Appleton, 1929); Philip S. Foner, *History of the Labor Movement in the United States*, Vol. I (New York: International Publishers, 1947).

45. A short account of the Mollie Maguires appears in John R. Commons and associates, *History of Labor in the United States*, Vol. 2 (New York: Macmillan, 1918), pp. 181–91. A longer and more recent account is Arthur H. Lewis, *Lament for the Mollie Maguires* (New York: Harcourt, Brace & World, 1964). A fictional treatment is Conan Doyle's "Valley of Fear."

The Abuses
of Power—
A Tragedy in
Three Acts

For a good many thoughtful Americans, there was nothing golden about the year 1876, nor any glow at all unless that of the red flames of destruction. New Year's, a brief false dawn, yielded quickly to the gloom of political realities that invited despair for the nation. The nation did survive. But there is a poignant irony in the contrast between what it had been hoped the year would be, as the great Centennial of the nation's independence, and the betrayal of democratic ideals that marked its progress.

If power corrupts, it corrupts in variable fashion. The United States has no power, not even in its Presidency, to corrupt absolutely, but corruption has sometimes approached the absolute, and never more closely than in Ulysses S. Grant's final year in office. Grant himself was like a dying king in a classical drama, no more able than the audience to halt the action, yet forced to accept the role of prime villain. On December 5, 1876, his final message to Congress was an abject apology; he blamed the failures of his administration on his own inexperience but said he was guilty of "errors of judgment, not of intent." Many, knowing this, were still unable to forgive him—at least, not yet. Nor was the drama over after Grant's final message, for the last act was yet to come; the final curtain did not fall until March 5, 1877.

What follows is a selective account, not the whole sordid story; dramaturgical demands must be considered. Villains are numerous, heroes few. The nation's editors comprise a Greek chorus, or rather two choruses, Republican and Democratic. The helpless victim is the national honor. The scene, for Acts One and Two, is laid chiefly in the national capital; in Act Three it extends to include the entire nation. The time is the year 1876 as it unfolds week by week.

I

THE WHISKEY RING

Whiskey is seldom numbered among British contributions to American civilization, but there is no question about it: however we spell it—with an *e* for domestic types or without one for imports—it is chief among our alcoholic beverages. Monasteries in England first made it in the eleventh century, and by the sixteenth it was being commercially distilled. During much of America's Colonial period, rum, a distillation of molasses, was no doubt more popular, and gin, first developed in the Netherlands, became attractive as a poor man's substitute. But whiskey, whether produced by legitimate firms or illegally as moonshine, has long been the great American drink. Our thirst for the stuff seems unquenchable and the effort to avoid payment of excise taxes on it has been a virtual constant in the nation's life.

The hardy Scotch-Irish in western Pennsylvania, hostile to Alexander Hamilton's excise tax of 1791, expressed their opposition to taxation in the famous Whiskey Rebellion of 1794. A later Secretary of the Treasury, Grant's Benjamin Bristow, was to owe his position as the leading Reform candidate for President in 1876 to his effective crackdown on organized tax evasion and graft within the industry.

By the 1870s, millions of dollars that the United States Treasury should have received from the federal tax on whiskey had been systematically diverted into private pockets. Honest distillers were few enough to be exceptions proving the general rule. In an industry the size of the whiskey industry, there was big money for men at every level. Federal officials, placed in distilleries to see that tax stamps were properly affixed to every bottle, were poorly paid and susceptible to bribes; once bribed, they simply ignored the forged internal revenue stamps and issued false reports of the amount of spirits made or rectified. There were, it later developed, whiskey rings in every distilling or rectifying community in America. At a higher level, there were within the Bureau of Internal Revenue certain officials who accepted continuing retainer fees for tipping off the rings whenever an investigation was planned. At this level, it was to be discovered that the Whiskey Ring included some of President Grant's closest advisors.

Tax evasion in the whiskey industry had long been suspected, but until Benjamin Bristow entered Grant's Cabinet in mid-1874, the Treasury Department was so lax in enforcing the law, and so reluctant to investigate specific charges mentioned by the newspapers, that the criminals had become ever more brazen and grasping. Bristow, however, turned out to be rare among Grant's Cabinet members in taking his oath of office seriously. He sent secret agents to investigate the charges. Their report, however, indicated that nothing was amiss; the tip-off system had worked too well. In fact, Bristow's very efforts at first proved a bonanza for the government grafters, who used them to extort even higher blackmail from distillery owners and employees.

When sample routine checking of shipments showed clearly that more whiskey was being shipped than the tax receipts indicated, Bristow realized that his agents had been gulled. Not knowing which men in his department might be informers for the rings, he next decided to stage a widespread raid, confiding his plans only to a trusted member of his staff. The raids, on May

10, 1875, were so successful that the books of sixteen distillers and sixteen rectifiers in Milwaukee, St. Louis, and Chicago, and the records of all collectors of internal revenue, were seized and placed under seal until Secretary Bristow could examine them personally. If just one of the men assigned to this raid had tipped off the ringleaders, the entire elaborate effort might have failed. But Bristow was lucky and this time the guilty men had no chance to replace their records with falsified duplicates.

What canny journalists and the few honest men in the industry had long suspected, and had reported without the satisfaction of seeing any effective government action, proved from the confiscated papers to have been all too true.

The local ring in Milwaukee included E. W. Keyes, Wisconsin's Republican boss of patronage; and every single prominent Republican in the state of Illinois. The most flagrant thievery proved to be in St. Louis, where the Collector of Internal Revenue, General John McDonald, was both illiterate and so morally weak that Missouri Congressmen had protested his appointment. His chief qualification for office, in fact, was the friendship of President Grant himself.

The ring that McDonald organized collected at least two and a half million dollars. He developed some very interesting methods. He would tell distillers that they were guilty of minor infractions of the law and then blackmail them into partnership in the ring by giving them the choice of legal prosecution or cooperation in the graft. Honest men, guilty only because the revenue laws were extremely complicated, could thus be forced into corruption unless they preferred to retire from business. Most of them could not afford to retire. The leading Washington agents of the ring turned out to be William Avery, Chief Clerk of the United States Treasury, and Colonel Orville Babcock, Grant's confidential secretary, who had his hands in many guilty ventures but none, perhaps, more lucrative than the St. Louis whiskey ring. Rare liqueurs, valuable diamonds, free hotel rooms, and a girl known as "Sylph" to help him while away his hours in St. Louis were all subsequently reported, along with thousand-dollar bills transmitted in cigar boxes that totalled, according to McDonald's subsequent testimony, about $25,000.

So naive was Grant, and so certain that no close friend of his could do wrong, that he accepted the insinuations against Bristow that Colonel Babcock and other grafters now poured into his ears. Bristow was pictured as the darling of the reformers, ambitious for the Presidency, and acting solely to discredit the administration and Grant himself. True, Bristow did aspire to the top office, but so did many other men. In fact, it was Grant's obtuseness on questions of official morality, his habit of trusting any personal friend even after his honesty had been questioned, that may, more than any other single fact, explain the virtual collapse of his administration and its continuing reputation as the most corrupt in the nation's history.

When Secretary Bristow ordered General McDonald transferred to Philadelphia, Grant revoked the order at the urgent request of McDonald himself, who said the shift would hurt the party organization in St. Louis. Then, early in June, 1875, federal grand juries indicted about 350 distillers and officials, McDonald among them. But the trials took time, and meanwhile Colonel Babcock, the President's personal secretary, was caught in Bristow's efficient net. Telegrams in code had been widely used by the members of the ring. Several sent from Washington to McDonald, signed "Sylph," strongly suggested that Babcock was their author. A St. Louis banker, W. D. W. Barnard, sent Grant a detailed denunciation of federal agents investigating the corruption. The President, impressed, forwarded the letter to Bristow with a note on the back of one page: ". . .*Let no guilty man escape if it can be avoided.* . . . No personal consideration should stand in the way of performing a public duty." Bristow, with or without Grant's permission, made this letter, marked "Confidential," available to the newspapers.[1] The key words, "Let no guilty man escape," were to come back to haunt Grant later on. Meanwhile, he kept Babcock on, and was more receptive to his version of events than to Bristow's. Bristow, blunt and honest, was no match for Babcock in the art of adorning, inventing, and manipulating evidence. When at a Cabinet meeting in October, 1875, Bristow formally produced the "Sylph" telegrams, Grant summoned Babcock to explain and accepted what he said, that Sylph was a St. Louis woman intent on blackmailing the President.

Babcock, faced with Bristow's charges, insisted he was innocent and, as a former army officer, demanded a military trial. But when further evidence of his complicity emerged from the drawn-out McDonald trial in St. Louis, he was indicted by a grand jury in that city. Grant had already appointed a tribunal consisting of three generals—Sheridan, Terry, and Hancock—but the civil prosecutors refused to surrender the evidence to them. The day Babcock went on trial, February 8, 1876, Grant showed anger at a Cabinet meeting and said he wanted to testify in person, a procedure that Hamilton Fish, Secretary of State, most strongly opposed as being altogether improper. "The President," Fish recorded privately, had "expressed his determination to go to St. Louis, to start either this evening or tomorrow morning. . . ." One Secretary, Robeson of the Navy, at first spoke in favor, but he eventually saw the light and, faced with the unanimous disapproval of his Cabinet, Grant reluctantly abandoned the idea. He sent instead a deposition taken on February 12 by Chief Justice Waite in the presence of attorneys for both sides; it comprised a firm endorsement of Babcock's character. Largely because of this deposition, Babcock, alone of the Whiskey Ring defendants, was acquitted. He impudently showed up at the White House to resume his old position, and Grant did not dismiss him for several days, despite Secretary Fish's indignant insistence that he do so. He acceded March 1, when he named his old friend Inspector of Lighthouses.[2]

The convictions were especially significant because on January 26, 1876 Attorney-General Pierrepont, at Grant's request, issued a circular letter to all federal attorneys revoking immunity for defendants who turned state's evidence.[3] Pierrepont's action was dubious in the extreme, for the immunity clause has always been a prosecution weapon, providing for the testimony of accomplices. Grant, it seemed, had crippled the prosecution to benefit his friends; but the evidence was too strong, and too carefully prepared in Bristow's office, for the defense to override it.

When McDonald was found guilty, Grant was apparently pleased that such treachery was being punished. But when a jury convicted William McKee, owner of a Ring newspaper, the President exploded at a Cabinet session, bitterly condemning Bluford Wilson, the Treasury solicitor who had led the McKee prosecution. Bristow courageously defended Wilson, and for a long tense moment the two men, Grant and Bristow, sat grimly glaring at each other.[4]

Grant could, of course, have dismissed Bristow at any time, but he feared the public reaction that would certainly have resulted had he dropped the man now best loved by the reformers. Bristow, for his own part, would have liked to resign, but, he held on partly at the urging of Hamilton Fish within the Cabinet and Carl Schurz on the outside. On February 15 Schurz wrote to Bristow advising him to remain and make Grant responsible for his removal. It was an uncomfortable position, Schurz acknowledged, but he pointed out that the American people thought of Bristow as their representative in the present administration; to resign would be to let the people down. Bristow acknowledged the letter promptly, admitting that the situation was very hard on him.[5] He held on until the Republican convention in June before doing so.

Rings were a familiar part of political life in the 1870s. New York had two of the most notorious—the Canal Ring, involving prominent politicos in upstate counties, and the Tweed Ring in New York City, both dispersed by 1876. Corruption in public life, in fact, was pretty much taken for granted as a price that had to be paid for the democratic system. But too much was too much; there was a limit to what was tolerable, and the usually indulgent public could become very indignant when grafters exceeded that limit. The Whiskey Ring exposure came at a time when the public mood had already been strongly affected by the Canal Ring and the Tweed Ring and this new ring seemed worse than the others because it was not local but national. Worst of all, men very close to the President were implicated, so close that many people suspected Grant himself.

Voters by the thousands would have liked to see Benjamin Bristow in the White House. But in the context of political realities he had no chance at all. He was a political newcomer, without even a state governorship to his credit. True, he had a good military record, but this was a commonplace in 1876. Indeed, whatever was working for Benjamin Bristow, the fact was crystal clear that his very effectiveness in smashing the Whiskey Ring made him an enemy of the Republican leaders who held the power; he was obviously not a man who could be manipulated.

Thus, Act One in the drama of the Whiskey Ring ends with the certain public awareness of corruption at the highest level of public life. This was bad enough, but worse yet was the public awareness, confirmed at the Republican convention, that the chief reformer could not be rewarded. From the moment Grant accepted his resignation, Bristow was as dead politically as the conspirators he had sent to prison.

2

GRAFTERS IN THE CABINET

William Worth Belknap was born in Newburgh, New York, in 1829. He graduated from Princeton, studied law, and then commanded a Civil War division under General Sherman, reaching the eventual rank of major general. After the war he served as Collector of Internal Revenue for Iowa from 1865 until Grant named him Secretary of War in 1870. He was to become the arch symbol of the corruption of the Grant administration.

Belknap's appointment had been a typical Grant appointment. Never a man to concern himself about political questions or legalistic theory, Grant had hoped, as the overwhelming people's choice for President, to base his administration on the famous epigram that concluded his letter accepting the nomination: "Let us have peace." If the professional politicians could be kept at bay, he seemed to think, the country could move along peacefully, for politicians were only trouble-makers. During the four months between his election and his inauguration, he tried to avoid men who wanted Cabinet posts or had candidates to propose, and when he could not avoid them he listened non-committally. Nobody who was likely to overshadow him had a chance; anybody who was a good friend, preferably an old friend, had a definite advantage. Few of these old friends had had any prior experience in politics.

When Grant nominated him for the Cabinet in 1870, General Belknap was virtually unknown in Washington. Without a strong endorsement from General Sherman, the Senate would almost certainly have rejected him, for there was now considerable Senatorial indignation over Grant's habit of consulting nobody. But as it was the appointment went through.

Belknap, described as "a pouchy-cheeked, beetle-browed, curly-haired man with a tremendous flowing beard and the air of an unctuous politician," [6] kept out of the limelight until 1876. Early in 1872, it is true, Senators Schurz and Sumner accused him of violating the neutrality laws by selling arms to France. Schurz's chief concern was the possible bad effect of the action on the German vote in Missouri. But a committee friendly to the administration had reported no violation of either American or international law. The committee report did, however, prompt suspicion that the War Department was grossly careless, and perhaps corrupt, in handling its affairs.[7]

Grant's reelection in 1872 was as great a personal triumph as his first election had been, but in four years he had come to appreciate the importance of politicians, and in his formal acceptance letter he pledged himself to earn the approval of "the great party which elected me." [8] Such a declaration offended the Republican liberals, who read it as an endorsement of the men close to Grant who had won control of the party, and as an invitation to more brazen corruption. When Grant decided to send federal troops to Louisiana, to keep order before the election of 1874, he quite properly asked Belknap to insist that the officer in command refrain from partisan activity, but the ensuing confusion was so great that the liberals construed the troop commitment as a deliberate effort to keep Louisiana safe for the ruling clique, and to ensure a third term for Grant. A mass meeting at Boston's Faneuil Hall, on January 16, 1875, adopted a resolution condemning Secretary Belknap,[9] although it is a little hard to see how he was greatly at fault.

Whether or not Belknap acted with any awareness of abetting Grant's third-term hopes, his sudden exposure as a grafter of the first magnitude, early in March, 1874, suggests that he had been too engrossed in his own crooked affairs to give much thought to Grant. At the same time, he apparently never considered the possibility of exposure. But two years later, in 1876, the Democrats elected a majority of the House of Representatives, the first time in sixteen years that they controlled either chamber of Congress.

It was not easy to be a Democrat in Congress during the Grant period, when the Republicans could always revive the tired old charge that during the Civil War the Democrats had been the party of treason. The basis for this charge was the obvious fact that most Confederates had been Democrats, and that during the War the Democrats, as the minority party, had opposed the Republicans who were conducting the Union effort. Now, as one Southern state after another regained full sovereignty, and sent to Washington men who were both Democrats and, usually, former Confederate officers, Republican editors expressed the fear, which they may honestly have felt, that the South would gain through Congress what they had lost in battle—control of the nation. It was partly to prove their loyalty to the nation, and partly because they were hungry, after so long a period of starvation, for the sweets of political control, that the Democratic leadership of the House, when Congress organized on December 5, 1875, immediately announced a series of committee investigations of the Grant administration.

The Republican press took delight in referring to "the Confederate House" and accusing the House Democrats of partisan self-interest. But even if self-interest had been the uppermost motive, the results of the committee probings proved beyond question how very much corruption there was.

Grant was at first contemptuous of the proceedings. Having no notion of the extent of the graft, he disparaged the investigations as mere dragnets being used in the hope of finding something for partisan advantage. But like the Muckrakers in the first decade of the twentieth century, the net-draggers found plenty beneath the surface to shock the nation. The worst fears of the Liberal Republicans proved true; the wildest, least responsible Democratic editorials were shown to be valid.

One House committee, investigating the War Department,

had as its chairman, Congressman Heister Clymer of Pennsylvania, who had been Secretary Belknap's roommate at Princeton. It is easy to imagine Clymer's anguish when, on the afternoon of March 2, he interrupted a House debate on a treaty with Hawaii to ask that Belknap be impeached for high crimes and misdemeanors. It is also easy to believe the report of "great excitement and unusual stillness of the House" as the sorry tale unfolded. Clymer had with him copies of Belknap's letter of resignation. Grant's acceptance was given at 10:20 A.M. "I would not if I could," Clymer said, "and I could not in my present condition if I would afford to silence the facts just reported to the house . . . They are so plain that . . . throughout Christendom, wherever the English language is read or spoken, they will for long years constitute a record of official corruption and crimes such as there is no parallel for in our history, or in that of any other country that I know of." [10]

The story was on every front page the next morning. The banner headline had not yet been invented, but a story's importance was indicated by the number of subheads, which in this case, came halfway down the column. For the moment there was no partisan division of opinion, though in time the Republican editors rallied. The cold hard fact of the matter was the testimony given the committee by one Caleb Marsh that he had paid Secretary of War Belknap $20,000 for the post tradership at Fort Sill in the Indian Territory.

After his revelation, Caleb Marsh fled to Canada. One quick result of his flight was the establishment of a guard at Belknap's fine house on J Street to discourage any such thoughts by the Secretary and his family. The news reports continued to multiply, with hints of worse revelations to come. Soon enough, too, a body of sympathy developed. Living was costly in Washington; Cabinet members were expected to entertain with some lavishness, and Belknap's salary, $8,000, was far short of what a man in his position required. Some commented that wifely social and sartorial ambitions, as appeared to be part of the problem in this case, could wreck any man's career.[11] In general, indignation varied in proportion to individual degrees of idealism. Carl Schurz, the Republican Senator from Missouri, represented the highest degree, shared by a good many other disenchanted Republicans.

Now other men came forward with further charges against Belknap: he had pocketed $90,000 from contracts for headstones on Union graves; he had sold five other post traderships for large sums. His estimated total take now reached a million dollars.

During these proceedings, President Grant maintained his composure in front of his Cabinet. Perhaps the presence of Benjamin Bristow, by now his open enemy, deterred him. Perhaps he remembered, painfully, that his own brother Orvil had applied in 1874 for four post traderships and had been given them at once, but had never done a stroke of work for his share of the profits. If by some chance Grant had forgotten this, the Clymer committee was quick to remind him by reporting the fact on March 9.[12] But if Grant remained discreet, his wife did not. She asked the entire Cabinet to see her after one of its meetings and implored them to show sympathy for the wretched Belknap family. Hamilton Fish was shocked by this, and further shocked when he learned that three of his colleagues—Postmaster-General Jewell, Secretary of the Interior Chandler, and Secretary of the Navy George Robeson—had all called on the Belknaps; Robeson had gone twice with the excuse that he and Belknap were fellow Princetonians.[13]

The Whiskey Ring scandal had been bad enough. But because Belknap was a Cabinet member, his exposure created an even greater general sense of incredulity. One editor observed that the shock was so great "because there had been no suspicion." [14] Public opinion, always quick to shift, now suspected that the entire Cabinet was corrupt. Somebody revived an old charge against Bristow, concerning some army mules, but he was able quickly to answer it. Someone else invented corruption by Representative Clymer, a useful means of discrediting an enemy, but he too was able to clear his name. George Robeson could not; it developed later in March that he had exacted money enough from Navy contracts in four years to build up a bank account of $320,000.[15] But the wholesale suspicion of the Cabinet was not justified; Bristow and Jewell were well in the clear, and Hamilton Fish, with the longest tenure in the cabinet, was a very symbol of uncorruptibility. The triphammer exposures of specific graft, however, had the unjustified effect of totally discrediting the entire administration.

The Belknap case continued to hold the public attention, partly because it was the first in a series of Cabinet scandals but also because of a moot point of law that soon became a concern: did the Senate have jurisdiction to try Belknap for his crimes?

On the morning of March 2, Belknap, having learned what the Clymer committee had discovered about his affairs, had hurried to the White House, blurted out his wish to resign, and left with Grant's letter accepting the resignation. A reliable biographer of Grant describes Belknap as having been agitated to the point of incoherence, and Grant as having been misled into thinking that some illegal act by Mrs. Belknap had so entangled her husband that only his resignation could save her honor. After Belknap left, two Senators brought Grant a true version of the events, and Grant realized that he had been tricked; instead of shielding a lady's honor he had helped a criminal to escape.[16] Asked at a Cabinet meeting the next day why he had acted so promptly in accepting the resignation, he lamely explained that he did not realize, until later in the day, the enormity of the crime; had he known, he said, he would of course have acted differently. This unanswerable statement was possibly true, although Grant had a long record of doing all in his power to help his friends. He told his Secretaries that as a young lieutenant he had greatly admired Belknap's father, "one of the finest officers of the old army." But he then went on to say he did not know that acceptance of a resignation was not a matter of course.[17] This was either sheer stupidity or a lie that compounded his guilt in helping forestall Belknap's impeachment.

When Congressman Clymer made his dramatic announcement in the House, his colleagues promptly passed a resolution of impeachment and sent it to the Senate, where impeachment trials are conducted. For some weeks the Senate deliberated on whether or not it had jurisdiction, finally deciding, by a vote of thirty-seven to twenty-nine, that it did and on August 1, despite overwhelming evidence of his guilt, Belknap was acquitted. Almost all the twenty-five Senators voting for acquittal admitted that they voted as they did out of a sincere belief that the Senate lacked jurisdiction in the matter. Only three, at most, believed that Belknap was not guilty as charged. Belknap was not present when the vote was taken.[18]

Whether or not the trial was valid, and despite the inconclusive verdict, Belknap nevertheless stood convicted in public opinion. The other Cabinet members subsequently exposed were no less guilty, but Belknap was the first, and the impeachment trial accentuated and prolonged his notoriety. For men like Hamilton Fish, deeply concerned for the national honor, the Belknap case was the straw that broke the back of the Grant administration. But the administration itself, shattered though it was, and bereft of public confidence, had to carry on for more than six months longer—until the following March, 1877, when a new administration would take office.

The question that had troubled the Senate and that led to Belknap's acquittal has a continuing relevance. Senator Roscoe Conkling of New York, who came as close as anyone else to being Grant's spokesman, consistently opposed the trial of Belknap as an exercise in partisan politics. But another Senator, Justin Morrill of Vermont, forever honored as the author of the Land-Grant Act of 1862 in support of higher education, offered what may be the clearest opinion on the subject. Speaking of Belknap he asked, during the debate, "Can he solely by his own act defeat our jurisdiction?" He for one thought a miscreant should be tried whether or not he had resigned.

> The alternative presented looks to me far more formidable, and that is, to leave all officers of the United States at liberty to burrow in corruption, to betray the honor and the highest interests of their country, to sell justice, to accept bribes, to embezzle the public funds, and then, after destroying the records of guilt, if that be possible. . . . they can resign and defy all the remedies provided through the dead forms of impeachment. . . .
>
> The doctrine of resignation and avoidance, so far as I am able to comprehend it, fritters away all the power there is of real substance in the Constitution relating to impeachments, and, if it shall prevail, the torn shreds of that power will hang dangling in the air as a mere scarecrow, but scaring nobody.[19]

The human scarecrow, torn and dangling, should by rights have been Belknap. The acquittal must have relieved him greatly, for a guilty verdict would have meant three years' imprisonment and repayment of twice the amount he had stolen. Instead, he was free to start a new life, and he did, as an attorney in Washington. Nothing was lost but honor.

3

THE DISPUTED ELECTION

ON JUNE 25, 1876, on a Montana hillside, there was enacted in a matter of minutes the tragedy that was to be forever memorable as "Custer's Last Stand." It was the very stuff of which national legends are made. It had an elemental quality, not easily forgotten, as men in other lands and other times could not forget the final hours of Roland, or Arthur, or Leonidas. But in 1876, and in America, what happened to Custer and his troops actually meant far less than another "last stand," that of Ulysses S. Grant and his administration, which after seven fat years were now facing extinction. This drama, indeed, might fittingly be titled, "Grant's Last Stand."

The nation had first witnessed the scandal of the Whiskey Ring. Next came the exposure of corruption in the government itself. Thus the national emotions were already drained when, the day after the Presidential election in November, 1876, the result was challenged, creating a turmoil and uncertainty for the nation that was to continue for the following four months. Whether the election hassle was really worse than the exposure of the Whiskey Ring or the Belknap scandal is a bone for historians to pick over. Allan Nevins has suggested that the hardly bearable climax led people to overlook what was really worse, the collapse of the Presidency. At the time, however, no such objective judgment was possible. In the 1876 election, both parties nominated candidates pledge to reform. But the contest was fought with all the methods known to political corruption, and the final result was decided by sheer power politics.[20]

In 1872, a few Republicans were already so disenchanted with the Grant administration that they had formed a new party, the Liberal Republicans, and nominated as their candidate for President the influential newspaper editor Horace Greeley. But even though the Democrats had also named Greeley, Grant, the nominee of the regular Republicans, had won his second term handily —such is the political magic of a great general's name. By 1876, the same group of reformers had even more reason to be disenchanted with "Grantism." Some of them became independents. Others deserted to the Democratic Party; one of these, Charles Francis Adams, taking the extreme step of accepting the Democratic nomination for governor of Massachusetts. Still others organized a pressure group to persuade the Republicans not to name a Grantist candidate. The moving spirit behind this group was Senator Carl Schurz.

Carl Schurz was one of the few public figures of the time who was not native-born of old stock. At the age of nineteen, in his native Germany, Schurz had taken part in the abortive revolution of 1848. Reaching the United States in 1852, he plunged at once into the anti-slavery movement. After serving in the Civil War he tried his hand at journalism, first as correspondent for Greeley's New York *Tribune*, and later as editor of newspapers in Detroit and St. Louis. Elected to the Senate from Missouri, for the term 1869–75, Schurz at first supported Grant, but he gradually shifted to an independent position as he learned more and more unsavory facts about the administration. As a former Senator in 1876 he was in an ideal position to exercise his independence. "It is painfully apparent to every candid man," he wrote to an acquaintance the day after the Belknap scandal broke, "that the machinery of the Government is fairly honeycombed with corruption. The Republic stands before the world in an attitude of unprecedented humiliation and shame." [21] On April 6, 1876, he released to the press a circular letter, signed also by the noted poet, critic, and editor, William Cullen Bryant and three other liberal Republicans, announcing a conference at the Fifth Avenue Hotel in New York to consider what might be done to secure the election of an honest President.

Nothing was said in this letter about the possibility of a third-party candidate; from the very outset the liberals had decided not to repeat their 1872 maneuver in this respect. Schurz confided to Secretary of the Treasury Bristow his opinion that the Republicans would nominate a reform candidate only if they saw that the alternative was defeat,[22] and it was the major purpose of the conference to persuade the party leaders that defeat was indeed the alternative. "To this," Schurz wrote to a Michigan editor, "only those Republicans will object who desire to continue the existing abuses of party government and who will find us a stumbling block in their way." [23]

There were various negative reactions to the conference. One editor called it "a sort of gunpowder plot"; another pronounced its members "reckless idealists," as if "practical politicians" were obviously and always more reliable. One state governor observed that "honest government can be laughed down as 'barren ideality.' " If so, Schurz felt, "we may tremble for the future of the Republic." [24]

The conference met again in mid-May and drafted an "Address to the American People." In this Centennial year, the "Address" began, "memories of our past history are rising up before us in a new glow of life, forcing upon us comparison of what the Republic once was, what it was intended to be and what it is . . . Never was there cause for keener mortification, and keenly does it strike every patriotic heart. How can we avert such dangers and wipe off such shame?" Simple honest integrity was not enough. The next President must have the courage and the will to weed out evils and replace spoilsmen by honest, able officials. "Our generation has to open the second century of our National Life, as the Fathers opened the first. Theirs was the work of independence, ours is the work of reformation." [25]

What Schurz and his Conference provided was a spearhead for the growing revolt. William Cullen Bryant had been one of the founders of the Republican party in 1854. He now wrote to a British friend that significant differences no longer separated the two parties: both included all opinions, and both were corrupt.[26] John Hay, Lincoln's secretary and eventual biographer, had said in 1875 that "there is really no Democratic or Republican Party left, and a man can with perfect consistency favor the one in one State, the other in another." [27] William Howard Taft, the most prominent sophomore at Yale, and in time the twenty-sixth President of the United States, wrote his family that Blaine and Conkling, the leading Republican contenders, "smell too much of rings"; [28] and later in the year he gave a campus oration on the vitality of the Democratic party, somewhat embarrassing, it may be supposed, to his father Alphonso, Grant's final Secretary of War.

Grant would have liked a third term, and his supporters, the Radical Republicans, hoped he would get one. In December, 1875, the House of Representatives passed a resolution opposing third terms by the overwhelming vote of 233–18, and in the next few months several other resolutions of like nature were debated though not brought to vote. But their hopes were forever buried by the triphammer exposures of corruption in the Cabinet. By May, 1876, Grant saw that he was through. A new item on the twenty-third, that he was planning a trip around the world after his term ended,[29] removed the last fear—or hope—that he might run again. He now let it be known that he favored Roscoe Conkling, the Senator from New York, and the state's Republican boss, as the Republican candidate for the Presidency.

The Republican organization of New York had no doubts at all about Conkling's chances. Andrew D. White, the founder and first president of Cornell University, said in public that Conkling would not win, only to draw a rebuke from the state Republican leader: "I do not believe that he *can* be beaten." [30] The state convention endorsed him as a man "steadfast to equal rights and financial honesty, and the unflinching exponent of Republican principles." [31] At the national convention all but one of the seventy New York delegates voted for Conkling; the maverick was George W. Curtis, editor of *Harper's Weekly*, who seconded the nomination of Benjamin Bristow of Kentucky.

The front Republican runner, however, was not Conkling but Congressman James G. Blaine of Maine. He too was a Radical, but of a different faction of the party. Originally both factions had been in agreement, especially in their punitive attitude toward the former Confederates. They had also agreed in their permissive attitude toward business and the industrial barons.[32] But they had split on the question of who should control the handing out of political plums; and the "Stalwarts," Conkling's faction who were mostly members of the Senate, had gradually gained the upper hand.

Blaine's faction, called the "Half-Breeds," were more often Congressmen than Senators. In general they took their duties as representatives of the people more seriously than the Stalwarts, and the exposures of 1876 shocked some of them, at least, into a higher level of patriotism. Of all the Half-Breeds, however, only Blaine closely approached the Stalwarts in arrogance and in his individual corrupt behavior.

James G. Blaine was supporting only one man for the Presidency—James G. Blaine. In the early months of 1876, he drew attention to himself, again and again, by insulting his Democratic colleagues in the House. It may be doubted whether any other Congressman has ever exceeded Blaine in sheer boorishness. He made political capital of the fact that the public viewed him as the chief enemy of the Stalwarts, a reputation he had won quite easily by calling Senator Conkling a "turkey gobbler."

When the Republican delegates met in Cincinnati for their convention on June 14, 1876, in typical convention weather— unseasonably hot, Robert Ingersoll, the "great agnostic," nominated Blaine in one of the most famous nominating speeches in history. The climax of his colorful verbiage came when he compared Blaine to a knight of old: "Like an armed warrior, like a plumed knight, James G. Blaine marched down the halls of the American Congress and threw his shining lance full and fair against the brazen foreheads of the defamers of his country and maligners of his honor." [33] The *New York Times*, for one, was not impressed. The editor wrote that "if Blaine is nominated, let us find some handy potter's field to bury the Republican party with such honors as we can." [34] Edwin Godkin, the idealistic Irish-born editor of *The Nation*, noted aciduously: "Blaine I have watched in the House, and he cuts a very poor picture, shows a feminine waspishness, and screams over every trifle that comes up." [35] Petulant, often ridiculous, and obviously insincere is how Blaine may have seemed to shrewd observers, but less discriminating voters admired him as a consummate actor.

For any other man than Blaine, perhaps, the setback that came in April would have ruined his popular standing. Two newspapers in Indianapolis, the *Sentinel* on the eleventh, the *Evening News* on the twenty-first, accused him of profiting from a deal with the Union Pacific Railroad.[36] Actually, it turned out to be another railroad—the Little Rock and Fort Smith. But investigators unearthed commissions totalling $157,000 paid to Blaine in 1871 when he was serving as Speaker of the House. On June 1, 1876, one James Mulligan of Boston testified that Blaine, on hands and knees, had begged him not to ruin him, had spoken piteously of Mrs. Blaine and the six Blaine children, and had promised him a consulship as a reward for silence. Then, when Mulligan softened, Blaine had taken the damaging letters and had refused to return them. Mulligan's testimony was given to the investigating committee on a Thursday, and the normal procedure would have been to hear Blaine's answer the following day. But Blaine kept the committee waiting until two o'clock that day, and when he finally arrived, he declined to yield the letters. Over the weekend he now had time to plan his strategy, which provided, on Monday and Tuesday, an amazing exhibition. He read from the letters, explaining some passages, obviously omitting others, using every trick in his well-developed repertory to confuse and mislead his opponents. One of them, Proctor Knott of Kentucky, chairman of the Judiciary Committee, became so indignant that at the close of the session he said to Frye of Maine, "Mr. Frye, your friend Blaine is the G-d d---dest scoundrel in America!" Frye replied, "You forget yourself, Mr. Knott," and Knott apologized.[37] We are left wondering how many Americans, reading the accounts of the incident, agreed with this appraisal made in anger and how many were actually delighted by Blaine's play-acting.[38]

With the nominating convention only a week away, Blaine now turned to stalling the hearings. On Sunday, June 12, he fainted at church and was unconscious for five hours. It was a welcome reprieve, for now he could legitimately request a postponement of the hearings until after the convention. But on the other hand his sudden ailment raised the question of whether he was physically well enough to carry the burden of the Presidency.

In the early hours of the Republican national convention, on June 14, George W. Curtis asked permission to read the "Address to the American People." [39] Somebody objected to the reading, but the convention shouted down the objection and heard the statement, which censured Grantist corruption and called for reformation throughout the government.

The convention now turned to consideration of the candidates. After Blaine and Conkling, the third strongest candidate was Benjamin Bristow, the choice of the militant reformers. Also put in nomination were Governor Hartranft of Pennsylvania, Governor Rutherford B. Hayes of Ohio, Senator Morton of Indiana, and Marshall Jewell, the Postmaster-General. On the first seven ballots, Bristow was either second or third. On the dramatic seventh ballot, which looked at first like a Blaine landslide, Indiana withdrew her favorite son, Senator Morton, and divided, twenty-five to five between Hayes and Bristow. Kentucky, fearing Blaine and realizing that Bristow had little chance, switched unanimously to Hayes, and so did most of the remaining delegations. The Stalwarts did not want Blaine, the reformers wanted Bristow and could brook neither Blaine nor Conkling. And so the nomination went to a political dark horse: Rutherford B. Hayes.

The term "dark horse" may be a misleading one to apply to Hayes. For one thing, he had known that his election as Governor of Ohio had made him a Presidential possibility. "He desired the nomination, and sought it," but accepted a friend's advice to remain passive. In November, 1875, Chief Justice Waite had bracketed him with Bristow "on the upper rungs of the ladder" and Hayes had tried to get on record the fact that he supported Bristow, knowing this would boost his own chances. For he was aware that he alone of all the contenders was not hated by the followers of other candidates.

As for positive action, Hayes had encouraged a friend, William Henry Smith, to help locate the Mulligan letters that had put Blaine on the defensive.[40] But the term "dark horse" can be used with regard to Hayes in the sense that he had never been in the national limelight. A good many Republicans felt that the convention had chosen a loser.

"The nomination of Hayes," the Auburn *News* said editorially, "falls like a wet blanket on the party." [41] At best a compromise candidate, Rutherford Birchard Hayes, former Congressman and currently in his third term as governor of Ohio, had few of the external qualities that could rouse popular enthusiasm. Two uncles, it was reported, had left him bequests totalling more than half a million dollars; [42] he could therefore be assumed to be above the gross temptations of graft, which was something.

When the campaign began, Senator Conkling made a single campaign speech for the slate, in Utica on October 3. His biographer reports that after that he was taken ill and spent seven weeks in a darkened room, unable to speak and too proud to explain what looked to the public like indifference. [43] Radicals in general swallowed their disappointment and worked, but more for the party than for Hayes. The Liberals were more-or-less satisfied; their only fear was that Hayes was not strong enough to lead the work of reform.

The Democratic convention took place in St. Louis on June 27–28. There were only two ballots. The first permitted the usual gestures toward favorite sons—two Senators, a general, and Governor Hendricks of Indiana. Above all other candidates loomed the figure of Samuel Jones Tilden, Governor of New York. Hendricks, a Western soft-money man, was nominated for vice-president by acclamation. The one excitement of the convention was a speech by John Kelly, a Tammany leader, strongly opposing Tilden; but everyone except a few purblind Republican editors knew how little love was lost between Tilden and the dominant group in Tammany.

If Hayes was an obscure figure, nominated virtually by default, a man of unknown capacity for leading political reform, Samuel Tilden was his complete opposite. He had many qualities that would have made for a strong candidate in any election. A highly successful lawyer in New York, he embodied a conservative soundness which stilled any fears that a Democratic victory would mean rule by irresponsibles. He was a rich man and a friend of rich men, and a firm believer in hard money. His political prominence had begun in the course of his active support of Martin Van Buren, President from 1837 to 1841. During the Civil War he was a sharp critic of federal financing. Elected state Democratic chairman in 1866, he became prominent as the man who broke the Tweed Ring, and as Governor, 1874–76, he had dispersed the Canal Ring as well, and sending several important politicians to prison.

The cold logic that contributed much to Tilden's success was a distinct asset, but his lack of warmth was also a liability. When the state Democratic convention at Utica endorsed him for President, there was little applause; he was simply the logical choice. But people who could not like him trusted his honesty, his acumen, his courage in the cause of political reform. He had enemies, of course. William C. Whitney, New York's Corporation Counsel, felt that Tilden was not a reformer at all, but a scheming politician who took the credit for what other men did.[44] The Tammany sachems could never forgive him, and fought him every inch of the road. Some people were suspicious of his wealth; the Richmond *Dispatch* called him "the candidate of a club of New York swallow-tails." [45]

Everyone had known for some time that Tilden would be the Democratic candidate, but only after his actual nomination did the full-scale partisan attack begin. He was accused of using an obsolete portrait, one that did not show the paralyzed lid of his left eye. The rumor was kept alive that he was in poor health, a part truth, for he was far from robust and had never married for just this reason. But, as his subordinates knew too well, he overworked himself and expected others to do the same. His bachelor status made him the natural butt for many rough quips. One editor, taking cognizance of the several rumors of brides, supposed that he would have to join the Mormons. He drove a spirited pair of horses; he was accused of reckless driving. He served good whiskey to his guests; this made him a heavy drinker. (Hayes, rather a puritan, was a teetotaler.)

More serious were accusations about Tilden's financial dealings. The Utica *Herald* early in July remarked that "the whole history of Tilden's business life bears the indelible imprint of fraud. His political career is of the same piece." And it became a kind of game among his opponents to think up fitting nicknames: Soapy Sam, Slippery Sammy, Ananias Tilden.

A bonanza to the opposition was a lawsuit filed with embarrassing timeliness by the Terre Haute, Alton, and St. Louis Railroad. Reviewing it editorially under the heading "Tilden's

Millions," the *New York Times* (the bitterest Tilden-hater in the business) called him on August 11 "a shrewd, cunning, tricky railroad lawyer." A sworn affidavit filed in the case gave Tilden's 1862 fee from the railroad as $10,000, although in his tax return for that year he had sworn to a total income, from all sources, of only $7,118. He had explained the discrepancy by saying he had given large sums to his brothers that year, but the Republican editors insisted that income is income, whatever one does with the money, and gleefully used the device, day after day, of printing in parallel columns the texts of the affidavit and the tax declaration.

On September 3, however, the device lost some of its sharpness when the Toledo Sunday *Democrat* printed a detailed accounting of *Hayes's* local tax declarations for 1874 and 1876. Hayes had neglected to mention a fund of $50,000, which was his to hold for three years, several mortgages, and his piano, the pride of the neighborhood. In the long run such charges, on either side, were not very effective, for two reasons: tax evasion was almost respectable in those days, and both Tilden and Hayes were generally accepted as men of honor.

The campaign was waged not by party against party or Hayes against Tilden but by Tilden against a handful of Republican leaders. Abram S. Hewitt, Peter Cooper's son-in-law, who was the new chairman of the Democratic National Committee, was ostensibly Tilden's campaign manager, but it was Tilden himself who planned the strategy, supervised the activities, and provided most of the cash for the campaign. State by state the organization was almost perfect. A "Literary Bureau" and a "Speakers' Bureau" ground out printed and verbal statements; a "Correspondence Bureau" kept in touch with party workers. Tilden depended more on ideas than on money, and with his habitual parsimony kept the expenses down, although Republicans conjured up visions of barrels of money being sent to certain states. It was easy for Republican editors to point to identical editorials in pro-Tilden papers and to ridicule the word-mill that supplied the copy. But it was good copy, well written, which soundly reviewed the record of Grantist corruption and the failure of the Republican program for Reconstruction in the South.

The Republican offensive, directed by the national chairman

Zach Chandler, was less effective. For one thing, it persisted in linking Tilden with Tweed and Tammany, an absurd exercise in light of Tilden's reform activities. Tilden was a Tammany member and a one-time sachem; but this did not make him a crony of Tweed, or of John C. Kelly, who bitterly opposed the Tilden nomination. With better logic the Republicans reminded voters of the Democratic war record in opposition to Lincoln. Perhaps the best point made was the peculiar split in the Democratic team: Tilden for hard money, Hendricks for soft. But sound reasoning of one paragraph might be abandoned in the next for such dubious arguments as that since the Confederates were Democrats, all Democrats must be disloyal, Tilden among them.

However effective this latter gambit may have been in the 1876 election, its chief result was a damaging legacy to the Republican future. The charge rankled in every Democratic heart, but whereas Northern Democrats might soon forget it, the effect on Southern thinking was permanent. Coming as it did on top of Reconstruction and what most Southern Whites viewed as prolonged vengefulness, it served to cement what was called in that campaign first "*a* solid South" and, quickly enough, "*the* solid South." Early in October, for example, the *New York Tribune* began a lengthy editorial by asking "A solid South— what does it mean? Why does it alarm all thoughtful men?" A few days later Bristow attempted an answer: "Now, what does this solid South mean? I insist, my fellow citizens, that it portends mischief for the country." [46] The South was not yet as "solid" as it later became, but only because the process of re-establishing firm local control was not yet quite complete.

Rutherford Hayes was in a frustrating position, pledged to rout the corruption of just such men as were conducting the campaign to elect him. His self-estimate was humble. He knew he was no great leader, and he was not optimistic about his chances of election. Perhaps his greatest virtue was listening to the right people. The man he most heeded in 1876 was Carl Schurz, who was not reticent in offering advice. On June 21, only six days after Hayes was nominated, Schurz wrote him a long letter. The issue was highly uncertain, he insisted, if the Republican party depended on its record. In his acceptance letter, Hayes should give his own interpretation of the platform's reform plank and of his duties if elected. Above all, Hayes should make this *his* campaign and, by relieving it of the party's recent record, make it "a campaign worthy of this centennial year." Two days later Schurz reiterated the importance of a broad, bold, determined purpose; "Only the strongest personal assurances of reform will keep [many voters] from looking for a change through a temporary success of the opposite party." [47]

William Dean Howells, an old hand at campaign biographies, ground out a campaign life of Hayes, one of three to appear. Howells wrote to Mark Twain on August 5, tongue-in-cheek, "You know I wrote the Life of Lincoln that elected him." Hayes was Howells' wife's cousin, "and *she* thinks that anyone who votes for Tilden will go to the Bad Place." Twain promised to read the biography but said he was convinced already by the acceptance letter—especially by Hayes's promise to serve only one term. "If Tilden is elected," Twain wrote, "I think the entire country will go pretty straight to Mrs. Howells' bad place." He was quite confident: "Don't you worry about Hayes," he wrote on October 11. "He is as bound to go to the White House as Tilden is to go to the devil when the last trump blows." But he hoped the victory would be sweeping.[48]

Howells wrote the campaign biography in twenty-two days, reading for it as he wrote, and he had no reason to be chagrined at its poor sale—about three thousand copies. He urged Twain to speak out, but Twain was fearful that as a humorist he might do more harm than good—and he may have been right. He agreed to introduce General Hawley at a Hartford Republican rally on September 30 but spoke a little too frankly about Grantism. "We will not hire a blacksmith who never lifted a sledge [or] a teacher who does not know the alphabet . . . we even require a plumber to know something about his business, that he shall at least know which side of a pipe is the inside [yet] we put the vast business of the custom house in the hands of a flathead who does not know a bill of lading from a transit of Venus—never having heard of either of them before." Consuls were appointed "who speak no language but their own" and speak that ungrammatically.

Howells called Twain's speech "civil service reform in a nut-shell," but the Boston *Transcript* said of Twain that "somebody should have led him off the platform by the ear." In reporting the speech, however, the *New York Times* said it was followed by great and prolonged applause, and the Elmira *Daily Advertiser* reprinted it with a favorable comment.[49]

Party regulars might be incensed by Twain's humor, but the recent scandals had alerted the better elements within the party, if not the public at large, to every action by the Grantists and Grant himself. On July 14 Grant removed Postmaster-General Jewell, an honest official, for no other apparent reason than that his replacement, James Tyner, would enhance Republican chances in Indiana. Soon after, Bluford Wilson, former Solicitor of the Treasury, confirmed Grant's undue influence in securing the acquittal of Babcock. "And this is the Administration," said the Democratic Auburn *News*, "endorsed by the Cincinnati convention and Governor Hayes! What do honest Republicans think of it?" [50] Next came Belknap's acquittal by the Senate on August 1, and Grant's too-prompt acceptance of his resignation.

The final month of the campaign was focused on Southern war claims. The Republicans asserted that a Democratic victory would loose a flood of claims for indemnity that would cost the taxpayers millions, perhaps billions of dollars. Tilden in reply wrote a masterly letter, widely circulated in the press, discounting the likelihood of any overwhelming increase in payments and noting that a great deal of money had already been paid out under Grant's administration. An enterprising Democratic editor, moreover, revealed the existence of thirteen Northern war claims, ranging from $3,395 to $270,000.[51]

Now finally it was Tuesday, November 7, Election Day. The election itself was orderly. In New York, rain fell from lowering skies. Tilden, dressed in black with a red lapel flower, received guests at his home in Gramercy Park. Outside, despite the rain, a crowd gathered.[52] As the day progressed, Tilden's private telegraph wire brought increasingly good news. The next morning it appeared that he had won.

The doubtful states—New York, New Jersey, Connecticut, and Indiana—had all gone Democratic. Though the returns were not yet in from Oregon, Florida, Louisiana, and South Carolina, Tilden already had 184 electoral votes, just one short of a majority. Hayes, in Cincinnati, was in fact certain that he had lost. To suppose that he could secure all twenty-two of the doubtful votes seemed almost insane, and in a special dispatch to the New York *World* he was quoted as saying, "I think we are defeated, I am of the opinion that the Democrats have carried the country, and elected Tilden." Most newspapers agreed. The Chicago *Tribune*, the leading Republican newspaper of the Middlewest, editorialized mournfully: "The true cause of the terrible defeat we have experienced was 'Grantism.' Republicans by the thousands voted for Tilden because they were sick and tired of the corruption and jobbery which have found countenance in Washington under Grant's administration."

But the election, in fact, was by no means settled. It was not to be settled for four agonizing months. In its Thursday morning edition, the *New York Times* carefully tabulated the state returns and asserted: "This leaves Florida alone in doubt. If the Republicans have carried that state, as they claim, they will have 185 votes—a majority of one."

Late on election night John C. Reid, the *Times*' news editor, had received a note from Democratic headquarters asking the outcome in the three Southern states and Oregon. If the Democratic leaders were in doubt, Reid wondered, why should the Republicans give up? He hurried to Republican headquarters in the Fifth Avenue Hotel. No one was there, but on the street he met William Chandler, the one-time railroad lobbyist, now a Republican committeeman. They tried to rout out Zach Chandler, the Republican National Chairman. Too exhausted to join them, he authorized them to act in his name. What they did was to send telegrams to Governor Chamberlain of South Carolina, S. B. Conover in Tallahassee, and S. B. Packard, the Republican candidate for governor of Louisiana. All three telegrams were no doubt the same as the one sent to Louisiana:

> Hayes is elected if we have carried South Carolina, Florida, and Louisiana. Can you hold your state? Answer immediately.

Some hours later, refreshed by a little sleep, Zach Chandler sent other telegrams, including this one to Florida's Governor Stearns:

> Florida must be made Republican. Troops and money will be furnished.

The Tallahassee telegraph operator, obviously a Democrat, released the text to Democratic editors (and lost his job for doing so). Chandler did not wait for replies but later in the day issued his famous statement, "Hayes has 185 votes and is elected." From this bold assertion the Republican National Chairman never wavered.

A comparison of newspaper reports on Wednesday and Thursday shows the change in mood that Chandler's claim produced. On Wednesday the Indianapolis *Journal*, a staunch Republican organ, conceded defeat: "Tilden is elected. The announcement will carry pain to every loyal heart in the nation, but the inevitable truth may as well be stated." On Thursday, however, a headline proclaimed "A Change," and an editorial pictured the Republicans emerging "from the valley and the shadow of dark despair into the sunshine of hope. . . ."

Mark Twain, as a Hayes supporter, responded to the changing news in his own way, in two telegrams to William Dean Howells. The first, on Wednesday, slightly reworded a hymn: "I love to steal awhile away from every cumbering care and while returns come in today lift up my voice & swear." The second, the next day, was simply the doxology with the added words, "The congregation will rise & sing." [53]

Both parties at once sent "observers" to the three Southern states, ostensibly to see that the opponents committed no fraud in counting the returns but also to influence the results by any means they could command. On Friday, November 10, the day he closed the Centennial Exhibition, Grant issued an order, reproduced in virtually every newspaper, directing General Sherman to "preserve peace and order" in the state canvasses by adequate military supervision. Most of the Republican "observers" were sent at government expense; the Democrats had to pay their own way.

The procedural details of counting the vote show how little the "observers" could do. The commissioners in each county appointed three inspectors per polling place, who were required to count the votes and send certificates of the result to the clerk of the circuit court and the county judge. These two officials, together with a justice of the peace, were to canvass the county returns within six days, record the result in a book kept by the clerk, and send duplicate certificates to the governor and the secretary of state. Within thirty-five days after the election the final accounting was to be made by the board of state canvassers. If men actively sought to influence the returns, there were therefore three levels to consider: the individual polling places, the county canvass, and the final state canvass.

Most of the tampering, as a subsequent Congressional investigation showed, was at the precinct and county levels. The Democrats, eager to regain the control of their states that Reconstruction policies had forcibly taken from them, and sincere in believing that Negroes were inferior beings who should not vote, had felt justified in using intimidation on Election Day itself. If threats of economic reprisals were not enough, groups of armed whites near the polls, and rumors that the Ku Klux Klan would ride again, discouraged all but the bravest Negroes from voting. Some Republican intimidation of Democratic Negro voters was also reported. If a Negro ignored the threats, he might then be told when he reached the polls that his registration was irregular or had expired, or he might be duped into putting his X in the wrong column. It was found that one enterprising official had actually exchanged party symbols in order to beguile the illiterate.

The most effective measures, however, were taken after the polls had closed. The three local inspectors at each voting place could readily certify a false return, and the county canvass could yield a false report. Which direction the manipulation went depended on whether the county had Republican or Democratic officials. Sometimes even that didn't matter, because a secret midnight visit to the courthouse could alter the certified count, or could insert evidence of irregularity that would justify the State Canvassing Board in rejecting the vote of certain precincts, or even of entire counties. The total vote of Manatee County, Florida, ten to one for Tilden, was rejected because of an "entire absence of any and all legal steps in preparation for the election and in holding same." The Democrats in this case strongly suspected that the county's Republican officials had deliberately disregarded the election laws in the hope of just such a rejection. But even a single violation could be taken as reason enough to void a return: Precinct No. 3 in Key West favored Tilden by

401 votes to 59, but the vote was thrown out because the precinct tellers did not complete the count until after an adjournment. Thus one dishonest partisan at the next higher level could set the efforts of honest officials at naught.

The state canvassing board in Florida had a Republican majority which could and did make partisan decisions. The one Democratic member of the board, Attorney-General Cocke, took repeated exception to the board's decisions but was overruled by his two Republican colleagues. After seven public sessions, at which, under the eyes of the party "observers," they examined affidavits and listened to oral arguments, the board met in private for the final canvass on December 5. Only twenty-six county returns went unchanged. The state return as submitted by the board gave Hayes 24,337, Tilden 24,292—a majority of just 45. General Barber, a Republican observer sent by Grant, honestly attempting to do a fair job, concluded that Tilden should have won and urged one of the Republican members of the board to concede the point; but he, too, failed.

Subsequently, the Tilden electors sent their own return, and in January a new board of Canvassers sent a *third* return to Washington.[54]

The Florida manipulation was sordid enough, but it was mild compared with what occurred in Louisiana and South Carolina, the two other Southern states still under federal, i.e., Republican, control. Some Democratic editors in the North wrote darkly of the possibility of Southern violence if Tilden were not inaugurated, and the phrase "Tilden or blood" gained such currency that the *New York Herald*, a Tilden organ, thought it wise to caution the nation's Democrats to avoid responsibility for a second civil struggle. The New York *Sun* took the same tack. The favorite Republican gambit of reminding the country that Democrats had started the Civil War made Democratic leaders sensitive to the possibility of being newly blamed for disorder. Of all the Democratic leaders, moreover, Tilden was perhaps the most sensitive to this charge, and his lack of aggressiveness in the course of the dispute alienated some of his supporters. "It will come out all right," he said in an interview widely quoted. "Our people may run to extremes for a time in moments of excitement, but they are always right in the end and you may rest assured that they will never sustain any such attempt as is now being made to destroy the republic." Tilden appeared to prefer defeat to a victory based on the same kind of tactics that were used to defeat him.

The state of Louisiana had been close to anarchy since 1866. Pre-election disorders in 1872 had killed or injured more than two thousand people. The current Republican governor, William P. Kellogg, was particularly resented by the Democrats, who could not forget that he had been elected with the aid of a federal judge's "midnight restraining order" and had assumed office behind rows of federal bayonets. The 1876 state canvassing board had four Republican members, all of them obnoxious to the Democrats.

The subsequent Congressional investigation of the election revealed every conceivable irregularity in Louisiana before, during, and after the election. About eight thousand more Negroes (i.e., Republicans) were registered in the 1876 election than were counted, four years later, in the 1880 census. One effective device was sending out "sewing machine circulars"; the name of any registered white man (i.e., Democrat) reported by the mail carriers not to be at his given address was stricken from the list of eligible voters. Then, after the election, the returns were delivered in person instead of by mail as the law required. Despite all this Republican maneuvering, the vote as cast gave the lowest Tilden elector some seven thousand more votes than the highest Hayes elector. Yet the state board juggled the returns until they showed a majority for Hayes.

With even an inkling of these wholesale illegalities, the electoral counters in Washington should by rights have rejected the entire Louisiana return. They must have chosen to ignore the fairly well-substantiated report that the chairman of the Louisiana board had tried to sell the election, first to the Republicans and later to the Democrats, for a cool million dollars. When the first offer failed, they had made a second one for $200,000. Tilden also reportedly turned down a similar offer from South Carolina for $80,000. Even if he had been willing to engage in so noisome a bargain, men so dishonest could hardly have been relied on to carry out their part of the agreement. It may have been a comfort to Tilden when, in 1877, the Louisiana board members were all indicted for fraud. But there is no evidence that Hayes, the victor through their fraud, ever offered to surrender the Presidency to Tilden.

In South Carolina, after a summer marked by bloodshed in three riots, the state canvassing board, even while the Northern "observers" looked on, voided several thousand Democratic votes and announced the electoral count for Hayes. Again, the Democrats submitted an alternate result. More than a month after Hayes was inaugurated, a special Congressional investigation unseated Chamberlain and declared Wade Hampton governor; but it was too late to reject the state's vote for Hayes, which would seem to have been an obvious parallel. There was, quite clearly, so much satisfaction among Southern whites over regaining control that they weren't overly distressed by the national result.

The dual reports sent from Oregon were the result of a local struggle for control. One report gave Oregon's three votes to Hayes, the other gave two to Hayes and one to Tilden.

By prescription spelled out in Article II of the Constitution, and in the Twelfth Amendment adopted after the tie vote of 1800, the electors in each state meet on a date fixed by Congress, cast their vote, and send it properly certified to the President of the Senate (the Vice-President), who, in the presence of both houses, opens the returns, counts the votes, and announces the result. Now confronting acting Vice-President Ferry were multiple returns from Louisiana, Florida, South Carolina, and Oregon. Instead of simply confirming facts long known to everybody, Congress in 1876 had to determine what the facts were. There was no precedent for this situation. A special procedure had to be devised, and it had to be devised by men all of whom were partisan. Sanguine historians point with satisfaction to the handling of the disputed election as an instance of the ability of Americans, at a time of such great stress, to resolve the issue peaceably. The more cynical view it as a ruthless exhibit of the workings of political machinery, with the issue never really in doubt.

Almost at once after convening on December 5, both houses of Congress established committees to investigate the election. The eventual result was testimony totaling thirteen thousand

pages, of interest to historians but with no bearing on the outcome. Since the House of Representatives had a Democratic
majority, the majority reports of its investigating committee
favored Tilden in the doubtful states, and the minority reports
favored Hayes. The reverse was true in the Senate, with its
Republican majority. Meanwhile, the daily sessions of both
houses were dominated by the debate, but neither side could
budge the other from its position. Outside of Congress, the
election had been the dominant topic in newspapers and in
conversation ever since Election Day. There was talk of im-
peaching President Grant for his part in controlling the Southern elections. This possibility was even discussed in the House,
but Southern Democrats, fearful of violence and possible war,
were strongly opposed. Rumors spread that the Southern rifle
clubs were preparing to help inaugurate Tilden, and in eleven
states, mostly midwestern, Tilden Minute Men were actually
enrolled, through the Democratic Veteran Soldiers Association.
As if verbal claims had some magical value, Hayes asserted on
December 12, "I fully expect to be inaugurated," and the next
day the Democratic chairman Hewitt "announced" the election
of Tilden.

Out of the wrangling in Congress, several concrete proposals
emerged. The most significant was a House resolution proposing
a House committee to join with a Senate committee in drawing
up a plan. Tilden opposed this move as a surrender, and the
Democrats held several caucuses early in January and passed
warlike resolutions that threatened to kill the spirit of compromise. But the Senate finally passed a similar bill.

Now the joint committees, meeting in secret, drew gradually
nearer a practical plan. On January 10 a bill was finally offered
suggesting the establishment of a fifteen-member Electoral Commission, with five men each from the House, the Senate, and the
Supreme Court. The bill passed the House on the twenty-fifth
and the Senate on the twenty-sixth. The Democrats were its
most ardent supporters because the probable fifth Justice, representing the Supreme Court, David Davis, though presumably
nonpartisan, was felt to lean slightly toward the Democrats.
Tilden consistently opposed the method selected to choose the
five Justices—the four first chosen named the fifth—as a kind of

lottery, but with the bill as passed he stood an excellent chance of becoming President. As soon as President Grant had signed the bill, the two houses named their members and the four Justices named their fifth member, but it was not Davis. In a move denounced by Democrats in general, Davis had decided to leave the Supreme Court to run for an Illinois office. Named instead was Joseph P. Bradley, who was closer to the Republican party than to the Democratic.

On Thursday, February 1, 1877, the two houses met together to begin the offical count. When the alphabetical roll call reached Florida, its three certificates and the affidavits objecting to each were referred to the Electoral Commission. Few judicial arguments in history have attracted such an array of legal talent, and the detailed record of the proceedings makes fascinating reading. It took until February 6 to determine what would be admitted as evidence, but what mattered most was that in this first decision Justice Bradley voted with the Republicans, and on February 10 the Commission gave the Florida vote to Hayes.

Louisiana's four certified returns were next referred to the Commission; again, by a relentless eight to seven majority, it reported for Hayes. By now the original Democratic enthusiasm for the Electoral Commission was wholly dispelled. Oregon's two returns were next duly considered by the Commission; a decision for Hayes was reached on February 23. Inauguration Day was now only nine days away, and a dangerous delaying action on the part of Democrats now developed in the House. It was curtailed by the Democratic speaker, Samuel Randall, who rose above the partisanship to rule that when a duly enacted law prescribes a clearcut procedure "it is not in order to . . . obstruct or impede its . . . execution . . ." Congressman Clymer spoke bitterly of the infamous eight as betraying and crucifying the rights of the people. Congressman Woodworth of Ohio chided the Democrats for being poor losers, and noted that the Commission's seven-man minority had clearly been no less partisan than the majority. Futile objections were offered to isolated votes in a number of states. The last real Democratic hope was South Carolina, but it was by now the thinnest kind of hope. Jeremiah Black's closing statement before the Commission was hardly an argument at all: it was rather a denunciation of the

Commission itself, couched in bitter invective that has seldom been equalled. "If this thing stands," he cried out, "we can never expect such a thing as an honest election again. If you want to know who will be President by a future election, do not inquire how the people of the states are going to vote. You need only to know what kind of scoundrels constitute the returning boards, and how much it will take to buy them."

The Commission's verdict on South Carolina came on February 28. Again it favored Hayes. There was now talk of a Democratic filibuster, but it did not take place. In a series of conferences between Hayes men and responsible Southern Democratic Congressmen, the latter reputedly pledged themselves not to filibuster in exchange for a Hayes pledge to free the last Southern states from federal control. How much this meant to Southern Democrats few Northern Democrats could perhaps quite realize. But the Northern group were sobered by the knowledge that if Inauguration Day arrived without a President and Vice-President, Morton—the Indiana Radical Republican who would be the new Senate president—would assume the Presidency. Few Democrats anywhere would have preferred him to Hayes.

Despite the agreement between Hayes and the Southern Democrats, the very last days before the Inauguration were chaotic. As the roll call of states continued, Democratic Chairman Hewitt challenged the Vermont return. The Senate promptly accepted it, but in the House a resolution was proposed to refer the matter to the Commission, which threatened to delay the proceedings until after March 4. The House session on Thursday, March 1, was one of the stormiest in the history of Congress. Desperate members shouted, gesticualted, and pushed forward to badger Speaker Randall; the crowded galleries roared as the irreconcilables shouted their arguments. The resolution was finally defeated. The returns of Virginia, West Virginia, and finally Wisconsin were duly accepted, though the last was challenged and once more the houses separated to deliberate. The Representatives argued it out until four o'clock on the morning of Friday, March 2. The diehards loosed their final bitter blasts. One reminded his colleagues that on another Friday long ago Christ had been crucified, as "justice, honesty, fair dealing, manhood, and decency were suffering crucifixion now." Another said that today was not only Friday but hangman's day and a fitting time that this "bogus, pretentious, bastard brat of political reform . . . should be strangled to death, gibbeted higher than Haman." After the joint session reconvened and the final result was announced, the Senate retired, the galleries quickly emptied, and the House itself adjourned. Rutherford Hayes dined with President Grant the next evening, March 3, and after dinner took the oath of office, administered by Chief Justice Waite. His formal inauguration took place on Monday, March 5.

There are still families in America who are convinced that Samuel Jones Tilden was the nineteenth President of the United States and that Rutherford B. Hayes held office as an interloper. In their view the election was not "disputed" but stolen, and though cautious historians agree to use the former term, their considered judgment supports the latter. That Tilden did not serve as President illustrates at least as well as the worst scandals of the Grant administration the ever-present potentiality that government of the people, by the people, and for the people can be subverted by determined special-interest minorities. For a year that began with such high hopes, and that so bravely celebrated a hundredth anniversary, it was a dark, inglorious, and deferred conclusion.

Footnotes for Chapter Five
THE ABUSES OF POWER

1. Allan Nevins, *Hamilton Fish: The Inner History of the Grant Administration*, revised edition (New York: Frederick Unger, 1957), Vol. II, p. 788. Many of the details in this chapter, drawn from Hamilton Fish's private diary, in which he recorded the action in Cabinet meetings, are made available in the Nevins biography. The most informed, complete, and lucid contemporary account of the Whiskey Ring was by H. V. Boynton: "The Whiskey Ring," *North American Review*, 123 (Oct., 1876), 281–327. Publication of this article caused an irreparable break between the editors of the magazine, Henry Adams and Henry Cabot Lodge, and the publisher; the subscribers to this venerable quarterly were treated to this unusual "Publisher's Note" beneath the table of contents:

"The editors of the 'North American Review' having retired from its management on account of a difference of opinion with the proprietors as to the political character of this number, the proprietors, rather than cause an indefinite delay in publication, have allowed the number to retain the form which had been given it, without, however, committing the Review to the opinions expressed therein. JAMES R. OSGOOD & CO."

2. Fish diary, in Nevins, *Hamilton Fish*, II, pp. 798, 799, 803.

3. The circular letter was printed in newspapers throughout the nation.

4. Nevins, *Hamilton Fish*, II, p. 794.

5. See Schurz to Bristow, February 15, 1876, and Bristow to Schurz, February 18, 1876, in *Speeches, Correspondence and Political Papers of Carl Schurz*, ed. Frederic Bancroft, Vol. III (New York: G. P. Putnam's Sons, 1913), pp. 220–21. This work is subsequently cited as Schurz, *Writings*.

6. Nevins, *Hamilton Fish*, II, 806. The Belknap story is part of Chapter 23, "Babcock and Belknap at Bay," pp. 790–810.

7. *New York Times*, Feb. 18, 22, Mar. 2, 1872.

8. New York *Tribune*, Nov. 27, 1872.

9. New York *Tribune*, Jan. 16, 1875.

10. Congressional summary news, Elmira *Daily Advertiser*, March 3, 1876; the editor, a Republican, began the column with these leaders: "Let No Guilty Man Escape / A Cruel Humiliation to the Country."

11. *Harper's Weekly*, Mar. 18, 1876.

12. New York *World*, Mar. 10, 1876.

13. Nevins, *Hamilton Fish*, II, p. 806.

14. *Harper's Weekly*, Mar. 18, 1876.

15. Nevins, *Hamilton Fish*, II, pp. 815–16.

16. William B. Hesseltine, *Ulysses S. Grant, Politician* (New York: Frederick Unger, 1957), p. 396.

17. Fish diary, Mar. 3, 1876, in Nevins, *Hamilton Fish*, II, p. 805.

18. "Forty-Fourth Congress. Belknap Discharged," Elmira *Daily Advertiser*, Aug. 2, 1876.

19. William Belmont Parker, *The Life and Public Services of Justin Smith Morrill* (Boston: Houghton Mifflin, 1924), p. 247.

20. The standard work on the 1876 election is P. L. Haworth, *The Hayes-Tilden Disputed Presidential Election* (Cleveland: Burrows Brothers, 1906). Numerous scholarly monographs and journal articles have modified Haworth's findings, especially C. Vann Woodward, *Reunion and Reaction* (Boston: Little, Brown, 1951).

21. Schurz to B. B. Cahoon, Mar. 3, 1876, in Schurz, *Writings*, III, p. 222.

22. Schurz to Bristow, Mar. 31, 1876, *Ibid.*, pp. 226–28.

23. Schurz to L. A. Sherman, editor of the Pt. Huron *Times*, Apr. 15. 1876, *Ibid.*, pp. 230–31.

24. "To a Republican," in Schurz, *Writings*, III, pp. 236–39.

25. "Address to the People" was not only released to the press but was printed as a pamphlet for wide distribution. The text appears in Schurz, *Writings*, III, pp. 241–48.

26. Bryant to a British friend, Feb. 16, 1876, in Parke Godwin, *A Biography of William Cullen Bryant, with Extracts from His Private Correspondence* (New York: D. Appleton, 1883), Vol. II, Chapter 48, "The Closing Years."

27. Hay to Whitelaw Reid, Oct. 1, 1875, in William Roscoe Thayer, *The Life and Letters of John Hay* (Boston: Houghton Mifflin, 1908), Vol. I, pp. 426–27.

28. Henry F. Pringle, *The Life and Times of William Howard Taft* (New York: Farrar & Rinehart, 1939), Vol. I, p. 43.

29. Elmira *Daily Advertiser*, May 23, 1876.

30. A. B. Cornell to Andrew D. White, Mar. 30, 1876, in White Papers at Cornell University.

31. *Appleton's Cyclopedia* for 1876, p. 601.

32. Seward's remark is quoted in Matthew Josephson, *The Politicos* (New York: Harcourt, Brace, 1938), p. 171.

33. Harry Barnard, *Rutherford Hayes and His America* (Indianapolis: Bobbs-Merrill, 1954), p. 290.

34. *New York Times*, June 16, 1876.

35. Godkin to Charles Eliot Norton, Mar. 22, 1876, in Rollo Ogden, *Life and Letters of Edwin Lawrence Godkin* (New York: Macmillan, 1907), Vol. I, p. 309.

36. Indianapolis newspaper stories reported in Elmira *Daily Advertiser*, Apr. 12 and 22, 1876.

37. Elmira *Daily Advertiser*, June 2, 3, 6, 7, 8, 1876.

38. Charles Edward Russell in his *Blaine of Maine: His Life and Times* (New York: Cosmopolitan Book Corp., 1931), called Blaine the greatest opportunist in American political history, and concluded: "No cause of humanity was the better or stronger for his service to it; . . . nothing was gained by his pilgrimage here." Eulogistic biographies of Blaine also exist.

39. Elmira *Daily Advertiser*, June 10, 1876.

40. Barnard, *Rutherford Hayes and His America*.

41. Auburn *News and Democrat*, June 22, 1876.

42. Elmira *Daily Advertiser*, June 27, 1876.

43. Alfred R. Conkling, *The Life and Letters of Roscoe Conkling* (New York: Charles L. Webster, 1889), pp. 495–515.

44. Alexander Clarence Flick, *Samuel Jones Tilden: A Study in Political Sagacity* (New York: Dodd, Mead, 1939); Mark D. Hirsch, *William C. Whitney, Modern Warwick* (New York: Dodd, Mead, 1948).

45. The opinion of the Richmond *Dispatch*, and other editorial remarks cited in this section, were dutifully reprinted in the Elmira *Daily Advertiser*, a loyal Republican organ, on various dates.

46. New York *Tribune* editorial on "Solid South and Bristow's Answer" in Elmira *Daily Advertiser*, Oct. 9, 12, 1876.

47. Schurz to Hayes, June 21, 23, 1876, in Schurz, *Writings*, III, pp. 251–53.

48. Howells to Twain, Aug. 5, and Aug. 20; Twain to Howells, Aug. 9, Oct. 20 in *Mark Twain-Howells Letters*, ed. Henry Nash Smith and William Gibson (Cambridge: Harvard University Press, 1960), Vol. I, pp. 142–46, 157–59.

49. The Boston *Transcript* comment on Twain's Hartford speech is in a footnote to Howells to Twain, Oct. 1, in *Mark Twain-Howells Letters*, Vol. I, p. 156. The speech appeared in the New York *Times* on Oct. 1, and in the Elmira *Daily Advertiser* on Oct. 6, 1876.

50. Auburn *News and Democrat*, Aug. 10, 1876.

51. Northern war claims reported in Auburn *News and Democrat*, Nov. 2, 1876.

52. Flick, *Tilden*, p. 323.

53. Twain's telegrams to Howells, in *Mark Twain-Howells Letters*, Vol. I, pp. 162–63.

54. The most reliable account of the manipulations in Florida is Jerrell H. Shofner, "Fraud and Intimidation in the Florida Election of 1876," *Florida Historical Quarterly*, 42 (Apr. 1964), pp. 321–30.

6

The Southern
Question

PRESIDENT LINCOLN had directed the federal campaign against
the Confederate States of America on the basic premise that the
United States were one and inseparable and that no state had the
privilege of withdrawing from the Union. The Union victory
posed the question of how to restore the seceded states to their
former status, and a military problem, solved in four years, gave
way to a political problem that took a dozen years to solve. By
1876 three states—Florida, Louisiana, and South Carolina—still
remained under federal control.

The people of the states in secession, once the Confederacy
was crushed, desired nothing so much as to regain control of
their states. Federal control, or "occupation," or "military government"—whatever term might be preferred—was a constant
reminder of their lost privilege and status. So great was their
dissatisfaction, that by the thousands they joined together in
underground resistance to harry the federal forces, while newspaper editors and other spokesmen used every weapon at their

disposal to discredit the Republicans who were managing the process of Reconstruction.

By the 1870s, even Northerners were now beginning to have questions about Reconstruction. An administration as manifestly corrupt as Grant's, could hardly, in the thinking of growing numbers of people, be governing the Southern states still under federal control with wisdom and efficiency. James Russell Lowell reflected the dissatisfaction of a large number of citizens when he wrote to a friend in October, 1876, "We are deliberately trying to make an Ireland of the South, by perpetuating mismanagement there." [1] Some Northern Republicans expressed their disaffection by becoming Democrats, enough of them, in fact, to give the House of Representatives a Democratic majority in the 1874 election. Smarting under the often-repeated Republican charge that they were the party of treason, the Democrats now had the chance they had long desired to prove, by responsible action, that they could be as patriotic as anybody else. And to Southern Democrats this was the chance they had been waiting for, to present their position with some assurance of a sympathetic hearing.

The weakening of Northern support for Reconstruction policies did not, however, carry with it any blunting of rivalry between the two political parties. And although substantial hope existed for harmony between the Democratic House and the Republican Senate there was always the danger that some demagogue, especially in the election year of 1876, would put personal interest first and shatter the hopes of peace.

On Thursday, January 6, 1876, the House adopted a resolution citing the national harmony as "a most auspicious inception of the centennial year" and urging members to "do no act which would unnecessarily disturb the patriotic concord now existing and increasing, nor wantonly revive bitter memories of the past." Who could have voted in the negative? The resolution passed unanimously, 198–0.[2] But it was not a harbinger of things to come.

The Speaker of the House, Democrat Samuel Randall of Pennsylvania, had previously introduced a bill to grant amnesty to the few ex-Confederates, about 750 in number, who had not been included in the general pardon of 1872. The traditional interpretation of Reconstruction, describing Northerners as brutal and vindictive toward the South, has tended to overlook the federal government's magnanimity in pardoning the rebels. Indeed, it would be very hard, if even possible, to find a parallel in any other nation that has had a civil war. The only officer of the Confederate Army tried and executed for war crimes was Wirz, the commander of the Andersonville army prison, for mistreatment of captured Union soldiers. A few civilian officials were imprisoned briefly, but they were released without trials. The 1872 act, a Republican measure, had restored full civil rights to most Confederate leaders. Randall's bill in 1876, a Democratic measure, was intended to remove the remaining restrictions.[3]

The "harmony" resolution of January 6 had no doubt been intended to discourage exactly what happened when Randall's bill went before the House. To such an opportunist as Congressman James G. Blaine, then the front runner for the Republican nomination for President, the resolution served only as an invitation to sow dissension among the Democrats. As soon as he learned that Randall intended to bring his bill to a vote, Blaine read a substitute measure, identical in wording except for a clause specifically excluding from amnesty Jefferson Davis, the Confederacy's former president.

After extended parliamentary skirmishing, Randall failed to win the two-thirds support needed to bring his bill to a vote, and debate began. Blaine spoke at length on his own version. He wished to exclude Davis, he said, not because Davis had been "the head and front of the rebellion" but on the ground that he was "the author, knowingly, deliberately, guilty, wilfully of gigantic murder and crime at Andersonville"—crime greater, Blaine insisted, than that of the Duke of Alva, the Spanish Inquisition, or the massacre of St. Bartholomew's. Any government in Europe would have tried Davis long since and shot him within thirty days. "France, Russia, England, Germany, Austria, any of them would have done it. The score of victims would demand his death for brutal treatment of prisoners. But I always thought it was a weak movement on the part of our government to allow Jefferson Davis to go at large and hang Wirz." Davis, by a wave of his hand, by a nod of his head, or even by a wink, "could have stopped the atrocities," and it was shameful, Blaine said in closing, to think of "crowning with the honors of full American citizenship the man that organized that murder."

There was loud applause for Blaine on the Republican side of the House and in the galleries, then Samuel Sullivan Cox of New York rose to answer. "Sunset" Cox was an interesting man. He served in the Congress for twenty-four years, eight of them as Congressman from Ohio, 1857–65, and the other sixteen as Congressman from New York. He owed his nickname to a striking description of a sunset that he had written for an Ohio paper in 1853. Cox had a way with words, and whenever he spoke his colleagues listened. No one had worked harder than he to rid the Democratic party of its pro-slavery stigma, and Blaine's words were particularly offensive to him.

"You," he said to Blaine, "are like the small boy in Memphis, who undertook to twist the mule's tail; you will never again be as handsome as you were; but you will know a good deal more than you did." In a more serious vein he said that Blaine had seen proper in this Centennial year to tear away the plasters from the green and bleeding wounds of the late civil conflict, and was "raking up all the embers of dead hate." (In the November election Cox was returned to Congress by the astounding margin of 17,098 to 41.[4])

Cox's words hit closer to the mark than the full-dress Democratic reply the following day, which proved only how successful Blaine had been in putting his opponents on the defensive. By far the ablest Southern spokesman was absent—Lucius Quintus Cincinnatus Lamar, to give his improbable full name, of Mississippi. People remembered his eulogy of Charles Sumner on April 27, 1874, when, after a mediocre statement by E. R. Hoar of Massachusetts, he had electrified the House audience with his concluding words: "My countrymen, *know* one another, and you will *love* one another." There had been a long silence, hardly bearable, and then a thunder of applause. But Lamar was ill, as he often was this year, so often that people commonly supposed he was close to death (though he survived for a subsequent career in the Senate, Cleveland's cabinet, and the Supreme Court).[5] Chosen to speak in his absence was Benjamin Hill of

Georgia, a tall and powerfully built old man with a grim face, angular gestures, and a loud, harsh, passionate voice.

Lamar would certainly not have committed the tactical blunders that followed. Hill began well enough, drawing applause by disclaiming any Southern desire to reopen the breach between North and South. "There are no confederates in the south; there are no confederate ambitions, desires or purposes in this house; but the south is here to stay, and here she intends to remain." But he quickly descended to a lower level. If Reconstruction were a fair sample of the Republican magnanimity mentioned by Blaine then Hill prayed God to save the nation from such in the future. Two hours before his execution, Wirz, the Andersonville commandant, had been offered commutation of his sentence if he would implicate Jefferson Davis. "What Wirz would not say for his life," Hill went on, "the gentleman from Maine says to the country for the sake of keeping his party in power." If Davis was guilty, Grant was no less guilty for his part in the whiskey frauds and deserved not a third term but twenty years in prison.

Hill then charged that the prison camp at Elmira, New York, had been just as bad as the one at Andersonville. He read into the record a letter written by a Confederate surgeon at one time imprisoned in the camp. This last spelled disaster for Democratic unity. It immediately drew the retort from Congressman Platt, a Democrat whose home was thirty-six miles from Elmira, that the statements were unqualifiedly false.

Blaine, listening, must have been delighted: his ploy had successfully divided the Democratic majority on an extremely sensitive issue. On Thursday, January 13, he badgered Hill and other Democrats, and drew frequent laughter from the crowded galleries with an amazing performance which he kept at a very low level of dignity. In his hands he had copies of speeches made by Congressman Hill and others, before, during, and after the war. He quoted from them whatever suited his purpose, and ignored the protests that he was quoting out of context. At one point, charging Hill with wanting another war between North and South, he so exasperated Cox that he broke in to say, "Oh! Blaine, dry up." A little later Blaine reminded the House that Cox had voted during the war against an exchange of prisoners.

Mr. Cox (interrupting): The honorable hyena from Maine.

Mr. Blaine: I am not to be interrupted . . .

Mr. Cox: Well, bellow away; you are a hyena.

Blaine must have realized, however, that the Randall bill was certain of passage, since the Democratic majority in the House was substantial. A vote to end debate, on January 14, was 182–97, just short of the two-thirds required. Twelve Republicans voted aye, but there were many abstentions, and so the debate continued. Blaine sorely tried Speaker Randall's patience when he said, "I am for a practical amnesty. I am for an amnesty that will go through." Randall replied contemptuously, "Oh! You are not sincere in the least degree."

But whatever other Congressmen might have thought about Blaine and his relative sincerity, it says something about Centennial standards that his clowning and rudeness, as reported in detail in the nation's daily papers, rather than lowering him in the public estimation actually improved his chances for the Presidency. Other men on other occasions have "waved the bloody shirt," but none with more skill, or more electrifying effect, or in a way better calculated to enhance a personal image.

Andersonville was (and still is) a sleepy Georgia hamlet, but Elmira was one of the larger cities in New York, and one with a high degree of local pride. Charles Walker, the Democratic Congressman for the district, now won Republican plaudits for denying categorically Hill's charges of poor conditions at the Elmira prison camp. "We wish to be prompt," wrote the editor of the city's Republican daily, "in according Mr. Walker the credit which is his due. . . . It required courage for a Democrat to make this statement." [6] This newspaper in the next few weeks printed numerous letters and telegrams sent by former Confederate inmates of the prison attesting to the courteous treatment by the Union officials and to the generosity of the women of Elmira. Elsewhere in the nation, all the Civil War prisons were compared. Blaine's choice of Andersonville as an issue had been as shrewd as it was disruptive of national harmony. The horrors of Andersonville had been drilled into Northern magazine readers; it was a name as familiar to them as Bull Run or Gettysburg. The Buffalo *Express* no doubt correctly interpreted predominant Northern thinking when it observed, "Next to the assassination of Lincoln the Andersonville cruelties were the hardest thing for the North to forgive and forget." [7] Blaine had indisputably scored.

The debate over amnesty deferred consideration of the Centennial appropriation bill. Kentucky, Jefferson Davis's native state, adopted a resolution declining to take part in the Centennial Exhibition unless universal amnesty were voted, and in most parts of the former Confederacy the animosity stirred up by Blaine simply confirmed earlier decisions not to participate. On January 18, when the Exhibition appropriation bill was at last presented, Waddell of North Carolina, appealed for unanimous approval of the recommended $1,500,000 federal appropriation to "promote the honor and advance the interests of the country, and the peace and happiness of the people." But opponents argued that nothing in the Constitution warranted such an expenditure. Let the country's rich men bear the cost. The debate dragged on until January 25. An amendment required repayment in full to the government before any dividend could be distributed to the stockholders. Congressman Lucius Lamar was effective in a speech grounded in solid Constitutional argument and ending with a reiterated plea for sectional good will. The bill finally passed 37–20 in the Senate, 146–130 in the House. But the margin was close and the damage had been done. The Exhibition did not represent all the states, and the harmony it was supposed to restore was again deferred.

No number of Congressional resolutions could have forced Republican editors to refrain from castigating the South. Phrases like "treason incarnate" and "the unregenerate hearts of pardoned rebels" were common, and during 1876 what had earlier been called "the ex-Confederate House" was shortened to "the Confederate House." Blaine's adroit toying with Hill of Georgia, and the resentment it caused both in the House and throughout the South, showed how real the Southern question still was in 1876.

"Southern question" is somewhat inept as a term for the continuing mutual hostility, smouldering just beneath the surface and often erupting, that made national harmony so elusive in 1876. On either side there were deep-grained suspicions and doubts: could the other side be trusted? was there really good will? Such questions have only gradually evaporated—but not entirely. The fact that certain fundamental controversies remain unresolved, a century after the Civil War, attests to their virtually irreconcilable nature, and indicates how much greater they were, as divisive forces, at the first Centennial.

The classical Southern position, best expressed by John Calhoun of South Carolina, was that the Union was an association of sovereign states, each one a member by its own choice and each free to withdraw, at any time it might choose to do so. Men firmly committed to this interpretation thus justified the secession that catapulted the country into civil war. It was argued during Reconstruction that the federal government, and not the seceding states, had violated the Constitution in 1861 by instituting military measures. Confederates, whether military or civilian, had no sense of acting treasonably. Instead they believed they were defending the most sacred rights of Americans against the violation of those rights by the federal authority. Defeat by superior Northern power did not alter their belief in this political philosophy.

The federal position, best represented in action by President Lincoln, was simply that the Union was inviolable and that the federal authority had the supreme responsibility for its preservation. Once the war ended, Lincoln hoped for prompt reinstatement of the defeated Southern states. His leniency, reflected in the generous terms of the surrender at Appomattox, may stand as his noblest action. The Southern view that less lenient, more vengeful men controlled the federal government after Lincoln's assassination, and deliberately held back the restoration of the states that had seceded, caused much of the bitterness that Lincoln had hoped to minimize.

On another lofty level is the religious argument; but its loftiness is compromised by its close relation with racial attitudes. At its first organizational meeting in Nashville in 1867, the Ku Klux Klan, asserted that the Maker "has intended to give us over inferior races a dominion which no human law can permanently derogate." Again and again, apologists for the Klan fell back on this position: federal legislation to give freed slaves civil equality with whites was blasphemous, since God had made the races different in capacity and had meant whites to be forever superior and blacks forever inferior. Southerners viewed with growing alarm the immigration from European countries other than England that by 1876 was threatening to end the nation's Anglo-Saxon majority. This majority was divinely intended to create not only a white man's country but an Anglo-Saxon country as well—so went the old argument of the whites in the one region little affected by new immigration and still predominantly of English derivation. The Civil Rights Acts, and the Fourteenth Amendment, were construed by loyal Southern whites as deliberate efforts to humiliate the racial group that God intended to be supreme, by forcing equality with the group God meant to be at the very bottom of the human scale—if the blacks were human at all, as many white Southerners sincerely doubted.

The several Congressional enactments, the "invasion" of the South during Reconstruction by federal agencies such as the Freedman's Bureau, and by employees of private Northern churches and philanthropic societies, in addition to the federally appointed administrators and the soldiers sent to support them, seemed in conservative Southern opinion further proof that the North was bent on defying divine intent by subverting Southern tradition. This being so, resistance, open or secret, was widely approved as a defense of true religion. The open resistance was expressed chiefly in public orations, sermons, and newspaper editorials; the secret, underground resistance was to be found in the Ku Klux Klan and other organizations willing to use violence of every sort against the unwelcome agents of the North.

The Klan, organized in Pulaski, Tennessee, on Christmas Eve, 1865, given a national form at Nashville in the spring of 1867, officially disbanded in 1869 by its first Imperial Wizard, Confederate General Bedford Forrest, but sporadically active thereafter, reached an estimated peak strength of half a million—almost exactly the size of the defeated Confederate Army. Most of the Grand Dragons, in charge of states, were former high officers, usually generals, in that army. It was first hoped that the Klan could achieve its objectives by mere intimidation, but local dens, free of any effective restraint, engaged with mounting frequency in acts of violence—whipping, raping, castrating, branding, hanging, burning, shooting—against both Negroes and white Northerners. Southern opinion was sufficiently sympathetic to the Klan to ensure the acquittal in the trials of men arrested for such crimes: arrests, however, were very rare. For one thing, many Klansmen were either law enforcement officers themselves—sheriffs, deputies, constables, and the like—or relatives or close friends of these officials. For another, Klansmen took extreme care to avoid arrest because, as former Confederates, so many of them had sworn allegiance to the Union and strict obedience of all laws as the simple price of regaining their full citizenship, and identification as a lawbreaker meant exposure of the worst sort. The ends desired, however—the expulsion of hated carpetbaggers, and preservation of the old racial balance —were incentives enough to make Klan members run that risk.

In 1870, in the face of the growing Klan violence, Congress staged an investigation, the results of which were reported in thirteen volumes referred to as "The Ku Klux Conspiracy." [8] Few Northerners read this final compilation, but newspapers reported the investigation's proceedings day by day. The extent of Klan activity, the sensational nature of some of the incidents, and the undeniable fact that Klansmen included some paroled Confederates, made an enduring impression on the North. Editorial phrases of the sort mentioned earlier, "the unregenerate hearts of pardoned rebels" and the like, were thus not mere groundless partisan accusations. No doubt unjustly, many Northerners in 1876, remembering the Klan atrocities, thought of the entire South as a place of unrestrained violence and actually feared for the nation's safety as more and more former Confederates were elected to Congress. Violence in the South during 1876, especially during the elections at year's end, further strengthened this fear. The common Southern response was that the violence was stimulated by the mismanagement, corruption, and brutality of the federal Reconstruction program.

All of this, of course, played its part in the contested election of 1876. In general, the Klan was relatively quiescent by 1876, largely because by that year most of the former Confederacy had been "redeemed" for local white control. But where there was still a struggle for control between Democrats and Republicans, as in Louisiani, Florida, and South Carolina, meaning the three states with Republican governors who owed their position to the federal government, local Klansmen roused to do their part in helping the Democrats. Negroes were taken from their cabins at night and threatened with the noose if they voted for other than Democratic candidates, or if they ever reported these threats. Another effective tactic was the surrounding of Republican rallies by a dense line of mounted, robed Klansmen; very few Negroes were brave enough to cross such lines. There was a sense of great urgency, for if the Democrats could not carry their states in 1876, Negroes would earn the privilege of voting in subsequent elections, and would be more likely to vote Republican than Democratic. Since voting was one of the traditional privileges supposedly limited to the superior race, along with unrestricted travel, ownership of land, and the right to bear arms, then extending the vote to the freedmen was one of the Northern crimes that justified Klan violence.

In Florida, violence was generally expected, but somehow avoided. The state superintendent of instruction, William Hicks, and William Saunders, a Baltimore Negro and former barber, stumped the state urging Negroes to vote "early and often" for Republican candidates, and strongly hinted of their return to slavery if the Democrats won.[9] Republican Governor Stearns warned Negroes that a Democratic victory would lead to war, and to a closing of the schools. Most Florida whites, he intimated, paid taxes to support education only because the Republicans forced them to.[10] It was also alleged, weeks after the event, that the Republican boss of Alachua County (home of the University of Florida) had advised local Negroes to carry guns on election day.[11]

In Jefferson County, Florida, a Republican state senator, a mulatto ex-slave, was fired upon by an unidentified gunman a week before the election.[12] But most intimidation was economic. Democrats owned most of the land and were the principal employers; threats of eviction and dismissal were easy ways to discourage Negroes from voting Republican. A railroad recently taken over by the state was accused of discharging Negro employees for attending Democratic meetings, and of levying assessments for the Republican campaign treasury.[13] Another railroad, owned by Democrats, retaliated by handing numbered Democratic ballots to employees and threatening discharge if the ballots did not show up at the polls.[14] Democrats in Jackson and Columbia counties slyly adopted the Republican emblem for their own ballots and passed them out to Negro voters, most of whom could not read.

Most of the partisan accusations of fraud appeared in print only after the election, when its disputed result gave unanticipated importance to the vote in Florida. Earlier, the charges and counter-charges were limited to the local papers. After the election, some of the same incidents, plus many new ones, found their way by "exchange" into papers in the North. As Southern elections could be judged, during the Reconstruction decade when Republicans challenged the Democratic monopoly, the Florida election of 1876 was no more corrupt or marked by violence than others. The real corruption began only after the election, as reported in Chapter Five.

It was quite another story in South Carolina, where Negroes constituted almost two-thirds of the population, and where the struggle for political control saw three contending groups: the Radical Republicans, extremist white Democrats, and, in the middle, the white moderates led by Wade Hampton, the chairman of the state's Democratic Executive Committee. The election of President Grant in 1868, and the subsequent seizure of power by the "black Republicans," had the effect in South Carolina of firmly establishing Radical Republican control until 1876. An election called and superintended by the military governor produced the legislature that convened on July 6, 1868, with a majority of Negro members—eighty-four of them, as compared with seventy-two whites—which has been made famous by the traditionalist historians and is still being used in textbooks as a horrible example of Radical misrule. That most of the Negroes were men of ability was ignored. No Negro, in the classical argument of White Supremacy, could possibly be the equal of a white. Specific details of graft among the legislators have been magnified into a wholesale indictment, as if no legislative body with a white majority had ever engaged in graft.

The eight Negroes in the Forty-Fourth Congress were probably, as a group, superior to the eighty-four in the notorious South Carolina legislature. One of the eight made no impression whatsoever, and a second performed so wretchedly that his Negro constituents, at the next election, rejected his bid for re-election and chose a white man instead. But Congressman

James Rainey of South Carolina was an extremely fluent speaker who won wide respect in the House, and Jeremiah Haralson of Alabama has been called the best "natural politician," of any race, that Alabama has ever produced. All but one of these men had been born slaves, and only one had attended college. But in their committee assignments, and in floor debates, the eight exhibited roughly the same range of effectiveness as any eight white members of Congress.[15]

The Radical success in South Carolina was so great that it intensified the determination of the white conservatives—the Democrats—to regain control. The moderate Wade Hampton appealed to the voters to correct what, in the overwhelming white opinion, was an intolerable situation; but he was helpless until 1876. The state's governor from 1874 to 1876 was Daniel Henry Chamberlain, a Yale graduate who had moved to South Carolina to become a planter after serving in the Union army. By selling no pardons and granting none for political reasons, and by vetoing eighteen bills, he alienated the support of many Radicals, especially such men as "Honest" John Patterson who was supposed to have announced, in 1873. "There are still five years of good stealing in South Carolina."

Patterson was the kind of Northerner in the South who justified the epithet "carpetbagger." Chamberlain, an honest man, had the bad luck, shared by all honest Northerners in Southern politics, of being tarred with the same brush, and the ironic result of his courageous administration was to give the conservatives the opening they had been hoping for. Clubs of reputable Democrats were organized to back the governor's efforts, but by June, 1876, there were two strong factions, the "Straight-Outs," intent on eliminating all Radicals, Chamberlain among them, and the moderates, supporting him. Wade Hampton threw his influence to the latter group. But when the "Straight-Out" leader, General Gary, asked Hampton to be the Democratic nominee for governor, he agreed, and the decision of necessity pitted him against Chamberlain. He was no doubt the one man in the state strong enough to hope to be elected.[16]

During the summer, when Hampton was away on vacation, violence broke out. The "Hamburg Massacre," a term invented by the Republican press, took place at Hamburg, South Carolina, across the Savannah River from Augusta, Georgia, on July 8. A Negro militia company had been accused of obstructing a highway on the Fourth of July, and its commanding officer had been arrested. The gathering of several hundred whites at his trial so incensed his men that they formed ranks, and firing broke out; eight of the Negro militiamen were killed, and three whites. Northern papers, preoccupied with such events as Custer's death, Blaine's elevation to the Senate, and Hayes's letter accepting the Republican nomination, gave the incident scant attention. On July 19, Governor Chamberlain conferred in Washington with Secretary of War Cameron and Attorney-General Taft, who told him that the federal government expected to take stern action to punish the individuals responsible; and on July 26 Grant wrote to Chamberlain to express full agreement with his distress and his proposed prosecution of the culprits. "The scene at Hamburg," Grant wrote, "as cruel, bloodthirsty, wanton, unprovoked and as uncalled for as it was, is only a repetition of the course that has been pursued in other Southern states within the last few years, notably in Louisiana and Mississippi." In the final paragraph of his statement, however, he offered only the hope that "the better judgment and cooperation of the citizens" of South Carolina would rally behind Chamberlain to bring the offenders to trial, "without aid from the federal government." [17] It is possible that Grant delayed his message to the Senate until he heard that on August 1 a coroner's jury charged fifty-odd South Carolinians and thirty Georgians with murder, and instructed that warrants be issued for their arrest. The very next day a jury indicted seven of the men; but they were never put on trial, probably because Chamberlain failed to secure additional federal troops. He made a second attempt in October, sending to Washington a delegation of Republicans, but General Sherman discounted the need of further troops. [18]

The Straight-Outs, accusing Governor Chamberlain of using the killings as a lever to get more troops in order to improve his chances of re-election, were considerably benefited by the outcome: Grant refused the troops, and the state's whites rallied to the Democratic side. Hampton's unanimous nomination for governor, at the party convention in August, closed the Democratic split. But a new split developed, between those advocating violence and those supporting Hampton's more moderate slogan of "force without violence." Rifle Clubs (on foot) and Sabre Clubs (mounted)—the famous Red Shirts—were organized but Hampton was generally able to keep their enthusiasm within bounds. When the Straight-Out leader proposed a mass circling of a Republican rally, Hampton vetoed the plan. All he was willing to permit was organized hissing at Republican speakers.

But just two days after General Sherman gave his opinion that no more troops were needed, violence disrupted a political rally at Cainhoy, nine miles south of Charleston. Two white men came to blows, one of them fired a shot, and the Negro militiamen promptly seized their muskets and advanced upon the few whites on the fringe of the crowd. The upshot was two men killed and fourteen wounded.[19] The next day representatives of the state Republican Club called upon Grant, the Cabinet discussed the matter in plenary session, the Attorney-General composed a proclamation for Grant to sign disbanding the Rifle Clubs, and Secretary of War Cameron ordered General Sherman to send all available troops to South Carolina in the hope that "a collision may thus be avoided." It seems clear that a skirmish leaving nine dead in July carried less weight in Washington than one leaving two dead in mid-October, when the election was three weeks away.

The Southern Question, which in the 1876 election focused national attention on the three Southern states still under federal control, magnified the degree of corruption in those states, the campaign violence, the contending power groups, even the personal rivalries; these things made good copy, but the printed reports left the impression that irregularities and dramatic incidents were a Southern monopoly, as if states outside the South all had orderly campaigns and electoral counts wholly devoid of fraud. One real difference between North and South was that the Northern counts were not challenged elsewhere; and thus, the customary veil of obfuscation was not pushed aside before the eyes of the national audience. The second substantial difference was the coexistence in the South of two races, one aspiring to human dignity, the other intent on limiting that aspiration. The end of federal control meant redemption of the South by the local whites, and, for the nation at large, a satisfying solution of the Southern Question. Only later would people realize that the solution was only a partial and temporary one. The spotlight of national attention on the garish election drama left in darkness the borders of the stage, where Negroes stood by helplessly as their most cherished hopes dwindled and, at the final curtain, were shattered.

In Louisiana and Mississippi violence also marred the 1876 election. Not even as strong a man as Lucius Lamar could repress violence in every part of his state. Historians, in assigning responsibility for major events, have seldom mentioned one of the most heinous acts of Klan violence to occur during Reconstruction. This was the liquidation of William Wallace Chisolm.

Georgia-born, Chisolm had lived in Mississippi from the age of sixteen. In 1858 he was elected magistrate for his township, and two years later he became probate judge. Prior to 1865, before Negroes had the vote, Chisolm owed his position to the confidence of local whites, even though he was known as a Unionist. However, his equitable treatment of Negroes in his courtroom had the predictable result, first, of enlisting almost total Negro support, and then of rousing the ire of conservative whites. In 1869, as first deputy to his brother John, Kemper County's sheriff, he had the specific responsibility of collecting taxes to support the public schools—about as unpopular an assignment as could be imagined in a state that had never had public schools until the Radicals in Washington insisted upon them, and in a state almost bankrupted by the Civil War. Yet Judge Chisolm stayed politically alive. He served a two-year term as sheriff, 1873–75, and in 1876 was the Republican candidate for Congress. Klansmen, using their familiar device of forming a ring around Republican rallies, harassed his campaigning, and, for two nights just before election day, serenaded his home, discharged cannons, and broke windows, preventing all sleep. On the second night, a band blared out "Dixie," the Klan theme song, and "The Bonnie Blue Flag," the Confederate "national anthem." Chisolm was defeated (no Republican candidate had much chance in 1876), but instead of merely retiring from public attention, he persuaded his Radical supporters to bring the offenders to justice. A federal grand jury indicted thirty Klansmen for violating the federal Enforcement Act, which guaranteed the freedom to campaign without interference. The state press, almost entirely Democratic, vilified this indictment as the most inhuman and uncalled-for act of tyranny and oppression ever enacted upon a free people. The logic of this would have escaped most Northerners but was apparently quite clear to Southern conservatives.

Before the trials could begin, all the records were stolen from the courthouse, and legal action could not be pursued. After a lengthy stay in Washington, Chisolm returned home on March 29, 1877, and that very night a former sheriff was murdered near Chisolm's home. Chisolm was arrested as an accessory and taken to the county jail in DeKalb. The jail was promptly besieged by some two hundred Klansmen. In the ensuing battle, one Klansman was killed, Johnny, Chisolm's thirteen-year-old son, had an arm shot off and was then killed, and a daughter was severely wounded, as was the judge himself, so severely that the Klansmen thought he was dead and allowed his wife to take him home. When it was learned that he was still alive, Klansmen besieged his house once again. Chisolm died on May 13, his daughter two days later. They were buried, along with Johnny, near a church but with no clergyman brave enough to read a funeral service.

A friend, Arthur Wells, published an account of the murders in 1878, entitled *The Chisolm Massacres;* this was countered in 1879 by James Lynch, in *Kemper County Vindicated.* Wells concluded that "the people of the South are governed by passion and prejudice more than by reason or law." Lynch attributed the responsibility for Chisolm's death to Chisolm himself, for being a notorious Radical. One Northerner saw fit to honor Chisolm's memory in concrete form: J. C. Sigmond of Clinton County, Pennsylvania, bought a cemetery lot for a Chisolm monument that remains a curiosity of the region. But whether Wells, in defending Chisolm, or Lynch, in condemning him, presented the better case, no two books quite so well illustrate the cleavage between Northern and Southern (or Mississippian) ways of thinking which made the Southern Question so baffling and destructive.

Northern disillusionment with Reconstruction and the resurgence of Southern power in Congress may both be measured by the repeal, in 1876, of the Homestead Act. Adopted in 1866, chiefly to help the freedmen toward independence, the Act opened up for homesteading 47,700,000 acres of public land in five Southern states—Alabama, Arkansas, Florida, Louisiana, and Mississippi. By paying a five dollar fee, moving onto the land, and working it, a freedman could have eighty acres. The Act halted real estate speculation in the areas involved, but relatively few freedmen were benefited. Few of them had the money for tools and other farming necessities; also, the land was not very good for farming. But the chief deterrent was the old Southern tradition that land-owning was a privilege reserved for white men. As with voting, it took a courageous Negro to apply for a homestead grant.

Southern representatives in Congress put pressure on their colleagues, and as one of the final actions of the session, in June, 1876, the Senate by a large majority and the House by a small margin passed a bill repealing the Act, and President Grant allowed the repeal to become law without either signing or vetoing it. Although there was a stipulation that the homesteaders would not be forced from their farms, intimidation in fact drove many of them off. In Florida, for example, of 2,012 homesteads listed in 1876, only 1,063 remained after three years. But the story ends with a grim irony. Immediately after the repeal of the Act, land speculators, mostly nonresident, rushed in and acquired the land, holding it for eventual profit and depriving white Southerners of its use and development.[20] By heeding the demands of Southern members, Congress had inadvertently hurt the Southern cause more than it had by its Reconstruction programs.

Footnotes for Chapter Six
THE SOUTHERN QUESTION

1. Lowell to Mrs. S. B. Herrick, Oct. 9, 1876, in *Letters of James Russell Lowell,* ed. Charles Eliot Norton (Boston: Houghton Mifflin, 1904), II, pp. 405–06. Martin Duberman, *James Russell Lowell* (Boston: Houghton Mifflin, 1966), pp. 456–57, fn. 30, points out

that Lowell's political opinions for this period are taken from his letters to Mrs. Herrick, "A southerner, an admirer, and a woman."

2. Unless otherwise noted, all references to Congressional proceedings are drawn from "Telegraph News. Forty-Fourth Congress," in the Elmira *Daily Advertiser*, hereafter designated by *EDA*.

3. A substantial number of Confederates refused, on principle, to swear allegiance to the Union, and thus did not qualify for the general pardon; such men lived out their lives, proudly and defiantly, as "unreconstructed rebels," but by their own decision, not any act of the government.

4. David Lindsey, *"Sunset" Cox: Irrepressible Democrat* (Detroit: Wayne State University Press, 1959); and *EDA*, Jan. 11, 1876.

5. Wirt A. Cate, in *Lucius Q. C. Lamar: Secession and Reunion* (Chapel Hill: University of North Carolina Press, 1935), p. vii, calls Lamar "the first truly reconstructed statesman either North or South." Albert D. Kirwan, in *Revolt of the Rednecks* (Lexington: University of Kentucky Press, 1951), is less enthusiastic, reporting that Lamar, as virtual boss of Mississippi after 1876, applied an iron rule to ensure Democratic control.

6. *EDA*, Jan. 14, 1876.

7. "Elmira and Andersonville," editorial in Buffalo *Express*, reprinted in *EDA*, Jan. 14, 1876.

8. *The Testimony Taken by the Joint Select Committee to Inquire into the Condition of Affairs in the Late Insurrectionary States* (House Report no. 22; Senate Report no. 41, 42d Congress, 2d Sess., 1871–72), 13 vols. 1872.

9. Reported in the Tallahassee *Floridian*, Apr. 11 and Oct. 18, 1876. This summary of the Florida situation is based largely on Jerrell H. Shofner, "Fraud and Intimidation in the Florida Election of 1876," *Florida Historical Quarterly*, 42 (Apr., 1964), pp. 321–30.

10. Reported in the Tallahassee *Weekly Floridian*, Nov. 14, 1876, with the editorial comment that such remarks were grounds for an indictment of the governor.

11. Tallahassee *Weekly Floridian*, Dec. 5, 1876.

12. *Ibid.*, Oct. 31, 1876.

13. Quitman (Ga.) *Reporter*, Sept. 14, Oct. 12, 1876.

14. Tallahassee *Weekly Floridian*, Sept. 19, 1876.

15. Samuel Denny Smith, *The Negro in Congress 1870–1901* (Chapel Hill: University of North Carolina Press, 1940).

16. This account of Hampton's progress toward the South Carolina governorship is drawn from Hampton Jarrell, *Wade Hampton and the Negro: the Road Not Taken* (Columbia: University of South Carolina Press, 1949), a book with an obvious pro-Democratic bias.

17. Grant's letter of July 26 to Chamberlain, together with a special message sent to the Senate on July 31 and copies of pertinent reports on the Hamburg incident, given in full in *EDA*, Aug. 2, 1876. Chamberlain himself wrote about the situation much later in "Reconstruction in South Carolina," *Atlantic Monthly*, 87 (Apr., 1904), 473–84; his conclusion was that the ballot had been debauched in 1876, and that the Negro race was used as a tool and then thrown aside.

18. *EDA*, Oct. 14, 1876.

19. "Another Collision in South Carolina," *EDA*, Oct. 14, 1876; a further report, Oct. 21, 1876.

20. C. Vann Woodward, *Reunion and Reaction; the Compromise of 1877 and the End of Reconstruction* (Boston: Little, Brown 1951), pp. 53–54, and Rembert W. Patrick, *The Reconstruction of the Nation* (New York: Oxford University Press, 1967), pp. 231–32. See also Kenneth M. Stampp, *The Era of Reconstruction, 1865–1877* (New York: Knopf, 1965), and Paul W. Gates, "Federal Land Policy in the South, 1866–88," *Journal of Southern History*, 6 (Aug., 1940), 303–30.

7

Good
and Faithful
Servants

THE HARD FACT that refused to be ignored in 1876 was that government of the people, by the people, and for the people could be manipulated to yield government by a corrupt handful for sordid personal profit. The facts were especially painful because the year had opened in such a glow of pride, with all the world invited to share in the celebration. But what neither the visitors nor the host citizens could miss, alongside the proud displays at the Centennial Exhibition, was an unprecedented exhibition of corruption at the highest level of the government.

In one interpretation of the period, the tide of public morality was at a low ebb, pushing to the surface, and to Grant's attention, individuals weak in moral fibre, unqualified for major responsibility, and talented only in devising methods of defrauding the government. At some other time in history, presumably, the moral tide, running higher, would have brought to the surface, and to Grant's attention, Cabinet prospects of administrative competence and personal integrity. By this reasoning, Grant was as much a victim of the period as of his own impetuous method of choosing his lieutenants.

If public morality was indeed so low in the mid-1870s, and if corrupt men were the rule and not the exception, only a change in administration could have prevented complete collapse of the government. This argument was heavily used by the Democrats in the 1876 election, and also, earlier, by the Liberal Republicans in their fight for nomination of a candidate pledged to reform. Grant's administration, both groups argued, was so badly damaged by the corruption that "collapse" was not too strong a word, though some spoke instead of "paralysis." Historians have generally echoed this contemporary judgment. A single major scandal in the Cabinet would be enough to cast a shadow over any administration; the multiple scandals of 1876 plunged Grant's reputation into almost total darkness. To assume, without further testing, that the darkness extended to every part of the government is fatally easy—but hardly fair.

The United States government did not collapse in 1876. In the language of a later age, a "credibility gap" became a very wide chasm, yet the day-to-day functioning, at most levels, was not greatly affected. Partly, no doubt, simple momentum kept the machinery going, as people showed up each morning, did their customary work, went home at night, and drew their accustomed salaries. But this is not the whole story: some men, despite what may have seemed to them, as to the public, a crumbling of the upper structure, were loyal enough to perform in outstanding ways, bringing valuable projects to completion, undertaking new ventures for the public welfare, and notably advancing the common welfare.

Salary scales were low throughout the government, and some men were susceptible to bribes and other inducements. Yet the same poor salaries did not prevent most federal employees from doing their work adequately, or a few from doing it brilliantly. In fact, perhaps astonishingly, some of the best minds of the period were at the public disposal. Good and faithful servants of superior ability, who might have earned much more money in private employment, were contributing more to national progress than the few rascals exposed in 1876 were able to do in impeding it. If morality *was* at low tide, the public did not deserve the solid good work of these men.

The government in 1876 was hardly the mammoth it has since become, but it had grown substantially since 1789. The Constitution provided for five Executive departments—State, War, Treasury, Justice, and Post Office—and for the creation of others when they should prove necessary. Congress acted to establish the Navy Department in 1798, the Interior Department in 1849, and the Department of Agriculture in 1862. Grant's Cabinet in 1876 consisted of the executive officers of all these departments except Agriculture, which until 1889 was assigned only a commissioner. Numerous independent agencies, bureaus, and officers also existed, directly responsible to the President; they were a violation of organizational logic, but so was the assignment of yet other agencies to particular departments.

The War Department, for example, included two divisions that had drifted away, gradually, from their original military function: the Signal Bureau, which in 1870 assumed the duty of weather forecasting, and the Engineer Department, more often called the "U. S. Engineers" or the "Army Engineers," increasingly active in river and harbor improvements that sometimes had no connection with national defense. The Navy Department had undergone parallel developments: its Bureau of Hydrography was best known for the Kane Arctic expeditions and for the apparatus it developed for observing the transit of Venus, less important for the Navy than for scientific determination of the earth's distance from the sun. Few men in the Navy, moreover, could have felt any departmental kinship with Simon Newcomb, the Nova Scotian who in 1861, at the age of twenty-six, was named professor of mathematics in the Navy and who in 1873 was put in charge of the twenty-six-inch equatorial telescope built under his supervision.

Within the Treasury Department were the United States Coast Survey, the Bureau of Weights and Measurements, the Light-House Board, and the Supervising Architect of the Treasury, with jurisdiction over all federal building. Interior included the Patent Office, Census Bureau, Indian Bureau, Bureau of Education, and the Geological Surveys of the Territories. Agriculture was divided into three Sections—Chemical, Natural History, and Statistical. Independent agencies in 1876 included the Government Printing Office, the United States Fish Commission, and the Smithsonian Institution.

Most conspicuously absent from the panoply of federal agencies was machinery for the control and regulation of private enterprise. It seems reasonable to suggest that a larger fraction of the total governmental effort went into direct service to the public in 1876 than it does in the present century. In prevailing Centennial theory, service was the proper interpretation of the "welfare" clause in the preamble to the Constitution; but it may equally be reasonable to observe that much of the service the government provided was, like the new directions given by radical educators to universities, less in response to public demand than what intellectuals conceived as worth undertaking.

One notable achievement in 1876, well publicized in the newspapers, was the completion of the geological survey of Colorado, which came to be known as the Hayden Survey. Ferdinand V. Hayden had been trained as a geologist at Oberlin College and as a physician at Albany Medical College. He served as a Union surgeon in the Civil War, but when peace was restored he found more absorbing challenge in surveys conducted by the Department of the Interior. Among his other achievements, Hayden is given major credit for the establishment in 1873, of Yellowstone National Park, the nation's first. The geological survey of Colorado was chosen for completion in 1876 because regions further north were the scenes of Indian uprisings. In addition, the discovery of important lead deposits in the area multiplied the demands for a thorough going exploration (and accelerated Colorado's admission, on August 1, 1876, as a state). One byproduct of the survey was the climbing and measurement of Colorado's mountains, some of them previously unknown. The loftiest point reached by the survey crews was Blanca Peak, tentatively measured at 14,464 feet and thought to be the highest elevation in Colorado.[1] The survey confirmed what a few pioneers had been derided for suggesting, that Colorado had more than fifty peaks higher than 14,000 feet. It also described areas never before penetrated, with great canyons, broad tablelands, and beautiful remote valleys. Fifteen drawings by Thomas Moran, the pioneer artist of the Yellowstone, added a special touch to the summary account written by Hayden; the detailed mapping was in six large sheets.

At the same time that Hayden's hardworking crews were busy in Colorado, other crews were at work, in the Far West, for the Coast Survey of the Treasury Department, under the direction of George Davidson. Few other men have ever devoted so much of their lives to public service, with such complete enthusiasm, as George Davidson. In 1900, at the age of seventy-five, he remarked, "In fifty years of official life I took less than fifty days leave of absence and worked every holiday and Sunday for forty-five years of that time. And I continue ceaselessly to work because I love it, because I have the constitution to stand it, and because I believe that I can add something to human knowledge and especially to benefit the young." A native of Philadelphia, Davidson first went to California in 1850. At first he disliked the place intensely. "Combine all the worst features of New England, make every hill barren—no roads, no timber, no houses—and you will get a country in which no man will work while he can live elsewhere." In time, however, he overcame this repugnance. He gave names to a great many places in the Far West, wrote an important long report on Alaska in 1868, and in 1874 and 1875 made a world tour inspecting irrigation and reclamation programs. After the tour he returned to California and issued a summary report of his trip in eight articles published in the *San Francisco Bulletin* from April, 1876, to February, 1877. During the Centennial year he also co-authored a report on San Francisco Harbor, accepted a Ph.D. degree from Santa Clara College, and, as president of the California Academy of Science, maintained his pressure on wealthy men to donate cash for a new Academy building. His campaign paid off when the industrialist James Lick left part of his three-million-dollar estate to the Academy. Lick's name is kept alive primarily by the Lick Observatory atop Mt. Hamilton, and his reputation as an eccentric is embodied in the answer he gave shortly before his death when asked if he wished to be cremated: "No, sir! I intend to rot like a gentleman!" [2]

Another scientist in government service, even more illustrious than Davidson and Hayden, was Joseph Henry, the one-time

Princeton professor of physics who discovered the principle of induced current for which Michael Faraday, publishing first, reaped the principal fame. When Congress, after delaying ten years in accepting the half million dollars willed by James Smithson, an English mineralogist, for "the increase and diffusion of knowledge," finally authorized the Smithsonian Institution, Joseph Henry was the logical choice for its director. His annual report for 1876, the penultimate year of his life, is a volume of 488 pages covering the many activities of the Institution that he had been chiefly instrumental in organizing: the library, the National Museum, scientific expeditions and collecting trips, a voluminous international exchange of scientific publications, the Smithsonian's own *Contributions to Knowledge* and *Miscellaneous Collections*, and laboratory services for other federal agencies, especially photography and chemical analysis.[3]

Henry's staff in 1876 numbered fifteen besides himself: an assistant secretary, an assistant curator of the National Museum, four scientists in charge of divisions (Mineralogy, Conchology, Ornithology, Ethnology), a photographer, seven clerks, and a janitor. The operating budget of roughly $50,000 was easily covered by Smithson's endowment, which had grown by occasional small bequests to about $700,000. Congress was occasionally invited to supply funds for various projects, but when costs exceeded appropriations, Henry could make up the difference from the endowment. At a time when most branches of the government had budgets in the millions—enough, in some instances, to encourage large-scale thievery—the Smithsonian was providing remarkable public service at almost no cost to the taxpayers. Its major assignment during 1875 and 1876 was planning and preparing displays at the Centennial Exhibition for all federal agencies. It required twenty-two freight cars to transport the displays from Washington to Philadelphia, and even more space for materials collected by the Smithsonian from all over the country. Spencer Baird, the superintendent of the National Museum, was in charge of the project. It was hard work, and the only thing he liked was the opportunity it gave him to meet eminent scientists visiting the Exhibition from many foreign countries.

Professor Henry was hardly a man to be excited about the

Exhibition, or to derive any keen satisfaction from the ten citations given for Smithsonian displays. He stayed in his Washington Office, tending to what he considered the major work of the
Smithsonian. He had seen to it, however, that the specimens
gathered here and there about the nation would be added to the
permanent collection; he encouraged waste of neither tangibles
or staff energy. The National Museum he seemed to view as a
nuisance, and in his 1876 report he urged its separate financing
and administration as soon as possible. Like T. H. Huxley,
Henry was primarily interested in search and discovery, not in
mounting results for the public to gawk at. Anybody, he felt,
could perform the custodial function; research was what increased the fund of knowledge.

Henry liked to accumulate data in a specific field and then
hand-pick a man to work it into an article for the Smithsonian's
Contributions to Knowledge. The two volumes of the *Contributions* published in 1876 exhibit this procedure. "Tables, Distribution, and Variations of the Atmospheric Temperature of the
United States," is by Charles A. Schott, a German-born assistant
in the United States Coast Survey. Henry not only furnished the
data for Schott's article but added his own commentary. A
major potential beneficiary of this work was the nucleus of a
weather bureau that existed in the Army's Signal Bureau. The
other volume included two extended monographs, one on the
Antiquities of Tennessee, the other on the archeological collections in the National Museum. In the *Miscellaneous Collections
for 1876* were *Birds of Southwestern Mexico, Catalogue of the
Fishes of the Bermudas,* and a classification of the animal resources of the United States. Also issued, specifically for the
Centennial, was a large outline map of the United States in
twenty sheets which measured roughly fifteen by seventeen feet
when assembled. The cost of the enormous map, as the prudent
Henry managed things, was shared by the various federal
agencies that had practical uses for it—the Post Office, for example, and the Light-House Board. No immediate utility, however,
can be imagined for the Smithsonian's compilation of all planet-
oidal discoveries made in 1876. Nor would it be possible to trace
the uses made of the huge number of scientific documents exchanged during 1876; during the year the Smithsonian mailing

room handled thirteen thousand separate parcels weighing eighty-thousand pounds and maintained correspondence with 2,275 foreign institutions.

In the kind of government we condemn today as bureaucratic, employee initiative is not encouraged. Under such a system Joseph Henry and others like him would have had no freedom to experiment and no applause for devising new ways of serving the public. But during 1876, as in many other years, the American government often resembled the new state universities in providing services that the public had not demanded, and whose value had never been imagined. Weather, for example, had always been viewed, for good or for bad, as an unknowable force. When in 1870 somebody in the Signal Service, a unit of the War Department, decided to try predicting the weather, the public showed little initial interest. Newspapers were slow to adopt the daily figures that the Signal Service provided without charge; the New York *Herald* was typical in declining to print the forecasts until May 5, 1871. But within five years the novelty became an American institution. Weather forecasting was not entirely new, however, even in 1870. Some years earlier the New York *Tribune* had begun reporting readings from several points within a hundred-mile radius of New York. During 1876 both houses of Congress passed resolutions asking the Secretary of War to estimate the cost of weather forecasting; there was strong sentiment for transferring it to the Treasury Department. A general economy move, that summer, forced the closing of several weather stations, but without any serious effect on the program.[4]

The unidentified Signal Service employee who first suggested weather reports may well have been inspired by the mounting loss in severe weather, of shipping vessels, especially on the Great Lakes where commerce was multiplying. In 1869 nearly two thousand ships were sunk or beached in gales on the Lakes, and almost as many on the sea coasts.[5]

Railroads were less at the mercy of the weather than were ships, but railroads, like farms and riverside communities, could suffer from floods, and one unforeseen value of weather forecasting was that floods could now be predicted in advance. Serious floods in 1876 occurred in eastern Connecticut, in the

Columbia River Valley, in Colorado, and in Texas, but thanks to the forecasting there was minimal loss of life and property.[6] Tornadoes were another matter. It would be years before scientists learned how to predict their formation. The Centennial Year was fortunate in having no tornadoes as destructive as the one on March 20, 1875, which roared along a path two hundred miles long in Georgia and South Carolina, or the one on June 4, 1877, which killed sixteen people in Mt. Carmel, Illinois.[7] Pioneering work for the shipping industry was also being done by another unit in the War Department—the Engineer Bureau. During 1876 its most spectacular project was the blowing up of New York's Hell Gate.[8]

Hell Gate was the one weak point in New York's superlative harbor. It was a passage notorious among mariners for its swift tidal currents, its treacherous eddies and its complex of reefs, most of them hidden. It was even more notorious for its frequent wrecks. New York's merchants dreamed of a Hell Gate cleared of reefs and widened to slow down the currents. Steamship lines dreamed of a safe channel for ships in trans-Atlantic service.

In 1848 two Navy lieutenants were assigned to survey Hell Gate. They identified and measured the major hazards, recommended the elimination of three reefs by blasting, and proposed fenders to keep ships off the underwater rock. Encouraged by their report, a group of New York citizens collected $14,000 in 1851 to begin the work; but the technology of the time permitted blasting on exposed rock surface only, and the results were disappointing. The next year Congress appropriated $20,000 for the project, only enough to lower one reef, Pot Rock, by two feet. In 1856 a special advisory council reviewed the situation and decided that surface blasting was futile; the only hope lay in drilling blast holes into the rock below the surface.

Nothing happened, however, for the next ten years. Then in 1866, Lt.-Col. John Newton of the Army Engineers made a fresh survey, and in 1868 Congress voted $85,000 for a fresh start. That sum, and larger appropriations in subsequent years, were poured down the Hell Gate drain as one experiment after another failed. Diving bells were swept away by the currents. An oval iron caisson proved too unwieldy. But a domed caisson with adjustable legs worked better; by 1872 Diamond and Coentie's reefs were broken up, and by 1874 three others had been lowered enough to pose no further danger. Then Colonel Newton tackled Hallett's Point Reef, a formidable obstacle 720 feet long, 120 feet wide, containing an estimated 110,000 cubic yards. Instead of piecemeal drilling and blasting, it was decided to create a network of tunnels and galleries, eventually totalling 7,425 feet, in preparation for one huge blast that would literally raise the roof. The tunneling removed 47,000 cubic yards, almost half of the reef. The target date was Saturday, September 23, 1876. Delay in delivery of explosives forced postponement to Sunday, September 24.

Some pious individuals were critical of such a desecration of the Sabbath, but most New Yorkers awaited the big day with bated breath. Ten years of study, trial and error, along with more than $1,700,000, had been spent on the baffling monster, Hell Gate, and hopes were now high for success. But as the big day neared, anxiety developed. One editor reported "a justifiable dread about the effects of the explosion," and observed that if the calculations were faulty, and "buildings be freely demolished and great injuries inflicted . . . it would have been better not to get rid of Hell Gate reef." [9] Most houses in the vicinity were deserted on the big day, and doors and windows left open to avoid shattering from the explosion. But curiosity was greater than fear, for large crowds gathered along the shore despite a hard rain. And Ward's Island, just to the south, and other choice positions, were reserved by the city for ticket holders. A heavy police contingent was on hand in case of a panic.

Newton's calculations proved correct. Two warning shots were fired before the blast, the second just thirty seconds before the switch was closed at 2:51 P.M., the moment of full high tide. The waiting thousands saw water and rock fragments leaping into the air, fifty feet at most, then black smoke and shattered timbers before the dull sound and underfoot tremor were noticeable. Boats of every size converged quickly on the spot, although nothing could be seen beneath the surface on so dark a day. Not a single window pane had been broken, but the earth tremor caused by the blast extended as far as Springfield, Massachusetts. The venture had finally met with success.

Hard core pessimists were left with one thing to worry about:

what if some of the nitro-glycerine had gone unexploded? Might some innocent boating party sometime in the future be blown to bits? But the common sentiment was of satisfaction: the channel was measurably safer, and the New York public had witnessed a rarity—a visible and exciting display of how their tax dollars were spent. These War Department ventures were both notable successes, but the War Department, in other respects, was in a sorry condition. One reason was the old national habit of opposing a standing army, generally regarded as a possible threat to individual liberty and as an unnecessary luxury. Armies were thought to be justified only in emergencies. People put greater reliance on local militia before the Civil War and volunteer state troops afterwards. There was no interest at the time in military theory; the only prominent officer in 1876 at all concerned about it was General Sherman, and even his concern was so slight that his memoirs, published in 1875, dropped only scattered hints of possible minor changes. Like most Americans he was a man of action. The first real student of military theory in America was Sherman's protegé Emory Upton, whom he sent around the world in 1875 to inspect the military systems of major nations, and whose great work, *The Military Policy of the United States*, had an influence, more harmful than good, that endured almost until World War II. Upton, contemptuous of militia and "citizen soldiers," argued for a Regular Army of highly trained cadres of "expansible companies" modeled after the efficient German army; and thus, from a premise the exact opposite of traditional popular thinking, contributed to the maintenance of a very small army: the authorized strength reached its low of 25,000 men in 1876, and stayed at that figure until 1898.[10] The deployment of so small a force, together with wholly inadequate Congressional appropriations, taxed the ingenuity of those in command. In all the East, there were only three army installations of more than three hundred men. Civilians there rarely saw a soldier. Most of the army was in posts and forts in the western half of the nation; forts, when Easterners thought of them at all, were the scattered relics of former frontier warfare, of historic interest only.[11] The Indian campaigns of 1876 were, for many editors, prime material for jesting; here's one example, from March: "Sitting Bull. Generals Custer and Crook to Fetch him up Standing." [12] But perhaps the punning editors were right; perhaps pioneering of weather forecasting by the Signal Service and such aids to navigation as the blowing up of Hell Gate, by the Engineer Bureau, were more important for Centennial Americans than fighting recalcitrant Indians, and a better gauge of the War Department's public service. Railroaders in the West, and homesteaders, might not have agreed.

It would be grossly unfair to the War Department not to mention Henry M. Robert, who was eventually to become its chief engineer. A West Point graduate, Robert was for many years in charge of river, harbor, and coast improvements in one part of the country or another. None of this good work is remembered, however, by the millions who know and use as a kind of bible a book he brought out in 1876, *Pocket Manual of Rules of Order for Deliberative Assemblies*. No publisher would risk its publication, and Robert had to have it printed at his own expense. But the first edition of 4,000 copies, priced at seventy-five cents, was exhausted in six weeks,[13] and of all the volumes that bear the Centennial date, *Robert's Rules of Order* seems least likely to go out of print.

The Navy Department showed a comparable range of interests and activities. The Navy as such had 10,046 officers and men, plus 1,980 Marines.[14] The largest ship in use was the "Franklin," 3,173 tons, with thirty-nine guns. It was one of the Navy's five "first rate" ships; there were twenty-seven "second rates," thirty "third rates," and six "fourth rates." In addition were twenty-two wooden sailing vessels, the largest being 2,800 tons, two torpedo-boats, twenty-four iron-clads, and twenty-seven tugs and other small craft. Of the larger vessels, most were receiving ships or training ships, or were laid up or under repair.[15] The Navy had actually taken a step backward, in 1872, when it asked for and got permission to rebuild wooden ships despite the common knowledge that they were useless in war. Their one function, shared with most other ships in the Navy, was distant patrolling.[16] On May 16, to be sure, the Navy landed a small force of sailors and marines at Matamoros, Mexico, at the request of the United States consul in that city, to protect American citizens and property after revolutionaries had evacuated the city and before government troops arrived. This was the only action of the Navy recorded, in a standard chronology, for 1876.[17]

The "Virginius" affair provided a better measure of the relative power of the Navy, and also of the country's pacific mood. A filibustering vessel with no real right to fly the American flag, the "Virginius" was captured by the Spanish navy in 1873 and taken to Santiago de Cuba, where the crew and passengers were divided into groups, tried in nominal courts-martial, and executed by firing squads. There might have been time for a show of force to halt the killings, but no effective Navy ships were available. Tardily, the United States issued an ultimatum to the Spanish government, which surrendered the ship and paid $80,000 to be distributed to families of the dead men. At some other period, the incident could well have led to war; that it did not in the mid-1870s was fortunate, in view of the dilapidated Navy.[18]

As with the War Department, the Navy Department's best service to the public issued through its specialized divisions—such as the Hydrographic office, the Nautical Almanac Office, and the Naval Observatory. The Department was fortunate in having on its payroll two scientists of considerable eminence: Simon Newcomb in the Naval Observatory, and William Ferrel in the Nautical Almanac Office. The British Admiralty had pioneered in 1767 in publishing its first quadrennial *Nautical Almanac*. The United States entered the field in 1855 with its annual *American Ephemeris and Nautical Almanac*. William Ferrel, by profession a meteorologist, wrote extensively about tides, currents, winds, and storms. His major books were *Tidal Researches* (1874) and *Meteorological Researches*, issued between 1875 and 1881. The question that occurs sooner or later to everybody who watches the water draining from a bathtub—why is the swirling clockwise?—is answered by Ferrel's Law; moving bodies are deflected to the right north of the equator and to the left south of it. The more serious application of the law is in its application to air currents.

The two service academies—the United States Military Academy at West Point, established in 1802 and put under the War Department in 1866, and the United States Naval Academy, at Annapolis since 1845 and reorganized under that name in 1851

—were in the doldrums in 1876. Higher education everywhere else was in rapid transition; the two academies were conspicuous exceptions, clinging to traditions. To a good many Centennial Americans, they were not colleges at all; to a small but significant group, they were fit objects for political interference. Their curricula were obsolete, their faculties reactionary, their equipment nominal. The professors were often officers retired from active duty who held onto their posts for life. They never changed the required textbooks, and they ignored what was happening elsewhere in the nation. The bright spot of the Annapolis year was the annual cruise aboard the famous "Constellation," launched in 1797, and used as a training ship from 1871 to 1893.[19]

The Centennial Year did witness one advance in service education, the establishment of what is now the Coast Guard Academy. The Coast Guard takes pride in its antiquity; it began as the Revenue-Marine, in 1791, with ten cutters, whose purpose was to enforce collection of import duties and to prevent smuggling. The Revenue Cutter Service (changed to Coast Guard in 1915) inaugurated a cadet system in 1876 under Congressional law. The first cadets were appointed from nineteen men who went to Washington on December 12, 1876, to take the first entrance exam.[20]

The Army and Navy were shrinking, but other Departments were growing—rapidly. Paid civilian government employees numbered 51,000 in 1871, and almost twice as many, 100,000, ten years later. Only about a sixth of them were based in Washington, but if the postmasters, clerks, and carriers on the Post Office payroll were subtracted from the total, the fraction would be closer to one-third. Much important work had to be done elsewhere than in Washington, of course. For example, the New York Custom House employed about 1,400 people (one of whom in 1876 was the novelist Herman Melville, who was paid four dollars a day.) A doubled federal payroll in a decade of such growth and expansion as the 1870s was easily justified by the many services provided for the public, especially what we call the business community. The prevailing laissez-faire philosophy did not rule out what the government, in manifold ways, was doing to benefit business. Government employees minted the money, carried the mail, surveyed new regions, gave land away, issued patents, kept the peace, and did much more besides. What they were not supposed to do was to interfere. Thoreau had stated the case for unrestricted free enterprise when he wrote, in his essay, "Civil Disobedience," that the government best served the people by its speed in getting out of the way. And laissez-faire was the subject of countless Centennial sermons and editorials, books and magazine articles, orations and college lectures. God had provided all these resources and opportunities for ambitious men to seize and use. An obstructing government would have been guilty of heresy.

This attitude was not quite universal, however, even in 1876. A few men could see a limit to America's natural resources, under the ground and above it; unregulated exploitation, they realized, could lead to exhaustion. Their somewhat vague fears were given focus by a book that appeared in 1874: *The Earth as Modified by Human Action,* by George P. Marsh, a brilliant lawyer, philologist, diplomat—the kind of person we call a universal genius. In this book, which was a revision of his *Man and Nature* published ten years earlier, Marsh asserted that roughly half of the Roman empire had become virtual desert—North Africa, Syria, Mesopotamia, Arabia, Greece, Sicily, and parts of Italy and Spain—through disregard of the laws of nature; and Americans seemed ready to repeat history's mistakes. Marsh urged scientific building of shelterbelts, defended snakes and song birds as destroyers of harmful rodents and insects, and argued that the ground water level depended on forest cover. All of these ideas were foreign to prevailing American thinking, with its residual fear of the forest as the habitat of hostile savages and dangerous animals, its quite practical view of trees as obstacles to agriculture—the commonest means of a livelihood—and its belief that profit from lumbering was part of the American promise of unlimited opportunity.

It would be highly gratifying, in a chapter devoted to the beneficial services of the national government in 1876, to report bold action for conservation, in one federal agency or another. What can be cited is the appointment in 1876 of Franklin B. Hough as a special advisor to the Department of Agriculture on forest policy. Hough, a physician by training with long experi-

ence which made him aware of resource depletion, offered a
resolution at the 1873 meeting of the American Association for
the Advancement of Science, urging federal recognition of forestry problems, and the Association adopted it. But it took three
years for even this smallest of possible beginnings to take tangible form, largely through the prodding of the American Forestry Association, organized in 1875.[21] Hough's work prepared
the way for the creation of a Division of Forestry, and eventually to the Forest Service and the concept of National Forests.
But the 1870s were too early for conservation-mindedness on
any effective scale. Carl Schurz, appointed Secretary of the
Interior by Rutherford Hayes, was the first to be seriously
concerned about natural resources or protection of the public
domain, but his efforts were foiled by flagrant disregard of even
the mildest efforts to regulate. What Vernon Louis Parrington
later called the Great Barbecue, meaning the eager feasting on
natural wealth, by means honest or dishonest, had too much
momentum for anyone to slow down in 1876, much less bring to
a halt. The government was not supposed, in dominant Centennial opinion, to stand in the way of opportunity.

In some parts of the nation, however, trees were scarce and
highly valued—in the plains states, for example, where a seedling
had to be carefully nurtured if it were to grow at all. On April
10, 1872, Sterling Morton, the governor of Nebraska, instituted
Arbor Day and was probably astonished by its quick acceptance, in thousands of communities, as a day each year for planting trees. In the same year James Arnold left $100,000 to Har-
vard for what became the Arnold Arboretum, and New York
State established a Forest Commission. But real conservation, on
the scale needed to reverse the progressive rape of the nation's
forests, had to await until a young Yale graduate, Gifford Pinchot, began in 1891 to demonstrate at Biltmore, the seven thou-
sand-acre Vanderbilt estate near Asheville, North Carolina, that
scientific forestry could be profitable. The results, put on display
at the Columbian Exposition in 1893, attracted nationwide interest. But that was seventeen years and one world's fair after the
period of our immediate concern. The one object at all related to
conservation that was shown at the Centennial Exhibition—or
rather outside the fence, among the peripheral attractions—was a

cross-section of a California redwood, seventeen feet in diameter; but it served rather as an incentive for cutting than as a goad to preservation.

Within the Exhibition grounds, the exhibits of the various federal departments were among the most popular with the viewing public; the Smithsonian men had done their work very well. The Post Office, the one government agency that touched the daily lives of all Americans, was given added attention in 1876 by a popular book, well-illustrated, P. H. Woodward's *Guarding the Mails; or, The Secret Service of the Post Office Department.*[22] Woodward, who had served as chief special agent under Postmaster-General Jewell, to whom he dedicated the book, was able to breathe excitement even into his preface with its raw statistics. Of 410 arrests made in the year ending April 30, 1876, 162 were of officials, including even members of the Secret Service; but the Department had cleaned house, he reported, and the public could be reasonably confident in the future. More than half the arrests were for embezzling from the mails; other offenses included using the mails for fraudulent purposes and mailing obscene materials. Ninety-one of the arrests had led to convictions. The twenty chapters of the book are human-interest accounts of particular crimes and their solutions, over a period of years. The heroes are the special agents in charge of ensuring the safety of the mails; they are pictured as intrepid, persistent, resourceful, and incorruptible, with a code of honor all their own. The villains, no less resourceful, are victims of temptation and evil influences. The stories meet all the requirements of melodrama; but the fact that all of them were true must have convinced many readers that government employees, by and large, were honest men intent on protecting the public—which was probably much more often the case than not.

Because the scandals of 1876 did so much to undermine public confidence in the government, it is regrettable that books for other federal agencies were not written and published. But while exciting stories might have renewed faith in the Coast Guard, or the Light-House Service, or the Army Engineers, it would have been difficult to glamorize others: the Supreme Court, for example, which seemed unable to make up its mind whether to favor corporations or the consuming public. In the Slaughterhouse Case of 1873, the Court under Chief Justice Salmon Chase showed an undeniable shift away from the extreme nationalism of the preceding period; the decision denied the federal government's right to override state legislation creating a monopoly. Critics of the decision thought that it denied to individuals—in this case, most of the butchers in Louisiana—the protection of due process provided by the Fourteenth Amendment.

Justice Chase died in 1873 and was replaced, in 1874, by Morrison Waite. The drift away from nationalism continued, partly because the prewar conflict over states' rights in relation to the national interest gave way to the interrelationship of government and business. This was inevitable, considering the nation's rapid business development after the Civil War. The big questions were now whether the government should control capitalism and, if at all, how much. Laissez-faire theory opposed any control, of course; and during the rest of the nineteenth century the Court in general agreed. But on occasion the Court outraged the prevailing business sentiment by ruling against companies and for the consumer.

So it was with the Waite Court's most important business of 1876. Midwestern railroads and grain elevators had been fixing rates that hurt their grain-producing clients, especially during the Depression of 1873. These farmers, acting through the Patrons of Husbandry (better known as the Grange), put pressure on state legislatures to limit the maximum rates that could be charged for storage and transportation. In contemporary business thinking it was quite proper for firms to set rates but quite improper for states to do so. Railroad and elevator companies sought to have the state laws invalidated, and in time the lawsuits reached the Supreme Court for final judgment. Arguments were heard in October, and November, 1875, and in January, 1876.

The Court's decision on the most famous of these Granger cases, *Munn* v. *Illinois*, was handed down on March 1, 1877,[23] and was as offensive to the country's capitalists as the original state legislation had been. Waite wrote for the Court's majority that "when private property is devoted to a public use, it is subject to public regulation." If individuals disliked a law, they should try to change it by electing legislators who agreed with them, rather than seeking redress through the courts. This decision reflected the philosophy of "self-restraint" that is at the opposite pole from "activism." The leading Court activist at the moment was Justice Stephen Field, whose rigorous dissent suggested that the majority had opened the gates to state control of all business. If, as in this case, a state could regulate a grain elevator, what would prevent some other state from subjecting landlords to the unthinkable extreme of rent controls? In more recent times, activism implies positive Court action on behalf of the consuming public; but its basic meaning is positive Court action to influence national affairs, whether on the side of business or against it. Field, an advocate of laissez-faire, certainly sided with business.

What Field may not have fully comprehended was the loophole the Chief Justice provided when he said that "under certain circumstances" a regulatory statute might be so arbitrary as to be unconstitutional. This concession proved to be of great value to attorneys for corporations. It was a kind of "promissory note" for laissez-faire to cash in at any time—which it chose to do quite soon. The Court under Waite, in its decision in *Munn v. Illinois*, had not been nearly as hostile to laissez-faire as it had seemed.

Whether the Supreme Court served the country better in its moments of self-restraint or activism, and whether it retarded progress or helped it by favoring corporations or their clients, may be questions open only to partisan answers. The Justices, in any event, enjoyed a freedom shared by no other federal employees. They could not lose their jobs, no matter how they decided key questions; and presumably they could act always on principle, as they saw it, without regard for expediency.

They were also very well paid, receiving $10,000 a year, with $500 added for the Chief Justice. The only larger salaries were those of the President, $50,000; eleven diplomats with the rank of Envoy Extraordinary and Minister Plenipotentiary, four at $17,500, seven (including George P. Marsh in Italy) at $12,000; the top three military officers—General Sherman and Admiral Porter at $13,000, Lt.-Gen. Sheridan at $11,000; and Chester A. Arthur, Collector of the Port of New York, whose $12,000 was more than double the salary of any other collector and $4,000 more than that of his superior, the Secretary of the Treasury. All Cabinet members were paid the same salary, $8,000. A major difference between 1876 and the present is that a wide gap in salary separated the top man from all his staff including the second in command; the Vice-President, for example, was paid $8,500, while second highest salaries in executive departments were, with almost no exceptions, less than half the top salaries.

The men singled out in earlier parts of this chapter as making significant contributions to knowledge and the public welfare worked for salaries so low as to be out of all proportion to their merits. Simon Newcomb at the Naval Observatory drew a salary corresponding to that of a Navy Captain—$2,800. William Ferrel, in the Nautical Almanac office, had to be content with $1,200. The men in survey work fared somewhat better: Ferdinand Hayden, as United States Geologist, drew $4,500, George Davidson $3,730, and William Henry Jackson, classified as photographer, $2,100. Spencer F. Baird, the superintendent of the National Museum and the man in charge of federal displays at the Centennial Exhibition, earned $2,700. One man of distinction not mentioned earlier was Benjamin Peirce, Consulting Geometer in the Coast Survey, whose $4,000 salary represented only part-time work; his chief position was that of professor of mathematics at Harvard, but he had served as superintendent of the Coast Survey from 1867 to 1874 and must have been considered indispensable.[24]

Academic salaries, it is only fair to say, were seldom better than government salaries. But professors had extended vacations, freedom of choice in research, the constant stimulation of colleagues with multiple intellectual interests, and, even in those days before tenure rules were enforced, a high degree of job security. They were expected and encouraged, moreover, to push back the frontiers of knowledge; only a few government positions, even in 1876, offered comparable opportunity and challenge.

Those few positions could, however, attract and keep men of great talent, whose presence on the federal payroll was the nation's good fortune. The abuses of power in 1876, by venal men at the upper echelon of government service, have left an unjustified notion that the government was corrupt and inefficient from top to bottom, and paralyzed during Grant's final months as President. Good, solid work went on despite the scandals, and if there were precise scales for measuring good and evil, a long-range judgment might well reveal that the good work performed outweighed the wickedness. Perhaps as a people we take for granted efficient, loyal service, even the outstanding productivity of the most capable, while we magnify the relatively few instances of corruption, remembering Belknap and Babcock and Orvil Grant, and forgetting that Henry and Hayden, Ferrel and Newcomb, Marsh and Davidson and Colonel Newton were in the same Centennial government.[25]

Footnotes for Chapter Seven
GOOD AND FAITHFUL SERVANTS

1. Subsequent remeasurement established Blanca Peak's altitude at 14,317 feet, the fourth highest mountain in Colorado.

2. Oscar Lewis, *George Davidson, Pioneer West Coast Scientist* (Berkeley: University of California Press, 1954).

3. 1876 *Annual Report of the Board of Regents of the Smithsonian Institution* (Washington: Government Printing Office, 1877).

4. Donald R. Whitnah, *A History of the United States Weather Bureau* (Urbana: University of Illinois Press, 1961).

5. Ivan Tannehill, *The Hurricane Hunters* (New York: Dodd Mead, 1955).

6. William G. Hoyt and Walter B. Langbein, *Floods* (Princeton, N. J.: Princeton University Press, 1955).

7. Snowden D. Flora, *Tornadoes of the U. S.* (Norman: University of Oklahoma Press, 1953).

8. Summary account of the Hell Gate project: "Improvement of Hell-Gate," *Appleton's Annual Cyclopedia for 1876*, pp. 377–82.

9. Elmira *Daily Advertiser*, Sept. 21, 1876.

10. Russell Weigley, *History of the United States Army* (New York: Macmillan, 1967), pp. 275–281; Upton's book on Military policy was not published until 1904 but it circulated in manuscript form 1880 on; C. Joseph Bernardo and Eugene H. Bacon, *American Military Policy: Its Development since 1775* (Harrisburg, Pa.: Military Service Pub. Co., 1955). The actual Army strength in 1876, as given by *Historical Statistics of the United States, 1789–1945* was 2,151 officers and 26,414 enlisted men, or a total of 28,565.

11. Francis J. Prucha, *A Guide to the Military Posts of the United States 1789–1895* (Madison: Wisconsin State Historical Society, 1964).

12. Elmira *Daily Advertiser*, Mar. 1, 1876.

13. Julius Mattfield, *Variety Music Cavalcade 1620–1961*, rev. ed. (New York: Prentice-Hall, 1962).

14. *Historical Statistics of the United States 1789–1945*.

15. *United States Official Register for 1877*. This is a biennial register, with no issue for 1876.

16. Walter Millis, *Arms and Men* (New York: G. P. Putnam's Sons, 1956), p. 139.

17. David M. Cooney, *A Chronology of the U. S. Navy: 1775–1965* (New York: Franklin Watts, 1965).

18. Samuel Flagg Bemis, *A Diplomatic History of the United States*, 4th ed. (New York: Holt, 1955).

19. Stephen E. Ambrose, *Duty, Honor Country: A History of West Point* (Baltimore: Johns Hopkins University Press, 1966), Chapter X, "Stagnation"; U. S. Navy Dept., *Centennial of the U. S. Naval Academy*, 1845–1945 (Washington: Government Printing Office, 1945); and Capt. W. D. Puleston, *Annapolis, Gangway to Quarterdeck* (New York: D. Appleton-Century, 1942).

20. Riley Hughes, *Our Coast Guard Academy, a History and Guide* (New York: Devin-Adair, 1944).

21. David Cushman Coyle, *Conservation: An American Story of Conflict and Accomplishment* (New Brunswick: Rutgers University Press, 1957), p. 26; Gifford Pinchot, "How Conservation Began in the United States," *Agricultural History*, XI (October, 1937), 255–65. Hough's 1876 appointment as special agent is also cited in *The Forestry Primer* (Washington: American Tree Association, 1926), but Hough is not listed as a federal employee in the *United States Official Register* for 1877. His *Report upon Forestry* was printed by the government in 1878, in two volumes.

22. A volume of 586 pages, published by Dustin, Gilman & Co. of Hartford. A reprint edition has been made available by the Johnson Reprint Corporation of New York.

23. *Munn* v. *Illinois*, 94 U. S. 113. The text of the majority and dissenting opinions may be found in *The Supreme Court; Law and Discretion*, ed. Wallace Mendelson (Indianapolis: Bobbs-Merrill, 1967), pp. 65–77. The case is discussed in Charles Warren, *The Supreme Court in United States History*, Vol. 3 (Boston: Little, Brown, 1923) and Robert G. McCloskey, *The American Supreme Court* (Chicago: University of Chicago Press, 1960), pp. 127–34.

24. Salaries, presumed to be the same for both years of the biennium 1875–77, reported in the *United States Official Register* for 1877.

25. A thorough historical survey of the development of research and applied science in federal bureaus may be found in A. Hunter Dupree, *Science in the Federal Government: A History of Policies and Activities to 1940* (Cambridge: Belknap Press of Harvard University Press, 1957).

8

The Exhibition

THE very first world's fair, London's Crystal Palace in 1851, was conceived by a man named Henry Cole; he passed along his brilliant idea directly to Prince Albert, the man in all Britain best able to turn the idea into actuality.[1]

It was not that simple in America, where the idea of a world's fair to commemorate the centennial occurred, like the telephone, to two men at the same time, both in the year 1866. One was John L. Campbell, professor of mathematics, natural history, and astronomy at Wabash College. In 1866 he wrote suggesting a Centennial Exhibition to one of his Senators and to the mayor of Philadelphia. The other was General Charles B. Norton, the United States Commissioner to the 1867 Paris Exposition, who, while in London in 1866, proposed a centennial exposition in an article published in an English periodical. Two other men also suggested an exposition, only a little later: John Bigelow, New York's Secretary of State, and Richards Mucklé, a Philadelphia socialite. While it may seem of slight consequence now, this first great fair in America was important enough, to cast a special aura around the men who first proposed it, and all four of these men were honored.[2]

The suspicion of governmental interference did not rule out federal help; support but not control, in a land of free enterprise, was the slogan. The contemporary circumlocution was that identification of the Exhibition with a particular city or state might be fatal to its acceptance as a national project. It also seemed necessary to have some kind of legal sanction, from the highest possible source.

When enough sentiment developed in Philadelphia for the fair to be held there, the Pennsylvania legislature was prodded into memorializing Congress, which first considered the matter in March, 1870. A year later the Congress passed an Act favoring "an exhibition of American and foreign arts, products, and manufactures" but carefully avoiding financial responsibility. On June 1, 1872, in a more definite action, Congress established a Centennial Board of Finance and authorized the sale of ten-dollar shares, to a limit of ten million dollars. In 1874 two bills were passed, one asking the President to invite foreign nations to exhibit, the other waiving import duties on what those nations might send. An outright appropriation of $3,000,000 was defeated, but half a million was voted for a United States building. The final effort at federal support, in the form of a credit of $1,500,000 to ensure that the fair would open free of debt, succeeded as we have seen, at the last possible moment, in January 1876, after lengthy debate and by a very narrow majority.

A world's fair needs considerable executive ability if it is to have any hope of success. Two important positions went to the co-fathers of the Centennial, Professor Campbell and General Norton, but their assignments were more than mere rewards. Campbell was no obscure Hoosier schoolmaster. Among other things in 1864 he had been the principal speaker at the Galileo tercentenary staged by the Smithsonian Institute. When the Centennial Commission was organized in 1872, he was chosen as Indiana's member, and the next year he became its permanent secretary. Wabash College rejected his letter of resignation and granted him, instead, an extended leave of absence. General Norton was named secretary of the Centennial's board of revenue. The presidency of the Centennial Commission went to

Joseph Hawley. Hawley had served a term as governor of Connecticut, and was elected to Congress in 1872 and again in 1874. As owner of the Hartford *Evening News*, which had recently merged with the *Courant*, he was obviously a man of considerable business commitments, and could hardly give his full attention to the Exhibition. The active chief executive was the director-general, Alfred Goshorn, a lawyer and later a paint maker. The respected Philadelphia merchant John Welsh was named president of the board of finance. He was responsible for every contract, every disbursement, and for the half-million dollars in surety bonds which his solid fellow Philadelphians endorsed.

These men—a general, a college professor, a paint-maker, a merchant, and a newspaper magnate—were a fair sampling of types within the dominant Anglo-American element of the population. They performed their unusual duties with laudable efficiency and honesty.

The Exhibition differed in important ways from other large enterprises. Its span of existence was too brief—officially, only the six months from May 10 to November 10—to encourage bureaucratic entrenchment, the accumulating of red tape, a spoils system overstaffing by incompetents, or jockeying for future advantage: there *was* no future to think about. The full glare of publicity may have minimized any latent impulse to cheat; and in addition, a record of good work done in such limelight was a quickly earned enhancement to personal reputation. On the other hand, planning had to be done with utmost detailed accuracy; there could be no resort to trial and error.

On March 4, 1872, the day after Congress gave the Exhibition its official blessing, the members of the Centennial Commission held the first of a great many meetings in the Common Council chamber in Philadelphia. Most of the states and Territories had anticipated Congressional action by naming their Commissioners and alternates earlier, and thirty attended the initial meeting. Protocol took the first day: with ceremonial greetings, from mayor and governor, and other formalities. Then the Commission got down to business. Fairmount Park was accepted as the site. All recent fairs were reviewed—those in New York and Dublin, Paris, London and Vienna—and the group was divided into preliminary committees. Officers were elected and permanent committees named: plans and architecture, finance, foreign affairs, legislation, classification, opening ceremonies. The duration of the Exhibition was fixed for the period from May 1 to November 30, 1876; it was later changed to April 19–November 30, and finally to the half year from May 10 to November 10. Engineering surveys of the site were authorized. Stock certificates were prepared for sale. Privileges of exhibitors were discussed and determined, and procedures were developed for applying for space. Drawings and floor diagrams had to be submitted and approved, along with regulations and specifications of every sort. Admission and other fees were determined, and the sums to be charged for concessions. International judges and juries were defined, with their duties, and the system of awards sketched out. All these things and many more were done by February, 1873, when the Commission reported to Congress and Congress ordered the report printed.[3]

From April to December, 1873, the grounds were prepared—grading, leveling, drainage, installing of gas and water lines, ventilation—and streets and building sites were staked out roughly. March 4, 1874, was the deadline for acceptance by foreign nations wishing to participate, and April 1 for final plans for all structures, most of them due for completion by November, 1875. Catalogue material had to be submitted by February 1, 1876; display material had a deadline of its own for delivery. The several committees and their professional staffs worked steadily to meet their specific schedules; much of the planning took years before anything tangible could be begun, and the public had no knowledge of what was going on until the first buildings began to rise. It was like an iceberg, the six months the Exhibition was open resembled the ninth part visible, while the preparation was the submerged eight-ninths.

By October 1875, Machinery Hall, the second largest building at the Exhibition, was completed. The largest, called the Main Building or simply Main, on December 2. All the other principal buildings were well underway by New Year's. Chance early visitors could judge only by what they saw, and what they saw was apparent chaos. John Lewis, at the time of his Christmas visit to Philadelphia, went out to the site and was less than enthusiastic:

I went over one day to see the Cent. buildings—2 quite
finished—the 3 others nearly so. The land is a reddish yellow
sticky clay & was horrible, but asphalt roads were being made
& an immense amount of work being done. The buildings are
grand & immense; they cover about 48 acres. I was told that
there were 200 buildings going up all directly connected with
the exhibition, minor shows of manufacturers, womens products, offices for foreign & home commissioners &c &c. The
English one is much admired but I did not go near it—it
appears to be the old familiar brick & oak frame house with
many gables so common in Shropshire, & inside is said to be
a marvel. Uncle Sam has also a building but there is nothing
there yet except a 20-inch bore gun, and that has been care-
lessly left out of doors as if to tempt some one to steal it.[4]

The timetable was being closely followed. On January 5 the
first exhibits arrived, and visitors to the grounds could now
watch not only the construction of buildings but also the un-
loading of crates and boxes of every size and shape, and could
speculate about their contents. Visitors were few, however, until
winter gave way to spring. Then it became fashionable for
Philadelphians to ride out to Fairmount Park to see how their
fair was coming along. On fine sunny days the inquisitive
crowds somewhat hindered the workmen, but the officials were
tolerant. One visitor remarked that the early spring weeks at the
grounds were "a marvelously curious and attractive period."

Public interest elsewhere in the nation was not so easily roused
as in Philadelphia. The general interest was stimulated by news
releases, sparse through January but steadily increasing in volume as the opening date approached. In Elmira, for example, the
Daily Advertiser printed only four facts about the Exhibition
during January. The volume of national news items rapidly
increased in February, until, with one or more items every day,
the random shots hit a wide variety of individual interests. The
mail contract had been awarded, stipulating five wagons and ten
horses of specific color and adornment. The Japanese workmen
used no hammers, and worked in silence. Centennial cards, with
pictures of the buildings, were being used by business firms, as
handout advertisements. A gale on February 1 did little damage
except to the roof of Agricultural Hall. A moving sidewalk was

reported, at fifteen or twenty miles an hour. (It was never built.) Philadelphians were reportedly buying smallpox signs to ward off visitors. Atlantic steamship companies were fearful of a lean summer, with everybody flocking to the fair. A Mound Builders exhibit was to be sent from St. Louis. The Press Building cost $20,000. The Women's Centennial Union was bursting with pride over Richard Wagner's agreement to compose a grand march. Centennial striped stockings in red, white, and blue were becoming a fad. Philadelphia was in danger of over-reaching itself by setting exorbitant prices on hotel rooms and meals. William Evarts was announced as the Centennial Orator, Bayard Taylor as the Centennial Poet. Letter boxes on the grounds would be inscribed in six languages. Bowditch's *Navigator* in Japanese would be on display; also a steel file eight feet long. Dr. W. A. Washington of Denison, Texas, had sent a box of Washington relics, while Queen Victoria and her daughters had sent samples of their own needlework. The official Catalogue was ready: the cost, $1.50. A potpourri, indeed; but a world's fair *is* a mammoth potpourri, if one ever existed. Elmira's special pride was the quartet of La France fire engines that would be shown; since every city that made anything was certain to be represented, visitors from every city had a special reason to visit the Exhibition—to view with pride what they may never have bothered to look at back home. If the product in question happened to win a medal, which was a strong possibility, that alone would make the Exhibition a success in the visitor's thinking.

But it is impossible to please everybody. One early decision, to close the grounds on Sundays, won the approval of the Protestant orthodox; it was a notable victory for sabbatarianism. But people who worked all week—at a time when the customary working week was seventy-two hours—were outspoken in their opposition. In consideration of their feelings, the management set aside several half days for workingmen, at half the usual admission, but the concession was meaningful only for those in and near Philadelphia. For the pious, meanwhile, the Sunday closing was a Pyrrhic victory in view of two other decisions, one to permit the sale on the grounds of alcoholic beverages, the other to forbid the sale of religious tracts. Smoking was banned on the grounds, which suggests that pipe, cigar, and cigarette interests were as yet too weak to oppose entrenched piety. No rule forbade chewing. The Catholic Total Abstinence Union had its own impressive symbol, a Memorial Fountain dominating the northwestern angle of the grounds. Visitors gratefully drinking its water on hot afternoons could be inspired by a marble Moses, sixteen feet tall, topping a group of Europeans famous for aiding the patriot cause in 1776—Lafayette, Pulaski, De Grasse, and others; but what their connection was with abstinence remains a puzzle.

The Memorial Fountain, which survives today, was only the largest of a great many meccas for the pious thirsty. The most popular fountain was one described by John Lewis that forced water past large cakes of ice to make it the coldest commodity in the entire Exhibition. There were also numerous soft drink stands, offering a considerable variety of flavored syrups diluted with water or, less commonly, with carbonated water. Charles E. Hires not only displayed his Root Beer but gave demonstrations of how he made it, with dried roots and spices.[5] The standard price of a soft drink was three cents, handy enough because the three-cent piece was one of the standard coins. The soda water concession alone cost $50,000. The cold drink vendors had no reason to be bitter about the very hot summer. Shade was at a premium; trees acquired a sudden popularity. Nowhere on the grounds was there quite the home comfort of quiet back yards, wisteria-enclosed verandas, rooms with drawn shades; on the worst days of that torrid July and August, in all America there was *no* place like home, and potential visitors to the Exhibition showed their good sense by staying away. But if one were hardy enough—trained, perhaps, by a lengthy sojourn on the Sahara Desert—such days would have been ideal for a visit, when a mere ten thousand people ranged an area that easily accommodated one hundred thousand a day in November and was not overtaxed even on September 28, Pennsylvania Day, when the turnstiles clicked off the peak figure of a quarter million.

The officials were right in criticizing the early newspaper pessimism, which was based on the apparent chaos of preparation. Work did remain to be done after the opening on May 10, but it was minor compared with what was ready. William Dean Howells, on May 17, got a bad first impression; it was a raw, drizzly day and the mud discouraged him. "Keep off the grass" signs on newly seeded plots struck him as absurdly optimistic. But there is a vast difference between even an obvious incompleteness and the inability to open; and open the Exhibition did, as scheduled, on the tenth of May. Some people, however, were so sure it could not open on time that they believed it did not. Jacques Offenbach was typical of this group: "Like all world's fairs, the Centennial Exhibition was late in opening. Announced for the first of May, the gates were finally opened on May 11. But nothing was ready." [6]

Eleven springs before, Philadelphia had shrouded itself in black for the body of Abraham Lincoln passing through on its long slow final journey. Now, for an event dedicated to binding in new brotherhood the sections that Lincoln had held together by force, the city was bright with gay bunting. One enthusiast reported dogmatically that "no feast or carnival in Europe or the Orient ever showed brighter decorations." [7] The weather had been bad and it was raining at dawn on the tenth, but the ringing of the Liberty Bell for half an hour was evidently all that was needed to bring the sun out by eight. The pealing magic could not dry up the streets, however, and the vast parade that formed on Broad Street churned the mud into a quagmire. Governor Hartranft of Pennsylvania, a few minutes before eight, led his "brilliantly accoutred" staff west on Walnut Street from Broad. At the residence of George W. Childs, near Twenty-Second Street, President Grant and the members of his Cabinet, in carriages, swung into the line of march. The governors of several other states were there, and many a smartly clad corps of cadets. At the gates of the Exhibition all cavalry had to halt, but there were foot troops enough to fill the space between Main and Machinery. In front of Main, a platform for four thousand people had been erected, facing an inner platform for a thousand musicians and other performers.

By ten o'clock the stands were packed, the roofs of nearby buildings were crowded, and all the statues were draped with men and boys. Theodore Thomas, the German-born violinist who was by now the country's foremost condctor, led an or-

chestra of 150 through a medley of eighteen airs, sixteen foreign
and two American, in the alphabetical order of the nations
represented by exhibits; as each piece began the chief delegate of
that nation was escorted to his place. Last to enter were Grant
and the two Commission presidents, Welsh and Hawley. The
Centennial Grand March was played, perhaps the worst music
that Wagner ever composed, and then Methodist Bishop Simpson offered a lengthy prayer. "May the new century be better
than the last," he intoned. "More radiant with the light of true
philosophy, warmer with the emanations of world-wide sympathy." The Grand Chorus sang the first and last verses of the
Centennial Hymn—words by John Greenleaf Whittier, music
by John K. Paine. Welsh formally presented the Centennial
buildings to Hawley. Dudley Buck[8] conducted his Centennial
Cantata, for which Sidney Lanier had written the words. Hawley presented the Exhibition to President Grant, who accepted
in the name of the nation, and, at the stroke of noon, declared it
open. The notables then toured the grounds. Grant and Dom
Pedro, the Emperor of Brazil, together turned the valves to start
the great Corliss engine, while the Empress formally opened the
Woman's Pavilion.

As such things go, it was a success. General Hawley's speech,
one reporter noted, was "the only one loud enough to be heard
with satisfaction." The fact that all the speeches were read from
manuscript, no doubt a necessity if the time was to come out
right, had a deadening effect. Grant, when his turn came, rose
from his seat beside the imperial Brazilian couple, fished his
speech from out his tail-coat pocket, and read it with a modest
voice, getting "almost as much applause as Welsh and Hawley."
So wrote John S. Ingram, author of one of the voluminous
histories of the Exhibition. The reporter for the *Atlantic
Monthly*, safely anonymous, said that Grant got no applause at
all, and added, "Let the truth be told in spite of the reporters:
there were more groans and hisses than huzzas, as he finished his
brief address. Ten years ago earth and sky would have shaken
with the thunder of his welcome. What a sublime possession to
have thrown away, the confidence and gratitude of a nation!"[9]

Be that as it may, the Exhibition was now duly opened under
the highest possible auspices. Visitors could begin to view the

actuality against what the crescendo of newspaper stories had led them to expect. Perhaps there is no ideal way to view anything so large and multi-faceted as a world's fair; it may take the first day just to become familiar with the layout. William Dean Howells spent *his* first day in aimless wandering about, overwhelmed and not yet oriented.[10] He might have taken the steam elevator to the observation platform in one of the four central towers of Main. Better yet, he could have ascended the Sawyer Observatory, on the Belmont Plateau west of the grounds, for an excellent bird's-eye view of a hundred feet above the tallest building.

In its main outline the plan of the Exhibition resembled a huge lop-sided "A" with all three of its lines extending beyond the points of intersection. The left line of the A, running east and west and paralleling Elm Avenue outside the fence, was named Avenue of the Republic; it followed the north walls of Main and Machinery. At the Catholic Total Abstinence Fountain, a little beyond the northwestern corner of Machinery, it intersected Fountain Avenue, the right side of the A, extended northeast to Horticultural Hall. A small stream flowed down through the A, widening into a pond just above the crossbar and then descending rapidly into the ravine known as the Lansdowne Valley. Whether awareness of the A-plan helped the visitors in 1876 is doubtful, however, with the thousand-and-one eye-catchers on every side.

Most out-of-town visitors reached Philadelphia by train and stayed in hotels, either the regular ones downtown or the large temporary structures which had been erected near the main gates. Collectively the hotels could accommodate an estimated 150,000 people. Besides the two railroads with Centennial depots, there were steamboats on the Schuylkill River that left a downtown wharf every ten minutes. The most picturesque means of local transport were probably the horsecars, three hundred in number, using newly laid tracks and able to carry twenty thousand passengers an hour. There were also omnibus and hack lines. Fares, set by the city, were prominently posted in each vehicle in four languages.

The main entrance, facing the end of Belmont Avenue, had thirty-three money gates, two gates for holders of complimen-

tary tickets, three for exhibitors and employees, and one for
wagons, and thirteen exits. A second entrance had fifteen money
gates, and eleven others had from one to five. Visitors were
instructed to have in hand the exact entry fee, either a silver
half-dollar or a fifty-cent note; if they had neither, there were
money-changing booths nearby. Complimentary tickets and the
booklets given to exhibitors and employees had to be left at the
entrances to keep the daily attendance figures exact.

Just inside the main entrance was the Grand Plaza, with Main
to the right and Machinery to the left. Main was the chief
building and, reputedly, the largest structure in the world—
1,880 feet long, 464 feet wide, and twenty acres in area. Apart
from its sheer immensity, visitors were apt to be aware, first of
all, of the organs—the Hook and Hastings organ at the east end,
the Hilborne L. Roosevelt organ in the north transept, and the
Electric Echo organ in the English Tower. The only time all
three were silent was when some other music was scheduled,
usually in the bandstand in the very center of the building. The
second likely impression was of the fountains, some of them
scented with cologne, each one, if possible, less attractive than
the last.

Having noted these phenomena, the visitor could start detailed
inspection of the exhibits, either on foot or seated in one of the
wheelchairs available for hire. How much he could take in on
this first visit depended on his stamina, for the displays numbered
in the thousands, and covered, literally, a lot of ground. If James
McCabe, one of the Exhibition's historians, was correct, the
visitor would "remark a certain unstudied harmony of dissimi-
larity produced by the kaleidoscopic mingling of . . . our composite American life." [11]

The kaleidoscope was made up of Yale locks, Scott stamps,
carpets, linoleum (a novelty), hardware, cutlery, iron and steel
products, guns, safes, toys, pottery and porcelain, fabrics, slate,
bridges, watches, uniforms, clothing, ropes and cordage, clocks,
Pullman berths, inks, perfumes, glassware, silver, gas fixtures,
jewelry, chemicals, paints, and books, to give only a sampling.
But it was not only American products that mingled in unstudied harmony; many of the displays were foreign. Howells liked
the Norwegian silver work and lifesize groups but thought that

Italy's products, to anyone who had lived in Italy, as he had during the Civil War, seemed meagre and bric-a-brackish. Meissen china was conspicuously absent; so were the best French products, but even for mediocre or trashy products the French provided very attractive settings. Belgian wood-carving and Swedish crockery got considerable attention. Great Britain had extensive but somewhat disappointing exhibits, although British magazines were present in force. Canada had sent a large display. The Japanese work astonished all who saw it. The Carriage Annex, with its historical parade of wheeled vehicles from the most primitive to the latest "Pullman Palace Cars," proved to be one of the most fascinating parts of the Exhibition.

At a certain point even the most indefatigable visitor must have been ready for a change, and Machinery Hall offered just that. Here the only music was the restful steady hum of the Corliss engine and the varied lesser sounds of the machines which the Corliss powered by shafts and pulleys. Cornell University's department of mechanical engineering vied for attention with printing presses which ran off the New York *Herald* and the *Sun* from stereotype plates brought daily from New York, and a London *Times* press that turned out a daily edition of the *New York Times*. Benjamin Franklin's venerable hand press was also there, and a section of the Brooklyn Bridge cable, and a Tuscan column made of thirty-eight grindstones, all different, topped by an eagle. The Pyramid Pin Company had a machine, run by a little girl, which could and did stick 180,000 pins into paper every day. There were steamship models, sugar clarifiers, ice yachts, automatic switches, a machine that made forty thousand bricks a day, an hydraulic ram, fire engines, candy and popcorn machines, a chewing-tobacco machine run by four Negroes who sang hymns while they worked, and a typewriter, described by McCabe as "an ingenious machine for printing letters or manuscripts instead of writing them with the pen." [12] A crowd always gathered at the machine making Centennial stamped envelopes. Sweden displayed stoves and a narrow-gauge locomotive, the "Nyhammer." Belgium displayed a well-borer. Germany displayed some Krupp guns. A man named Bell displayed a telephone; the Emperor Dom Pedro happened along one day, listened, and dropped the receiver with the comment, "My God, it talks!" [13] Elisha Graves Otis was less lucky with an elevator that he tried to interest people in. American technology, if anybody needed to be convinced, was on the march.

The Exhibition had a railroad of its own; in the Railroad Age, why should anybody walk? John Lewis thought the little train wonderfully convenient and restful; [14] Howells wrote that it "coughs and writhes about the grounds," and complained of its excessive speed. Donald Grant Mitchell ("Ik Marvel") agreed with Howells, calling the railroad "a constantly recurring pest, by reason of its half-hourly blockade of one of the most important thoroughfares," and complaining of its employees as "a noxious and noisome exception to the generally civil and courteous conduct of all the servants of the Exhibition who wear uniform." [15] The fare was considerably lower than fares outside —five cents, even if one stayed aboard for the complete four-mile circuit. There was first the long straightaway past Main and Machinery, then a sweep around the southwest corner of the grounds, between several model factories and past the encampment of West Point cadets, then a meandering run north-north-east past the main row of State buildings, and a great loop around Agricultural Building, in the northern angle. The return followed Belmont Avenue—the crossbar of the lop-sided A—between the Woman's Pavilion on the left and the United States Government Building on the right. Horticulture was the only large building not on the line.

Once the Exhibition had opened, firsthand reports began to appear in newspapers and magazines. Their volume increased gradually, with the crest coming at the very end of the period, if not after the closing, as in two *Harper's Weekly* articles by Rebecca Harding Davis on November 18 and 25. Most of these letters and articles began with descriptions of Main and Machinery, but there was no agreement about what to see next, or the best order for inspecting the rest. The miniature railroad served several reporters as the means of deciding, or of recovering energy while waiting to decide.

Agricultural Building had what state and county fairs have always had—plows and reapers and binders, and foodstuffs of every sort, but also a few surprises—stuffed birds and mammals, fishing craft, aquaria refilled daily with salt water. On a perch, proudly surveying the horse-shoes, the baking powder, the tobacco, the silkworms, the spice-grinders, sat "Old Abe," the eagle mascot of the Eighth Wisconsin Regiment, twice wounded in the Civil War. If the Agricultural Building was of special interest to farmers, all taxpayers found something fascinating in the United States Government Building, which showed better than charts and figures where the tax money went. The only department not represented was State, diplomacy being difficult to put on display. There were Post Office railroad cars, famous Indians in papier-mâché, totem poles, a wooden model of a monitor turret with a pair of fifty-two-inch guns, various small boats (one of them from the famous Kane Arctic expedition of 1853–55), guns of all sorts, the instruments used by the Navy in observing the transit of Venus in 1874, and a great many more of the multiform and multipurpose gadgets used by various federal divisions, bureaus, and services. People who had seen lighthouses in operation were glad to inspect, at first hand, one of the large rotary lamps with multiple reflectors. The weather instruments used by the Signal Service were even more popular, but the largest crowds of all gathered to see the camp equipment that George Washington had used on his campaigns. Howells especially liked this and the other Washington relics at the Exhibition, and used them as peg for a remark that there was, unfortunately, "no modern worthy thus to hand down a coat and a hat to the admiration of posterity."

Howells was not the only reporter of the Exhibition who saw fit to snipe at Grant, although it may seem out of character for "the gentle realist." He gave more attention to the various State buildings, whose purpose eluded him: "In a country where for the most part every State is only more unrepresentative than another, it is very difficult for the buildings to be representative." He excepted Mississippi's, built of logs and draped with Spanish moss, and the Old Colony House of Massachusetts, also of log construction; both, incidentally, contributed to the persistent and popular Log Cabin Myth. Most of the other State buildings, as their portraits indicate and as the one survivor, the Ohio Building, demonstrates, were merely different versions of the same modified Gothic, or Queen Anne, that might have graced High Street in Upper Suburbia. Howells was also perplexed by the Woman's Pavilion: "Those accustomed to think of women as the wives, mothers, and sisters of men will be puzzled to know why the ladies wished to separate their work from that of the rest of the human race." Why not a "Man's Pavilion" too? John Lewis was of the same opinion, adding that the women working in the watch department in Machinery Hall gave a better notion of the skills that women could achieve.

One building that everybody noticed was the Department of Public Comfort, which provided not only toilets and washrooms but quite a variety of other facilities. There was a large reception room, abundantly supplied with chairs and sofas, with a large register where visitors could sign their names. There were barber shops, shoeshine rooms, check rooms, dressing rooms, desks for writing letters, an Art Gallery, and an open-air terrace with a canvas awning where friends could meet. One wing housed the Commission offices and the press, and the opposite wing accommodated the Exhibition's telegraph office. Most of the services were free of charge, but the sale of stationery, postage stamps, and opera glasses, and the renting of umbrellas, which during the dog days were a leading symbol of the Exhibition, made the operation very profitable to the company that had paid a mere $20,000 for the concession.

An area outside the grounds, variously dubbed Shantyville and Dinky-Town, had a number of catchpenny establishments. A "museum" featured wild men of Borneo, wild children from Australia, Fiji Islanders, a fat woman (602 pounds), a two-legged horse and a five-legged cow. There were also sausage stands, lemonade booths, and shooting galleries. One reporter hinted darkly of dens of vice, but he did not elaborate, and nobody else thought them worth investigating. But whether or not there was any threat to morals, the flimsy construction posed a constant threat of fire. On September 9 a fire did start, and it rapidly spread. If the wind had been from the south instead of the northwest, Main might have caught fire; as it was, the turnstiles at the Belmont Avenue entrance were scorched.

Several of the attractions outside the fence were hardly objectionable: the model of a Pennsylvania oil well, for example, and a section of a California redwood. There was a panorama called

"The Siege of Paris," and nearby was Operti's Tropical Garden with its cascade, rocky nooks, beds of rare flowers, and sixty-piece band. It rivalled Theodore Thomas's beer and concert garden at the Forest Mansion and the "Offenbach Garden" especially prepared for the visiting French maestro.

Three restaurants outside the grounds—Wiley's, Doyle's, and Tischner's—escaped the criticism heaped on some of those inside, which early became known as extortionate and found it hard to correct the impression even after lowering their prices. John Lewis, who knew his groceries, was indignant at the high prices but excepted the Vienna Bakery and Cafe, just to the east of Memorial Hall, as a kind of paradise with its fine crusty bread and proper coffee. Donald Grant Mitchell, however, said of it that "by its extortionate charges, it keeps vividly in mind some of the worst aspects of the Vienna Fair" (of 1873),[16] and Howells considered it the worst of all the foreign eating places, with wretched coffee that cost a whole quarter of a dollar. *De gustibus.* Howells liked Lauber's German restaurant, near Horticultural Hall, and the Lafayette, beside the pond, but described the Trois Frères Provenceaux as "impudently extortionate." That adjective was rather overworked during the summer. The anonymous reporter for the *Atlantic* said he never ate anywhere else once he had tried the American Restaurant, in front of Agricultural Building; he found it cooler, cheaper, better, and cleaner than all the others; it was also the largest, capable of seating five thousand people at once.[17] The Southern, at the far end of the Belmont Avenue cross walk, was managed by an Atlantan and staffed entirely with Negroes; it was a favorite rendezvous for Southerners.

There were several smaller restaurants, and in addition some of the exhibitors sold or gave away food—the Caffé do Brasil, the popcorn factory, the Dairy (fittingly near the Bible Society building) with milk, buttermilk, and ice cream, Jacob Kohn's pavilion (Hungarian wines and liquors), the Butter and Cheese Building, the Tunisian Coffee Tent, and the Tea and Coffee Press Building. *Harper's Weekly* advised people to bring their own lunch, and eat it on the banks of the Wissahickon.[18] This good advice was hardly needed, for from the beginning a goodly number of visitors squeezed through the turnstiles with sizable hampers of food. Eating beside the Wissahickon posed certain problems, however; that stream was part of Fairmount Park, all right, but it was a substantial distance from the Exhibition grounds. Most of the hamper-toters, especially during the low-attendance days of July and August, could find attractive spots in the Lansdowne and Belmont ravines, under trees so large that New Yorkers were envious: Central Park, in contrast, would not have such fine old trees for many decades.

At the Kohn pavilion the waiters wore the Hungarian national dress. Howells regretted that more national costumes were not worn, but the jostling of foreigners on the Philadelphia streets, especially the Japanese, had convinced most of them of the prudence of abandoning their native garb. The *Atlantic* correspondent was particularly attracted by the Japanese, "the sweetest-voiced, gentlest-mannered folk," and he thought that their display made everything else at the Exhibition seem vulgar.[19] John Lewis on his first visit had admired their tools and their method; and everyone admired the Japanese Building, a far cry from the ubiquitous Victorian. It had its drawbacks, however: its unoiled and unpainted wood, however suitable for the climate of Japan, made it impractical for the summer climate in Philadelphia.

The jostling of foreigners was probably not so much rudeness as curiosity and a counterpart of the attention paid to visiting celebrities when recognized. But even celebrities were lost in the crowd unless they had special duties on special occasions, such as State days. Governors, Senators, Congressmen, Cabinet officers, generals, and socialites were conspicuous in the many parades because they rode on horses. It may have been the Railroad Age, but any man of distinction knew how to ride a horse. The crowning event of the Exhibition, as of the Centennial Year, was the Fourth of July; the Exhibition may have fallen somewhat short of other goals, but it did revive the spirit of the Fourth as a prime occasion to make loud noises, give speeches or cheer them, and pay tribute to the Stars and Stripes. For the moment, the nation was willing to be distracted from all that had happened since New Year's to defeat the noble hopes of cementing sectional brotherhood.

In Philadelphia, the celebration of the Fourth was given to the

Centennial Commission to manage, and the Commission decided that Independence Square was the logical setting. All business in the city was suspended for the first five days of July. On July 1, a Saturday, biographic memoirs of the Revolutionary leaders were presented, various Centennial hymns and odes were sung, and Leverett Saltonstall of Massachusetts gave the principal address. The Committee for the Restoration of Independence Hall was very much in evidence.

Sunday was quiet, and so was most of Monday. At about half past eight that evening a torchlight procession began to form, made up of workingmen's delegations, commissioners from foreign countries, several state governors, Army and Navy officers, civic and political organizations, and Commission officials. Along the line of march fireworks were set off and the crowds cheered. The main streets, especially Chestnut and Broad, were bright with thousands of colored lanterns. It all seemed carefree and spontaneous, but it was so well timed that the head of the procession arrived in front of Independence Hall exactly at midnight. The Square was already crowded; somebody estimated that a quarter million out-of-town visitors joined with Philadelphians for the occasion. As the minute hand of the tower clock reached the exact zenith, there was a breathless silence, and then the new Liberty Bell rang out—thirteen times. The crowd now roared—independence was a century old. Throughout the city and throughout the nation, every bell rang, every whistle blew, and guns of all sorts were fired—it was New Year's Eve all over again. In the Square, an orchestra and chorus struck up "The Star-Spangled Banner," followed by the Doxology. This was meant as the finale, but a good portion of the crowd stayed until about two o'clock, simply enjoying themselves too much to leave.

At sunrise, not much more than two hours after the last revelers had gone home, cannon thundered from the Navy Yard, from Fairmount Park, and from Swedish, Brazilian, and American warships anchored in the Delaware. Since the day was certain to be a scorcher, the parade formed soon after seven. Among the military units were the West Point cadet corps, the Black Hussars, selected companies from Detroit, three from Virginia, and "visiting troops from Texas." A "Centennial Legion," commanded by General Henry Heth of Virginia, was composed of detachments from all the thirteen original states. On the reviewing stand in front of Independence Hall were William Tecumseh Sherman, in command of all United States armies, Prince Oscar of Sweden, Lieutenant-General Saigo of Japan, a sprinkling of governors, and General Hawley. When the parade ended—the route had been shortened because of the heat—the four thousand invited guests took their places in the great stand, and the crowd cheered the celebrities, especially Dom Pedro. The only flaw in the entire occasion was that President Grant had not come. James McCabe, scrupulously objective in his treatment of every detail of the Centennial Exhibition, departed from his sober matter-of-factness on this occasion only:

> It was hoped that the President of the United States would be present and preside over the ceremonies; but General Grant declined the invitation to do so, which it was at once his privilege and his duty to accept, and remained in Washington, preferring his selfish ease to a little patriotic exertion and exposure to the heat on this grandest of his country's festivals. His absence was generally remarked and severely condemned by his countrymen.[20]

The anonymous reporter for the *Atlantic* was even more indignant: "The president's absence put the finishing stroke to the sum of his offenses; it was the most condensed yet crudest statement of his estimation of the dignity of the country, the occasion, and his office. The credit of the day and nation could only gain by his absence. . . ."[21]

Vice-President Thomas W. Ferry served as Grant's stand-in and spoke his lines at the proper time. Richard Henry Lee of Virginia, grandson-namesake of the man who had offered the resolution that "these United Colonies are and of right ought to be free and independent States," read the Declaration of Independence from the faded original manuscript; but the crowd could not keep quiet and few heard the words. Bayard Taylor read a "noble ode" and the Hon. William M. Evarts of New York delivered a grandiloquent address. The choir sang the "Hallelujah Chorus," and finally, at Ferry's suggestion, everybody who knew it joined in singing the Hundredth Psalm. That wound up the great day, except for a fireworks display, after dark, on the Exhibition grounds.

Later in the summer and continuing into the fall, consecutive Thursdays were set apart to commemorate particular events and to honor those states near enough Philadelphia to ensure good attendance. October 12, the 386th anniversary of Columbus's New World landfall, was Italian Day, climaxed by the unveiling of a twenty-two-foot Columbus monument designed by a Florentine. The next Thursday, the anniversary of the surrender of Cornwallis at Yorktown, was in honor of Delaware, Maryland, and Virginia and was memorable for an old-time Southern Tournament, with sixty thousand people on George's Hill watching fifteen knights compete at ring-spearing. The Knight of Delaware (a Baltimorean) won handily, spearing eight rings out of a possible nine. Later, a Virginia girl was crowned Queen of Love and Beauty. Although her State was among those not officially represented at the Exhibition, a pretty girl is better, any day, than a mere governor.[22]

The days set apart for New York and Ohio, logically enough, were marked by appearances of the candidates for President who happened to be their governors. It was no doubt only coincidence that Ohio Day, with Rutherford Hayes the stand-out attraction, was also the date of a convention of the nation's leading business executives. Other special days, too numerous to list, were assigned to particular interests, sports, and organizations. The international billiards tournament, encampments of various military units, reunions of foreign-born citizens, and assorted conventions all stimulated interest—and boosted gate receipts. Perhaps the greatest peripheral attraction was the Grand International Regatta of rowing clubs on the Schuylkill, from August 22 to September 6. Philadelphians soon lost count of the parades and the famous names. A Brazilian frigate celebrated mass on board every Sunday morning, with military music. A Swedish couple were married in Agricultural Hall. In September 722 dogs were assembled for a dog show, and 246 horses were on exhibit, 176 of them from Canada. Thieves stepped up their petty larceny with the cooler fall weather. A fire at Lauber's German restaurant early in October caused a

$26,000 loss. A committee of Philadelphia businessmen asked the Park Commissioners to save Main Hall from demolition but "met, to the astonishment of all, with a flat refusal." [23] Talk of deferring the closing also led to nothing; but the grounds did stay open, unofficially, for ten days beyond November 10.

The final days of the Exhibition occasioned a good deal of premature nostalgia. All too soon the daily routine would stop forever. No lines would start forming by half-past six in the morning, and early risers would not witness the Exhibition police force entering by squads, or the gray-clad rolling-chair attendants, also in military formation. The machinists, the restaurant cooks and waiters, the bootblacks, the many vendors, would come no more; neither would the butchers' wagons, the ice carts, the mail-carriers, or the beer vans. There would be a different set of sights and sounds as the exhibited goods were crated and taken away and most of the buildings dismantled, sold to the highest bidder. Memorial Hall was to remain, as a permanent art gallery, and Horticulture as a vast greenhouse. England gave her buildings to the city of Philadelphia—and the largest still stands, a handsome red-brick dwelling, close by the Catholic Total Abstinence Fountain.

President Grant, though he missed the festivities on the Fourth, appeared for the closing. It was a rainy day, that Friday in November, suggesting to the superstitious that Nature joined in mourning the demise of the year's great spectacle. The ceremonies began with a thirteen-gun salute. D. J. Morrell paid tribute to the work of the Centennial Commission. A "Te Deum" was sung. Welsh paid "eloquent tribute" to the memory of the past century. An orchestra played Beethoven's Fifth Symphony. Goshorn paid tribute to the foreign commissioners. A choir sang the Hallelujah Chorus. Hawley reviewed the difficulties that had been overcome and paid tribute to practically everybody. "America" was sung. John Paul Jones's original flag was unfurled. Grant paid tribute to nobody, limiting his speech to a single sentence: "Ladies and Gentlemen:—I have now the honor of declaring the Exhibition closed." That was at 3:37; telegrams were sent out at once to the principal cities of Europe and America. In Machinery Hall some fifteen thousand people waited for Grant to stop the Corliss engine as he had started it six months before, but he never got there. A gong sounded, two engineers threw the switch, and the giant rested. In the Judges' Hall, the assemblage sang the long-meter doxology. The spectacle of the year was over. The rain continued.

Judged soberly, the Centennial Exhibition was a success as a spectacle. If it seems so in retrospect, how much more so it must have been for the thousands of visitors, especially those from farm and village unused to bigness as such or shiny machines or fountains or fireworks or notables or foreigners. In a nation with almost no paving at all, even the asphalt walks were a marvel to write home about. The more daring could tell of a ride in an overhead car. Few saw anything more than a remote kind of magic in Mr. Bell's telephone, and though the Corliss engine always attracted a dazed and reverent crowd, almost nobody foresaw that similar engines would some day bring electricity into private homes. In all subsequent world's fairs, American visitors have been aware enough of technology to view the gadgets as promising something to their own future; the Centennial Exhibition came at a point of time before the public was conditioned to look for miracles. It was still a time of orientation to the past, to the century of independence and to *its* record of progress. Above all, the Exhibition fully confirmed the sense, newly born in 1876, that the American nation had a past—a glorious past, one to be proud of and to commemorate. The present was dark, and as for the future, the election held three days before the Exhibition closed blocked out all thought except the big question of which man, and which party, had actually won. Settling *that* problem was what the future, just then, meant for most Americans.

Footnotes for Chapter Eight
THE EXHIBITION

1. Christopher Hobhouse, *1851 and the Crystal Palace* (London: John Murray, 1950).
2. The original proposers were singled out, though not in the same order, by the major contemporary works on the Centennial Exhibition: John S. Ingram, *The Centennial Exhibition Described and*

Illustrated (Philadelphia: Hubbard, 1877), John D. McCabe, *The Illustrated History of the Centennial Exhibition* (Philadelphia: National Publishing Co., 1876), and the eleven-volume official summary cited herein as *Exhibition Reports.* A more recent study is Christine Hunter Davidson, *The Centennial of 1876: The Exposition, and Culture for America* (unpublished Ph.D. dissertation, Yale University, 1948).

3. U. S. Centennial Commission, *The National Celebration . . . to be held in 1876,* compiled by H. D. J. Pratt (Washington: Government Printing Office, 1873), U. S. 42d Congress, 3d session, House Miscellaneous Document No. 99.

4. John Lewis to his brother, Jan. 14, 1876, in Lewis Letters at Cornell. Lewis's full report on the Exhibition is available in Randel, "John Lewis Reports the Centennial," *Pennsylvania Magazine of History and Biography,* 39 (July, 1955), 364–74.

5. John J. Riley, *A History of the American Soft Drink Industry: Bottled Carbonated Beverages, 1807–1957* (Washington: American Bottlers of Carbonated Beverages, 1958).

6. Offenbach, *Orpheus in America,* p. 25.

7. Ingram, p. 74.

8. The managers of the Exhibition had sought to enlist the nation's best available talent for all the ceremonial occasions; in music they had succeeded, for John Knowles Paine and Dudley Buck were the only two native composers of the first rank, according to Louis C. Elson, *The History of American Music,* rev. ed. (New York: Macmillan, 1915).

9. "Characteristics of the International Fair," *Atlantic Monthly,* 38 (July, 1876), 85–91; hereinafter cited as "Characteristics."

10. William Dean Howells, "A Sennight at the Centennial," *Atlantic Monthly,* 38 (July, 1876), 93–107. All Howells quotations in this chapter are from this article.

11. McCabe, p. 345.

12. McCabe, p. 453.

13. Floyd L. Darrow, *Masters of Science and Invention* (New York: Harcourt, Brace, 1923), p. 288.

14. John Lewis to his brother, Aug. 7, 1876, in Lewis Letters at Cornell.

15. Donald Grant Mitchell, "In and About the Fair," *Scribner's Monthly Magazine,* 12 (Sept., 1876), p. 774; this was the first of three installments.

16. Mitchell, "In and About the Fair," *Scribner's Monthly Magazine,* 13 (Nov., 1876), 115–24.

17. "Characteristics."

18. Note in *Harper's Weekly,* June 17, 1876.

19. "Characteristics."

20. McCabe, p. 671.

21. "Characteristics."

22. Ralph Waldo Emerson, on a trip South in July, remarked that Virginia girls were pretty, thereby giving proof that at the age of seventy-three his faculties were undimmed, but prompting an editorial question of whether he could go home and "confront the maidens of the modern Athens, after such a speech?" (Elmira *Daily Advertiser*, Oct. 23, 1876).

23. Elmira *Daily Advertiser*, Oct. 20, 1876.

9

The Quality
of Life

JOHN GREENLEAF WHITTIER, composing *Snowbound* for publication in 1866, breathed into it nostalgia for a rural way of life
he thought was dead. But his mourning was premature, for rural
self-sufficiency was still alive in 1876, and even much later. It
had been two centuries and more in the making, and was not
something to be discarded overnight.

The urban pattern was as old as the rural, if not older, but
until the advent of industry, after 1800, cities were hardly a
source of worry to the countryside. But accelerating migration
from farm to city after the Civil War caused great misgivings.
Whittier was hardly alone in thinking that cities were not quite
in the American tradition. To rural Americans, rural America
was the best of all possible worlds.

With all due respect to individual opinions about the quality
of life, however, it seems reasonable to say that life on the farm
was pretty dull. People who knew no other pattern may not
have thought so; but people today who move back to the land
accept the dullness as a welcome change from urban stresses.

Sabbatarianism, the nadir of dullness, had one advantage in 1876; it forced a suspension of the ceaseless labor of the other six days of the week. Much of the resistance to lowering the factory work week to less than the standard seventy-two hours stemmed from the rural necessity of working even longer. If farmers had to work that much, why should factory hands work less? Eating and sleeping were the other uses of time. Even the occasional socializing was work: barn-raising, corn-shucking, quilting-bees.

Virtually everything of interest in Centennial America existed elsewhere than on the farm and in the villages. Much of the interest stemmed from the rapidity of cultural change. Rural life was static; urban life was in constant flux. People knew who they were in the country, and where they stood; urbanites were either uncertain or didn't care. But the biggest difference between country and city was that cities created wealth and leisure and the challenge of finding ways to use them. A sampling of how people faced this challenge in 1876 is surely in order.

In the rural areas, clothing was a simple matter: work clothes and one good dress or suit for church and trips to town. Fashion was an urban phenomenon. The Princess Eugenie style (after the French Empress from 1853 until 1870) dominated feminine attire: high waistline, full blouse, bouffant sleeves, skirts almost to the ground, and small pert hats. Men wore informal suits with vests, and unpressed trousers. Formal evening wear was white tie and swallow-tails. With increasing travel by train, "country clothes" became fashionable—especially rough tweed jackets. And the spread of sports required more additions to wardrobes, especially for tennis and croquet. London, not Paris, set the modes.[1]

Recent converts from rural to urban living, uncertain as to how to behave, were grateful for books on etiquette. One such book, *Decorum: A Practical Treatise on Etiquette and Dress of the Best American Society* by John A. Ruth, devoted a thirty-page chapter to clothes: evening dress, morning dress for the street and for home, attire for riding on horseback and in carriages, dress for church and theatre, concert and opera, croquet and skating, country and seaside, calling and being called on, and going to Europe. And of course the special outfits for weddings. The author condemned all makeup, because it contained poisons "inducing paralytic afflictions and premature death," and considered negligence in dressing an affectation of millionaires who thereby betrayed their "miserly penuriousness of disposition." [2]

Ruth's remarks on "The Toilette" tell us something about contemporary home life. Well-arranged dressing rooms were, he noted, a must in the best society, one for the husband, a second for the wife. Although male wardrobes were not extensive, it was wise to have plenty of drawers to hold vests and pantaloons; boot-jacks and boot-hooks were essential. A case of seven razors was advisable for shaving, one for each day of the week; also, shaving soap, shaving brush, a small tin pot for hot water, and a package of paper to wipe the razor on. The lady's dressing room needed, among other things, a hairpin cushion, a washstand with large bowl and pitcher, a small pitcher and tumbler, a sponge basin, a bottle of ammonia, and a footbath beneath the washstand. Body baths were desirable at least once a week, but better yet were a douche or hip-bath every morning and a sponge bath every night before retiring. It was wise to wet the head with cold water and sponge the pit of the stomach before beginning the bath, and afterwards to apply the hair glove or flesh brush to stimulate the skin before toweling. As for shower baths, only the most vigorous constitutions could endure them. [3]

One intriguing passage in this volume concerns the etiquette of boating. The proper boating attire for men was white flannels; for women, skirts barely touching the ground, no crinoline under the skirts, flannel Garibaldi skirts, and little sailor hats; for both sexes stout boots. Corsets were not mentioned by name, but the author did say "it is impossible for anybody to row with comfort or grace if she laces tightly." In social boating, only the men were to row. However: "If you cannot row, do not scruple to say so, as then you can take your seat by the side of the ladies, and entertain them by your conversation." [4]

The author did not choose to discuss the use of chewing tobacco. Chewing was not a Centennial peculiarity; the entire nineteenth century might be dubbed the Chewing Tobacco Era, replacing the colonial period's addiction to pipes. Some of the famous trade names were "Cherry Ripe," "Wedding Cake," "Winesap," "Bouquet," "Uncle Sam," "Diadem of Old Virginia," and "Daniel Webster." So much did the manufacturers of chewing tobacco dominate that they produced also, as side-lines, most of the nation's pipe tobacco and snuff. With chewing so popular, spitting was common. As one recorder puts it, chewing and "its attendant expectoration" were not out of place in a society of slovenly male dress and crude personal habits, despite what all the authors on etiquette had to say. Some men, of course, did not chew; but the ubiquity of the spittoon, noted by one of our French travelers, was a necessity.[5]

Cigars had been introduced by German immigrants, from 1848 on, and by 1860 cigar-making was widely scattered—Philadelphia, New York, Baltimore, Cincinnati, Hartford, St. Louis, Newark, Albany, New Orleans and Hampden County, Massachusetts. Tobacco shops were distinctive for the wooden figures outside their doors, an idea borrowed from English shopkeepers. The famous wooden Indian, however, was by no means alone; there were also wooden Turks, Scotch Highlanders, Negroes, even an occasional wooden figure of Jennie Lind. Zinc and cast iron were also increasingly popular for these figures, perhaps because their greater weight made kidnapping difficult. By the 1890s their use, alas, had all but disappeared.[6]

Tobacco growing grew in importance with the increase in smoking. For many years Connecticut led in the production of cigar wrappers, but York and Lancaster Counties in Pennsylvania became rivals after 1860, and Gadsden County, Florida introduced the superior Havana Leaf in 1875. The fourth major growing area was around Janesville in southern Wisconsin. By 1876 Americans were buying and smoking more than two billion cigars a year, which meant a hundred cigars a year for each American male.[7]

Cigarettes were far less popular. As early as 1845, somebody accused ladies of smoking them secretly, but the habit grew quite slowly. At first, cigarettes were rolled by hand, using tobacco from Virginia, Kentucky, North Carolina; a cigarette-making machine was patented in 1872 and put in operation in 1876. It was to be many more years before Americans took to them, however; only about half a billion cigarettes were made in 1880, a fifth the number of cigars.[8]

Alcohol was a perennial object of reforming zeal. Some states already had prohibition laws by 1876, and the legislatures of other states considered the pros and cons that year. On December 12 one of New Hampshire's Senators, William Henry Blair, introduced a bill proposing *federal* prohibition of the liquor traffic, but it got nowhere. The Women's Christian Temperance Union had been organized in Cleveland in 1874, by delegates from seventeen states who had been stimulated by the forceful lecturing of Dr. Dioclesian Lewis of Boston. But the Anti-Saloon League was not founded until 1893, and Carrie A. Nation did not begin her dramatic activism against alcohol until 1900. Temperance and the woes of drinkers' families were themes of much popular sheet-music of the 1870's. Some of these sentimental delights were "Papa Don't Drink Any More," "A Cup of Cold Water" by an off-and-on reformed lush named John B. Gough, who made a fair living by temperance lecturing, and at least one with a happy ending, "Father Drinks No More." Children were often sent to buy liquor or beer to take home; a pint of raw whiskey might cost as little as ten cents. As a concession to the proprieties, girls sent for a "growler" of beer (a two-quart container) entered by the side door [10]—as one of our French visitors learned to do in his hotel on a Philadelphia Sunday.

Vice was rampant in Centennial cities, especially among the children. In the chaotic maladjustment after the Civil War, home for thousands of children meant congested squalor in old houses converted into crowded tenements, and play meant whatever they could find to do in the streets. Despite school attendance laws, large numbers of children never went to school at all, and their training for life lay rather in picking pockets, stealing lead pipe from empty buildings and selling it to junk peddlers, or rolling drunks for whatever cash they carried. Girls in the slums became professional early; as a cover they sold matches or flowers, but men knew that the question, "Give me a penny, mister?" meant that more than matches and flowers were for sale. The elite among this pathetic group were called the "hot corn" girls; they wore gay calico dresses and plaid shawls, went barefoot, and offered corn on the cob to knowing customers.[11]

In Philadelphia, the sorriest section was St. Mary's Street, where there were all ages, all colors, and all conditions except prosperity. Junk shops and "old-do" stores were numerous, and the Bedford Street Mission provided more than three thousand lodgings in four years and eighty thousand free baths in eight years. For two hours at midday free tickets were available to the soup house in Griscom Street; most of the diners were children. The mission was a welcome outlet for philanthropic impulses in the City of Brotherly Love. In June, 1876, a group of ladies organized a festival for the Mission children at Horticultural Hall, and on the fifteenth provided a picnic.[12]

Ohio had many notorious centers of vice. In fact, in the larger Ohio cities, crime and vice were so overwhelming that reformers saw little hope. The "Flats" district of Cleveland, along Lake Erie, was notorious, and so were three areas in Cincinnati—"Over the Rhine," "Blazing Stump," and "Rat Row," all near the Ohio River, and the "Sun Saloon," surrounded by tenements, factories, and warehouses, was as famous in 1876 as any dive in Dodge City or Deadwood.[13] It is a moot question, moreover, whether the marshals in wilderness towns, hired for their records as gunners and doubling as professional gamblers, were any less efficient than the police in many Eastern cities. There were never enough of them, they had no training, and they had never heard of scientific methods. Mack Sennett was accurate when he put their likeness on film—long-tailed, brass-buttoned blue coats, high rounded helmets, oak or walnut batons—or when he showed them commandeering private vehicles as auxiliary patrol wagons. The greater the city, it seemed, the worse the conditions. No city in all Ohio, for example, had an adequate water supply, a decent public health program, or a building code worth the paper it was printed on. And all too often efficient employees, especially firemen, were dismissed to make room for political hacks.[14]

Horatio Alger, Jr., was doing his very best, in a steady flow of dime novels, to prove that the right kind of boy could rise above even the most hostile urban environment. His millions of readers may have been convinced that it was the boy, not the environment, that really counted. In the Alger view, the congenitally vicious, unable to rise in a land of unlimited opportunity, deserved to be poor and remain in the slums. Through quite different methods Anthony Comstock was seeking to impose on the nation the moral standards of his own rural Connecticut. He

agreed with Alger that, if a boy had what it took he could
overcome poverty, but he lumped Alger's fiction with the other
forces that were diverting children from the proper moral road
to adulthood. Slum children were the easiest prey of the purvey-
ors of vice, but Comstock's concern was for the moral purity
of children in every social class. Like Josiah Holland, Comstock
served as an activist agent of the uneasy rural fears for the future
of America, and like many a reformer he honestly thought he
was divinely appointed for his campaign.

Anthony Comstock spent forty years crusading for morality,
beginning in 1872 when the Young Man's Christian Association
of New York formed a Commission for the Suppression of Vice.
The next year he persuaded Congress to pass a federal anti-ob-
scenity law, which was promptly dubbed the "Comstock Law,"
and he was appointed a special agent, without pay, in the Post
Office Department. With unflagging energy he collected evidence, passed it along to grand juries and public prosecutors, and
served as government witness in trials that over the years found
three out of four defendants guilty. It is unlikely that any other
reformer ever impounded so many examples usable as prosecution exhibits—tens of thousands of books, pamphlets, pictures,
and "articles made of rubber for immoral purposes."

Comstock's success drove him to ever more strenuous action.
On July 12, 1876, Congress at his behest amended the "Comstock Law" to give it more teeth. But by then the nation's
liberals were aroused—not because they favored vice but rather
because they resented Comstock's often shady methods, and
because they took issue with the comprehensiveness of what he
considered vicious. If he had confined his activities to breaking
up lotteries and other illegal schemes, nobody could have objected; but his concept of what was lewd and lascivious seriously
threatened all the arts. To refute his critics he published *Frauds
Exposed* in 1880, with solid evidence that fraudulent schemes
existed on every side, and *Traps for the Young* in 1883, which
confirmed the worst fears of his opponents. One example of a
trap was candy with a prize inside the wrapper; or printed
wrappers which, when a child had enough of them, could be
exchanged for a numbered ticket with an even chance at a
drawing.

There was organized gambling too, but it was apparently no worse, in Comstock's opinion, than the candy wrappers. From a New York policy maker's account book that came into his possession he was able to report some astounding figures: for 1876, out-of-town sales, in eight cities, of $465,445.23, expenses of $347,609.29, and a profit of $118,333.04.

Comstock was convinced, as he wrote, "that *Satan lays the snare, and children are his victims*," and because of this conviction he was able to see vice almost everywhere. What he could not see, and what the dominant rural class he represented could not see, was the overwhelming crime of society against the children in the cities—the almost total indifference to the causes of poverty, malnutrition, and ignorance; individual philanthropy that gave superficial attention to some of the symptoms without penetrating to the causes; and the general failure to accept responsibility for the cities—a failure freshly evident in the urban racial violence of the 1960's.[15]

American society has made better progress since 1876 in certain other areas, including the legal rights of women. Divorce was still rather uncommon in the 1870s; it was a subject not even considered entirely appropriate for polite conversation. T. S. Arthur, most famous for his *Ten Nights in a Bar Room* (1854), wrote what was probably the first novel on divorce, in 1858: *The Hand but not the Heart*. Howells, and no doubt many of his readers, thought he was daring when he used the theme in 1882 in *A Modern Instance*. The first play on the subject, Augustin Daly's *Divorce*, opened at the Fifth Avenue Theatre on September 5, 1871, and ran for two hundred nights; the second divorce play was Dion Boucicault's *Belle Lamar*, at the Booth Theatre in 1874.[16] In general the novels and plays followed conventional thinking that divorce was a last resort justified only by extreme conditions. The record of divorces granted in 1876 shows relatively few in the East and most in the Middlewest: of 14,800 divorces granted, Illinois stood first with 1,659, Ohio and Indiana next with 1,153 and 1,014, followed by Iowa, Michigan, Texas, Missouri, Pennsylvania, and New York. State laws differed, but the most common legal grounds were adultery, cruelty, desertion, and drunkenness.[17]

Henry Adams, lecturing in 1876 on "The Primitive Rights of

Women," argued that in primitive cultures women were equal
members of the clan, but that the church had reduced them to a
position of subjection. This was the enlightened conservative
position of the period. Much less conservative was the position
taken in lectures by such women as Susan B. Anthony and
Elizabeth Cody Stanton. In 1876, the National Woman Suffrage
Association took bold steps to promote their position. Barriers
for women existed everywhere. In Pennsylvania, for example, a
member of the Association trying to rent a hall ran into a state
law requiring her husband's consent—and he refused to give it.
But Susan B. Anthony, being single, could sign the lease. At
Fourth of July Festivities at the Centennial Exhibition, no
woman was scheduled to speak, and a request for permission to
present a Declaration of Rights for Women had been rejected.
When the audience rose to greet the Emperor Dom Pedro, a
phalanx of five women headed by Miss Anthony went to the
platform and handed a parchment copy of the Declaration to
Vice-President Ferry, who was startled but took it. The women
then walked out, scattering handfuls of broadsides, and Hawley
had to shout for order. Outside, Miss Anthony read the Declaration to the crowd while a friend held an umbrella over her head
and more leaflets were distributed. A special meeting at the first
Unitarian Church attracted a large audience. A special hit was
the song, "A Hundred Years Hence," describing a time when
women would have equality with men and government would
no longer be all-male. Meanwhile, the national association was
concentrating on state-to-state efforts for a woman suffrage
amendment to the Constitution—which had to wait, as it turned
out, until 1920.[18] Women were no longer expected to stay at
home, but demanding the vote was going too far. Wasn't it
enough that they were free to be admired in public?

To the foreign admirers of feminine pulchritude cited earlier
another may be added: General Bartolomeo Galletti, who said in
his book that he found four things outstanding in America—ap-
ples, women, oysters and white bread.[19] Traveling as he was with
Adelaide Ristori, the celebrated Italian tragedienne, he may
never have had the chance to learn that these four were closely
linked—in Centennial kitchens.

The American kitchen had been radically changed about

1850, when the fireplace was replaced by the wood-stove or range. By 1876, many of the old fireplaces had been bricked up or removed to make room for storage space, and the range had become the pride of the kitchen. But its invention seems to have exhausted kitchen technology for the rest of the century. The most sophisticated small utensils were the egg beater, the coffee mill, and the ice cream freezer. Woodenware and stoneware of older periods mingled on the work shelves with more recent tinware; the heaviest objects were the big iron griddles and fry pans. Women in Centennial America did much more than they do today. They made their own bread, butter, cheese, soap, and maple syrup. They salted meat or corned it in brine. They washed the family clothes with a scrub board set within a wash-tub, ran them through a hand wringer, hung them out to dry, and ironed them with irons of various shapes that they heated on the kitchen range. They scrubbed and mopped the floors. Until Melville Bissell invented the first practical carpet sweeper in 1876, they beat the rugs to get them clean. They grated their own horse radish, and they knew the many uses of Barbados molasses and Jamaica rum. Often, they took care of the poultry and the pigs and milked the cows. They prepared three heavy meals a day.[20] How any number of them found the time to saunter and be publicly admired is something of a mystery.

Even though peddlers brought to the door a variety of edibles, women did have to leave the house for most of the daily shopping. Most city food stores in 1876 were urban versions of the familiar country store, which sold almost everything under the sun. Not much canned food, however, but a little: the first successful sardine cannery opened in 1876 in Eastport, Maine, while canned salmon came from the Pacific Coast. The first chain store, the Great Atlantic and Pacific Tea Company, so named in 1869 when the owners, Gilman and Hartford, had thirty locations, already had a rival, the Jones Brothers Tea Company of Brooklyn, which started up in 1872 and later changed its name to Grand Union.[21] Most cities had farmers' markets, for the most direct transaction, from producer to con-sumer. Some of these markets were fabulous; at Philadelphia's Farmer's Market one could buy venison as well as more common meats; every kind of duck—mallard, teal, red-head, and canvasback in the fall; snipe in the spring and rail in the summer; and almost always reed-birds—bobolink from the north, rice bunting from the south, butter-bird from Jamaica, delicious whatever name was used. This market was also fabulous for the vendors with their singsong cries: "Hominy man come out this morning, with his sweet hommini-i-i," and "Peppery pot, all hot!" for a savory mess of tripe and dumplings. There were wholesale markets too, and oyster-wharves lined with numerous oyster-wagons; from all the evidence, nothing was more popular in Centennial America than the oyster, especially raw on the half shell.[22]

Whatever they preferred, there is no doubt that Centennial Americans were hearty eaters. Dinner at the Harvard commons regularly included a pound of meat, boiled on Monday and Tuesday, roasted the other five days; and a proper senior-class supper had seven courses. The "five o'clock ordinary" at the St. Nicholas Hotel in New York had eleven courses. The pioneering dining cars on the Chicago and Northwestern Railroad offered a table d'hote meal of oyster soup, hot and cold entrees, a choice of roasts, game, vegetables in season, pastry and puddings, then a "small pastry" and a dessert. In most homes the day began, typically, with a breakfast of sliced home-cured ham served with flour gravy, boiled potatoes, creamed codfish, and two or three eggs. Philadelphians often started the day with catfish and coffee, and broiled chicken and waffles was a supper favorite. Heartburn was common; it was attributed to "the hand of God."

The heavy diet did not escape criticism. Benjamin Franklin, after reading a vegetarian tract, had gone for years without meat. Somewhat later, Sylvestre Graham had tried to win over his countrymen to a flour made from whole-kernel wheat. He was only partly successful, but Graham crackers remain a staple on supermarket shelves. Next came Dr. James Jackson with "Granula," the first coldwater cereal and the ancestor of Grape-Nuts. In the early 1870s a Bellevue medical student, John Harvey Kellogg, tried to subsist on a diet of seven Graham crackers and an apple for breakfast and little more the rest of the day. In 1876 he published *The Use of Water in Health and Disease*, on the strength of which he was named medical superintendent of the Western Health Reform Institute at Battle Creek, Michigan, which the abstemious Seventh-Day Adventists had established in 1866. Dr. Kellogg was an expert surgeon, renowned for removing small scars, but what neither he nor America foresaw in 1876 was his impact, through the Kellogg health foods he later invented, on the nation's eating habits—particularly at breakfast.[23]

Heavy drinking, although by 1876 was less universal than formerly, because of the temperance movement, was still widespread enough. A current joke involved two freight drivers:

> *Inbound freighter:* What yuh loaded with?
>
> *Outbound freighter:* Twenty barrels of whiskey and a sack of flour.
>
> *Inbound freighter:* What in hell are you going to do with so much flour? [24]

Whiskey, as we have seen, was legion, and it had certain distinct advantages. It could be made from a variety of grains—wheat, corn, rye—all of which were abundant, and which never suffered, as wine grapes did, from diseased vines. California had suitable soil and climate for cuttings from French grape vines introduced in 1862, but a root louse plagued the growers. Rootstocks taken back to France in 1873 as curiosities in botanical gardens, had the alarming effect of hurting grape harvests until Louis Pasteur found the means of control. But neither a temporary advantage over French imports nor a steadily growing crop could bring American wine into favor. Over-production and thin demand in 1876 depressed the retail price to as low as fifteen cents a gallon.[25] Centennial Americans were simply not interested in wine and American wine in particular.

But hot weather made people thirsty, and the extreme heat of the Centennial summer was a boon to the soda water and soft drink industry. Hudnut's Fountain in the Herald Building dispensed as many as 3500 glassfuls of iced soda water on a hot day; and the fifty-odd bottling plants had to hustle to meet the demand. Soda fountains in drug stores had sold lemon and sarsaparilla soda as early as 1870, and each summer brought something new—ginger ale, birch beer, and assorted other flavors mixed with soda water. The first ice cream sodas were an immediate success in 1874, but the flavored soda water (tonic) was cheaper. The $50,000 price tag for the soft drink concession at the Exhibition was a measure of the popularity of the stuff.[26]

The Centennial spirit had an interesting effect on sports. The National League in baseball, the ICAAAA, and the Amateur Athletic Association, were all organized in 1876; and the year saw a forward thrust in virtually every sporting activity. Most sports and games of the time were importations with American alterations. Croquet, first introduced about 1870 in Norwich, Connecticut, as a society game, was widely popular. Roller skating, adapted in the mid-nineteenth century from the much older ice skating, got a boost in 1863 when James Leonard Plimpton invented a skate with two sets of parallel wheels. He built a $100,000 rink in New York, and had a virtual monopoly because of his patent.[27]

In 1876, two wealthy Bostonians built a court for court tennis, the ancient form of the game, on the present site of Back Bay Station. But lawn tennis, which calls for less capital outlay, had been known in the United States for two years. Mary Outerbridge, after watching British officers play the game in Bermuda in 1874, laid out a court that summer at the Staten Island Cricket and Baseball Club; and at Nahant, Dr. James Dwight of Boston laid out another. The first tournament, a handicap event, was played at Nahant in August, 1876.[28] Bowling (or ten-pins) was the oldest American sport; it was played in alleys indoors or on the lawns of the well-to-do. Cycling was a new sport: velocipedes (called bone-shakers) were introduced in 1868, and velocipede schools sprang up in all major cities. Improved English models shown at the Exhibition prompted some interest, but not until 1878 did the Bicycle Age begin in America.[29]

College competition was casual and informal until 1876, when delegates of fourteen eastern colleges met at Saratoga, July 21–22, to form the Intercollegiate Association of Amateur Athletes of America—the ICAAAA (or IC4A). At the time, the association limited itself to track and rowing. Cornell was currently supreme in rowing; and placed first in the Centennial regatta. Pennsylvania produced Horace Lee, the first man to run the hundred-yard dash in ten seconds. Football, for some reason, was handled separately. On November 23, delegates from Columbia, Harvard, Princeton, Rutgers, and Yale met at Springfield and formed the American Intercollegiate Football Association. A key question was whether soccer or rugby should be played; soccer was older, but rugby, introduced from England in 1874, was the collegians' choice. Another decision was to play the matches in the fall rather than the spring.[30]

Baseball entered 1876 under a cloud. The National Association of Professional Baseball Players, organized in 1871, had disbanded in 1875 after a public scandal created by dishonesty, gambling, and contract jumping among the players. During 1876, discussions and planning culminated in the creation of the National League of Professional Baseball Clubs, with a constitution drawn up by Judge Orrick C. Bishop of St. Louis. Franchises, costing $100 instead of the former ten dollars, would be given only to cities of more than 75,000 population. The teams in the new League in 1876 were Boston, Hartford, New York, and Philadelphia in the East; Cincinnati, Louisville, Chicago, and St. Louis in the West.[31] In the League's first game, on April 2, Boston beat Philadelphia, 6–5; and on May 23 Joe Borden pitched the first no-hitter.[32]

The year 1876 also ushered in the concept of a world's heavyweight boxing championship. Tom Allen, an American, boasted of himself as the world's champion, but lost to Joe Goss of England in a match on September 7, at Covington, Kentucky, that ended with Allen's disqualification for fouling in the twenty-seventh round.[33] On quite a different level and for quite a different audience, polo was introduced in 1876 by James Gordon Bennett, publisher of the New York *Herald*. He had learned the game in England from retired army officers who had learned it in India. When enough of his friends felt confident, they played the first outdoor match at Jerome Park. August Belmont took part but Leonard Jerome, suffering from a back strain, did not.[34]

Few people could afford a game like polo, but like international yacht racing it added a new dimension to the quality of American sporting life. Every few years, wealthy Britons and Americans competed for the *America's* Cup, named for the schooner that won the first International Yacht race near the Isle of Wight in 1851. Even though only a few people were lucky enough to watch these races, they roused great public interest. The challenger in 1876 was the Canadian-owned *Countess of Dufferin*. She lost the first race, on August 11, to the *Madeleine*, the American entry, over a triangular course near Montauk Point. The next day, on a windward and return course, she lost to both the *Madeleine* and the aging original *America*.[35]

Of all American sports, however, by far the most popular in the Centennial year was horse racing. It took two forms: the running race with jockeys or the trotting race with sulkies. Almost every community, large or small, had its track and its racing club. There was spirited betting, for more men were interested in gambling on the races than they were in the horse-flesh itself. On Washington's Birthday, 1876, a race at the three-mile Bay View Racing Course near San Francisco carried a purse of $30,000.[36] The first "big-time" track was built in 1864 at Saratoga by John Morrissey, the fabulous prize-fighter, politician, and gambling-room owner. Others followed soon—Pimlico near Baltimore in 1870, the Fair Grounds Course at New Orleans in 1874, Churchill Downs in Kentucky in 1875. By 1876 betting at the big tracks was being handled by bookmakers; at smaller tracks, however, the older practice of direct bets between owners and spectators prevailed. Paris had introduced pari-mutuel betting in the mid-1860s, but it was never popular in nineteenth-century America, and was adopted only after 1940.

August Belmont, who started the Belmont Stakes in 1865, was one of the nation's leading sportsmen. New York could also boast of Leonard Jerome, who developed Jerome Park, and leased it to the American Jockey Club from 1866 on. Jerome had long prided himself on skillful, showy driving, whatever the vehicle, and he kept a fine stable at his town house in Madison Square. Learning that the Duke of Beaufort had taken up four-in-hand driving in an effort to revive the old coaching days of England, Jerome had a coach built that quickly became one of the smartest sights of the city. His friend Belmont, however, outdid him with an even costlier coach. One early spring day in 1876, these two and others staged the first public parade of their new Coaching Club. Col. William Jay, "in bottle-green coat, yellow striped waistcoat, and silk topper and boutonniere, led the smartest array of turnouts New York had ever seen." Only the most impeccably clad ladies were invited. Their feathered hats and lacy parasols vied for public attention with the gaudy ribbons on the horses.[37]

The rich gave a glitter to life, wherever and however they spent their money. Small coastal and mountain villages became resorts because wealthy families first sought them out and made them desirable. The rich had a way of moving onward and upward, seeking their own kind at Bar Harbor and Newport, but the resorts survived—Ogunquit and York Harbor, Cape Ann and Hyannisport, Fisher's Island and Long Branch, all with fine ocean swimming tried by only a daring few. Inland, Saratoga still reigned supreme although it missed its Southern clients of the pre-war days, while rivals for the summer trade developed in the White and Green Mountains, the Berkshires and Catskills, Lake George and the Finger Lakes, the Poconos, Georgian Bay, and Duluth. The mid-South resorts were still in the doldrums, but Pinehurst and White Sulphur Springs were on the way back. Thomasville, in southernmost Georgia, basked in its reputation as the nation's oldest winter resort.

Few Northerners were yet ready to venture far into Florida, but Jacksonville was increasingly popular.[38] At the tiny village of Mandarin, upstream from Jacksonville on the St. Johns River, Harriet Beecher Stowe raised oranges for the Northern trade and served as a committee of one to lure visitors and settlers; her book *Palmetto-Leaves* (1873) was a model of touristic literature.[39] A little further south, at Tacoi, riverboat passengers could transfer to one of the shortest railroads in the nation for a fifteen-mile ride through scrub oak to St. Augustine, which William Astor of New York was trying to develop. In 1876 he bought the railroad, replacing the old wood and iron rails with steel and the mules with a locomotive.[40]

Atlantic City, about twenty years old in 1876, was both a resort and a summer suburb of Philadelphia. Merchants commuted in parlor cars; the ride was so short that they barely had time to read their daily papers. The cottages facing the ocean sported bright colors, balconies with scroll-saw elaboration, and roof shingles cut and stained to look like slate. The less affluent had their choice of a hundred boarding houses and a dozen hotels, the largest being the United States, Schauffler's, and the

Sea-View House. A footway of heavy planking laid on the beach, about two miles long, provided for the afternoon promenade that Philadelphians were accustomed to on Chestnut Street. Tiny cabins stood in lines or clusters on the beach, as changing rooms for the fashionable bathing hour, eleven in the morning. Fishing, crabbing, and sailing were the other chief sports.

Much nearer New York along the same Jersey coast was Long Branch, in high favor because the President and his family summered there; it catered mostly to New Yorkers. Philadelphians who were willing to go further than Atlantic City liked Cape May, the southern tip of New Jersey, where the hotels were more substantial. Congress Hall and The Stockton House rivalled the best at Saratoga—or so their clients insisted. Each resort had its particular customs: at Cape May bathers obeyed the eleven-o'clock tradition, as at other beaches, but everybody napped after lunch, dined about five, and then drove in carriages on the hard-packed beach or on oyster-shell roads in the country.[41]

Saratoga had its mid-continent counterpart at Hot Springs in Arkansas, which had the advantage of being open all year. A new hotel, the Arlington, was completed in 1875 at a cost of $80,000. The hot springs themselves, with their reputed value for various ailments, numbered fifty-eight. Some were hot enough to boil an egg in fifteen minutes.[42] Whether a particular water-cure center became a fashionable resort with sundry other attractions, as at Saratoga, or a sanitarium, as at Battle Creek, depended on the inclination of the men in control. The quest for health, however, was as great as the quest for amusement; and a third element, religion, was sometimes active, as on parts of the California coast.

Sometimes health and religion combined to lure visitors. Pacific Grove Retreat on Monterey Peninsula, begun in 1875 on the model of Ocean Grove, New Jersey, offered Methodist theology and solar therapy. Other beaches attracted hundreds of tent-campers, many of them foreign city-born people.[43] Louis Agassiz, on a visit to southern California in 1872, endorsed the mild climate, and the promotors of San Diego quoted him widely as part of an intensive publicity campaign. Pasadena was originally a temperance village. Other communities were established as health centers for members of particular churches. The invalids, "playing farmer" to occupy their time, pioneered orange growing and bee-keeping. Los Angeles, still very small in 1876, stressed health in its campaign for population; according to one of its newspapers, "The health-giving powers of our climate are attested by many of us, more or less invalids, being capable of working in the open air almost every day in the year, and not feeling as we might feel in other places, drones in the world's great hive." And in 1912 a California writer gave almost the last word: "I have lived in California since 1876 and have in consequence no desire to go to heaven." [44]

The quest for health was hardly new in 1876, but the year witnessed an increase in its exploitation as a business. In May, Dan Pinkham set out by boat from Lynn, Massachusetts, bound for New York with twenty thousand handbills and a barrel filled with samples of his mother's home-made remedy for female complaints. Within six weeks he spread the fame of Lydia E. Pinkham's Vegetable Compound among the city's druggists. Back home, he obeyed a sudden inspiration to put his mother's picture on the label, where it still is. Judicious advertising in Boston newspapers and in the programs of five Brooklyn theatres put the business firmly on its feet.[45]

Before the end of 1876, the Pinkham labels were registered at the Patent Office in Washington. There were no secret ingredients, only roots and herbs and, originally, 18 percent alcohol. It was a time of considerable argument about who should be allowed to make medicine, and under what kind of control. Most doctors made their own pills, powders, and plasters. Most druggists complained, saying they knew more about the subject and were equipped to be more precise. Doctors and druggists agreed, however, in detesting the medicine showmen, who sold nostrums from the back of wagons or carts, with a colorful spiel no longer, regrettably, heard in the land. Bottle collectors now highly prize some of the bottles that were used for the 456 identified varieties of bitters alone; there were also balms, balsams, compounds, cordials, cures, drops, elixirs, emulsions, liniments, mixtures, oils, sarsaparillas, specifics, syrups, and waters—most of them containing fixed amounts of alcohol. What the itinerant salesmen offered was proprietary, like the Lydia Pinkham compound, differentiated only by the trade name used. There were also patent medicines with secret formulas—and usually with even more alcohol.[46] The blue color favored for bottles prompted a popular song, *Blue Glass*, introduced in 1877 by Sam Devere, a well-known blackface banjo player.[47]

About 1,300 drug firms exist in America today, but only a handful were organized before 1876. During that year a Civil War veteran, Col. Eli Lilly of Indiana, dissolved his partnership with a dentist and started his own drug business, selling $4,470 worth of ethical pills, fluid extracts, elixirs, and cordials before the year ended.[48] But what gave the year its chief importance for drugs and medicines was the intensifying of Dr. Edward Robinson Squibb's campaign to revise the *U. S. Pharmacopoeia*, which had first been published in 1870 and which Dr. Squibb described in an 1873 review as little more than a catalogue, requiring a dispensatory. The Wood-Bache Dispensatory, the only one available, had not been revised for many years. At the 1876 convention of the American Medical Association he offered a resolution for updating and improving *Pharmacopoeia*; the motion was tabled. He then outlined his proposal before the Kings County Medical Society and the New York College of Pharmacy. In a pamphlet he finished on the last day of 1876 Squibb argued for a five-man "Pharmacopoeial Council" of A.M.A. members to supervise periodic revision of the *Pharmacopoeia*. But the A.M.A. rejected the idea, which did not bear real fruit until the passage of the Pure Food and Drug Act of 1906.[49]

Why the A.M.A. rejected Squibb's proposal is not clear, especially when we learn that the organization, from the time of its founding in 1847, had been trying in numerous ways to improve the quality of life for Americans—urging states to keep vital statistics, for example, working for quarantine and stronger public health agencies, and fighting against the vast commerce in nostrums. The campaign was going poorly, for in 1876 the general public had little faith in doctors, partly because people could not easily distinguish the trained physicians from the quacks. The low level of confidence may have reflected the slowness many physicians showed in adopting the recent new methods and instruments; medicine was just now in the process of being transformed from a speculative to an exact science.

Robert Koch, the great German bacteriologist, in 1876 proved beyond doubt that specific bacteria caused specific diseases; but the news filtered down slowly. Not every doctor was ready in 1876 to accept Lister's plea, made in 1864, for sterile hands and instruments, and clean air in operating rooms. The shortcomings of medical practice make absurd or pathetic the proud claims of a century's program in that year's *American Journal of Medical Sciences*.[50]

The best-known American medical man of the time was S. Weir Mitchell, forty-seven in 1876, who has been credited with inventing the rest cure and with foreshadowing psychosomatic medicine. Between 1870 and 1879 he published thirty-five papers on neurology (along with other professional papers, poetry, short stories, and novels—for he was a very versatile man). The most famous anecdote about him, unfortunately not dated, concerns his method of persuading a woman patient that her illness was imaginary. "If you are not out of bed in five minutes," he told her, "I'll get into it with you." Deliberately he removed his coat and his vest; but when he started taking off his trousers, she leaped angrily out of the bed.[51] Few doctors in any age would carry empiricism quite so far.

Nursing, under the stimulus of Florence Nightingale in England, was improving rapidly. The oldest training schools, Bellevue in New York, Massachusetts General in Boston, and New Haven, could hardly meet the demand as hospitals increased, and education was all too often sacrificed to the urgent need of ward duty.[52]

An outbreak of yellow fever in Southern port cities dramatized the inadequacies of preventive medicine. The epidemic was particularly severe at Savannah, Georgia, and inadequate funds made it very difficult to stem. For a century, the contents of privies in Savannah had been hauled up, dumped, and covered, until the soil was saturated. The city got its water from the Savannah River just at the point where several drainage areas met. On July 25, the first case of yellow fever was reported. By November, when a heavy frost brought relief, there were fifteen thousand ill and fifteen hundred dead—a severe blow both to Savannah and to the federal health service. A lesser epidemic at nearby Brunswick, where 122 people died, pointed up the scarcity of nurses and doctors and the inadequacy of preventive measures.[53] Almost as bad was the condition of veterinary medicine. The thirteenth annual meeting of the United States Veterinary Medical Association at Philadelphia in 1876, reported glaring deficiencies and the need for greatly expanded means of controlling tick fever and contagious pleuropneumonia in cattle, hog cholera, and the horse plague that had paralyzed traffic in New York streets in 1871–72.[54]

The paved streets we take for granted today in our cities was rare in 1876. Washington, after spending five million dollars on chemically treated blocks, was the best-paved city in the nation. Elsewhere, cobblestones were used in the East, wooden blocks in the West. Paris had begun using asphalt in 1854, London in 1868, but Americans, for all their vaunted progress and willingness to try the new, considered asphalt too expensive. Its use at the Centennial Exhibition smacked of luxury, especially for smalltown visitors who considered dirt streets good enough. It probably never occurred to them that dirt could have a direct connection with disease. Wooden block pavement wasn't much better. The wood absorbed and retained every foul element, and as it decayed it added its own foulness. Even stone blocks, although they resisted decay, were a hazard to health. Horse dung and urine collecting between the blocks were noisome in wet weather and, when dry, dispersed as dust.[55]

New York, however laggard in paving its streets, had begun experimenting with elevated railroads in 1871. In February 1876, Cyrus Field, George Pullman, Jay Gould and others were permitted to extend the tracks of the elevated, but the city stipulated "tasteful design" and the planting of vines at the base of the columns. The elevated's little steam locomotives, which were given such picturesque names as Aristotle and Xantippe, operated in the already dirty southern tip of Manhattan. Most riders paid the ten-cent fare for the novelty, for as yet the line was too short to be of real practical value.

The "El" in New York was a sensation comparable to the varied enterprises of Phineas T. Barnum. In the summer of 1875, Barnum had auctioned off the Hippodrome, his American Museum, dating from 1842, and his menagerie in order to enter the Centennial year with a single project—his traveling circus. In honor of the Centennial, he planned a celebration every day, with a battery of cannon to welcome each new morning with a thirteen-gun salute, a chorus of several hundred to sing the "Star-Spangled Banner" and "America," men and women costumed in Revolutionary period styles, a live eagle, and a fireworks display every evening. To transport so many people and properties, he had to use three railroad trains. One acquisition new in 1876 was Lucia Zarate, who was only twenty inches tall —five inches shorter than Tom Thumb, the most famous of Barnum's "Marvellous Living Human Curiosities." [57]

Several of the foreign visitors were particularly impressed by American fire engines. Their display and competition were standout attractions of the Exhibition. In a nation built largely of wood, their efficiency and that of the fire brigades, whether paid or volunteer, was of vital concern to the public. M. Bertie-Marriott, sent by *Le Figaro* to report on Centennial American life, was overwhelmed by an exhibition of that efficiency. One of New York's fire department officials, a Mr. King, took him to the Eighteenth Street station and bade him keep time as the men responded to a gong.

> At the door, Mr. King said to us: "Look out! Set your watches. Are you ready?" "Yes." He rang a little bell, a man opened and we entered. A superb machine was standing there, all shiny. In the rear, three horses were in their stalls with their harnesses on. The firemen were sleeping upstairs. A gong hanging on the wall was to give the alarm. "Pay attention and take your position against the wall to be out of the way of the horses." Clang! Clang! Clang! The three horses are hitched up; twelve men are there manning the pumping machine; the driver has said, "Ready!" "How long?" Mr. King asks us. It had been just six seconds and a half since the gong sounded! Without a single word, without one observation, the horses were put back in their stalls; the men went upstairs to bed. The inspector had wished to see if everything was in order, and that was his right. He had found out; they had done their duty.

Bertie-Marriott was satisfied, but King insisted on providing another demonstration. In Madison Square they stopped beside a post with a box attached, and pressed the button.

It was just midnight, the surrounding streets were still full of carriages. Suddenly, in every avenue, bells were heard accompanied by frightful rumblings. Everywhere the carriages pulled to the curb and stopped; the pedestrians were motionless. You could hear the cry, "Fire! Fire!"

At full speed they arrived roaring, whistling, panting, vomiting steam. Here they were, the firemen and the machines. "Where? Where?" asked the men. The horses were already unhitched, the hoses attached. Then they found that the Inspector was trying to see if the organization was perfect, and each returned to his post without a word, without one single mark of discontent.

"How long?" asked Mr. King.

"Four minutes and a half."

So in four minutes and a half six powerful machines with steam up and ready to pour torrents of water on the fire had arrived. Press another button and six others would have arrived, and all the machines in the city would have come if they were needed. As long as I shall live, never, no never, will I feel so poignant an emotion, so real an emotion as I felt that night.

"Do you want another demonstration?" asked Mr. King.

"No, no, this is enough. It is too exciting!"

And, in spite of myself, I saw in my mind's eye a fire in Paris, the shouts of the crowd, that absurd little cart with buckets hanging from it, those hand pumps, reaching the spot when the fire is already beyond control, our firemen running up, full of goodwill, it is true, but out of breath, exhausted from running.[58]

Not even the most efficient fire departments, however, could prevent great fires with their terrible toll of lives. *Harper's Monthly* had a special monthly feature called "Disasters." Only the worst were recorded: twelve deaths at Robinson's Theatre in Cincinnati on February 5; eighteen old men burned to death in Brooklyn on March 7, when a home for the aged caught fire; forty-two people drowned in a storm and flood at Rockdale, Iowa, on the Fourth of July; Castle Garden in New York destroyed by fire on July 9; seventeen passengers and ten crew members drowned the next day when the propellor "St. Clair" burned on Lake Superior; fifteen workmen killed in a boiler explosion at a nail mill in Pittsburgh on October 12; twenty patrons trampled to death in a panic at Union Theatre in San Francisco on October 31, after an alarm of fire. But by far the worst disaster of the year was the fire at the Brooklyn Theatre on December 5. A performance of "The Two Orphans" was within five minutes of its conclusion when people noticed smoke. Members of the cast urged the audience to be calm, but panic broke out. Most of the holders of orchestra seats escaped, but the one stairway from the gallery proved a fire trap, especially at the turn. In all, 292 died, mostly from smoke inhalation and suffocation. Four days later, at Greenwood Cemetery, the unclaimed dead were given a mass burial—a rather astonishing 103 of them. Two of the play's cast were among the dead.[59]

One long-range effect of the tragedy was sparse attendance at theatres for the next few years. The second worst disaster of the year, later in the month, seemed rather an anticlimax. A train of the Lake Shore Railroad fell through a bridge over the Ashtabula River in Ohio, and seventy passengers died. The sombreness of this event within two days of New Year's was symbolic, in a way, of the general darkness in which the year ended.

Of such as the foregoing would life have been in 1876 without the Exhibition, the government scandals, and the Presidential election, for the ordinary American, the man on the street, reading all about it in his daily or weekly paper. However much more has had to be passed over, even a sampling would not be complete without mention of Charles Ross. His kidnapping on July 1, 1874, was the mystery of the decade. Whatever people knew or didn't know, or quickly forgot, they had heard of that, and remembered it. The story was so well known that whenever an unidentified boy turned up people thought he was Charley. Early in January, 1876, a "claimant" in St. Albans, Vermont, was found to be only Jimmie Blanchard, formerly in a Boston orphan asylum; his mother, from Milford, New Hampshire, reclaimed him but even so, St. Albans was up in arms, certain the boy was Charley Ross. Early in February the same thing occurred in Tiffin, Ohio; the boy concerned knew he was Charley Schench, the son of a horse trainer, but nothing could dissuade the citizens that he wasn't Charley Ross of Germantown, Pennsylvania.[60] These were only two of the numerous such incidents over the years, reported from various parts of the country and from Europe, each one momentarily rousing the Ross family's hopes. Sympathy was universal; there was even a popular song, "Bring Back Our Darling." [61]

Perhaps the most unusual turn was the publication in 1876 of a book by Charley's father, Christian K. Ross: *The Father's Story of Charley Ross, the Kidnapped Boy*.[62] A brief introduction by the vice-provost of the University of Pennsylvania established the serious tone; this was no cheap way of capitalizing on a misfortune. Mr. Ross reviewed in detail all the circumstances of the kidnapping, reproduced the complete correspondence with the kidnappers, who proposed a ransom of $20,000, described every step taken by policemen, Pinkerton agents, friends, and himself in what proved to be a futile quest, and printed some of the numerous crank letters that all such cases seem to engender. The climax came when two men strongly suspected of the crime, Murdock and Douglas, were killed while committing a burglary; but the boy was never found. Until fairly recently, old men earned fleeting notoriety by announcing they were Charley Ross. It is one of America's most famous unsolved mysteries.

Footnotes for Chapter Nine
THE QUALITY OF LIFE

1. R. Turner Wilcox, *Five Centuries of American Costume* (New York: Scribner's, 1963).

2. *Decorum: A Practical Treatise on Etiquette and Dress of the Best American Society*, compiled by John A. Ruth (New York: J. A. Ruth Co., 1879), p. 266.

3. *Ibid.*, pp. 302–06.

4. *Ibid.*, pp. 156–58.

5. Joseph C. Robert, *The Story of Tobacco in America* (New York: Knopf, 1949).

6. *Ibid.*

7. Adrian Francis McDonald, "The History of Tobacco Production in Connecticut," in a pamphlet on the Connecticut tercentenary of 1936.

8. Robert, p. 140.

9. Levy, *Grace Notes in American History*, pp. 106–20.

10. Frank R. Donovan, *Wild Kids* (Harrisburg: Stackpole Books, 1967), p. 158.

11. *Ibid.*, pp. 153–54.

12. Strahan, *A Century After*, pp. 191–92.

13. *Leffel's Illustrated Miller's and Mechanical News* (Springfield, Ohio: April, 1875), cited in Philip D. Jordan, *Ohio Comes of Age, 1873–1900*, Vol. 6 of *The History of the State of Ohio* (Columbus: Ohio State Archeological and Historical Society, 1943).

14. *Ohio Comes of Age.*

15. Anthony Comstock, *Traps for the Young*, ed. Robert Bremmer, reprint edition (Cambridge: Belknap Press of Harvard University Press, 1967); the editor's introduction is especially significant.

16. James Harwood Barnett, *Divorce and the American Divorce Novel 1858–1937* (Philadelphia: University of Pennsylvania Press, 1939), and Donald Nelson Koster, *The Theme of Divorce in American Drama*, 1871–1939 (Philadelphia, University of Pennsylvania Press, 1942).

17. Carroll D. Wright, *Marriage and Divorce in the United States 1867–86* (Washington: Government Printing Office, 1889).

18. Eleanor Flexner, *Century of Struggle: the Woman's Rights Movement in the United States* (Cambridge: Belknap Press of Harvard University Press, 1959).

19. Bartolomeo Galletti, *Il giro del mondo colla Ristori* (Roma, 1876), cited in Andrew J. Torrielli, *Italian Opinion on America as Revealed in Italian Travelers, 1850–1900* (Cambridge: Harvard University Press, 1941), Vol. 15 in Harvard Studies in Romance Languages.

20. Helen Lyon Adamson, *Grandmother in the Kitchen* (New York: Crown, 1965).

21. Godfrey M. Lebhar, *Chain Stores in America 1859–1962* (New York: Chain Store publishing Co., 1963).

22. Strahan, *A Century After*, pp. 158–65.

23. Gerald Carson, *Cornflakes Crusade* (New York: Rinehart, 1957).

24. Quoted in Brown and Felton, *The Frontier Years.*

25. M. A. Amerine and V. L. Singleton, *Wine: an Introduction for Americans* (Berkeley: University of California Press, 1965).

26. Riley, *A History of the American Soft Drink Industry*, pp. 117 ff.

27. Edward R. O'Neill, *Roller Skating* (New York: Ronald Press, 1960).

28. Frank G. Menke, *The Encyclopedia of Sports*, 3rd ed. (New York: A. S. Barnes, 1963); Parke Cummings, *American Tennis* (Boston: Little, Brown, 1957).

29. Harvey S. Firestone, *Man on the Move: The Story of Transportation* (New York: Putnam, 1967).

30. Menke, *Encyclopedia of Sports.*

31. *Ibid.*

32. *The Encyclopedia of American Dates and Facts.* ed. Gorton Carruth and associates (New York: Thomas Y. Crowell, 1956).

33. *Ibid.* and Menke.

34. Anita Leslie, *The Remarkable Mr. Jerome* (New York: Henry Holt, 1954), p. 203.

35. Roland F. Coffin, *The America's Cup: How it Was Won by the Yacht America in 1851 and How it Has Been Since Defended* (New York: Scribner's, 1885).

36. David L. Phillips, *Letters from California in 1876* (Springfield: Illinois State Journal Co., 1877).

37. Leslie, *The Remarkable Mr. Jerome*, pp. 74–75.

38. *American Seaside Resorts*, ed. Charles L. Norton (New York: Taintor Brothers, 1871), 1877 edition.

39. Morita Mason Clark, "The Development of the Citrus Industry in Florida before 1895," unpublished M. A. thesis (Florida State University, 1947).

40. George W. Pettengill, Jr., *The Story of the Florida Railroads, 1843–1903* (Boston: Railway & Locomotive Historical Society, 1952).

41. Strahan, *A Century After.*

42. *A History of the North-Western Editorial Excursion to Arkansas* (Little Rock: T. B. Mills & Co., 1876), p. 127.

43. Pomeroy, *The Pacific Slope.*

44. Editorial in Los Angeles *Herald*, January 1, 1876, and Margaret Collier Graham in *Do They Really Respect Us?* (San Francisco, 1912), both quoted in John E. Baur, *The Health Seekers of Southern California, 1870–1900* (San Marino: The Huntington Library, 1959).

45. Jean Burton, *Lydia Pinkham Is Her Name* (New York: Farrar, Straus, 1949).

46. Larry Freeman, *The Medical Showman* (Watkins Glen: Century House, 1957).

47. Levy, *Grace Notes in American History*, pp. 148–151.

48. Tom Mahoney, *The Merchants of Life: An Account of the American Pharmaceutical Industry* (New York: Harper, 1959).

49. Laurence G. Blochman, *Doctor Squibb: The Life and Times of a Rugged Idealist* (New York: Simon and Schuster, 1958).

50. Bernhard J. Stern, *American Medical Practice in the Perspective of a Century* (New York: The Commonwealth Fund, 1945);

Richard Harrison Shryock, *The Development of Modern Medicine: An Interpretation of the Social and Scientific Factors Involved* (New York: Alfred A. Knopf, 1947).

51. Ernest Earnest, *S. Weir Mitchell, Novelist and Physician* (Philadelphia: University of Pennsylvania Press, 1950).

52. Richard Shryock, *The History of Nursing* (Philadelphia: Saunders, 1949).

53. [John M. Woodworth, M.D.] *Annual Reports of the Supervising Surgeon-General of the Marine-Hospital Service of the United States for the Fiscal Years 1876 and 1877* (Washington: Government Printing Office, 1878).

54. Louis A. Merillat and Delwin M. Campbell, *Veterinary Military History of the United States,* 2 vols. (Chicago: Veterinary Magazine Corp., 1935).

55. Q. A. Gillmore, *A Practical Treatise on Roads, Streets, and Pavements* (New York: D. Van Nostrand, 1876).

56. Rodman Gilder, *The Battery* (Boston: Houghton Mifflin, 1936).

57. P. T. Barnum, *Struggles and Triumphs; or, Forty Years Recollection* (Buffalo: Courier Co., 1876); "The Fat Man and His Friends," *American Heritage,* 17 (June, 1966).

58. Quoted by Offenbach in *Orpheus in America,* pp. 161–64.

59. *Harper's Monthly,* various dates, 1876–77.

60. Elmira *Daily Advertiser,* Jan. 4, 10, Feb. 2, 1876.

61. Levy, *Grace Notes in American History,* pp. 302–305.

62. Philadelphia: John E. Potter, 1876.

10

The Arts, Fine and Otherwise

I

THE LIVELY ARTS

THE CHARLEY ROSS MYSTERY proved a strong magnet when Augustin Daly borrowed it for the subject of a play, *Pique*, that opened on December 14, 1875, at the Fifth Avenue Theatre and ran for 238 performances, easily the longest run of the 1876 season. Charley's name was changed to "Little Arthur," played by Belle Wharton; others in the cast of nineteen were John Drew, Maurice Barrymore, and Fanny Davenport. During the week of March 13, when the performances passed the magic number of one hundred, ticket buyers got their change in silver every night except Friday, when gold coins were used. Since the smallest gold coin was a dollar, some of the audience came out ahead.[1]

Augustin Daly was one of the most successful playwright-producers of the Centennial period. He had a hand in writing or adapting about ninety plays, and as a producer he had a knack for discovering stars. This double role was not unusual—some men of the period combined acting with directing, managing, and producing. Nothing close to realism was presented on the stage in America. It would not be until James A. Herne risked fortune and reputation, in the 1890s, with *Margaret Fleming* and *Shore Acres*. European audiences of the 1870s were watching the "new drama" of Ibsen and Strindberg; American audiences watched melodramas, sentimental comedies, murder mysteries (a speciality of the Union Square Theatre), adaptations of foreign plays like Sardou's *Ferréol*, performed fifty times in the spring of 1876, or such imports as the super-sentimental *La Dame aux Camélias* by Dumas the younger. The star system, which could mean success or failure depending on the magnitude of the stars in question, led to the practice of writing plays for particular actors. One such was *The Mighty Dollar*, created by Benjamin Woolf as a vehicle for Mr. and Mrs. W. J. Florence, which ran for 183 performances despite general condemnation by the drama critics. One of the brightest stars of the period, Clara Morris, opened at the Union Square Theatre on November 20 in *Miss Multon*, an adaptation of a French version of *East Lynne*. It hardly mattered *what* was being acted if a real star trod the boards.

One curiosity of the period was the presentation of benefit performances for individual members of the cast—usually the star. A play enjoying an extended run would be replaced for one night by a different play as a "benefit." *Pique*, for example, gave way on May 20 "when James Lewis took a benefit," as the phrase went, with the year's first performance of *Charity*, and again at the May 24 matinée, when *As You Like It* was staged for the benefit of Fanny Davenport, who acted Rosalind and sang "The Cuckoo" in Act IV.[2]

Of numerous classics playing briefly in New York, Shakespeare's were the most numerous. *Hamlet* was given nine times during 1876, *Othello* and *Richard II* four times, *King Lear* three times, together with single revivals of *The Taming of the Shrew*, *The Merchant of Venice*, and *As You Like It*.

The new season opened in mid-September. The first two

plays offered were *Money*, with an English setting, and *Life*, adapted from a French play.

At one theatre, a blackface minstrel troupe opened the night after a play had completed its run. This was not unusual. As Joseph Hatton, our visiting Londoner, had remarked, Americans liked to be entertained; it only seemed odd to him that the same theatre would offer such diverse fare. Hatton was better pleased by a new theatre, the Madison Square, that Steele Mackaye had just completed. Any London theatre-goer, he thought, would be impressed. Each seat was roomy and well cushioned. In hot weather, air pumped over ice kept the temperature down. The drop curtain was a handsome expanse of needlework from a design by Louis Tiffany. The footlights, gas jets, were enclosed in glass. The orchestra was located above the stage; a bank of flowers replaced the usual orchestra pit. The stage was double, allowing unusual effects. But the play Hatton saw there, the venerable *Hazel Kirke*, struck him as mediocre—a melodrama of noble self-denial and virtue triumphant.[3]

Centennial Americans may not have had sophisticated taste, but everywhere they showed unlimited affection for the theatre. Jules Leclercq, one of the visitors from France, was dead wrong in reporting that Philadelphia had no music hall or legitimate theatre. He was right in saying that the Fox Theatre offered burlesque shows; but there were several theatres of a better sort, and the mammoth Academy of Music, built in 1857 in Italian Byzantine style, was regularly offering operas and plays in alternation. It was known for its perfect acoustics; the slightest stage whisper could be clearly heard in the most remote of its 2,900 seats.[4]

What was known in countless small cities as "the Opera House" provided fewer operas than plays. In Elmira, New York, for example, there were performances two or three times a week, usually "one-night stands." On Monday, January 17, *East Lynne* was presented, with Charlotte Thompson starring; on Friday, January 21, the Julia Matthews Comic English Opera Troupe gave *Lurline* and an Offenbach one-acter, *H.I.H.*; and so it went all year. There were lecturers, too, sent by Major James Pond and lesser booking agents. Not all provincial theatres, unhappily, were as modern as Mackaye's Madison Square;

and the Elmira editor regretted that Charlie Smith, proprietor of the Opera House, could not move an oil well from Bradford to Elmira, to cut down the noise of the seat hinges. The whole house knew when anybody arrived or departed. "Perhaps Charlie is in league with those who want to keep track of the fellows who go out 'to see a man.' "

Nor was theatre restricted to older communities: some new ones with money enough had lavish opera houses, and even the rawest new villages in the West demanded drama at once. Sometimes the "theatre" was no more than a small raised platform in the corner of a barroom. The Gem in Deadwood, in its own building, endured for many years and was widely known in the West. A brass band on a balcony played to attract an audience before the show began at eight o'clock. The usual program included singing, dancing, banjoplaying, burnt-cork comedians, and high-kickers. But occasionally touring companies provided a change. Some such groups were regional, like the Montana Minstrel & Variety Troupe, but others ranged over vast areas—the Denver Dramatic Troupe, the Boston Company, the J. W. Carter Company, the Hasenwinkles, and the Katie Putnam group. Comedy was preferred in the small Western towns, but audiences were receptive to such time-tested favorites as *East Lynne, Camille, The Octaroon, Uncle Tom's Cabin, Rip Van Winkle,* and *Led Astray.*[5] Buffalo Bill was always welcomed when he arrived with *The Right Red Hand*, an autobiographical melodrama built around his fight with Yellow Hand. He had interrupted his career as a thespian to serve as a scout in the Indian campaign. When he began his 1876–77 tour, he was joined by Captain Jack Crawford, the "Poet Scout," who enriched the program by reading from his own immortal works.[6]

Stage facilities varied with the size of the town and the wealth of its people. Central City, Colorado, and Virginia City, Nevada, had both the money and the inclination to erect gorgeous opera houses and to attract the finest singers. Salt Lake, under the leadership of Brigham Young, maintained a great interest in theatre and music, but more sedately and less as a social occasion. Citizens and visitors could attend good opera at the opera house and also hear good music at the Mormon Tabernacle, justly famed for its fine choir and for its great organ, completed in 1867.

At the opposite extreme was San Francisco, which clung to its reputation for wickedness. The first crude theatres there were adjuncts of saloons where men came to drink and, as an afterthought, to watch the performers. The struggle for separate theatres was long and difficult, but by 1876 it was reasonably successful. San Franciscans also loved the ostentatious, and delighted in costly gestures like importing an entire production from New York on a special train.[7]

Two new theatres were completed in 1876 in San Francisco. Wade's Opera House, at Mission and Third, blended Romanesque and Italian motifs. It had three entrances, a grand vestibule with skylights above, two curving staircases, and a lobby in black and white marble with a fountain in the center. There were twenty-two mezzanine boxes, twelve proscenium boxes, a dress circle, and three galleries. The decoration was in shades of blue. The stage had floor wells through which to lower scenery to a storage basement. The grand opening, on January 17, featured Anna Pixley in *Snowflake*, a dramatization of Snow White and the Seven Dwarfs. The other new theatrical miracle was Baldwin's Academy of Music, attached to the Baldwin Hotel on Market Street near Powell. It was replete with red plush, velvet draperies, crystal chandeliers. It opened on March 6 with Barry Sullivan, an Irish actor, in *Richard III*.[8]

If the expanding variety of stage productions is any measure, the quality of life was much richer in 1876 than at any time earlier. Minstrel shows, first tried in 1841, were still popular, although in New York and other large cities a white-face version, more elaborately staged, was drawing crowds. The white-face minstrels somewhat resembled the variety shows, pioneered in 1864 when Tony Pastor opened his Music Hall. The beloved English pantomime had some success in America, but did not survive beyond the 1870s.

Musical comedies are sometimes traced back to *The Black Crook*, which opened in 1866 at Niblo's Garden and was revived often until about 1900; but actually it was not in anyway a musical comedy in the modern sense. The burlesque *Evangeline*, introduced in 1874, also at Niblo's Garden, more closely resembled a musical; it borrowed from the patomime and other earlier forms, and ran off and on for thirty years. The author, Edward E. Rice, called it first "an American opera bouffé" and later "an American extravaganza." The prima donna in tights took the male lead, while a man played the feminine lead. A dumb actor, foreshadowing Charlie Chaplin and Jimmie Savo, convulsed the audience. The title role was played by two men teaming as a heifer; their eccentric dance was almost as well known in Centennial America as Charley Ross. This was the production's only connection with Longfellow's *Evangeline,* who owned a cow. The revered poet would have been startled by such stage effects as spouting whales, a balloon trip to Arizona, and a sphinx-like auction of "The Lone Fisherman." [9]

Jules Verne's *Around the World in Eighty Days,* adapted by the Kiralfys, three brothers from Hungary, was a great hit in the 1870s with scenes laid at Suez, the Taj Mahal, and Calcutta, and with the first use of cutout flats to give the effect, for example, of actual trees. Another new venture was the farce-comedy, introduced in 1875 by Nate Salsbury's Troubadours in *Patchwork.*[10] If as some have suggested the musical is America's prime contribution to the lively arts, it was beginning to take shape in Centennial America. One particular event in 1876 of future importance was the entry of Oscar Hammerstein, a cigar maker, into show business, as manager of the German-language Stadt Theatre in New York's East Side.[11]

In Europe, a theatre was for plays, an opera house for operas; and even these categories were broken down with some theatres for serious plays and others for light comedies, some opera houses for grand opera and others for *opera bouffé.* But while Offenbach was in New York, he conducted his best-loved light operas, *La Vie Parisienne* and *La Jolie Parfumeuse,* in Booth's Theatre, and his opening concert May 11 at the Hippodrome with its five thousand seats. Refurbished with tropical plants and cascades it was familiarly known as Gilmore's Garden. Offenbach's orchestra of 101 musicians was none too many for so immense a hall. The concertmaster was a young violinist John Philip Sousa. Much as Offenbach admired the United States (which he compared to a giant a hundred cubits high), he wondered why Americans, with all their vaunted knowhow, had not yet provided a secure basis for the arts. Talent existed but went begging, partly for lack of a long tradition but more, he thought, because of a paucity of established institutions. He found in New York no permanent opera company, no *opéra comique*, not even an established operetta theatre. Regular theatre lived from day to day, he noted, and actors were commonly nomads, rushing from city to city for very brief engagements, often one-night stands. He recognized the widespread prejudice against governmental support, but it seemed to him that such a prejudice should encourage, not preclude, private initiative. There was money enough, if it were systematically collected, to build and endow concert halls, opera houses, theatres, and art galleries, and also to establish schools of fine arts with the ablest of teachers. Within twenty years, he predicted, such a program would begin to produce great works and master artists, and Europe would be coming to America in quest of talent as America was now accustomed to seeking it in Europe.[12]

Offenbach's chef d'oeuvre, *The Tales of Hoffmann*, was still to be written, but his other light operas were as popular in the United States as in Europe. People knew he was a less significant composer than Wagner, but there were few genuine Wagnerians this side of the Atlantic, and if Americans attended Wagner's operas it was often as much from a sense of duty as for genuine delight. They liked other opera well enough, however, especially the wealth of Italian works. The Astor Place Opera House was the home of the Italian Opera Company directed by Maretzek, and Carl Strakosch kept another opera company alive in New York. German, Italian, and Swedish sopranos were imported in 1876, as well as foreign tenors. The dominance of European composers, directors, and performers was probably a necessity, considering the limited facilities for music education in the United States, but at the same time it helped perpetuate the sense of cultural inferiority. One American, however, Clara Louise Kellogg of South Carolina, had developed an extensive repertoire of soprano roles, and in 1876 she was touring the country with her own company, successfully producing French and Italian operas in English translation. In Europe, then as now, operas were produced in the local language; the American habit of using the original text has been yet another barrier separating ART from ordinary life.

Miss Kellogg was not, however, the only American-born prima donna making good in 1876. Minnie Hauk, rumored to be the illegitimate daughter of Leonard Jerome, who financed her musical training, reversed the usual order of things by becoming famous in Europe, in several Wagnerian roles but especially as the Carmen whom Bizet considered ideal. She was in Europe most of the time from 1875 to 1878, but returned briefly in the summer of 1876, and sang excerpts of *Carmen* for Mr. Jerome.[13] But at the same time, more European singers were ravishing the ears and eyes of American opera-lovers: Teresa Carreño, Anna del Belocca, Madame Poppenheim, Therese Tietjens. No American conductor was touring Europe, not even an American tenor or pianist.

Offenbach may not have realized the stubborn hold of cultural dependence on Europe, a greater deterrent to the progress of the arts in America than the lack of permanent institutions. Walt Whitman, while editor of the Brooklyn *Daily Eagle* a generation earlier, had argued for music instruction in the schools and for a native American music,[14] but this kind of nationalistic thinking roused slight response. Concert-goers showed the same preference for European music that wealthy art collectors showed for European paintings and sculpture, to the discouragement of talent at home. The only consistently successful American composers of the time were hymn writers. The picture was a little different in the theatre, where American plays were performed. But here again Americans were best, or were allowed by producers and patrons to do their best, at the lower levels only.

In both New York and in Philadelphia, where the Alhambra was temporarily renamed "Offenbach Garden," Offenbach was in direct competition with Theodore Thomas, the most celebrated conductor in the United States. When somebody asked Thomas why he put no Offenbach music on a program in honor of the French visitor he reacted violently: "What! Me conduct an Offenbach composition! Never will I do anything so degrading!" Offenbach, on hearing this, met the Teutonic malice with Gallic wit: "Please tell Mr. Thomas that I will not be so particular. I shall be most happy to conduct any composition of Theodore Thomas when he reaches the dignity of becoming a composer." And Offenbach proceeded to charm his American audience by writing a bravura waltz for the cornetist Jules Levy, naming it "The American Eagle Waltz." [15]

Thomas had particular reason in 1876 to be out of sorts: he had personally assumed the responsibility for the music at the Centennial Exhibition and it went so badly that he paid off the deficit only twelve years later. Wagner's *Fest Marsche*, played at the opening ceremonies, had begun the debacle. Because he had done a great deal to popularize Wagner in America, Thomas never forgave him for accepting the $5,000 commission and producing so dismal a composition.[16] As a conductor who was not afraid to use new works, Thomas in his long career had a considerable influence in the orchestral field.

Dudley Buck and John Knowles Paine shared the honor of being the most prominent composers of the day, the first serious American composers. Theodore Thomas's orchestra premiered Paine's Symphony No. 1 in C Minor in Boston in January 1876, thus proving that an American could turn out music in the classical form. Buck, an organist, composed choral works, especially cantatas.[17] Paine's professorship of music at Harvard, and Hugh Archibald Clarke's at the University of Pennsylvania, were both established in 1875.[18]

The one professional symphony orchestra, the New York Philharmonic, dated from 1842; not until 1878 was there another, the New York Symphony. Community orchestras existed, however: Columbus, Georgia (1855), St. Louis and San Jose, California (1860), and Belleville, Illinois (1866). The oldest college orchestra, the Harvard Musical Association, antedated even the New York Philharmonic, having been in existence since 1808. There were also numerous private groups, such as Boston's Handel and Haydn Society.[19] A partial list of 1876 concerts [20] shows the variety and the level of both performers and taste:

> *January 6*. Schubert's "Marche Héroique" given by the Harvard Musical Association, in Boston.
> *January 24*. American operatic début of Therese Tietjens, noted dramatic soprano, as Norma, at the Academy of Music, New York City, under Strakosch.

January 26. J. K. Paine's First Symphony, produced by Theodore Thomas, in Boston.

January 29. Saint-Säens's "Danse Macabre" given by Theodore Thomas in New York City.

February 3. Saint-Säens's Second Pianoforte Concerto (G minor) given by the Harvard Musical Association, in Boston, with B. J. Lang as soloist. Carl Zerrahn conducting.

February 17. Saint-Säens's Violoncello Concerto in A minor given at a concert of the Harvard Musical Association, in Boston, with Wulf Fries as soloist.

February 19. Cherubini's overture to "Faniska" given by the Philharmonic Society, New York City.

February 25. Teresa Carreño, great pianist, appeared as a singer in the part of Anna in "Don Giovanni," under Strakosch, at the Academy of Music, New York City.

February 26. Raff's "Suite in F" given by Theodore Thomas, in New York City.

February 28. The first part of Liszt's oratorio "Christus" given by the Oratorio Society, New York City.

April 17. American début of Anna del Belocca, contralto, in "Il Barbiere" at the Academy of Music, New York City, under Strakosch.

April 16. Handel's oratorio "Joshua" given by the Handel and Haydn Society, in Boston.

April 22. Chaikovsky's overture to "Romeo et Juliette" given by the Philharmonic Society, New York City, with Carl Bergmann as conductor (American premiere).

May 11. Wagner's "Centennial March"; Dudley Buck's "Centennial Meditation of Columbia"; and J. K. Paine's "Centennial Hymn" produced at the Centennial Exposition, in Philadelphia, under Theodore Thomas.

October 9. Saint-Säens's symphonic poem "Phaeton" given by Theodore Thomas, in New York City.

November 8. Wagner's opera "Il Vascello Fantasma" given in Philadelphia in Italian by Madame Pappenheim.

November 14. Madame Annette Essipoff, pianist, made her début at Steinway Hall, New York City.

November 25. Bach's Suite in C given by Theodore Thomas, in New York City.

The compiler of this list omitted at least two signal events: Von Bulow's farewell piano concert at Chickering Hall before setting out on an American tour,[21] and the introduction by Etta Morgan, of the Family's Ladies' Orchestra, of a new instrument, the saxophone. On January 17 she began a two-week engagement at New York's Olympic Theatre.[22]

For all its mellifluousness, or because of it, composers ignored the saxophone for serious music. If there was one instrument in universal regard, it was the piano—or "pianoforte" as many people persisted in calling it. There were more pianos in American homes than there were bathtubs; they were second only to the kitchen range as a status symbol. In the West, the family piano often was transported by riverboat, until the railroads offered competition. In 1871 all but twenty-seven of the 274 pianos and organs shipped to Minnesota came by railroad.[23] American piano manufacturers were known throughout the world. The 157 piano factories in the United States in 1870 produced about 25,000 pianos, and about 700 church organs were made.[24]

Albert Bolles, in his book on American industry, expressed pique over European ignorance of American culture:

> In distant Europe the people expect very little of the United States in an art point of view. They look upon the country as half-savage yet. They think everybody carries a revolver, and drinks a great deal of whiskey straight, and can go out of town into the country any day, in any part thereof, and kill a wild Indian or a rampant buffalo within a few miles of the city. They look upon the United States somewhat as they do upon Siberia, whose only value to Europe consists in its producing savage dogs of great size and beauty; or as a barbaric country, from which it is absolutely out of the question to expect any product of genius and high artistic culture.

Such European attitudes, Bolles thought, made it possible for the Rev. H. R. Hawes of England to write *Music and Morals* in 1875 without mentioning the existence of an American-made instrument, even though, as Bolles insisted, "the American piano, organ, and violin are conceded the best made in the present age of the world."

At the risk of overstepping the bounds of what is art, some of the popular sheet music of 1876 may at least be mentioned: *Grandfather's Clock* ("as sung at Kelly & Leon's Opera House,

23rd Street, New York"), *I'll Take You Home Again, Kathleen, See That My Grave's Kept Green* by Gus Williams, *Rose of Killarney, My Dearest Heart* with music by Sir Arthur Sullivan, and such religious songs as *The Ninety and Nine* and *Trusting Jesus, That Is All*, both by Ira Sankey, *It Is Well with My Soul*, and *What a Friend We Have in Jesus*.[25]

2

THE VERBAL ARTS

The American book trade exhibit at the Centennial Exhibition, representing ninety-six firms, owed much of its success to the efforts of R. R. Bowker, the aggressive editor of *Publisher's Weekly*. In his lead editorial on January 1, 1876, he expressed his hope that the magazine would become the focus of the nation's entire book trade and a forum for discussion that would improve understanding, reform abuses, and raise the standards in every branch of the business. He was enough of an optimist to suppose that the book trade would one day rank where it properly belonged, second only to the learned professions.[26]

To anybody familiar with the writing and distribution of books in 1876, this was a tall order. Abuses were general, the worst being piracy and underselling. Domestic copyright had prevailed for some years, but it could not prevent the widespread practice of issuing American books abroad, and foreign books in America, without paying royalties. Even though William Dean Howells reviewed *Tom Sawyer* in the May *Atlantic Monthly*, Mark Twain deferred the book until fall in order to secure simultaneous English and American publication, the surest way to foil the pirates.[27] A few reputable firms in both countries refrained from piracy, but their decency only made it easier for less scrupulous competitors to turn a ready profit.

Effective international copyright could not be secured until all branches of the book trade were sufficiently interested to unite in pressuring Congress for legislation—which they eventually did, successfully, in 1890. The authors, who had most at stake, pushed hardest for a law that would end piracy, and some of the publishers were cooperative. But opposing them in 1876 were other publishers, almost all the typographers, and certain economists who argued that ideas were free and should not be treated as personal property for personal profit. Josiah Holland, in the October *Scribner's*, clearly and forcibly described the inequities resulting from the current situation: every other occupation prospered in the United States, he asserted, but except for three or four individuals, authorship was a "have-not" profession, to the obvious detriment of American literature.[28]

The other chief source of dissatisfaction was the way books were sold. The list price meant very little. A *Harper's Weekly* supplement advertised all Harper books currently for sale, grouped by price: 75 cents to $1.00, $1.25 to $2.00, $2.50 to $3.00, $3.50 to $4.00, $4.50 to $6.00, and $7.00 to $18.00. For a depression period, this scale was steep—but it was also artificial. Teachers, librarians, and clergymen were automatically entitled to a 20 percent discount, and so was any "large buyer," a term loosely applied to anyone buying more than one book at a time. But most bookstores were willing to bargain, and some habitually ignored the prices set by publishers. The logical result of this chaos was public suspicion of everybody including the authors. In self-defense, some writers, to control the price and the profit, sold their books by subscription only. Mark Twain chose to sell *Tom Sawyer* by this method.

One phenomenon of the Centennial book trade was the very cheap book, paperbound, quarto, not in copyright. Donnelly, Loyd and Company of Chicago pioneered the species in 1875, with its Lakeside Library priced at ten cents a volume. Almost at once other "sides" made their appearance: the Beadle and Adams Fireside Library, the Riverside Library, the Seaside Library, along with Frank Leslie's Home Library. Standard works of Sir Walter Scott, James Fenimore Cooper, Charles Dickens and their peers cost a dime for a "single," twenty cents for a "double." At such prices the publishers could not ensure a good text: printing errors were abundant, and chapters were sometimes in the wrong order or even omitted. Excepting Scott and Cooper and Dickens, most of the titles were of the sort that gave the "dime novel" its enduring bad name. Jesse Pomeroy, who flared briefly in the Centennial news as "the Boston Boy Fiend," was reported to have read sixty dime novels.

Such were some of the conditions of the business that Bowker thought should rank next to the "learned professions." One fact he did not mention, perhaps because it was generally known, was that the four great book-trade centers were Boston and New York in the East, Cincinnati in the Middlewest, and San Francisco on the West Coast. Bowker lent his enthusiastic support to any group organized to foster the same hope as his, like the American Book-Trade Association, which was formed in 1873. Its 1876 meeting was scheduled for Niagara Falls but was shifted to Philadelphia, as were numerous other meetings that year, to permit delegates to see the Exhibition. The membership, seeking oceanside relief from the heat at Atlantic City, chartered a five-car train, flaunted a huge banner reading "American Book-Trade 1876," and steamed proudly across New Jersey, stopping at Egg Harbor City to sample the local wines.

Bowker was particularly helpful, in 1876, in the organizing of the American Library Association, but there was little he could do about the kind and quality of American writing. Here the book publishers and the editors of literary magazines came into their own, and even more than these, the literate public—Centennial American as reader.

Literary history, with its advantage of hindsight, regards the quarter century following the Civil War as a period of "recovery, re-orientation, re-dedication," and hesitancy,[29] of major redirection, from romanticism to realism, from reverence for tradition to experimentation with the vernacular, and from East to Middlewest as breeding ground of talent. Little of this redirection was visible in 1876; the great bulk of imaginative writing that got into print was about as close to realism as the eclectic architecture and over-decorated furniture were to native functionalism. Even the younger generation of authors that are now bracketed as pioneer realists—Edward Eggleston, Mark Twain, William Dean Howells—had slight awareness of sharing a common mission, and even less awareness that John W. DeForest, in

1867, had blazed the trail toward realism in *Miss Ravenel's Conversion from Secession to Loyalty*. Mark Twain, in his voluminous correspondence with Howells, never mentioned De-Forest even though two DeForest novels, *Honest John Vane* (1875) and its 1876 sequel, *Playing the Mischief*, treated Grant-ist corruption as Twain had done a few years earlier in *The Gilded Age*.

Busy though he was in building the one major career among the pioneer realists, Twain showed in his reading an avid interest in anything except realism. During 1876 he eagerly awaited each new *Atlantic* installment of Charles Dudley Warner's adventures in the Near East.[30] Warner's *Mummies and Moslems* and *My Winter on the Nile*, reminded him of his own travels in the Mediterranean world, which he had reported in *Innocents Abroad*, his first book. He also held Thomas Bailey Aldrich in special regard; his short story "Marjorie Daw" particularly impressed him, as a perfect *jeu d'esprit*. A persistent Twain myth pictures iconoclastic rebellion which he held in check only with difficulty and with the help of his wife and his friend Howells. But his letters to Howells reveal a rather astonishing respect for older writers and for contemporaries who, by a subsequent logic, were among the chief opponents of emerging realism. In writing to Howells in October about their project of a series of novels with a single plot, he suggested "that Aldrich devise the skeleton-plan" and that Warner and Bret Harte might follow; then he asked if certain others might not fall in line with the idea: "Won't Mr. Holmes? Won't Henry James? Won't Mr. Lowell? & some more of the big literary fish?" [31]

The plan failed, like so many others that Twain's lively imagination produced. Howells had enough respect for his genius to pay him more per *Atlantic* page—twenty dollars—than he paid any other author. He kept after Twain but was too careful an editor to use everything his friend sent. The February issue carried "A Literary Nightmare," best remembered by its rhyme for streetcar conductors, "Punch, brothers, punch with care,/Punch in the presence of the passenjare." June brought "The Facts Concerning the Recent Carnival of Crime in Connecticut," an early example of the indictment of the human conscience that Twain later perfected in *The Mysterious*

Stranger. In December came "The Canvasser's Tale," an absurd yarn about a man who collected echoes—Twain at his most farcical. Meanwhile one book of his, *Sketches New and Old*, was selling steadily all year. But what gave the Centennial Year its real significance, as far as Twain was concerned, was the appearance of *Tom Sawyer*.

In his premature review, Howells called it "incomparably the best picture of life in that region as yet known to fiction." For Twain, however, its regionalism meant less than his decision that the book should be one for boys, and as he wrote he worried unduly about its improprieties. He leaned heavily on Howells, who was usually ready and able to suggest a paraphrase less likely to offend. But part of the taking down was by Twain's own effort: Tom's comment at one point, "they comb me all to hell," drew no objection from Mrs. Clemens or her mother, when Mark read the passage to them, or from Howells; but even so, he confided, "that dern word worries me some nights." And he gladly deleted a phrase about a poodle "with his tail shut down like a hasp," which Howells called "awfully good but a little dirty." [32]

It was the inclusion of just such wording, however, that set the newer writing most clearly apart from the older, the more formal, the more traditional. In the year's list of bestsellers,[33] *Tom Sawyer* stood third, behind *Helen's Babies* by John Habberton and *The Royal Path of Life* by Thomas L. Haines and Levi Yaggi. (The next three in American sales, not quite up to the arbitrary figure of 375,000 copies sold, were George Eliot's *Daniel Deronda*, which was serialized during the year in *Scribner's Monthly*, Jules Verne's *Michael Strogoff*, and AnnEliza Young's *Wife No. 19*, an exposé of Mormon plural marriage.) Twain was particularly irritated by *Helen's Babies*, with its sentimentally artificial baby-talk; but the book was a sure momentary success and not likely to be banned, like *Tom Sawyer*, for "bad English" and for disrespect toward institutionalized piety.[34] Among the Protestant middle class that did most of the reading, many had a pious abhorrence of fiction as something not true, while others objected, even more strongly, to fiction that broke the rules by being actually true to ordinary life. The twenty-eight volumes of Jacob Abbott's "Rollo" books had conditioned an entire generation to didacticism, while thrillers and sentimental stories that postured as fact enjoyed freedom from reader censure. To many Centennial readers, great literature was not supposed to be a mirror to nature but something quite different, like the decoration concealing a building's function.

The same public that admired eclectic architecture and added frills to their modest houses idolized Bayard Taylor, whose facile warmed-over Romanticism made him the best-loved contemporary poet and the heir-presumptive to the immortal Longfellow. When in 1876 he parodied Whitman in *The Echo Club and other Literary Diversions*,[35] hardly anybody objected, for Whitman had committed the cardinal sins of rejecting traditional form and glorifying the commonplace. A representative editorial opinion was that "Walt Whitman, having broken down the barriers between decency and dirtiness, will next endeavor to break down those between prose and verse." Few "good" people had any use for him, and found just one more reason for disliking him in his concept of art, expressed in *Democratic Vistas* (1873): he reproached America not for failing to equal Old World culture but for not realizing that Old World models were "exiles and exotics here." Art, he thought, was not surface decoration but the expression of man's basic beliefs—a radical notion, in Centennial America.

Still rather lame from the paralysis of his left arm and leg three years before, Whitman was regaining his good spirits in 1876. He spent happy hours on horsecars, sitting beside the driver, riding to and from the Exhibition and enjoying the crowds—his *en masse*—even if nobody knew who he was. He was also regaining his energy and his productiveness. He issued an Author's Edition of his works in two volumes, *Leaves of Grass* and *Two Rivulets;* new poems assigned to 1876 include "Eidólons," "With All Thy Gifts," "To a Locomotive in Winter," and "By Broad Potomac's Shore." He also wrote "A Death Sonnet to Custer" that Whitelaw Reid published in the New York *Tribune;* not every American deprecated him.[36] But so many did that a letter from Bram Stoker in Dublin was particularly welcome: "We have just had tonight a hot debate on your genius at the Fortnightly Club. . . . We hope to see you in Ireland." [37] A different sort of foreign homage was represented during 1876 by the arrival of Anne Gilchrist, who in 1870 had published *A Woman's Estimate of Walt Whitman* and who had rather embarrassed her idol by a series of love letters. She called him "My Mate," but during her three years in America the mating was strictly platonic.[38]

Whitman at least had some recognition abroad; he was not so totally neglected as Herman Melville. Melville's six-hundred page narrative-philosophical poem, *Clarel*, appeared in 1876— and got no reviews at all. In this poem Melville was facing the issues raised for religion by the new findings in science, as perceptive poets were doing in Europe, but the current religious complacency in America would have condemned the effort even if *Clarel* had been easy to read. Something of the intellectual tenor of the times can be gleaned from the grudging nature of the homage paid to Ralph Waldo Emerson, dimly remembered as a radical, and the almost total ignorance of his mentor, Bronson Alcott. Concord idealism was satirized, to the delight of many readers, in "Transcendental Wild Oats" which Alcott's daughter Louisa included in her *Silver Pitchers*, published this year. In contrast, there were no doubts at all about Henry Wadsworth Longfellow, who was always lofty in tone and who never seriously challenged his reader's brains or defied convention. To be great, by Centennial standards, was to be understood— though not on the Emersonian level of the street and the barn. Emerson made two visits to the Exhibition, the first on his way to the University of Virginia to give a commencement address, "The Proper Functions of a Scholar," the second on his way back to Concord. The Exhibition, he wrote, "dazzled and astounded" him.[39] Longfellow spent an entire week there, blinking at the bulk of Main and admiring the fountains and the borrowed paintings, some of which he had seen on trips abroad. The three hundred West Point cadets fascinated him; but the industrial exhibits left him cold.[40] His poem "Nature" appeared in 1876, adding to his reputation as America's beloved household poet—intimate, homey, sentimental, and readily understood.

For better or worse, the editors and publishers in New York and Boston were virtual dictators of literary standards, and most of them were provincial in outlook, conservative in taste, or both. Of the quality magazines then being printed, only *Harper's Monthly* and the *Atlantic* survive; Centennial readers could turn also to *Scribner's, Appleton's, Lippincott's,* and the *Galaxy.* All six were published in the Northeast. If there was a Solid South (a term first used in 1876), its solidity created no reader loyalty to its own writers and periodicals. The *Southern Literary Messenger,* in its time, had been one of the nation's best, but it was no longer being issued. Southern taste was more old-fashioned in 1876 than it had been in 1840; Scott was still widely read and Tennyson was the favorite poet. With no regional journal to turn to, new Southern writers had to conform to the dicta of Northern editors. One surefire genre was local color; Sara Orne Jewett's "Deephaven Excursions," in the September *Atlantic,* was the prototype. A writer of genuine talent who could not or would not do what the editors demanded was, like Sidney Lanier, apt to go unrewarded. In December, visiting Florida for his health's sake, Lanier with pathetic pride reported checks for $24, $15, and $10—the last for his "Evening Song."

The best that Lanier could hope to do was keep a foothold on the fringe of recognition. A conversation with Daniel Coit Gilman left him with the flowing possibility of lecturing on English literature at the Hopkins if he could prepare himself adequately; but it was a race with time, for death had one hand on his shoulder. Bayard Taylor used his influence to give Lanier the commission to write a cantata for the Exhibition's opening ceremonies. "The Centennial Meditation of Columbia" in sixty-one lines, was showered with abuse after its appearance in *Lippincott's;* and Lanier, sitting beside Taylor at the opening, was in agony lest it fail. But it was intended to be sung, and the actual performance, with Dudley Buck's music and conducted by Buck, silenced the critics. "Psalm of the West," also printed in *Lippincott's* (and filling twenty pages), was much better received by readers. Buck asked Lanier for more short poems to set to music and was particularly taken with "Evening Song," finding it "simply lovely and as new as lovely." He composed the music for it at a single sitting.[41] Modern readers find it a little *too* lovely, but it is several cuts above most of the poems written in what George Santayana later dubbed the Genteel Tradition.

Another commission that came Lanier's way was to prepare a

biography of his friend Charlotte Cushman, the actress, who died on February 18, 1876; but a certain Miss Stebbins of Chadd's Ford, Pennsylvania, was too ill to do her part in going over the Cushman letters and the project collapsed—just the sort of frustration that Lanier had grown used to. A five-page sketch in *Scribner's* gave the actress her due as the best-known woman in American history, having been seen and heard by millions in her forty-year career, and as having been unsurpassed in tragedy, especially in the role of Lady Macbeth.[42]

Lanier was too modest to envy the great success of his patron Bayard Taylor, and by the same token he was spared the doubts that were beginning to plague his friend. Taylor complained to Paul Hamilton Hayne in August, 1876, that it was "the blackest period ever known since we began to have a literature," and in December he was worried enough about his own career to tell Thomas Bailey Aldrich that in twenty-five years of writing he had never had to work so hard.[43] The realization that fame founded on easy writing does not endure was a shattering experience for him. It was much the same with Helen Hunt Jackson, at the height of her fame in 1876 but increasingly aware of failure. During the year she published thirty-four short magazine pieces and two books—*Bits of Talk in Verse and Prose for Young People*, published under the pseudonym "Saxe Holm," and *Mercy Philbrick's Choice*, published anonymously. She had submitted *Mercy Philbrick's Choice* to *Scribner's* as an eighty-page novelette, and when *Scribner's* rejected it she expanded it to 296 pages for the Roberts Brothers' "No Name" series. Reviewers were caustic, but it sold eight thousand copies in four months. Like most of her novels, *Mercy Philbrick's Choice* was a hash of sentiment and artificiality. Men fell on their knees to kiss the hems of women's garments; women talked archly and fainted on slight provocation. The critics, if not her readers, were now pointing out flaws with a frankness that wounded, and both pseudonym and anonym were no doubt efforts to evade the mounting adverse criticism. She had won the fame she wanted, but too easily, like the architects, by pandering to popular taste and ignoring new materials. She lived to write better things: *Ramona* and *A Century of Dishonor*, reviewing the tragic treatment of the Indians; but nothing would have astonished her more than the posthumous fame of the gentle, retiring friend of her Amherst girlhood, Emily Dickinson, who never conceded anything to popular taste.[44]

Criticism in any age is seldom a fulltime profession. The most active critics in 1876 were journalists, editors, novelists, or professors of literature. James Russell Lowell, Longfellow's successor as Smith Professor of Modern Languages at Harvard, could have been an outstanding critic of contemporary American writing, but was preoccupied instead with European literature. *Among My Books* (Second Series) came out during 1876, with long discursive essays on Dante, Spenser, Wordsworth, Milton, and Keats. An illness, the first in his life, had kept Lowell from revising it as well as he wanted to, and in his discouragement he thought it "third rate," but it was favorably received and enhanced his reputation.[45] Edmund Clarence Stedman, poet and journalist, struck closer to the present with his *Victorian Poets* but did not satisfy William Dean Howells, who wrote in his *Atlantic* review that "our criticism of literature will never rise to the heights demanded of it until it concerns itself with the forces that lie back of literature. . . ." Stedman, Howells felt, was very good on the esthetic level, as in comparing Swinburne and Browning; but literature is related to life as well as to art, and it "demands criticism which is historic and ethic as well as aesthetic." [46] Howells was obviously no herald of the New Critics.

It is interesting to note how much Swinburne was disliked in Centennial America. A squib that made the newspaper rounds reported his joining the church and added the hope that as one result he would stop writing poetry.[47] A long review of his "Erechtheus" in the May *Scribner's*, no doubt by Josiah Holland, the editor, called him a "study poet" with no popular following, and observed that Emerson, whom Swinburne deprecated, wrote "lines that have gone into the language, and Longfellow, with a fraction of Swinburne's imagination, has been honored in the same way." Too great and too narrow a preoccupation with the Classics was suggested by the reviewer as a major reason for the public antipathy toward Swinburne.[48]

Harper's Magazine began in 1875 a series of articles about various facets of the century of progress. The article on literature, by Edwin P. Whipple, is well-balanced and temperate, with no touch of arrogant self-praise. When Whipple approached the present and named some of the younger writers, he backed away from specific judgments; and the article concludes: "It would be presumtuous (sic) to anticipate the verdict of the next generation as to which of these will fill the expectations raised by their early efforts. That pleasant duty must be left to the fortunate person who shall note the Centennial Progress of American Literature in Harper's Magazine in 1976." [49]

But it is always safer to criticize dead writers than living ones. The first significant biography of Hawthorne appeared in 1876, written by George Parsons Lathrop, his son-in-law.[50] Lathrop also contributed to the *Atlantic Monthly* a thoughtful review of "Early American Novelists," among them Charles Brockden Brown, John Neal, James Fenimore Cooper, James Kirke Paulding. Poor as most of their novels were, Lathrop insisted, they did not deserve the sneering remark made by the British critic Sidney Smith, "In the four quarters of the globe, who reads an American book?" The question had rankled patriotic hearts in 1820, and Lathrop's protest may be evidence that it could still be resented in 1876.[51]

What critics and reviewers might say in print was less important to contemporary writers, however, than the opinions of several large elements in the society—the militant pious, the defenders of tradition, and the great number of readers who resented being made to think. Whitman and Melville had defied all three groups and were now obscure and unread.

But there are other ways of alienating potential readers, and Henry James was so gifted in this respect that he ran no risk of too easy and too early a popularity. James was preoccupied with, and wrote for, the handful of sophisticates of the Eastern seaboard who could fit readily into European modes of living and thinking. His *Roderick Hudson* was published in 1876 after its serial run in the *Atlantic Monthly*, and *The American* was unfolding, month by month, in that magazine. The hero of *The American*, Christopher Newman, was a type that might have had general appeal to the public, for he was a Westerner who had made a fortune, but his defeat at the hands of a decadent French family was hardly what the generality of Americans relished reading about. It was an age of innocence when people were not eager to have their civilization disadvantaged, even in fiction. Furthermore, James's addiction to living abroad, like the painters Sargent and Whistler, was an implicit slap at Americans who stayed at home. But perhaps the greatest sin that James committed was to write about people who did not have to work; for work was a duty, in the prevailing Protestant ethic, and though God supposedly crowned the good work of the virtuous with success, enjoyment of leisure was uneasily viewed as sinful.

James could write for the wider public when he wanted to. His friend John Hay, in an effort to get him established, persuaded Whitelaw Reid to commission him to do a series of essays on Paris for the *Tribune*. James brought all his skill to the project and sent twenty letters, urbane and often amusing, about the people of Paris and their cultural interests; in many ways they foreshadowed his later fiction. But when Reid suggested they were unsuitable for a newspaper, James answered, "If my letters have been 'too good' I am honestly afraid that they are the poorest I can do, especially for a newspaper!" [52]

One gifted American critic was Lafacadio Hearn, who was living in Cincinnati in 1876. His gruesome reporting of the Tan-Yard Murder and other horrendous crimes had earned for him a local notoriety which he magnified by marrying a mulatto. The scandal led to Hearn's dismissal from the *Inquirer* in 1875, but it did not prevent his joining the rival *Commercial* almost at once, as police reporter, and continuing his lurid descriptions of murders, slaughterhouse techniques, and suicides. He also kept alive the paper's "Literary Notes." [53]

Josiah Holland, bigoted and narrow as he showed himself in *Every-Day Topics*, his salute to the Centennial, was a successful editor, attracting fresh talent and shaking *Scribner's* loose from the Eastern provincialism prevailing among the leading periodicals. He was alert enough to hire as his engraver, the English-born Timothy Cole, who arrived in America penniless in 1875, and in 1876 a new publisher, Theodore de Vinne, gave the magazine a professional competence hardly approached by its rivals. Some of the magazine's loyal readers may have lifted their eyebrows over a poem by Mary Mapes Dodge in the October issue, for it was favorable toward Walt Whitman. The poem, five stanzas of heptameter couplets with the title "The Two Mysteries," had a softening headnote: Whitman was pictured as sitting by the white coffin of his nephew, surrounded by children and with one little girl on his lap. Death is a mystery but, as Whitman had written, no more of a mystery than life; and "As life is to the living, so death is to the dead." Here was one facet of Whitman that Holland must have decided was outside the area of general censure. He had pretty thoroughly discredited the poet, however, in May, in his column "Topics of the Times." Using a technique he enjoyed, he first selected what struck him as some of the worst lines in Emerson's new book, *Conduct of Life*, and in *Sartor Resartus*. Then, "having given a taste of Emerson's and Carlyle's poorest prose," he quoted comparable passages from Whitman and found them inferior. "The man is capable of poetry," he asserted, "and always ought to have written it. The best he has done has been to set down, in the roughest condition, the raw material. . . . We believe that in his theories and performances he is radically wrong—that he is doing nothing but advertising himself as a literary eccentric, and that he ought to have, and will have, no following." [54]

Time can be depended on to erode some reputations. Some of the authors very popular in 1876 are read today only by graduate students in seminars on cultural history. The Rev. Edward Payson Roe, whose book about the great Chicago fire, *Barriers Burned Away* (1872), made him momentarily famous, published two books in 1876: *Fiction Near to Nature's Heart*, in his typical moralizing style, and *A Manual on the Culture of Small Fruit*, on the face of it more of a contribution. Timothy Shay Arthur, author of one of the great classics of temperance, *Ten Nights in a Barroom and What I Saw There* (1854), was still productive, turning out other crusading novels in 1873, 1874, and 1879 but none in 1876. Mrs. E.D.E.N. Southworth was more cooperative; her 1876 work was *Self-Raised; or From the Depths—a sequel to Ishmael; or, Into the Depths*.[55] But the palm for writing most deserving of quick oblivion goes to a poet, Julia A. Moore, the "Sweet Singer of Michigan" who began her career in 1876 with *The Sentimental Song Book*. She served a real purpose: more than any other versifier she was the inspiration for Emmeline Grangerford in *Huckleberry Finn* with her

"Ode to Stephen Dowling Bots, Dec'd." One contemporary reviewer of *The Sentimental Song Book* was cruel enough to write that "Shakespeare, could he read it, would be glad that he was dead." [56]

The attrition of fame is no doubt merciful, but some authors get caught unfairly. Mark Twain's bright light of humor blinds us to humorists almost as good—like Max Adeler, who is virtually forgotten. His 1876 book, *Elbow-Room*, is a series of absurdities in Millburg, a typical suburban community: Wilberforce Fogg quiets a baby by mesmerizing it, a doctor has to undo the act, and Mrs. Fogg sues for divorce; the lamplighter, Mr. Bones, is on the job when the moon is full, neglects his duty in the dark of the moon, and is puzzled until he discovers that the almanac he's been going by is for the wrong year.[57] It is humor underplayed, closer to the modern classics than to Twain.

Frank R. Stockton was hardly started on his career as a humorist in 1876; his book of the year, *Tales Out of School*, was only apprentice work to *Rudder Grange* and *The Lady—or the Tiger?* Charles Follen Adams was making headway with the comic poems of "Leedle Yawcob Strauss" in what he called "scrapple English" (Pennsylvania-German). David Ross Locke, editor of the Toledo *Blade* and strongly Republican, was using his considerable talents as "Petroleum Vesuvius Nasby" to swipe at the Democrats and the Bourbon South, in "letters from Confederit X-roads, Kentucky" that Republican editors gladly reprinted. *Nasby on Inflation* appeared in 1876.[58]

In the well-exploited field of juvenile literature, Horatio Alger, Jr. turned out two books in 1876—*Sam's Chance* and *Shifting for Himself;* [59] he was increasingly careless in his writing but his audience did not read for style. In 1876, the Elsie Dinsmore series by Martha Finley reached a peak of boldness; the Civil War was treated gingerly in *Elsie's Womanhood* (1875), but in the Centennial year *Elsie's Motherhood* came right out and excoriated the Ku Klux Klan. There are even dark hints that distant relatives of the Dinsmores are Klansmen—no-good drunkards and rabble rousers. In one climactic scene the Dinsmores meet the Klan with pistols and boiling lye; in another, a cousin routs a Klan gathering by a spectacular exhibition of ventriloquism.[60] The author, without realizing it, was pioneering the Klan novel; Albion Tourgee's *A Fool's Errand* did not appear until three years later.

Another woman writer was Marietta Holly (1836–1926), but she did not use her own name. Her first book in 1873, *My Opinions and Betsy Bobbet's* was issued as "by Josiah Allen's wife." It led to many more by "Samantha Allen"; *Samantha at the Centennial* (1877) tells of "goin' to Filadelfy to the Sentinal." Samantha gives advice to President Grant and Dom Pedro among others. *Samantha at Saratoga, or, "Racin' after Fashion"* (1887), was a runner-up for best seller. Samantha also reported on the Chicago fair of 1893 and the St. Louis exposition of 1904.

But none of these outsold *Helen's Babies;* John Habberton had hit upon a sure-fire formula. It sickened Mark Twain, but readers loved it and Josiah Holland, predictably, was extravagant with his praise: "We cannot have too many of such novels —if they will only supplant those of the lurid sensational variety with which the world is flooded." [61] What more need be said?

In 1876 there were no Children's Book Awards, no National Book Awards, no Pulitzer or Nobel Prizes. If the question had been asked, who were the greatest living American authors, the verdict must certainly have favored the eminent Victorians, whose citadel of fame younger men might assault with indifferent success. Mark Twain certainly thought of Oliver Wendell Holmes and William Cullen Bryant and Ralph Waldo Emerson as the Olympians, even though their writing gave him little pleasure. He much preferred William Dean Howells, his "only author," the one fellow writer, he once said, whose books he liked to read. An Olympian was someone to venerate, not to enjoy. Bryant, for example, wrote a long, lofty Centennial Poem, "The Flood of Years," printed in the August *Scribner's.* The poem sees life as existing on the crest of an ever-moving flood tide; behind the crest is a wasteland of desolate lifelessness, with wrecks and broken monuments, scraps of mementos and bits of paper, while ahead of the flood is "a mist where swarm dissolving forms, the Brood of Hope." Not too precisely located, beyond a dark barrier (death), is a soft, happy afterlife.

Bryant was so much of an Olympian that he looked over the Exhibition only before it opened; an increasing aversion to crowds kept him from a second visit.[62] Centennial readers were apparently both willing and able to ignore the revolution in poetry that Whitman had inaugurated in 1855, and could welcome, in the same issue of *Scribner's* as Bryant's effulgence, Richard Henry Stoddard's "Hospes Civitatis. Annus Mirabilis MDCCCLXXVI," an interminable ode replete with the approved poetic conventions. It turns out to be an American welcome to the nations on this great anniversary, and a prophecy of world leadership:

> Henceforth, America, Man looks up to Thee,
> Not down at the dead Republic! Rise, arise!
> That all men may behold thee. Be not proud;
> Be humble, and be wise;
> And let thy head be bowed
> To the Unknown, Supreme One, who on high
> Has willed thee not to die!
>
> . . . .
>
> The Commonwealth receives her honored guests—
> She celebrates no triumphs but of peace.

It might be difficult to say just what it was that Centennial America wanted in the way of literature. As had been true since 1800, or even earlier, patriots insisted upon foreign acknowledgement of American writing as the equal of Europe's but were not ready to understand that the imitation of foreign forms was not enough. Readers enjoyed the indigenous product—the works of Eggleston, Howells, and Twain—but did not see anything of art in it, any more than they did in their simple bridges and dwellings and utensils. Art was something beyond, somehow sacrosanct, not in the realm of the enjoyable. There was a clear and almost universal notion of what was *not* wanted in prose and poetry—the writings of Thoreau and Melville and Whitman, for example, and even Poe, who was still suffering, almost thirty years after his death, from charges of being addicted to drink and drugs. An immoral man could not produce great art, by Centennial standards. Instead of trying to understand Whitman, Centennial Americans admired Stoddard and the aging Bryant; they were indifferent to Lanier and fond of his patron Bayard Taylor; and they preferred *Helen's Babies* to *Tom Sawyer*. In general the literary picture, as at any other moment in our history, was one of great unevenness and diversity, ranging from

Emerson's *Letters and Social Aims* [63] to Holland's *Every-Day Topics—A Book of Briefs;* from Melville's *Clarel* to Will Carleton's bucolic *Home Ballads;* from Warner's *Mummies and Moslems* to P. Thorne's *Jolly Good Times; or, Child Life on a Farm.*

With a continent yet to be won and so much still to be done in the forging of a nation, books were thin as for idle moments, to compensate for the hard toil or for the ugliness of muddy farms and unfinished cities. If literature was lofty in language and moral in tone, it suited the pious, like sermons on Sunday. If it was comic or crude, it was something to chuckle over and forget. If it offended established ideas or ideals, it was to be ignored or condemned. American literature was rarely seen as part of an organic whole. There was not yet a single college course in American literature and literary criticism, despite the standard set by Poe four decades earlier, was generally underdeveloped, or devoted to the great writers of the past, or based on moralistic standards. Howells, alone among the reviewers, hinted that literature to be important must have some relation to current actualities; most critics and readers did not link art with life insisting, rather, that ART was forever set apart.

Whatever their view of literature, however, Americans were unquestionably interested in it in 1876. More literary magazines existed then than today, when the population is five times as large, and they carried much more literary material—poems, essays, short stories, serialized novels, and criticism—than do their modern counterparts. People, despite their tedious hours of work, had more time to read—and none of the modern gadgets of passive entertainment. Individual editors, moreover, had considerably more influence over the classes they catered to, and were better known throughout the country than editors today.

Newspapers, too, were more numerous, diverse, and influential. Few editors could relax, as today, in the absence of local competition and write the "non-think" of so many of our current editorials. In 1876 there were about seven hundred daily papers, sixty triweeklies, a hundred semi-weeklies, and six thousand weeklies. [64] Any city of more than a few thousand people had at least two papers, usually opposed politically and constantly sniping at each other. Most of the great editors were courageously partisan, although a few, including Samuel Bowles of the Springfield *Republican*, perhaps the best small-city paper, even more courageously tried to be non-partisan.

In 1876, William Cullen Bryant was semi-retired after almost fifty years in which he had made the New York *Evening Post* a distinguished paper. The New York *Herald*, taking advantage of the recently developed method of making paper from wood pulp, much less expensive than rag paper, lowered its price from four to three cents and its resulting increased circulation topped that of its rival the New York *Sun*. But the *Sun* was not doing badly, averaging 132,000 circulation daily in the summer of 1876. The editor, Charles A. Dana, was typically partisan: he was for Tilden and, after the verdict for Hayes, repeatedly wrote of "His Fraudulency Mr. Hayes." Whitelaw Reid at the *Tribune*, where he had succeeded Horace Greeley in 1873, was strong for Hayes, but not so violently pro-Republican as George Jones at the *Times*, who was both editor and majority stockholder and thus in no danger of being ousted. A new penny paper, the *Daily News*, was not yet a threat; it was notable in the 1870's for its coverage of lottery and policy drawings.[65]

In Philadelphia the *Public Ledger* reached a circulation of almost 100,000, and in Washington the *Evening Star* held the lead. The Boston *Herald* led in circulation and enterprise, but the *Globe* was beginning to look like a challenger in that city. Joseph Hawley's Hartford *Courant* was easily the leading paper in Connecticut. In the South, the Atlanta *Constitution*, which Joel Chandler Harris joined in 1876, had only one serious competitor, Henry Watterson's Louisville *Courier-Journal*. The Chicago *Tribune* gained a rival on January 3, 1876, when Melville Stone's *Daily News* issued its first number.[66]

Joseph Pulitzer of St. Louis was often in Washington and New York in 1876, conferring with such Democratic stalwarts as August Belmont, Manton Marble, and Abram S. Hewitt, and countering the statements of his former employer Carl Schurz; in December, as special correspondent of the New York *Sun*, he wrote a vigorous series about the electoral controversy. Not until 1878 did he become owner-publisher of the St. Louis *Post-Dispatch*, which he made into the leading Democratic organ of the Middlewest.[67]

Partisan rivalry often led to editorial invective, nowhere more so than on the Pacific Slope. What was known as the "Oregon Style" meant a kind of language that seemed to invite libel suits if not personal attack. Scandal-mongering was common, especially among the thirty-five newspapers being published in San Francisco in 1876. None of the thirty-five was above reproach, not even the *Chronicle*, which led in circulation. In Oregon, however, the Portland *Oregonian* proved that conservatism and moderation could pay off, for it led the state in circulation. But in Utah, perhaps surprisingly, there was deadly rivalry between the *Deseret News*, a Mormon mouthpiece, and the Salt Lake *Tribune*.[68]

For all their stress on politics, however, Centennial newspapers did not neglect literature. Poems, sketches, and stories did not appear every day, but their frequent inclusion provides one more bit of evidence for concluding that literature, whatever its quality, was amply served in 1876.

3

THE PLASTIC ARTS

In the dank, dark, and dingy basement of Memorial Hall stands a model of the Centennial Exhibition, in a glass case almost ceiling high and roughly thirty feet by twenty-five. Even the best maps and pictures and diagrams have their limitations; for the study of the Exhibition the model is a sudden welcome break-through to three-dimensional concreteness. In dust and disrepair, and dimly lit by small bulbs, there it all is, as it might have looked on one of the cloudier days of 1876.

Early in the planning stage, the directors decided to segregate the different kinds of exhibits in separate buildings, thereby pioneering the pavilion method at world's fairs. Next they settled on the number of major buildings—five—and announced an open competition for their designs; but after the competition ended and the prizes were given, they shelved all the submitted plans. Instead, they gave a free hand to their own engineer-architect, Herman J. Schwarzmann, and employed the firm of Henry Pettit and Joseph Wilson to serve as consultants. Schwartzman is given credit for Memorial Hall and Horticulture; Pettit and Wilson were responsible for Main. The deliberate effort of these men to fit the style of each building, insofar as possible, to the nature of its contents yielded a variety of styles that is particularly striking in the model.[69]

Siegfried Giedion offers no opinion of the major buildings in his authoritative *Space, Time and Architecture;* [70] but other critics have been free with their judgment, and most of it is caustic. Lewis Mumford, in *The Brown Decades*, found it "hard to conceive anything lower than the architecture of the Centennial Exhibition or," for that matter, "of the fashionable Newport villas of the same period." [71] The art historians are in general accord but seem unable or unwilling to agree on the adjectives to use in their condemnation. Oliver Larkin, for example, is unequivocal in his opinion of the Exhibition architecture: in his *Art in America* he uses an engraving that was made for *Harper's Weekly* from a balloonist's photograph, and remarks, "It shows the oddest collection of structures that had ever been assembled in America, and assembled in that rather careless way which was still a convention in landscape architecture." [72]

Memorial Hall, perhaps because it was the most consciously "artistic" of the five major buildings, has been a favorite target of the critics. Suzanne La Follette censures it as "a permanent monument to the bad 'French taste' of the period," and goes on to dismiss all the lesser buildings as "monstrous in everything except size," reflecting "the mélange of debased Classical and debased Gothic which was known as 'Queen Anne.' " [73] For Thomas E. Tallmadge, Memorial Hall was "contemporary French of the debased mansard variety." He considered the mansard one of the two chief inspirations for American builders in the 1870's, the other being the Victorian Gothic as it could be seen in Boston's New South Church (1876) and Harvard's Memorial Hall (1877). He disliked both. The genuine Gothic he liked well enough, in such New York examples as Trinity

Church, in the Perpendicular tradition, and St. Patrick's Cathedral, modeled after St. Ouen's in Rouen. What debased the Victorian Gothic, he asserted, was the addition of Italianate details in deference to Ruskin's enthusiasm for St. Mark's Cathedral, in his book *The Stones of Venice*.[74]

The inability of the critics to agree, or their insistence on individual vocabularies, parallels the confusion produced in America by the battle of the styles, in 1876 as in other years. The effort to domesticate one or another established form could not, of course, produce anything distinctively American. Ralph Waldo Emerson, notorious optimist that he was, had expressed as early as 1837 the hope that servile dependence upon foreign and ancient models would soon be rejected from American behavior; he asked for nothing less than an indigenous art. But in architecture at least he did not live to see it. If anything, the old habit of relying on borrowed forms was intensified in the four decades following his address. In the interplay between Transit of Civilization and Frontier—cultural diffusion versus meaningful adaptation to environment—it is an arresting thought, if not an outright irony, that cultural dependence should dominate so firmly at the very moment when the Frontier process was at its peak.

The art critics do agree, more or less, that the year 1876 marked a turning point in American architecture; but its relative importance in a long series of turning points may be a matter of individual judgment. Tallmadge asserts that the year saw the end of "that curious era of bad taste which hovered around the Civil War." He ascribes its demise not to the Exhibition in general but rather to the foreign influences there. "The beauty, taste, and skill of the foreign exhibits and the sumptuous manner in which they were displayed, compared with the crudity of our own exhibits . . . brought the blush of shame to the cheek of the hundred-percent patriot, and fired the soul of many a fifty-percent architect and craftsman to do better work."

Tallmadge betrays a certain inconsistency, however, when he proceeds to lavish praise on the Romanesque. In his words, the seventeen years "of high romance in architecture which filled the gap between two great world's fairs"—that is, between 1876 and 1893—produced "the first and most important movement that was not a copy or echo of a similar movement in Europe." [75] H. H. Richardson was the hero; his Trinity Church in Boston, completed in 1877, was the great monument. Since that church is Romanesque through and through, it represents a revival of the past that originated in America—an advance, no doubt, over merely adopting a revival of the past that began in Europe but still not the disavowal of imitation that Emerson had demanded in 1837.

One other style, the Queen Anne, figures prominently in the discussions of the year 1876 as a turning point. Vincent J. Scully, Jr., authority on the "Shingle Style" that was favored by many wealthy families in the 1870's, dates the Queen Anne from 1869 to 1876 but remarks that the Exhibition brought it into public prominence along with the colonial forms revived in conscious evocation of the past.[76] Fiske Kimball, in contrast, dates the Queen Anne *from* 1876 and specifically from the English Building at the Exhibition, which survives, along with Memorial Hall, for latter-day inspection.[77] It somewhat resembles the larger gabled dwellings of colonial New England, familiar to Centennial Americans less perhaps from actual observation than from illustrated editions of *The House of the Seven Gables;* but its Gothicism is more pronounced and its light warm colors set it apart from the sombre grays of natural weathering or the dark paint the Puritans sometimes used. It was carefully designed, with studied asymmetry, clustered chimneys, exposed beams within, and such other features reminiscent of the early eighteenth century as red brickwork and controlled half-timbering. While not of mansion proportions it is nevertheless a rather large house, commodious, built for comfort.

Gothic, Romanesque, and Queen Anne were not the only contenders in the Centennial battle of the styles. The Greek Revival, at its apex in 1825 and supposedly dead by 1850, killed off by the Gothic Revival, refused to stay buried. Visitors to the Exhibition, glancing eastward across the Schuylkill, could not have missed seeing on the skyline the city's best reminder of the Classical, the severe Doric of Girard College; but if they went downtown they could see another Doric building just being completed, the Ridgeway Library, while several of the smaller structures at the Exhibition were nothing *but* Greek. Memorial

Hall was late Renaissance. Horticultural Hall was Moorish. The two largest buildings, Main and Machinery, were nothing in particular, although both sported eclectic decoration; people forgave their lack of any recognizable style but had no way of knowing that their frank functionalism would one day become as much a label as Gothic. Neither Main nor Machinery was considered worth preserving; both were dismantled soon after the closing, with no chance of being portents of the functional revolution that had its first real beginnings a decade later.

Beginning with the works of Palladio, made available in English in the latter eighteenth century, American builders had always looked for guidance to foreign books on design. In the 1870's, the most influential was probably Charles Locke Eastlake's *Hints on Household Taste* (1873). Eastlake argued for a return to honest English craftsmanship, the kind that requires skill and time—and the kind that produced the English Building at the Exhibition. Attempts to achieve the same result quickly and at low cost could only cheapen the effect and earn the scorn that critics have heaped upon most examples of the Queen Anne in America. Tallmadge attributed the Queen Anne to Victorian Gothic modified by Eastlake but was savage in denouncing American architects, builders, and decorators for making a travesty of the product, with every detail writhing in architectural agony.

The popularity of the foreign authorities encouraged American imitators, some of whose books sold briskly. *Woodward's National Architect*, first issued in 1868, sold well enough to justify several subsequent editions; and *Hobbs's Architecture* appeared in 1873 and again in 1876. A little older, but still successful, was *Villas and Cottages* (1867) by a transplanted Frenchman, Calvert Vaux, who had some sensible ideas about house forms but was realistic enough to adapt his designs to the American desire for showiness. One result of these books was the building of Gothic castles, Italian villas, Shah's palaces, and other imitations of foreign models by people with money enough. Another result was the remodeling of existing houses, from the "vernacular" to the "cultivated" style. It was nothing new: Hawthorne had added an Italian tower to the Wayside when he returned from his long European sojourn in 1860, and his neighbor Bronson Alcott had doctored up his own good Concord house in a gesture of conformity not at all in keeping with his ultra-radical ideas. Organic, indigenous art existed without being recognized among such humble home-owners as could not afford to remodel. It did not exist among people educated to a self-conscious conformity and with the means of keeping up with their neighbors.

H. Hudson Holly, writing in *Harper's Monthly*, knew where the trouble lay but was resigned to it. Imitation of foreign models was utter folly, he wrote. "Until, however, we come to possess a vernacular style, we must content ourselves with copying." And he proceeded to show how adept he was by offering floorplans and sketches for Queen Anne houses in every price range. The largest might have been the plan for the New Jersey Building at the Exhibition.[78] If the tone of his article had not been quite serious, one might suspect that he was lampooning the popular books on house planning.

A sterner position was taken by the leading French architect, Eugene Viollet-le-Duc, two of whose books, *The Habitations of Man in All Ages* and *Discourses on Architecture*, were published early in 1876 in English translation. Architecture, alone of all the arts, had made no progress since the Renaissance—so thought the Frenchman. Modern homes were painful to the eye and worse than the habitations of people in countries generally dismissed as primitive and ignorant. "*Art* does not consist in this or that form, but in a principle, a logical method." Builders should adopt an attitude of absolute fidelity toward their materials. It was illogical to try to make wood resemble stone, and absurd to use new materials and methods to reproduce the Parthenon.[79]

There were stern-minded Americans, too. Wilson Flagg, writing on "Rural Architecture" in the April *Atlantic*, applied a kind of reasoning that can be respected today. After admitting he was no artist, he asserted, long before Frank Lloyd Wright, the radical notion that a house should be true to the people living in it. The best domestic architecture was the kind untouched by "art." "Many plain houses, when considered in relation to their rustic surroundings, and the simple manners and characters of their occupants, are far more beautiful in the eyes of a person of sensibility than any amount of decorative ornament could make them." A modest country couple, capitulating to the craze for "improving" their home, might well be a solecism in it; and the house itself would be false to the landscape. Counterfeit villas, ornate houses and grounds, revealed "a vicious love of fashion and display" and constituted "the most egregious folly." Architects, of course, did nothing to cure this esthetic monomania, which put money in their pockets. Good, simple buildings, Flagg concluded, "are rapidly disappearing, and in the same ratio is village scenery growing vapid and ostentatious." [80]

In the same tenor was an article on "House-Building" by John Burroughs, in the January *Scribner's*. What architects were doing to houses made him suspicious of all architecture except for public buildings. "I cannot see that architecture, properly speaking, has anything to do with the building of a house. I have never seen what might be called an architectural dwelling-house that was not a monstrosity. . . . A house is for shelter, comfort, health, hospitality—to eat in and sleep in, to be born in and die in." Added decoration was a bid for attention, not anything to do with living. The mansard style was all right for the city, perhaps, but it gave a country house a dapper, citified, unnatural appearance. He mourned the disappearance of the "picturesque." Fences, bridges, sheds, and log huts were picturesque, in his meaning of the term, because their construction principle was obvious and not concealed; but in most wooden houses the structural members were carefully covered from sight, often with cheap and hollow ornamentation and gingerbread work, the miserable result of the invention of the scroll-saw. "As yet, our people have shown no sense of the picturesque. When they builded from necessity, this quality often attended them; but when they builded for good looks, it retreated, and flew to the furthermost bound." Increasing wealth brought the end of simplicity and the beginning of pride and pretentiousness.[81]

As Giedion has pointed out, materials have been plentiful in America and skilled labor scarce, the reverse of the situation in Europe; and American builders in their impatience for profit encouraged the development of mechanical aids and relied on them much more than was either desired or possible in Europe. The railroad also made a particular contribution, bringing various materials together from distant places and obviating the local consistency that prevails in most of Europe and that can still be seen in American villages that reached their maturity before the railroad and have not grown since.

The supposed need for decoration to conceal the basic construction dictated the granite covers for the towers of the Brooklyn Suspension Bridge, with its 1,595-foot span, begun in 1869 and gradually taking form in 1876. Some notions die hard: the original plans for the George Washington Bridge of the 1930's also called for granite covers, and they would have been added if funds had been immediately available. The temporary cash shortage proved fortunate, for people had time to learn to appreciate the intrinsic beauty of uncovered steel, and no great bridge built subsequently has called for granite concealment of function. The Eads Bridge crossing the Mississippi at St. Louis, completed in 1874, was hailed as an engineering marvel; only later did people come to value the frank beauty of its three naked steel arches, two of 502 feet, the other 520. Not every engineering project, of course, was beautiful in adverse proportion to the effort to make it seem beautiful. Most bridges built in the 1870's were for railroads, and most were of iron truss construction although one, completed in 1876 for the Cincinnati Southern Railway, was cantilever—and for the moment the world's largest of the type. Few truss bridges had intrinsic beauty, but they were relatively cheap to build. Some were not very safe: it was an iron bridge only eleven years old that collapsed over the Ashtabula River in Ohio and plunged ninety passengers to their death.[82]

Steel, with a tensile strength much greater than that of iron, would have been an ideal material for tall buildings; but its use was deferred by the conventional thinking of architects and their clients. Not until 1883 was a steel skeleton used in a building—Chicago's ten-story Home Insurance Building, designed by William LeBaron Jenney. The invention of the hydraulic elevator, in 1857, had made lofty buildings feasible, but masonry construction set a limit of about fifteen stories because anything much taller required walls too thick at ground level to leave any usable space. The nation's tallest building in 1876 was the Western Union Telegraph Building in New York, with its tower rising 230 feet above the street. This, and the *Tribune* tower almost as lofty, had prompted the remark by Huxley that in Europe the churches dominated the skyline, in America, the agencies of intelligence.

The use of steel would have solved some of the most difficult problems faced by the designers of the Exhibition buildings, especially Main and Machinery. Memorial, using arches, pendentives, and the dome, gave Schwarzmann little trouble; there was plenty of precedent, going all the way back to the Pantheon in Rome. Some critics have wondered why Pettit and Wilson, designing Main as the largest building in the world, ignored the obvious precedent of the Crystal Palace in London, built in 1851 and still standing in 1876—it stood, indeed, until fire destroyed it in 1936. Every architect with any training at all must have been familiar with its lines and its structural principle. Joseph Paxton, its designer, had succeeded in spectacular fashion in enclosing a vast amount of space in glass; it was a gigantic greenhouse that gave visitors a sense of buoyancy and freedom, with the sky, far above, as the apparent ceiling. What the critics overlook is climatic differences: if sunlight is valued in London, shade is equally valued in most American cities in the summer heat. During that very hot summer of 1876 a Crystal Palace in Fairmount Park would have been unbearable, a veritable steam bath.

Pettit and Wilson did, however, adopt one important principle of the Crystal Palace—the use of multiple standard units, easily replaced and easy to dismantle and reassemble, if anyone had a mind to, at some other site. The Crystal Palace actually was moved, to Kensington Gardens, but Main Hall never was, though it could have been with equal ease. The multiple units greatly simplified the erection and reduced the cost, reflecting more awareness of engineering principles than was at all common among architects of the period. It was a very large building indeed—1880 feet long, 464 feet wide. Its perimeter, not counting buttresses and entrance protrusions, was 4688 feet, nearly a mile. The floor space could have been laid out in eighteen football fields, with room between them for benches, cheerleaders, and first-aid equipment. But even with all that space, it was essential to use as little of it as possible for interior supports. Steel would have helped tremendously; as it was, there were 672 wrought-iron columns set on masonry piles below floor level. The trusses were similar to those used in factories and warehouses. To provide plenty of light, the peripheral walls were bricked to a height of only seven feet, the remaining thirty-eight feet being mostly sash, some of it removable for ventilation. There were also large skylights in the roof, which was sheet tin laid over sheathing boards. Visitors had no complaints: the building struck them as airy, well-lighted, well suited to its purpose, and not clumsy despite its bulk. The question of whether it was beautiful never came up: it was not intended to be a thing of beauty, like Memorial or Horticultural. Art, people knew, was what they looked at in imitations of Moorish, Gothic, Renaissance, Classical; Main Hall had nothing to do with Art. Louis Sullivan's famous dictum, "Form follows function," still a decade away, would have been understood well enough as applying to Main; but letting function determine the form, in 1876, set any building clearly outside the domain of Art.

It would be more precise to say that Main was built with no thought of making it resemble any form recognized as traditional. Decorative details considered necessary were added without any relation to structural need. Four sizable towers surmounted the central crossing; one of them, reached by a large elevator, served as an excellent observation post, but the other three had no practical purpose. Neither did the smaller towers or turrets at the various corner angles, except perhaps to break the very long horizontal lines. Ornate entrance facades at the east end, the carriage entrance, and at the west end, opening onto the Grand Plaza, were a typical concession to the notions of the age.

Machinery Hall, less decorated than Main, was considered less attractive but even better suited to its purpose. It had six pagoda-like towers, two at each end, east and west, and one at either end of the north-south transept; but they did not rise much above the roof line, and since the length of the building, 1402 feet, was eighteen times its height, the general effect was of squatness. Whether the resemblance to a factory was a virtue or a defect, Machinery Hall was the most functional of all the major buildings, for it housed what factories usually house, machinery, and with all the machines operating it sounded like a factory. Like most factories, moreover, its interior columns and main roof supports were of wood.

"Surely here," one observer concluded after watching the machines at work, "and not in literature, science, or art, is the true evidence of man's creative power; here is Prometheus unbound." To this William Dean Howells added, "Yes, it is still in the things of iron and steel that the national genius most freely speaks." [83] The arts were of the future. The crowds gawked at the central object in Machinery Hall, the Corliss engine, awed by its naked strength and efficiency but unaware that it had anything to do with art. How could there be art without decoration? Sewing machines were thought to need dressing up with Greek or Roman motifs (or both at once), just as the Main Building needed ornate towers and entrance facades. A household organ shown at the Exhibition was praised for its "decoration subordinated to use," but its elaborately carved wooden case would today seem anything but subordination. John Kouwenhoven, in his *Made in America* and other writings, hammers away at this all too common failing: Americans have always done well when they have followed their own instincts but have too often been persuaded that they need to be saved from their own crudity by accepting the influence of the past and the foreign.[84]

In 1876 British-born Walter Smith was advocating this same idea to his new compatriots in the United States. As editor of the volume on industrial art in *The Masterpieces of the Centennial* he was interested in examples of household taste; his "beauty in fitness" is the functional principle in essence.[85]

The Corliss was only one of many exhibited engines which were devoid of ornament. The various machines made by Ferris & Miles of Philadelphia—steam hammer, upright drill, planing machine, and screwcutting lathe—were totally free of ornament; so were the Rumquist oscillating governor, the Twiss vertical engine, the patent car coupler. In contrast the Cottrell & Babcock drum roller printing press, though hardly offensive, had needless painted arches and draftsman's curves in its frame, and the mould-holding drum of Gregg's impact brick machine bore a design—a very simple design, to be sure, but with no slightest relation to function. The decorated machinery, to give it its due, was innocuous compared with the products of industry, which may suggest a higher level of taste among the designers of basic machinery or, more reasonably, the fact that much machinery was seldom in public view and was not thought to need so much decoration to make it acceptable.

American locomotives shown at the Exhibition were more flexible than those made in Europe, and were thus more utilitarian, yet they commonly bore extensive embellishment in the form of scrolls, flower motifs, and bands of geometric pattern wherever there was enough flat surface. The patent folding bed shown in the Main Building had the same richly carved protuberances as the household organs, and much of the other furniture gives the no doubt erroneous impression of being unusable. Perforated rattan chairs were a momentary fad; the perforations, of course, had to be in elaborate designs. The wheel chairs that visitors could hire, at sixty cents an hour, were of this perforated rattan, which had the real advantage on hot days of permitting a little air to circulate. Fireplaces were, if possible, more ornate than the furniture, and nobody exhibited a plain clock, although one was first put on the market in 1876. Chandeliers were marvels of decoration, but the supreme forms of elaborateness appeared in things with no utility at all—the *objets d'art*, including ornamental vases, bas-relief plaques, and jewelled fans much too precious to use. A tumbler drainer and water jet would have to be seen to be believed, and so would some of the soda fountains built by Chas. Lippincott & Co. of Philadelphia, which shared the Exhibition soda water concession with James W. Tufts of Boston. The display cabinets in all the buildings were also elaborately designed, even those in Agricultural Hall containing mounds of beans and jars of pickles.[86] Decoration subordinated to use? Not in 1876.

Agricultural Hall, like Machinery, was dedicated to practical human activities, but its designers thought it needed to look like something other than a barn. Howells considered it the "most exclusively American" building of the Exhibition; it may be wondered what American function he attributed to the pointed turrets flanking the ends of the long Gothic nave and the several transepts. Silos may have inspired them, but they were too slender for exhibit purposes and existed as pure decoration. Another touch quite alien to typical farm buildings was the effect of half-timbering given by non-functional diagonal timbers on the outer walls.

The most striking of the major buildings was Horticultural Hall, Moorish in theme but also labeled "Mauresque" and "Saracenic." It was mostly glass, a giant greenhouse, with such luxuriant foliage inside that on hot days it was a mecca, not a place to avoid. All the surface that wasn't glass was brightly painted, with a gay polychrome effect. The critics, lavishing their displeasure on Memorial, rather neglected Horticultural Hall until recently, when the editors of *Philadelphia Architecture in the 19th Century* [87] soberly praised it; but the praise came too late. It had been preserved for its utility but the colors had been allowed to fade through the years, and it was a mere ghost of its original self by the time it was demolished, regrettably, in the early 1950's.

The book on Philadelphia architecture, with its 105 plates, is particularly valuable as a reminder of the eclecticism of that and almost every other city in 1876. The Academy of Fine Arts at the corner of Broad and Cherry, completed in 1876, showed "a perverse delight in clashes of form" from the thirteenth to the eighteenth centuries. The new city hall, not yet finished, was also eclectic but most suggested the Napoleon III pavilions of the Louvre. The Tenth Presbyterian Church, finished in 1875, was a Byzantine rebuilding of an older structure. And the Broad Street Theatre, or rather the part of it built in 1876 as Kiralfy's Alhambra Palace, was lavishly Moorish, with sculpture, fountains, and grottoes. The eclecticism of the Exhibition was not, obviously, unusual. It may be significant that a lengthy 1876 article on American architecture by William Fogerty, a fellow of the Royal Institute of British Architects, hardly mentions Centennial eclecticism. Fogerty does speak of Girard College as Doric, and of the absurdity of Gothic exteriors enclosing interiors of a different period, but he liked Gothic verandahs, and he heaped praise on the Tribune Tower and its architect, Richard M. Hunt, who "skillfully and tastefully" combined Modern French, Gothic and Greek elements, while he called the Western Union Building an "advanced type of American Renaissance." He would have agreed with John Burroughs that villages had no architecture, but he did not consider the lack an advantage. American architecture was at its best, he thought, in the great town houses along Fifth Avenue: "City life is . . . the most attractive, elegant, and fashionable." [88]

An obituary article on Hunt, in 1895, reported that after his return from Europe in 1855 he had consistently tried to avoid the Gothic; but apparently he was not always successful. He had the genius, without question, to create a new style, had he thought of trying, and if his wealthy clients had assented; instead, his surviving buildings, including Biltmore, the great Vanderbilt mansion near Asheville so reminiscent of Blois Chateau, attest to his preeminence as the greatest eclectic architect of his time. His one pioneering step was putting the first elevator in a building, the Tribune Tower. [89]

Scott Fitzgerald once said to Ernest Hemingway that the rich were different, and Hemingway bluntly replied that they were, in having more money. In 1876 there were other differences. Most of the very rich had not been rich very long, and had never acquired much of any skill in how to be rich gracefully. As a class they agreed in condemning the strange new ways of the immigrant poor, but in their haste to spend their unaccustomed income they turned to Europe for guidance—when they sought guidance at all. The best of the mansions they built were copies of French chateaux; there were also reasonable facsimiles of Moorish and Oriental palaces. The best interiors were also reminiscent of the luxurious best abroad, like the room in the Rockefeller town house, preserved today in the Brooklyn Museum, with its ceiling copied from the Alhambra and with exquisite brasses from Turkey. [90] Nothing echoing the American past, or with any relation to native reality, would do.

Mansions were no monopoly of the urban rich; they sprang up wherever men were prospering. The South Texas coast, where large ranches were both feasible and profitable, could boast its share of show places. Two of the finest homes of the region were built by George W. Fulton and Charles M. Coleman, partners in a million-dollar cattle ranch. Fulton, who had been a civil engineer, designed a house that would last: a concrete foundation, hard pine planks two inches thick, spiked together, for partitions as well as for outside walls, interiors panelled with cypress before being plastered. A windmill supplied a tank on the roof; a trough of circulating water kept food cool in the basement; a furnace forced warm air through ducts to every room, coming out in mock fireplaces. In summer, the same duct system yielded primitive air conditioning. A gasoline-powered generator provided electric lights and heat for cooking and laundry. Venetian blinds, black walnut stairways and doors, slate hearths and marble mantels, a tower room with a view over Aranas Bay; French tubs and closet bowls, a dumb waiter, crystal chandeliers, costly carpeting, individually carved doorknobs—almost everything was brought in from New Orleans, Philadelphia, New York, or Europe, with no regard to expense.

The roof, of copper, was of the mansard design that John Burroughs condemned outside of cities. The construction took four years and, when completed in 1876, was locally estimated to have cost $100,000. At the opening reception, Mrs. Coleman informed her husband that she wanted a home just like it, only larger and costlier. Her husband complied. The Coleman mansion, at the Chiltipin Creek ranch, was completed in 1880; Coleman quit counting the cost when the outlay exceeded $80,000. The two mansions and the company office at Rockport were connected by a private telephone system, one of the first in the country. Although appreciably less expensive and ornate than the biggest palaces built elsewhere by the very rich, these two in Texas exhibited the same impulse of lavish expenditure, and the same eclecticism—almost none of the materials locally produced, and most of the details exotic.[91]

Lewis Mumford, probably the most caustic critic of the period, has attributed its lack of taste and general drabness to "the visible smut of early industrialism." What he had in mind was not the best the wealthy could do but the second best of the not quite so wealthy—the families unable to employ art critics to guide them in their adaptation of the foreign. Since wealth is always like a pyramid, there were many more people of this class than at the very apex. What most of them did in the name of ART has not inspired museum directors to preserve examples. Gaudy wall paper, heavy ornate furniture—especially curving tables topped with chocolate colored marble, corner what-nots loaded down with china hand-painted by the girls of the family, who also painted on crimson plush and on brass plaques, Rogers pieces, sentimental or humorous or both at the same time, and cast-iron animals on the lawn, where there was a lawn, all represented a compulsive desire for conspicuous consumption. The faddishness and eclecticism did not, however, pass without contemporary censure; Albert Bolles, our historian of industry, was contemptuous: "The one weak point in American furniture is the lack of originality in the more artistic pieces. Everything is borrowed from the ideas of the French or the English. Whatever happens to be popular abroad—whether it is the style of 'Louis XIV,' the 'Louis XV' patterns, the 'renaissance,' the 'rococo,' the 'Queen Anne,' the 'Eastlake,' or what not—is copied immediately and slavishly by the American people." [92]

People less swayed by fashion knew that sturdy, simple, and tasteful furnishings were being made and sold by the Shakers, who issued a catalogue in 1876. A chair with web seat, arms, and rockers, cost $8.00; if the back was also webbed, the price was $10.00. There were cushions in fourteen colors, "woven on hand looms with much effort," some of them made to fit the chairs. One particular advantage of the Shaker furniture was its lightness; the largest chair weighed only ten pounds. The catalogue also gave several Shaker songs; [93] and the Shaker display at the Exhibition was not entirely without propaganda, of a modest sort.

There is such a thing as instinctive good taste, which too few people have. Harriet Tilden had it—the "divine Harriet," jewel of the Cornell graduating class of '76; and her parents seem also to have had it. William Mason Tilden, a New Englander who served an Ohio apprenticeship in trade, moved to Chicago in 1868 and was quickly among the boldest of that City's entrepreneurs. "Don't tell your mother," he once said to Harriet, "but today I lost every cent I had in the world." If one gamble failed, the next succeeded, in an economic pattern that might have horrified Bostonians or Philadelphians but was amply approved for members of the Chicago Board of Trade. Tilden's chief operations were in cattle and he was more often successful than not. The chief evidence was the fine house on Wabash Avenue at Thirteenth Street, from which every weekday morning he rode to his LaSalle Street office behind high-stepping horses and a coachman in formal livery. Each afternoon his wife, wrapped in a silk dolman and holding a tiny fringed parasol, rode in a low-slung carriage along Michigan Boulevard which was already being dubbed "Boul' Mich" in proud self-conscious allusion to Paris. Mrs. Tilden readily adopted the role of society leader, competently dispensing an almost regal hospitality. Guests entered a drawing room that was magnificently upholstered in white satin and carpeted with white Axminster. The furniture was gilt, and so were the frames of pier mirrors and the cornices. Crystal chandeliers diffused and reflected the light of scores of candles. Sometime during the evening the guests would be shown the conservatory and birdroom, on the south side of the house, opening out of the family sitting-room; several kinds of birds in bright plumage, ranging from canaries to parrots, came to Mrs. Tilden's call, perching on her shoulder and eating from her lips. Between the house and Lake Michigan was a formal garden. It was a spacious sort of splendor that needed continuing income to maintain, and by the 1890's the money was gone, the gilt tarnished, the satin grey and soiled, the birdroom empty, and Harriet a divorcée, teaching school and selling baked delicacies to make life bearable for her widowed mother amid the faded glories.[94] In a land of unlimited opportunity, people can go both up and down on the stairs of success.

More serious than lavish expenditure, because its effects were permanent, was the unplanned and uncontrolled adaptation of space to human needs. For every individual with vision and competence like Frederick Law Olmsted, conscientiously trying to devise adequate forms for city parks and railroads and bridges, mill towns and whole cities, there were scores of short-sighted men exploiting space in the same way they exploited natural resources and the needs of a growing population, with no plan except to make money and make it fast. Legislation for planning was held in the same suspicion as all other kinds of government regulation, and the idea was lost in the flood tide of laissez-faire opportunism. Olmsted must be included among the "heroes" of 1876. New York's Central Park, which he and Calvert Vaux had designed, and which drew plaudits from many visitors, was completed in 1876. Olmsted's other productions during the year included a map of Buffalo for the Exhibition, plans for the new capitol at Albany, a report to the Johns Hopkins trustees on use of the Clifton Estate, advice to the Boston Park Commission on new sites for parks, and to Baltimore concerning the Washington Monument grounds. In May someone started a lawsuit to prevent his serving on the New York State Survey while holding the job of Landscape Architect of New York City.[95]

Parks pleased everybody in 1876, partly, perhaps, because they contrasted so sharply with the general urban ugliness. But more than one visitor noted how small most city parks were, and how many cities had no parks at all and not even any plans for parks. There was also criticism of the paucity of historic buildings (or monuments as one of the French visitors called them). Centennial Americans showed much more interest in reviewing their past than in thinking about the future, yet there was singular indifference to preserving historic sites and structures. The greatest interest in preservation, ironically, was in Minnesota and other new states that had, in 1876, the least part to preserve. It remains, regrettably, an American habit to tear down a building, however artistic or historic, if it can be replaced by one producing more income.

The immediate demolition of most of the Exhibition buildings was no great crime against art, presumably, although some Philadelphians thought they should be preserved for their historic interest. With the demolition of Horticultural Hall in the 1950's, the one surviving major building is Memorial Hall. Neither of these had any enduring influence on American architecture, Horticultural because it was too exotic, Memorial because it was an eclectic dead end. It is to be regretted that the Centennial Exhibition had no single building, and left none, as a milestone of art history—no Crystal Palace (London, 1851), no Eiffel Tower or Galerie de Machines (Paris, 1889), no Transportation Building (Chicago, 1893); yet it is fitting that this one building still standing, Memorial, is a monument to the contemporary passion for modifying established forms. The city of Philadelphia has patched its roof—it no longer leaks when it rains—and neighborhood youngsters play league basketball on the floor of variously colored marble in the east gallery; but the proposed restoration depends on more money than has been made available so far.[96] The exterior is in fairly good condition, although an 1876 visitor, if he could return, would miss the great horses flanking the low steps at the broad front entrance.

But Memorial was more than a venture in design; as the art gallery for the Exhibition it represented the considered Centennial opinion of painting and sculpture. The collection included the first Old Masters—not many, and none really great —that most Americans had ever seen, a great many other paintings that nobody ever looks at today, and a very few examples of what modern opinion judges the best that contemporary artists, European and American, were producing. The selection was made by officials of the contributing countries, who were unlikely to choose avant-garde work—French impressionism, for example. But the public had no knowledge of such work and did not miss it.

Germany sent a "Surrender at Verdun" that struck Howells as a gratuitous insult to French visitors; but he thought the French betrayed their own bad taste by hanging too many nudes. These were but two of the reasons why Memorial was the one major building that offended him. A plaster George Washington on an eagle (by Pietro Guanerio of Milan) he found excruciating. The eagle was life-size, but Washington from the waist up measured a good six feet. Howells was also appalled by a bronze "Emancipation" with "a most offensively Frenchified negro." Finally there was a wax Cleopatra with an arm that moved, explicitly advertising a Philadelphia museum of anatomy. The Cleopatra had a popularity, Howells remarked drily, "which the other two disgraces of the Art Hall have not." [97]

Other reporters also found this Cleopatra offensive, but she represented a major advance, whether for good or bad, that has been credited to the Exhibition. In terms of commercial art, the Exhibition provided a stimulus to visiting businessmen with its great variety of advertising techniques. Advertisements that the public had previously seen in newspapers, often as small boxes on a page, acquired a new meaning when seen in large size, with colors and sometimes in three dimension. The web press produced in 1871 by R. Hoe and Company, the steady advances in color lithography, and all the varied eye-catching devices tried out locally by ambitious merchants, were all brought together at the Exhibition, which helped to distribute the knowledge of them to all parts of the nation.[98]

Whatever the wisdom of placing examples of advertising art in Memorial Hall, their presence did serve to distract visitors from the prime purpose of the building, the display of paintings. Howells thought there were too many, and he was right: the walls were crowded. After a few holes were poked in canvases with umbrella tips, some of the paintings were removed, but there were *still* too many. Museum directors, the good ones, knew the value of showing only a few pictures at a time, the bulk of a collection being kept in storage; but the managers of the Exhibition did not have this option, and the great mass of art in Memorial Hall was likely to produce cultural indigestion. It was like the Louvre and the British Museum, not like the more enlightened and effective Victoria and Albert Museum at South Kensington, or the great industrial museum in Vienna.[99]

"No country but England," one observer noted, "has made an attempt to show its best things. Everywhere, outside of the English pictures, mediocrity is the rule." [100] Other visitors agreed, although by "best" they seemed to mean the work of famous artists, and the English display included works by Gainsborough, West, Landseer, Frith, Laurence, Reynolds, and Millais; some had been lent by Queen Victoria. In contrast, Spain sent one Murillo but nothing, for example, by El Greco. Italy, despite its vast collections, sent nothing by anybody important, while the best the Netherlands felt could be sent were some copies of Hals and Rembrandt paintings. As for French art, nothing of exciting contemporary impressionism could have been expected, for even in France it had no official sanction— and in each country it was officialdom that decided what art was to be shown at Philadelphia.[101] In any event, a day spent in Memorial Hall would have yielded a very incomplete view of the world's great art, and no view at all of what was making the latter nineteenth century a most remarkable period in the history of painting.

The selection committee for American paintings decided that the display should be both retrospective and contemporary. This meant a generous number of older classics—by Peale, Stuart, Copley, West, Alston—together with works by living artists. About a quarter of the 760 oils and 186 watercolors were by thirty-two members of the Hudson River School, evidence of the great respect in which this group was held even though it had almost closed its career. Yet the greater number of American-owned works of the group were shown in 1876 not at the Exhibition but at the National Academy of Arts and Design in New York, which had joined forces with the Metropolitan Museum of Art to mount a Centennial Loan Exhibition from July to November. The catalogue of the exhibit at Philadelphia shows awards of "eminence" to Albert Bierstadt, George Brown, and Sanford Gifford, and of "excellence" to Thomas Moran, Asher Durand, Jervis McEntee, and Worthington Whittredge; awards were given only to living painters. All members of the Hudson River School, living and dead, had studied art abroad.[102] Their preoccupation with scenic grandeur was linked by one contemporary with stress on the wild in the writings of Bret Harte, Mark Twain, and Joaquin Miller.[103] It also perpetuated the European notion of America as mostly wilderness.

Loan exhibits, as at Memorial Hall and the National Academy, were more important to viewers in 1876 than later, after museums became more numerous. The Metropolitan Museum of Art, founded in 1870, was still in temporary quarters—converted private dwellings. Boston had its Athenaeum, and in 1876 added a Museum of Fine Arts. Charleston, South Carolina, and Cincinnati had institutions that joined instruction with exhibition, like the National Academy in New York.[104] Visitors to Washington could hardly miss the National Art Gallery, in the Capital, but the more discriminating sought out the Corcoran Art Gallery and the Steverson collection of paintings and statuary. In Philadelphia, what had been the nation's first art collection, begun in 1784 in his own home by Charles Willson Peale, was currently in Independence Hall. The city's larger collection was at the Pennsylvania Academy of Fine Arts, dating from 1805; it was rather conservative, reflecting the notion that art needed the guidance of the rich and the great, as if esthetic judgment grew with a man's fortune. Samuel F. B. Morse, before he abandoned painting for a more rewarding career as a voice teacher, had argued for indigenous inspiration, but most museum directors preferred to rely on European models and esthetic traditions—and the Centennial Exhibition confirmed this reliance.[105]

The rich, in any event, owned most of the nation's art. In a magnificent folio twelve-volume compilation of the nation's art treasures, issued in 1879, the great majority of the reproduced paintings are identified as the property of wealthy individuals.[106] Most of them, moreover, were by foreign artists, and those by Americans were "safe." The conservatism of collectors, some younger artists thought, was matched by unprogressive policies of men who chose work to exhibit. One of the masterpieces of Thomas Eakins, "The Surgical Clinic of Professor Gross," was barred from Memorial Hall and was put, instead, in the Medical Section; Dr. Gross's hands showed blood.[107] Wyatt Eaton, two of whose paintings were rejected for the Exhibition, together with Walter Shirlaw, John La Farge, Augustus Saint-Gaudens, and Louis Tiffany, rebelled against the narrow, unprogressive policies of the National Academy of Art and Design, and in 1877 formed the Society of American Artists.[108] Tiffany had shown an untoward interest in oriental colors, which led him in 1875 to begin experimenting with stained glass. The National Academy was alone in the field, and very powerful, until the Society challenged it and broke its virtual monopoly of control.

Eakins, along with Eastman Johnson, famed for such *genre* work as "Old Kentucky Home" and "Sunday Morning," was doing what the pioneer literary realists were doing—working with the humble and the commonplace in the Dutch *genre* tradition, and getting at the actualities of American life instead of the sublime in wild nature. It may be noted that Edward Eggleston had been strongly influenced by Hippolyte Taine's *Art in the Netherlands*. But the "rebellion" of 1876 was even more concerned with the preference shown by collectors and galleries for foreign paintings. The rebels must have been encouraged when, at an auction on December 20, at Chickering Hall, an American painting, Frederick Edwin Church's "Niagara Falls," was bought by W. W. Corcoran of Washington for $12,500, more than was paid for any of the numerous foreign paintings. A Corot, "Path through the Woods," brought only $1000, not as much as Winslow Homer's "Prisoners from the Front." [109] It was a sign of better things to come, even if the Church painting *was* of the nature school. Homer, incidentally, in 1876 abandoned his prosperous career as an illustrator to devote himself exclusively to painting.

The American sculpture at the Exhibition, unlike the painting, showed both tradition and new departures. William Wetmore Story, the country's most noted sculptor, was living permanently in Rome; his work was on classical themes—"Medea," "Salome," "Cleopatra." The most popular sculptor was Erastus Dow Palmer of Albany, famed for his life-size "The Indian Captive" and "The White Captive." Neither was as famous as Hiram Powers' "Greek Slave," dating from 1843 and probably the most famous statue in the world in the mid-nineteenth century; it was a conspicuous success at the Exhibition. But a new generation of sculptors was also represented. Pierce Francis Connelly, living in Florence, sent several pieces, the best a half-size "Honor and Death" that now seems impressive although it won no medal. Howard Roberts of Philadelphia was luckier: his "La Première Pose," somewhat of a sensation for showing for the first time, a model self-consciously posing unclothed, won one of the three medals given. Others in what Lorado Taft calls the middle period, 1876–1903, were Augustus Saint-Gaudens and Daniel Chester French, famous for his Minute Man statue at the Old North Bridge in Concord, which he was commissioned to do when only twenty-three. [110]

One of the contemporary historians of the Exhibition was critical of Connelly but thought the work of Story and Rogers restored American supremacy in pure sculptural form. [111] John Rogers, one of the rebels against classical sculpture, had won fame and fortune for his "Rogers Groups," "sentimental situations in clay." They were faultless in execution and widely popular because everybody liked and could understand his subjects: "Country Post Office," "Charity Patient," "Parting Promise," and the like. Comparable work from abroad, by Eugene

Blot of France and by various Italians, with such titles as "Love's Telegram" and "Blind Man's Bluff," showed that Americans were not alone in liking such things. The Rogers pieces had one advantage: they were mass-produced and cost less than the imports.

One unexpected result of the Exhibition was that the mass of neo-classical sculpture exhibited there turned American sculptors away from this style of sculpture. If the year marked transitions in painting and sculpture, it also marked the beginning of an American school of wood-engraving that soon revolutionized magazine illustrations. By 1879 it was possible to collect in a volume eighty-three examples of American works engraved on wood.[112] It may be added that the work shown in Photographic Hall at the Exhibition gave many Americans their first inkling that photography had artistic possibilities, although the wet-plate process with its collodion negative prevented any wide use of it. William Henry Jackson's superb transparencies of the West, enlarged to twenty-eight by thirty-six inches, were among the artistic successes of 1876.[113]

From the evidence offered even in so cursory a survey as this chapter represents, it is hard to justify the censure heaped upon some of the arts of 1876 by recent critics. Judgments change, as even the strongest critic, Louis Mumford, remarks in *The Brown Decades*, and it is unfair to apply the standards of one period to another. At the same time, it is easy to be impatient with some of the thinking discernible in 1876, and with the behavior based on that thinking—especially the scorn heaped upon such innovators as Whitman and the resistance to artists who, in 1876, were venturing beyond what was accepted. It was an age of great unevenness, with some arts progressive and others, like music, quite static. It was also an age of uncertainty; people didn't know what they wanted and were not aware that an organizing principle was either missing or desirable. They also paid undue homage to aging giants of a period already dead, and they maintained a gulf between art and life. Are we confident, however, of satisfactory advance in the decades since? If the arts *are* flourishing today, the seeds were germinating in 1876, amid the weeds and the decay.

Footnotes for Chapter Ten
THE ARTS, FINE AND OTHERWISE

1. A larger variety of coins were in circulation in 1876 than later, after people got over their fear of paper money. Gold dollars and three-dollar pieces were coined until 1889; gold quarter-eagles ($2.50), half-eagles ($5.00), eagles and double eagles continued in production much longer. Silver in use in 1876 included a twenty-cent piece, a half-dime, and a three-cent piece—these last two not minted after 1873—in addition to the silver dollar, half dollar, quarter, and dime that have survived. Nickel was used for both five-cent and three-cent pieces, and bronze for both cent and half-cent pieces, although the half-cent, last minted in 1857, was becoming rare.

2. T. Allston Brown, *A History of the New York Stage from the First Performance in 1732 to 1901*, 3 vols. (New York: Dodd Mead, 1903), III, p. 13.

3. Joseph Hatton, *To-Day in America*.

4. Strahan, *A Century After*.

5. Briggs, *Frontiers of the Northwest*.

6. "J. W. Crawford: Poet-Scout of the Black Hills," *South Dakota Review*, 2 (Spring, 1965), 40–47, reprinted in *Provincial Drama in America, 1870–1916: A Casebook of Primary Materials*, ed. Paul T. Nolan (Metuchen: The Scarecrow Press, 1967), pp. 110–18.

7. Pomeroy, *The Pacific Slope*; Edmond M. Gagey, *The San Francisco Stage, A History* (New York: Columbia University Press, 1950).

8. Gagey, pp. 130–31.

9. Cecil Smith, *Musical Comedy in America* (New York: Theatre Arts Books, 1950).

10. *Ibid.*

11. Mattfield, *Variety Music Cavalcade.*

12. *Orpheus in America*, pp. 157–58.

13. Leslie, *The Remarkable Mr. Jerome*, pp. 81–83, 204; and Edward B. Marks, *They All Had Glamour* (New York: Julian Messner, 1944).

14. Robert D. Faner, *Walt Whitman & Opera* (Philadelphia: University of Pennsylvania Press, 1951).

15. *Orpheus in America*, pp. 159 ff.

16. Mattfield, *Variety Music Cavalcade.*

17. Louis C. Elson, *The History of American Music* (New York: Macmillan, 1915), pp. 166, 231–32.

18. *Ibid.*, pp. 351–52.

19. Paul Henry Lang, *One Hundred Years of Music in America* (New York: G. Schirmer, 1961), pp. 39–40.

20. Henry C. Lahee, *Annals of Music in America: A Chronological Record* (Boston: Marshall Jones, 1922).

21. *New York Times*, Jan. 1, 1876. Another event not on the list has repeatedly been assigned to 1876, most recently in the *New York Times*, Feb. 12, 1967—concerning Johann Strauss, the Waltz King, conducting an orchestra of 2,000 and a chorus of 20,000 in his "Blue Danube." There was such a monstrous concert, but it was in 1872, at the Peace Jubilee in Boston, *not* at a Boston Centennial celebration.

22. Mattfield, *Variety Musical Cavalcade.*

23. Donald C. Holmquist, "Pride of the Pioneer's Parlor: Pianos in Early Minnesota," *Minnesota History*, 39 (Winter, 1965), 312–26.

24. Bolles, *Industrial History of the United States*, pp. 534–41.

25. Marks, *They All Had Glamour*, pp. 268–69; Mattfield, *Variety Music Cavalcade;* Harry Dichter and Elliott Shapiro, *Early American Sheet Music, Its Lure and Its Lore*, 1768–1889 (New York: R. R. Bowker, 1941).

26. Edward McClurg Fleming, *R. R. Bowker, Militant Liberal* (Norman: University of Oklahoma Press, 1952), pp. 45–46.

27. Twain to Howells, Apr. 26, 1876, *Mark Twain-Howells Letters*, ed. Henry Nash Smith and William Gibson, 2 vols. (Cambridge: Harvard University Press, 1960), I, 132; Howells' review of *Tom Sawyer*, in *Atlantic Monthly*, 37 (May, 1876), 621–22.

28. Josiah Holland, "English and American Copyright," *Scribner's Monthly*, 12 (Oct., 1876), 900–901. An earlier Holland comment on the subject was "The Price of Books," *Scribner's Monthly*, 11 (Jan., 1876), 434–35; the author, he wrote, "takes what the publisher, who is in direct competition with pirates, is willing or able to give him." See also Janet B. Randel, *The Contribution of American Authors to International Copyright* (unpublished M. A. thesis, Florida State University, 1961). General Centennial book-trade conditions are discussed in Raymond Shove, *Cheap Book Production in the United States, 1870–91* (Urbana: University of Illinois Press, 1937).

29. Robert Falk, *The Victorian Mode in American Fiction, 1865–85* (East Lansing: Michigan State University Press, 1965), pp. 17–106, "The Seventies: A Decade of Hesitation and Literary Experiment."

30. Warner's 1876 articles in the *Atlantic* were "From Jaffa to Jerusalem" in August, "Holy Places of the Holy City" in September, and "Neighborhoods of Jerusalem" in October. A DeForest article

in the December issue, "Crumbs of Travel," apparently did not interest Twain enough to mention it to Howells, who of course had been responsible for its appearance. Twain's delight in Warner's readability was expressed in a letter to Howells on Aug. 9, 1876, in *Mark Twain-Howells Letters*, I, 145.

31. Twain to Howells, Oct. 12, 1876, *ibid.*, I, 160.

32. Twain to Howells, Jan. 18, 1876, and footnote 4, *ibid.*, I, 122–23.

33. Frank Luther Mott, *Golden Multitudes* (New York: Macmillan, 1947). The number of copies used as basis for inclusion was not the sale in a single year, but of the decade, while the number of copies is 1% of the decade's population.

34. Among libraries banning *Tom Sawyer* in 1876 were the Denver Public Library and the children's room of the Brooklyn Public Library.

35. Taylor's nine-line parody, "Walt Whitman," was reprinted in *The Rise of Realism*, ed. Louis Wann (New York: Macmillan, 1933), p. 210.

36. Whitman's note accompanying the Custer sonnet reveals no high estimate of its commercial value:

>   Camden, New Jersey
>   July 7, 1876
>
> My dear Reid,
>   I send a piece for the paper, on Custer's death. If you can give me $10 for it, well and good—if not, not. If it comes in time, get it in tonight, as earlyness is everything.
>
>   Walt Whitman

Quoted in Royal Cortissoz, *The Life of Whitelaw Reid* (New York: Scribner, 1921), Vol. I, p. 311.

37. Bram Stoker to Whitman, Feb. 14, 1876, in Horace Traubel, *With Walt Whitman in Camden*, ed. Sculley Bradley (Carbondale: Southern Illinois University Press, 1959), v. 4, p. 180–81.

38. Henry S. Canby, *Walt Whitman* (Boston: Houghton Mifflin, 1943), pp. 301–4.

39. Ralph L. Rusk, *The Life of Ralph Waldo Emerson* (New York: Scribner, 1949), pp. 496–98.

40. Herbert S. Gorman, *A Victorian American: Henry Wadsworth Longfellow* (New York: George H. Doran, 1926), p. 334.

41. Letters of various dates, in *Centennial Edition of the Works of Sidney Lanier* (Baltimore: Johns Hopkins University Press, 1945), Vol. 9. *Centennial Meditation of Columbia*, words and music, was published by G. Schirmer of New York in 1876.

42. John D. Stockton, "Charlotte Cushman," *Scribner's Monthly*, 12 (June, 1876), 262–66.

43. *Life and Letters of Bayard Taylor*, ed. Marie Hansen-Taylor and Horace Scudder (Boston: Houghton Mifflin, 1884), Vol. II. Sidney Lanier in his poverty would hardly have appreciated Taylor's complaints about money; Taylor had an annual salary of $6,000 from the New York *Tribune*, not to mention his royalties and payments for current poems and articles. His fine house at Kennett Square, "Cedarcroft," was an expensive showplace.

44. Ruth Odell, *Helen Hunt Jackson* (New York: D. Appleton-Century, 1939).

45. Martin Duberman, *James Russell Lowell* (Boston: Houghton Mifflin, 1966).

46. *Atlantic Monthly*, 37 (Jan., 1876), 112–14.

47. An exchange in Elmira *Daily Advertiser*, Jan. 15, 1876.

48. Review of "Erechtheus," *Scribner's Monthly*, 12 (May, 1876), 130–33.

49. Edwin P. Whipple, "American Literature," 16th paper in "The First Century of the Republic," *Harper's Monthly*, 12 (Feb. and March, 1876). The *Harper's* 1876 survey of American literature is calmly awaited.

50. George Parsons Lathrop, *A Study of Hawthorne* (Boston: J. R. Osgood, 1876).

51. Lathrop, "Early American Novelists," *Atlantic Monthly*, 37 (Apr., 1876), 404–14.

52. Cortissoz, *Whitelaw Reid*, I, 308–9; George Manteiro, *Henry James and John Hay: The Record of a Friendship* (Providence: Brown University Press, 1965); *Henry James, Parisian Sketches*, ed. Leon Edel and Ilse Duroir Lind (New York: New York University Press, 1957).

53. Vera McWilliams, *Lafcadio Hearn* (Boston: Houghton Mifflin, 1946).

54. Holland, "Is It Poetry?" *Scribner's Monthly*, 12 (May, 1876), 123–25.

55. Her most popular book *The Hidden Hand* appeared in 1859. A uniform edition of 42 of her novels was published in 1877.

56. Cited by Leo Marx in his edition of *Huckleberry Finn* (Indianapolis: Bobbs-Merrill, 1967), pp. 122–23.

57. Max Adeler (pen-name for Charles Heber Clark), *Elbow-Room* (Philadelphia: J. M. Stoddart & Co., 1876).

58. *Nasby on Inflation. A New Comic Book by Petroleum V. Nasby* (D. R. Locke), (Philadelphia: Barclay, 1876).

59. *Sam's Chance; or, How He Improved It* (Tattered Tom Series-second series); *Shifting for Himself; or, Gilbert Greyson's Fortune* (Brave and Bold Series). John Tebbel, *From Rags to Riches:*

Horatio Alger, Jr. and the American Dream (New York: Macmillan, 1963).

60. Janet E. Brown, *The Saga of Elsie Dinsmore; A Study in Nineteenth Century Sensibility* (Buffalo: Buffalo University Monographs in English, No. 4, 1945).

61. Review of *Helen's Babies* in *Scribner's Monthly*, 13 (December, 1876), 280–81.

62. Parke Godwin, *A Biography of William Cullen Bryant* (New York: D. Appleton, 1883), Vol. 2, p. 368.

63. A reviewer of Emerson's *Letters and Social Aims* in the *Atlantic Monthly*, 38 (Aug., 1876), remarked that "this last milestone . . . stands singularly close to the first" and was in places "extremely fatiguing reading," with limited appeal to a new generation with scientific habits of thinking.

64. Pettengill's *Newspaper Directory and Advertisers' Hand-Book* (New York: S. M. Pettengill & Co., 1878).

65. David C. Smith, "Wood Pulp and Newspapers, 1867–1900," *Business History Review*, 38 (Fall, 1964), 328–45; Frank Luther Mott, *A History of American Newspapers in the United States . . . 1690 to 1940* (New York: Macmillan, 1947).

66. *Ibid.*

67. W. A. Swanberg, *Pulitzer* (New York: Scribner, 1967).

68. Pomeroy, *The Pacific Slope.*

69. On Nov. 1, 1873, after forty-three designs had been reduced to ten for the final judgment, the competition ended with the granting of four prizes, $4,000, $3,000, $2,000, and $1,000; but for "various reasons" none of the prize designs were used. *Report of the Director-General*, in *Centennial Reports.*

70. Siegfried Giedion, *Space, Time and Architecture* (Cambridge: Harvard University Press, 1941), p. 262.

71. Louis Mumford, *The Brown Decades: A Study of the Arts in America 1865–95* (New York: Harcourt, Brace, 1931), p. 36.

72. Oliver Larkin, *Art in America* (New York: Rinehart, 1949), p. 241.

73. Suzanne La Follette, *Art in America* (New York: Harper, 1929), p. 252.

74. Thomas E. Tallmadge, *The Story of Architecture in America* (New York: W. W. Norton, 1927), Chapter 7, "The Parvenu Period 1860–1880," and Chapter 8, "The Romanesque Revival 1876–1893." Quotation from p. 5.

75. Tallmadge quotations, *ibid.*, p. 164.

76. Vincent Scully, *The Shingle Style: Architectural Theory and Design from Richardson to the Origins of Wright* (New Haven: Yale University Press, 1959), pp. 1, 4, 19.

77. Fiske Kimball, *American Architecture* (Indianapolis: Bobbs-Merrill, 1928), pp. 127–28.

78. H. Hudson Holly, "Modern Dwellings: Their Construction, Decoration, and Furniture," *Harper's Monthly*, 52 (May, 1876), 855–867.

79. Review of Viollet-le-Duc, *Discourses on Architecture*, in *Scribner's Monthly*, 11 (Feb., 1876), 587–88.

80. Wilson Flagg, "Rural Architecture," *Atlantic Monthly*, 37 (Apr., 1876), 428–35.

81. John Burroughs, "House-Building, "*Scribner's Monthly*, 11 (Jan., 1876), 333–41.

82. David B. Steinman and Sara Ruth Watson, *Bridges and their Builders* (New York: Putnam, 1941).

83. "Characteristics of the Fair" and Howells, "A Sennight at the Centennial," *Atlantic Monthly*.

84. John Kouwenhoven, *Made in America: The Arts in Modern Civilization* (Garden City: Doubleday, 1948).

85. *The Masterpieces of the Centennial International Exhibition*, 3 vols. (Philadelphia: Gebbie & Barrie, 1876–78). Vol. I, *Fine Art* edited by Edward Strahan; Vol. 2, *Industrial Art* edited by Walter Smith; Vol. 3, *History, Mechanics, Science* edited by Joseph M. Wilson.

86. Both of the major histories of the Exhibition, by Ingram and McCabe, were copiously illustrated with typical displays.

87. Theo B. White et al, *Philadelphia Architecture of the Nineteenth Century* (Philadelphia: University of Pennsylvania Press for the Philadelphia Art Alliance, 1953).

88. William Fogerty, "On the Condition and Prospects of Architecture in the United States," *Van Nostrand's Eclectic Engineering Magazine*, 14 (Jan., 1876), 61–74.

89. Montgomery Schuyler, "Works of the Late Richard M. Hunt," *Architectural Record*, 5 (Oct.–Dec., 1895), 97–180.

90. Betty Pepis, "Picture of a Period" (illustrated), *New York Times Magazine*, Dec. 13, 1953.

91. A. Ray Stephens, *The Taft Ranch: A Texas Principality* (Austin: University of Texas Press, 1964), pp. 37–40; photographs after p. 116.

92. Bolles, *Industrial History of the United States*, p. 516.

93. *Centennial Illustrated Catalogue and Price List of the Shakers' Chairs, Foot Benches, Floor Mats . . .* (Albany: Weed, Parsons & Co., 1876).

94. Olivia Howard Dunbar, *A House in Chicago*. Harriet Tilden became the wife of William Vaughn Moody in 1909.

95. Frederick Law Olmsted, Jr. and Theodora Kimball, *Frederick Law Olmsted, Landscape Architect, 1822–1903* (New York: Putnam, 1922).

96. For an opportunity to visit Memorial Hall, and particularly to examine the Exhibition model in the basement, the author is indebted to Mrs. Frederick L. Ballard of the Fairmount Park Commission.

97. "A Sennight at the Centennial"

98. Clarence P. Hornung, *Handbook of Early American Advertising Art* (New York: Dover, 1947).

99. The practice of museum management in the Centennial period is reviewed in Neil Harris, "The Gilded Age Revisited: Boston and the Museum Movement," *American Quarterly*, 14 (Winter, 1962), 545–66.

100. "Topics of the Times," *Scribner's Monthly*, 13 (Nov., 1876), 126.

101. The first public showing of impressionistic painting in Paris was in 1874.

102. Mildred Byars Matthews, "The Painters of the Hudson River School in the Philadelphia Centennial of 1876," *Art in America*, 34 (July, 1946), 143–60.

103. Edward C. Bruce, *The Century: Its Fruits and Its Festival* (Philadelphia: J. B. Lippincott, 1877).

104. The National Academy of Arts and Design gave free art instruction prior to 1876, suspended lessons during that year, and resumed with a tuition charge on Jan. 1, 1877. *New York Times*, Dec. 21, 1876.

105. Harris, "The Gilded Age Revisited. . . ."

106. *The Art Treasures of America*, ed. Edward Strahan (Philadelphia: George Barrie, 1879).

107. Nathaniel Burt, *The Perennial Philadelphians* (Boston: Little, Brown, 1963), p. 322.

108. Samuel Isham, *The History of American Painting*, new edition (New York: Macmillan, 1927), originally published in 1905.

109. New York *Times*, Dec. 21, 1876.

110. Lorado Taft, *The History of American Sculpture* (New York: Macmillan, 1903), Chapter 14.

111. Bruce, *The Century: Its Fruits and Its Festival*, p. 173.

112. Joseph Pennell, *Modern Illustration* (New York & London: G. Bell, 1895); George W. Sheldon, *American Painters: With Eighty-Three Examples of their Work Engraved on Wood* (New York: D. Appleton, 1879).

113. Robert Taft, *Photography and the American Scene* (New York: Macmillan, 1938), pp. 382–83.

I I

A Great Year
for Education

IT WOULD have astonished most Centennial Americans if someone had told them that as a people they made their best showing
during their Centennial year, and moved ahead most notably, in
the field of education. The Progressivist Movement began that
year, under the able leadership of William T. Harris of St.
Louis. The Morrill Land-Grant Act of 1862 was steadily increasing its impact, partly through the institutions it specifically
fostered, even more through the radical notion it embodied: that
practical education in agriculture and mechanic arts was as respectable and as worthy of support as the classical education of
gentlemen. Especially in the Middlewest, this notion was implemented by combining within a single institution all branches of
learning—everything, noted President Folwell of the University
of Minnesota "from hog cholera to Plato." Graduate study,
barely existing earlier, received its most significant impetus in
1876 with the opening of Johns Hopkins University in Baltimore, and faculty research, both basic and applied, was suddenly
recognized as the capstone of the entire academic structure.

American experience with education differed most from the European in the role of philanthropy. The so-called Puritan ethic, however much it retarded the development of a social conscience, prompted a sense of stewardship, and schools and colleges were the chief beneficiaries. Wealthy men from John Harvard to John D. Rockefeller believed they owed their wealth to God and felt duty-bound to repay the debt by supporting good works. Education simply happened to be the most attractive of all available good works.

Most early philanthropy for educational purposes was without limiting conditions. The chief desire of donors was to *have* a college; what and how it taught were secondary. Even when a specific stipulation accompanied a gift, it could usually be ignored if the college did not like the idea. Trustees, presidents, faculty members, and the families of students, if not the students themselves, generally agreed that the old classical tradition was best, for broadening the mind; training for a specific skill was considered a sign of narrowness.

After 1800, however, egalitarian thinking led to a questioning of the emphasis on producing gentlemen, at the same time that the broadening occupational base suggested the desirability of practical education. Instruction in Latin, theology, and logic, some people began to say, could never produce a Robert Fulton or a Samuel Morse. As business and industry developed, entrepreneurs replaced gentlemen in the control of the economy, yet very few college graduates were at all prepared for the new and growing needs. Some wealthy men, increasingly impatient with the conservative behavior of established institutions, founded new ones devoted to practical education, including Rensselaer Polytechnic Institute in 1824, Cooper Union in 1859, Stevens Institute in 1870, Rose Polytechnic in 1883, Pratt Institute in 1887, and Drexel Institute in 1891. Chauncey Depew, at the opening of Drexel, declared that the "culture" the classical college sought to impart had become "the veneer of the quack, and finally the decoration of the dude. . . . The old education simply trained the mind. The new trains the mind, the muscles, and the senses." [1]

If Depew felt he had to say such things in 1891, it is obvious that the radicals who made 1876 a great year for education had not killed off the old tradition. Classical education had so much momentum that it carried well beyond what should, perhaps, have been its proper demise. The radicals could not have failed to realize how formidable their opposition was, and how unprepared the tradition was to die. The radicals of 1876 were few in number and unable to carry the battle to every part of the nation. Their only practical course was to establish their new ideas in the patterns and practices of particular places, in the faith that their success would lead to general emulation. It took more time, however, than some of them must have wished. Discontent with the limited scope of most colleges had led to a decline in enrollments, yet the creation of new institutions that repudiated tradition did not quickly reverse the decline.

If by some miracle of ingenuity the educational revolutionaries had been able to translate their ideas into displays at the Centennial Exhibition, public awareness and acceptance might have been greatly accelerated. Ironically, the most effective educational displays at Fairmount Park were those from foreign countries, and specifically from Russia. The drawings, models, and tools developed for Russian schools by Victor Della Vos so impressed President John D. Runkle of the Massachusetts Institute of Technology that he at once organized instruction shops and persuaded his board of trustees to create a School of Mechanic Arts for students who wished to enter industry rather than become scientific engineers. Industrial training had formerly baffled educators; the Russian breakthrough simply separated instruction from construction, putting youngsters in instruction shops first as preparation for later work in construction shops. This made it possible to plan graded instruction in each vocational subject—joinery, carpentry, blacksmithing, or whatever. Another educator impressed by the Russian exhibit was Calvin M. Woodward of Washington University in St. Louis; he began planning a Manual Training School, the nation's first when it opened in 1879. The concept produced in time the slogan "teaching the whole boy"; it was officially confirmed in 1917 by the Smith-Hughes Act, and it has recently been extended to two-year vocational institutes on the college level, some of them independent, others within university structures. Even more important, because it affected the entire curriculum, was the Progressivist Movement, which ran its course from 1876 to 1955 but could hardly display itself at the Centennial Exhibition. It was the logical outcome of notions first propounded by Horace Mann before the Civil War that all children should be required to attend school to a fixed age and that the schooling should be financed by taxation. Once the strong opposition of the propertied classes had been overcome, state after state adopted compulsory attendance laws. But *if* all children were to be educated, the curriculum would have to be modified and made flexible to allow for individual differences and for such variables as socio-economic background and employment probabilities. Mann would probably have been uneasy about the inclusion of vocational training; William T. Harris, even after becoming United States Commissioner of Education in 1889, clung to Mann's preference for traditional courses. The Progressivists also shared with Mann the rather idealistic conviction that democratized schools would banish poverty, crime, vice, and even illness, and would bring something of a Great Society; Jeffersonian republicanism and Emersonian individualism both underlay this notion.[2]

The idea of public education that Mann pioneered and that Harris led the struggle to advance, assigned to public schools the function of transforming family and community life. John Dewey refined the thinking later in his Instrumentalist philosophy, and gave a new spur to the application of educational research to actual school problems. One valuable practical contribution made by William T. Harris was to professionalize public school teaching and administration. Earlier, it had been commonly supposed that anybody could teach and that no training was needed.

Horace Mann's ideal of education for all, though it no longer seemed wildly radical in 1876, was still visionary as far as actualities were concerned. The nearly nine million children enrolled in elementary and secondary schools comprised only two-thirds of the population between five and seventeen years of age. And enrollment and attendance were not the same: the average daily attendance was a mere 5,291,376. The average school year was 79.4 days—about sixteen weeks. Teachers numbered 259,618, three-fifths of them women, and the average annual pay was

$192. Few of the pupils went on to college—slightly more than 2 percent of the college-age group. At 1876 college commencements a total of 12,871 degrees were granted, including 835 master's and eleven doctor's degrees.[3]

States varied greatly, of course. In the Deep South, where the idea of tax-supported public schooling was still viewed as one more strange Yankee notion, and where most white people firmly believed that Negroes were ineducable, fewer than half the children ever saw the inside of a school, and then for only five or six weeks a year. No state elsewhere could be called typical, but Maine may be taken at random to show the educational practice in a state where education had long been considered important. In 1876 three-quarters of the population between four and twenty-one were enrolled in either the summer term of ten weeks, or the winter term of eleven weeks, or both. Women teachers greatly outnumbered men during the summer, 4,284 to 209; in the winter the numbers were almost the same, 2,351 women and 2,151 men. Wages showed a striking discrepancy; male teachers averaged $35.45 a month, female teachers only $4.26—the value of board and room not being counted. The state was already well advanced in teacher education, with two normal schools: Farmington, the largest college in the state, with 175 students, and Castine. The three private colleges, Bates, Colby, and Bowdoin, enrolled 114,109, and 97 respectively; the new College of Agriculture and Mechanic Arts, at Orono near Bangor, enrolled 91.[4]

Dry figures such as these were part of what could be reported at the Centennial Exhibition. Education had its assigned place there, in Group XXVIII, "Education and Science"—the last of the numbered groups. The critical, sometimes caustic opinions of the judges for this group may be found in the final volume of the official reports, just preceding the summary results of the fire engine trials, the rifle matches, and the regatta. This relegation of education to last place at the Exhibition seemed, to some educators, symbolic of the Centennial attitude toward education. John W. Hoyt of Madison, Wisconsin, who summarized the judges' report, certainly thought so. Exhibits of industry in the other groups, he remarked, were an excellent kind of education, "but of education proper much less can be said. A plain and candid statement would be the old story of a tardy Congress and an over-confident, procrastinating people, less appreciative of education, notwithstanding their claims on this score, than of their material progress and power." [5]

As early as January 1874, the National Commission of Education, seconded by the National Education Association, had called upon each state and Territory to participate in the Exhibition, and in 1875 both the NEA and the United States Bureau of Education issued pamphlets with suggestions for preparing school displays.[6] But there were handicaps. The federal government gave no financial support, while the Centennial Commission was slow to act—so Hoyt charged—and niggardly in the space it provided for educational displays. The judges were willing to concede, as a third handicap, a general inexperience in mounting such displays, although the excellence of some state exhibits was proof that ingenuity and determination could be good substitutes for experience. Of the thirty-eight states in the Union, "perhaps a half-dozen," Hoyt wrote, "should be admitted to have done themselves credit," but not a single city "made a full and thorough representation of its educational instrumentalities, condition, and progress." Public education, the judges apparently thought, was not very good in 1876 but was better than it was shown to be at the Exhibition.

Hoyt's summary set the tone of the separate reports that followed. The judges shared the admiration of William Dean Howells, Josiah Holland, and other journalists for the displays of the several federal departments—lighthouse equipment, postal devices, guns, ship models, maps and map-making instruments, and all the rest, as being notably educational; and they singled out for special praise the Smithsonian Institution and the Hayden Survey. The excellence of these displays put in the shade what most of the states had been able to do for their educational systems and progress, and emphasized the glaring omissions, incompleteness, and other faults.

The poor showing made by Connecticut was embarrassing to two Yale graduates among the judges, Andrew Dickson White and Daniel Coit Gilman. They thought that Yale itself could have done better than display a plaster statue of its president and 1,100 volumes written over the years by members of its faculty.

Neighboring Massachusetts, in contrast, amply fulfilled all hopes, but even more impressive was an exhibit showing the work, department by department, of the Illinois Industrial University (as the University of Illinois was then known), it had been planned and paid for by the school teachers and pupils of that state with not a cent from the state treasury. Indiana drew applause for a complete and accurate report of its school system, which the judges thought every state should have provided. Some states were damned by faint praise, while others were simply damned. "Of the State of Iowa but little can be said. The Exhibition made by it was comparatively small, and in no way remarkable." Kentucky "made her mark, but not much more," while Missouri showed "just enough to make the deficiency of the State very noticeable." California and Oregon, too distant to do much of anything at the Exhibition, and the Southern states that held aloof because of the current political acrimony, escaped the risk of censure by having no school exhibits at all.

Thus, Group XXVIII gave at most only a spotty picture of Centennial education in the United States. But even if every state and community had mounted a display, and every college and university, the Exhibition could hardly have hinted at the changes that in 1876 were shaking higher education to its very roots. Three university presidents in the East—White of Cornell, Eliot of Harvard, and Gilman of Johns Hopkins—were the principal revolutionaries; the presidents of several state universities in the upper Middlewest were not far behind. The changes these men were pioneering, which the Exhibition could not display nor contemporary laymen appreciate, were of an importance for the American future that would be hard to exaggerate.

Among the most interesting exhibits at Fairmount Park were the relatively few that specifically reflected the Centennial theme. Hampden-Sydney, fourteenth oldest American college, could celebrate its hundredth birthday along with the Declaration of Independence, and so could the Phi Beta Kappa Society. By limiting membership to students of time-honored subjects, the Society was a conservative force opposed not so much to the acceptance of new courses and curricula as to their recognition on the same level of dignity as traditional subjects. It was not the only defender of tradition but it represented in this country what T. H. Huxley had for years been belaboring in Britain as "the Latin fetish," meaning the insistence upon the classics as the *sine qua non* of educated men. The academic struggle of 1876 pitted loyal supporters of this view against men who, like Huxley, were radical enough to want room made for courses in scientific and professional subjects.

Huxley's field of research, and his prime interest, was biology. He argued at every opportunity that a knowledge of living organisms was more important than acquaintance with a dead language that had once been but was no longer the international means of communication. A major purpose of his 1876 visit to the United States, as we have seen, was to give the first public lecture at the Johns Hopkins University; he would have been an outstanding choice in any event, but the invitation reflected President Gilman's particular wish to emphasize science. Huxley was well acquainted with the virulent opposition of academic traditionalists, and also of religious bigots, but instead of trying to conciliate such people, he seemed to take delight in goading them to attack. It was an effective way to bring the issue into public awareness.

To such a man as Huxley, the frontier of knowledge was not at the Exhibition but elsewhere: in Professor Othniel Marsh's collection of fossil horses at Yale; in the private workrooms of scientist friends at Newport and Cambridge; at the annual convention, in Buffalo, of the American Association for the Advancement of Science; and in the modest converted dwellings in a shabby section of Baltimore, where the Hopkins laboratories were being readied for use. The Exhibition, in contrast, was well behind the frontier; it was a place where trophies of past victories could safely be shown, and where the public could gawk at the humming Corliss Engine and at Alexander Graham Bell's queer little gadget without a glimmering of what either was to mean, in the coming technological age.

The Hopkins trustees, some of them sincere Quakers, decided to omit the customary invocation and benediction at Huxley's address, a decision roundly condemned by the orthodox. "It was bad enough," one clergyman wrote to Gilman afterwards, "to invite Huxley. It were better to have asked God to be present. It would have been absurd to ask them both."

"Many people," Gilman reminisced years later, "thought that a university, like a college, could not succeed unless it was under some denominational control and were sure that Huxley's opening discourse was but an overture to the play of irreligious and anti-religious forces."[7] We would be spared vast confusion today if the two terms "college" and "university" were as easily distinguished as Gilman apparently thought they were; but he must have known he was over-simplifying, even for 1876, for some four-year colleges were already calling themselves universities, while others, notably the City College of New York, were publicly supported and tied to no denomination. But in general he was right, for the great majority of our institutions of higher education were then, as they still are, for undergraduates only and identified, however loosely, with particular churches. If some of their supporters attacked the public institutions as "godless," it was from a fear, much livelier in 1876 than today, that the small church-related colleges were in danger of being overwhelmed, if not snuffed out of existence altogether. But the fear proved baseless; the big universities, both state-supported and privately endowed, forced the small institutions to improve in every respect in order to produce students adequately prepared for the graduate and professional schools of the universities. The sturdy small colleges of the mid-twentieth century are a far cry from what they commonly were in 1876 with ill-prepared faculties, virtually no laboratories, and libraries hardly worthy of the name. Most small colleges today have better facilities, today, in fact, than some major universities had in 1876.

Johns Hopkins, being primarily a graduate school, though taking pride from the beginning in its undergraduate division,[8] was in a good position to ignore the religious bigots. It was quite otherwise at Cornell, where Andrew D. White, the Beau Brummell and Demosthenes of Centennial university presidents, had had to face a steady barrage of criticism from the time the university opened in 1868. Non-public higher education, according to a widespread article of contemporary belief, had to be under the aegis of some one sect; a tax-supported institution might be "godless" but an endowed institution that claimed to be nonsectarian was held in particular suspicion. White went to considerable trouble and expense to fill the pulpit of Sage

Chapel, one Sunday and another, with eminent clergymen of all denominations, Catholic and Jewish as well as Protestant, but he couldn't win: by the logic of bigotry, putting all religions on the same level of acceptance was to deny that any one of them had any priority of importance.[9] In 1876 White gave vent to his accumulated annoyance by issuing one of the major books of the year, *The Warfare of Science*, reviewing, with all his skill as a professional historian, the long sorry record of ecclesiastical opposition to advancing knowledge.[10]

Cornell owed its inception to the Morrill Land-Grant Act but in a rather curious way. Ezra Cornell and Andrew White were members of the New York State Senate in the middle 1860s. Cornell was chairman of the agriculture committee, White of the education committee. When the question of how best to apply the land-grant provisions came up, it seemed logical to appoint these two as a special committee to draw up a recommendation. Several existing institutions applied for the agricultural assignment but none seemed quite suitable to the special committee after its two members decided to found a brand-new university. Ezra Cornell owned a hilltop farm just east of Ithaca and a sizable fortune—roughly half a million dollars—gained from selling out his interest in Western Union. White, also a fairly wealthy man, knew something about higher education from his days as a professor of history at the University of Michigan. The institution they organized was an unusual combination of a private college, using the Cornell endowment, and a land-grant college, using the proceeds from selling the state's share of land-scrip.[11]

It might have been logical for New York to assign the Land Grant function to the "People's College" at Havana, which had been organized in 1858; its backers threatened a suit, but Ezra Cornell wisely made a cash settlement to avoid adverse publicity, and the Havana institution quickly died. This people's college was only one of several scattered around the country, all of them originally prompted by the hope that sons and daughters of working people might be trained for practical careers. The Gardiner Lyceum in central Maine was one of the earliest; it was sub-collegiate, and it was operative only ten years, 1821–32, but it inspired emulation in other states and some of its graduates became leaders in subsequent efforts to reform higher education.

In 1841, Captain Partridge of Norwich Academy, in Vermont, had proposed a forty-million-dollar federal appropriation to foster institutions with practical curricula. But another Vermonter, Justin Smith Morrill, conceived a better plan: a vast endowment in public land. He must have noted that all branches of American education, from the beginning, had been "land-grant"; in the absence of other forms of property, land had been given as the readiest form of capital endowment. And there was still plenty of land in the West, owned by the federal government and easily available. As a Congressman in 1857, Morrill offered a bill that rallied all the groups agitating for practical education and unified all the variant proposals; he had studied them carefully and his bill was "a generalized synthesis of all of them, the epitome of two decades of regional agitation and experimentation." Twenty thousand acres of federal land were allotted for each Senator and Representative—not the land itself but scrip that stood for the land and could be sold by each state for whatever it could get. Ten percent of the proceeds could be used to buy sites and experimental plots, but none of the money could be used to erect buildings or maintain them. The bulk of the money had to be invested, at 5 percent or better, and only the income used. President Buchanan vetoed the bill, but in 1862 Morrill, now a Senator, guided it to passage, and Lincoln signed it. Because each state had to provide an institution within five years, or forfeit its share of the grant, the sale of scrip was often hurried and the proceeds small—the average came to about $1.65 an acre.[12] Cornell got the best return, securing cash advances from wealthy friends of the university and deferring sale of the scrip until the price was better. During 1876, President White's correspondence included inquiries from administrators in other states, some of whom apparently felt that Cornell had circumvented the law.[13]

But the great benefit of the Land-Grant Act was less the actual cash it provided than the stimulus it gave to kinds of education not recognized, then or later, by Phi Beta Kappa and other champions of tradition. Setting up agriculture and mechanic arts alongside traditional subjects was not, however, the only innovation at Cornell; its initial popular reputation rested on its announced intention to make no distinctions based on race, sex, religion, or financial means. Twice as many candidates showed up for the first term as could be accommodated: the word had spread fast. Letters poured onto White's desk from lawyers, bankers, clergymen, and businessmen on behalf of young geniuses without money; the incidence of genius, one might suppose from the letters, was unusually high in those days. Part of the promise could not be honored at once, for no women were admitted until 1873, a long enough delay for the college to earn a reputation for virility, especially in rowing, and to establish a male prejudice against coeds that still lingers in Ithaca. Coeducation did not exist in any of the older Eastern institutions that Cornell men looked upon as rivals, and having to attend classes with women was publicly resented.

Privately, no doubt, exceptions were common. It has been suggested that half the male students in the mid-1870s shared a secret passion for Harriet Tilden of Chicago, "the divine Harriet," the girl who had everything—wealth, a striking blonde beauty, a first-rate mind, and so good a knowledge of clothes that a faculty novelist, Bjornsterne Bjornson, sought her advice in dressing his characters.[14] When she left Cornell, adding a luster to the graduation ceremonies of 1876, she caused no such mass suicide as followed Zuleika Dobson's departure from Oxford; instead, we find in the annual *Cornellian* this remark about coeducation: "And we of 1876, after a three-years' trial, are beginning to shake our heads."[15]

This official male opinion (or public myth) also had to overlook the national fame won earlier in the year by another coed, Julia Thomas. It is to be regretted that intercollegiate academic contests are no longer held, such as the one at the Academy of Music in New York on January 4, 1876, with contestants from Lafayette, Rutgers, New York University, City College of New York, Williams, Syracuse, Northwestern, Hamilton, St. Johns, Cornell, and Princeton. Cornell, despite its youth, won team honors with first places in Mathematics, Greek, and Essays, and a second place in Oratory.[16] For an institution better known for its athletic prowess, the result was astonishing, and drew this friendly comment from *Harper's Weekly:* "It will not have escaped attention that both the muscular and mental honors of the last year were borne off by one of the youngest universities of the country, and one which, for many reasons, has been the subject of harsh and even of jealous and illicit criticism." [17]

What most startled the public, however, was that the Greek prize went to a coed. Miss Thomas (or Mrs. Irving, for she was married) had transferred to Cornell from Antioch College in Ohio, where presumably she had learned most of her Greek, but this fact was not known to the authors of the many letters to President White praising Cornell for providing the kind of education that enabled a girl to win in a fair contest with men. One Martha Goddard of Boston expressed the hope that Cornell would go on to the point of humbling Harvard. "I make every woman I know," she wrote, "proud of Julia Thomas, but the doubters and dogmatizers here will not be silenced until she has children; they do not so much deny the possibility of a female mind, as declare that a woman can not have mind and body both, and if she chooses education she renounces motherhood." [18]

Beyond the Appalachians, where many an Eastern tradition was quietly dropped, and where frontier egalitarianism fostered coeducation at all levels, a victory comparable to Miss Thomas's caused much less of a furor. During the spring of 1876, in Chicago, an Interstate Oratorical Contest was won by a coed named Laura Ann Kent. She was the lone female contender, and competed with two young men who later became United States Senators—Albert J. Beveridge and Robert M. La Follette. [19] That she was a student at Antioch, Julia Thomas's original alma mater, spoke well for the caliber that some small colleges could achieve, but specifically for the experimentation begun at Antioch by its first president, the same Horace Mann whose public school ideas were being advanced in 1876.

Tradition, the great barrier to change and hence the chief target of the educational revolutionaries, was tenacious in the East, grudgingly permitting, on a few campuses, the compromise known as "coordinate education," an idea borrowed from Oxford and Cambridge, and stimulating the founding of separate institutions for women. In 1876 Smith and Wellesley completed their first year of operation; their opening, in the fall of 1875, had confirmed the principle of colleges for women and had strengthened the opposition to coeducation, in private institutions at least. Public higher education in the East, meanwhile, had never developed significantly because the private institutions were so much older and more firmly established. These basic differences in higher education, East and West, comprise what is still one of our most obvious examples of regional diversity. Cornell, located between the two traditions both geographically and psychologically, has always been transitional in this respect.

Some traditions are strong enough to resist all change, but others give way, slowly or suddenly, by evolution or administrative fiat. The university president most instrumental in replacing old with new was unquestionably Charles William Eliot of Harvard, who had the longest accumulation of campus tradition to contend with—240 years in 1876. His election as president of Harvard in 1869 followed a long debate among the Overseers, some of whom feared his radical tendencies. While still an assistant professor he had campaigned, successfully, for written examination to replace or at least complement oral testing, and he had installed gas lights in his dormitory against the strong opposition of President Walker, who preferred candles and considered gas dangerous. But the Overseers' debate centered on more important points and reflected the struggle on every campus between tradition and change. The conservatives wanted a president who was theologically sound and a curriculum with continuing stress on the classics, while the progressives argued for more science, more subjects of a practical nature, and more freedom of choice for students. The progressives won, and Eliot amply fulfilled their hopes and realized the fears of the conservatives.

The innovations took time; most of them belonged to the period rather than to the Centennial Year itself. Harvard's *Lampoon*, founded in 1876, the nation's first undergraduate humor magazine, was one of the few innovations not attributable to Eliot. Some of Eliot's innovations were readily borrowed: making all the deans responsible to the president, for example, and abolishing the proprietary pattern that determined a professor's income by the number of students he could attract, and putting all units of the university on the same academic calendar. The chaos of different calendars for various units, honored so long in practice, may be likened to the chaos of local time, called "sun time" and often defended as "God's time," that prevailed in 1876 and gave way only in 1884 when standard time zones were established.

Eliot led also in reducing the Christmas vacation to two weeks and extending the summer vacation to three months. One of his hardest won victories was permitting students to take books out of the library. He established the case method in the law school. In the medical school he increased the course to three years, with two terms each year instead of one, insisted on higher admission standards (in 1877 instituting the first entrance examinations), and for graduation required passing grades on written examinations, three hours for each subject, instead of the five passes out of nine by oral testing that had been the practice.[20] It is no wonder, as a writer for *Scribner's* remarked in 1876, that a medical degree from Harvard was "the most valuable procurable in this country." [21]

It is often hard to realize today that patterns long established in our colleges and universities were once alarming proposals whose advocates were viewed as enemies of all that was good and true—allowing students to choose certain courses for study. The elective system, for example, seemed radical in the extreme in 1876. Eliot did not invent it, but his eventual success with it, over stubborn faculty resistance at Harvard, gave it a prominence that stirred academia everywhere. Too many professors of established subjects righteously defended their subjects as "necessary to a gentleman's education" or as "an indispensable means of broadening the mind and disciplining the intellect." Eliot was patient, and besides, he preferred to be right than popular. In the course of time, subjects once universally required became elective, making it possible to increase the number of choices. Social studies and biological science were the chief beneficiaries. Another result of increasing courses was the emergence of subject departments: where one man had formerly been able to teach everything within a given discipline, two were needed, then three, and so on until some disciplines required large numbers of teachers (and eventually a formal structure with a head or chairman). Harvard had the first department of economics in the country, in 1871, and Henry Adams, by the time he left Harvard in 1877, had established a history department. Reliance on single specialists had greatly restricted scholarly productivity;

Francis James Child, for example, the great authority on the Scottish ballads, had to devote much of his time and energy to teaching freshman composition until Eliot could appoint a second man in English in 1876, Adam S. Hill.

The Harvard curriculum, before Eliot, was typical in its rigidity. As late as 1869, all freshmen took Latin, Greek, French, mathematics, elocution, ethics, and the history of Greece. All sophomores took physics, chemistry, German, more elocution, themes, 350 pages of Dugald Stewart (probably in his *Outlines of Moral Philosophy*), twenty chapters of Gibbon's *Decline and Fall of the Roman Empire*, with an added eight hours chosen from a list of four courses each in Latin and mathematics, two in Greek, one in Italian, and one in Anglo-Saxon. Juniors had roughly the same choices in addition to prescribed courses in Herschel's astronomy, Lardner's optics, Bowen's logic, Scots metaphysics in Walker's editions, writing forensics, and lectures (but no laboratory work) in chemistry. Seniors took five hours a week in history, courses in philosophy, economics, and written themes, plus two or three electives. The pattern was so rigid that a student who happened to have had eight years of Latin before matriculating had to wait until his senior year to read Juvenal, while another student equally well prepared in Greek could not read *Antigone* until his final year. Eliot, it should be said, never slighted the classics in one respect: although he forced them to retreat as the *sine qua non* of a Harvard education, he built a very strong department of classics.

Every departure from tradition had to be fought for by whatever methods a strong-willed academic revolutionary could devise. Charles William Eliot led; other presidents followed. His actions roused mixed feelings across the country—a good deal of admiration for his courage, much resentment, and something of despair at the standards he set—standards that called for much more money than most college presidents could ever hope to have at hand. Laboratory science, for example, was very costly; the great majority of institutions in 1876, lacking the funds for adequate laboratories, had to rely on demonstrations by professors. Money meant a great deal in faculty caliber, too. Harvard, with its steadily growing endowment, was able to enlist and keep a faculty so good that it was virtually beyond the reach of other institutions: among others, James Russell Lowell in modern languages, Francis James Child in English, Oliver Wendell Holmes in anatomy, Asa Gray in natural history, Josiah Whitney in geology, Wolcott Gibbs in applied science, Henry Adams in history, William James in physiology, Francis Parkman in botany, and the three Peirces—Benjamin in astronomy, James Mills in mathematics, Charles Sanders in philosophy.[22] It may be doubted whether any college or university, Harvard included, has ever, before or since, assembled a faculty of such rare quality; it was the opinion of Charles Darwin that at this time the Harvard faculty excelled the combined faculties at Oxford and Cambridge.[23]

Harvard also pioneered in doctoral work, creating its graduate school of arts and sciences in 1872 and granting the first American doctorates in 1873, two in philosophy and one in science. Courses labeled "primarily for graduates" first appeared in the catalogue of 1875–76. Nathaniel Southgate Shaler, Louis Agassiz's famous pupil, earned his S.D. (Doctor of Science) in 1874, and Henry Cabot Lodge his Ph.D., in history, in 1876, with a dissertation on Anglo-Saxon Land Law. Shaler stayed to teach at Harvard, and his "Geology 4" was quickly the favorite introductory course. The capable candidates were available, and the culture needed men thus trained in specialized knowledge; the chief thing lacking, with the lack just beginning to be met, was the means of such training. Eliot's answer to the criticism that graduate work would harm the undergraduate was typical of his thinking: without graduate facilities an institution had no means of breeding new scholars to replace the old, and he used the death of Louis Agassiz in 1873 to hammer the point home.

For more than a century, the lack of advanced education in America had driven would-be professors to Europe; Ticknor, Longfellow, and Holmes were among those who trained abroad for academic careers at Harvard. In 1876 many students went abroad to study, and particularly to Germany. Of the 488 students at Heidelberg that year, thirty-nine were American.[24] Costs were low at German universities, but this was hardly the major attraction. In France, the program of studies leading to the doctorate took about nine years; in Germany, only two. Americans had learned that science, though strong in England, was not centered in the universities. German science, which *was* a university concern, was at least as strong as the British. Each German university, moreover, had developed over many decades a preeminence in a particular subject, or in several; and the professors in those subjects were internationally famous. An American student could be confident of finding, on one German campus or another, professional training in whatever subject he wanted, and the training was good enough to ensure him a college position when he returned home with his doctor's degree. The great freedom of German universities was in itself an attraction, after the narrowness and restrictiveness of undergraduate life in the United States. Students not only lived as they pleased but selected their own seminars, listened to as many or as few lectures as they wished, chose their own thesis topics, and even set the times for their final oral examinations.

Before 1870, Americans went to German universities chiefly for training in natural sciences and medicine; by 1876 the emphasis had shifted to social sciences and the humanities. The German method, particularly the massing of details and the presentation of seminar reports, had a startling effect on American education when German-trained faculty members applied it to American teaching. The untravelled soon had reason to be alarmed. The hoary tradition of daily recitation from the same old texts, year after year, was on the defensive; a professor who did not undergird his teaching, in any subject, with constant research stood in danger of obsolescing—of being branded as the dead wood of a faculty. Some teachers who had studied in Germany did away with textbooks altogether, sometimes because, in new branches of a subject, none existed, and sometimes because the teachers were far ahead of the textbook authors. If textbooks were essential, as in literature, they had to be replaced fairly often as research gave improved texts and eliminated gross errors. Traditionalists resisted all changes, of course. One new practice that horrified them was paying graduate students, or some of them, as fellows. It did not require exposure to German education for men to realize that traditional methods were subject to review and possible modification or elimination. But the German experience accelerated the changes.[25]

Charles Kendall Adams probably pioneered the seminar in

America—the small group of students gathered for original research. His was a seminar in history initiated at the University of Michigan, in 1869. Henry Adams began his own more famous history seminar at Harvard a year later. Nor was the seminar *method* the only innovation; the specialization it encouraged led to the rapid increase in knowledge, which in turn prompted the creation of professional associations and specialized journals to disseminate the new findings. The American Chemical Society, for example, was founded in 1876, with John W. Draper of New York University, as president. (Draper was the first man to make a successful photograph of the human face.) Yet another result was a subtle shift in professors' loyalty from their particular institutions to their disciplines, and from the "ivory tower" concept to one of serving society through involvement in activities beyond the campus.

As in the lower schools, where William T. Harris was guiding teachers and administration toward professionalism, perhaps the chief long-range result of German training was the emergence of the modern professional professor—a specialist, a person committed to research and the publication of results, a member of national and international societies in his own field, an active participant in various social movements, and, for much less of his time than would have been possible or even conceivable before 1876, a classroom teacher concerned primarily with undergraduates. The phenomenon of "research professors," though such individuals were very rare in 1876, was an inevitable extension of this shift in the profession.

The German influence waned by 1900, particularly the reliance on the massive accumulating of facts as the heart of graduate instruction. Fewer men each year had to go abroad for training as our own graduate schools developed and more subjects became susceptible of doctoral productivity. The Ph.D. degree varies greatly in quality, but it is at least a help to presidents and deans in search of new faculty (and a kind of union card to applicants for college positions). In 1876, the virtual absence of this credential made the job of recruitment difficult, except for the fact that enrollments were still small and the need for new professors rather limited.

Most college and university presidents, upon assuming power, inherit faculties which contain some good men to encourage, some lazy men to stimulate, and some "dead wood" to be endured until death or retirement makes replacement possible. Daniel Coit Gilman was lucky: he was in a position to choose the entire Johns Hopkins faculty. He would have liked to pry from Harvard and Oxford their most eminent living professors, but he knew this was impossible. Instead, he went abroad to consult Jowett at Balliol, Von Holst at Freiburg, Ranke at Berlin, Mahaffy at Dublin, Kelvin at Glasgow, and, at London's famous "X Club," Tyndall, Huxley, and Spencer. Back home, he had plenty of advice from Charles William Eliot and Andrew White. His lure was very attractive: freedom for individual research, the chance to teach superior students in small seminars, and $5,000 a year, an unheard of salary in those days. The six original professors he employed were a remarkable team: the mathematician James Joseph Sylvester, "a stout Englishman of about sixty with rosy cheeks, and long gray hair,"[26] (who in 1883 resigned to become Savilian Professor of Geometry at Oxford); two classicists in their forties, Charles D. Morris, a former Oxford fellow, and Basil Gildersleeve, a Princeton graduate who had continued his studies at Berlin, Bonn, and Göttingen; and three scientists in their twenties—Ira Remsen in pure chemistry, who for two years had served as Fittig's assistant at Tübingen; the biologist Henry Newell Martin, first man to earn a Doctor of Science at Cambridge and author, while serving as Huxley's assistant, of the first course outlines in biology; and finally the physicist Henry Augustus Rowland, at twenty-five the youngest of the six, famous later for computing the mechanical equivalent of heat, refining the measurement of the ohm, mapping the solar spectrum photographically, developing multiplex telegraphy, and, for his achievements, winning the Draper and Rumford medals.[27]

In addition to the six professors there were twelve associates, ten distinguished visiting lecturers, and twenty fellows on salary, chiefly engaged in research. A representative original fellow was Herbert Baxter Adams, valedictorian of his Amherst class of 1872, who earned his Ph.D. at Heidelberg, summa cum laude, on July 14, 1876. Most of the Hopkins fellows later moved up to professorships in other institutions; Adams stayed and soon took over the seminar in American history, shaping it to the German pattern even more closely than Henry Adams had done at Harvard. In 1884 he was one of the founders of the American Historical Association, and its first secretary. But for all his German training and methodology, it is interesting to learn that his choice of history as a scholarly pursuit was inspired in a traditional American way: Amherst President Julius Seelye had fired his enthusiasm, as an undergraduate, with a single lecture.[28]

The need was great but unrecognized, to the exasperation of public university presidents eager to serve their states by improving instruction, diversifying subject offerings, and providing new kinds of trained leadership not produced by the traditional liberal arts colleges. There was a sudden urgency, with demand for professorial talent of the sort represented by the Ph.D. degree far exceeding supply, and with presidents often in despair when farm-belt legislators could see no reason to support highly-paid specialists, or when boards of trustees insisted that buildings be given first priority. Presidents who made their mark —such men as Angell at Michigan, Bascom at Wisconsin, and Folwell at Minnesota—bent their chief energies to the creation of strong faculties with research potential; brick or stone could be put together at any time.

The Johns Hopkins was a prime example of the new American emphasis on faculty strength; it opened with a few old buildings on Howard Street in Baltimore, almost as if the trustees were aware that Huxley, in his address on September 9, would heap scorn on governing boards that lavished money on buildings:

> It has been my fate to see great educational funds fossilize into mere bricks and mortar, in the petrifying springs of architecture, with nothing left to work the institution they were intended to support. . . . Administrators of educational funds have sometimes made a palace and called it a university. . . . A century hence, when . . . you have endowed all the professors you need, and built all the laboratories that are wanted, and have the best museum and the finest library that can be imagined; then, if you have a few hundred thousand dollars you don't know what to do with, send for an architect and tell him to put up a façade. If Amer-

ican is similar to English experience, any other course will probably lead you into having some stately structure, good for your architect's fame, but not in the least what you wanted.[29]

Brazil's Dom Pedro, for one, after visiting several of the nation's campuses, concluded that Americans *were* building academic palaces.[30] The institutions he saw were very likely the nation's oldest and best endowed, with the most numerous wealthy alumni vying for the fame attendant upon having buildings bearing their names. The Protestant Ethic had been at work a long time in the East, prompting liberal gifts for buildings as material evidence of individual piety, and the number of substantial structures on campuses was one obvious way of distinguishing older from newer institutions of higher learning. Harvard was at one extreme, Hopkins at the other, in 1876. But this was only one of numerous differences among institutions for higher education that must have puzzled visitors from abroad.

One major difference was in the methods of establishment. Some of the oldest institutions—Columbia, Dartmouth, and Princeton among others—had been chartered by the Crown of England. Others, including Harvard, Yale, and Pennsylvania, boasted Colonial charters, a practice followed after 1789 by state chartering of private institutions. In the early 1800s, many of these were organized as stock companies, but by 1876 most had become nonprofit corporations.

Of the remaining tax-supported institutions, only a few were municipal; the City College of New York, founded in 1847, and the University of Cincinnati, 1870, were the two best known. Most were state chartered and supported. Some of these were created by provisions in the state constitutions, stipulating either freedom from legislative control, as in California, Colorado, Michigan, and Minnesota, or direct control, as in Alabama, Nebraska, and Wyoming. In a larger number of states the public universities resulted from acts of the legislatures—Arkansas, Illinois, Indiana, Kansas, Kentucky, Massachusetts, Oregon, Virginia, Wisconsin. Just as no two states had identical constitutions, no two state universities were exactly alike, and close acquaintance with one would be no guarantee of recognizing another.

All colleges and universities, however, whether private or public, were alike in having lay governing boards, variously titled regents, trustees, overseers, visitors, governors, fellows, or "the corporation." In size the boards varied from as few as three, at Marquette, to as many as fifty-four, at M.I.T.; the average was about twenty. Some members served for life, others for as briefly as two years. New board members at private institutions were commonly "co-opted"—that is, selected by the board itself. For public institutions the usual procedure was appointment by the governor, with or without the advice and consent of the legislature. There were all sorts of patterns—and very few have changed during the course of their existence. Eight of the forty-four trustees of Northwestern University (1851) were chosen by four Methodist conferences, for two-year terms; the remaining thirty-six were co-opted. Notre Dame (1844) had a six-man Board of Trustees, with indefinite terms, and also a Board of Lay Trustees, three ex-officio and sixteen elected for six-year terms. M. I. T. may have had the most complex board: thirty-five of its fifty-four members were co-opted for life terms, fifteen were elected for five-year terms by the board on nomination of the alumni, and four were state officials—the governor, the chief justice of the supreme judicial court, the state commissioner of education, and the president of the corporation. Ex-officio members appeared most often on boards of public institutions, but were seldom numerous—sometimes only the university president, as at Minnesota, Colorado, and Michigan State; more often the president and one other, either the governor or the state superintendent of education, and sometimes none at all. Apart from presidents the faculties were almost never represented on boards; some charters even specifically singled out professors as the one group not eligible, although they presumably knew more than anybody else about higher education.[31]

It was therefore contrary to general practice for the University of California, founded in 1868, to have eight ex-officio members on a board of twenty-four—governor, lieutenant-governor, speaker of the assembly, superintendent of public instruction, and the presidents of the state board of agriculture, the Mechanics' Institute of San Francisco, the university alumni association, and the university. The sixteen appointed members served for terms of sixteen years, with two retiring each year and replaced by two new members appointed by the governor. In its early years, this pattern proved so frustrating that one president, Daniel Coit Gilman, felt his only course was to resign, as another equally eminent president was forced out almost exactly a century later. Political pressures could often, as they still can, make life miserable for presidents and professors, and inhibit the proper growth of service to the population; yet the very existence of a complex variety of public and private institutions instead of the unitary system in European countries, with total control centralized in ministries of education, gave both presidents and professors a mobility that insured against unbearable pressures, and at the same time enabled competing institutions to experiment endlessly with curricula.

State universities had existed since 1784, when the first one was chartered in Georgia, but their greatest growth came after the Morrill Land-Grant Act. The ways the several states implemented the Act provide one further example of American diversity. Illinois was admitted to statehood in 1818 but waited half a century before the Morrill Act prompted the people to organize public higher education: in 1867 they established what was known first as Illinois Industrial University but in 1885 was renamed the University of Illinois. In sharp contrast, Michigan organized its University in 1817, twenty years before statehood, but assigned the Land-Grant provisions to another institution, founded in 1855, which became the Michigan State University.

In Wisconsin, where state and university both date from 1848, President John Bascom won a major concession from the legislature in 1876, a millage tax that assured a steadily growing income for the university.[32] The struggle for adequate support had been a long one, typical, unfortunately, of what most state universities have had to wage in order to serve the public adequately. The luckiest presidents today are those whose predecessors were able to establish firm commitments of financial support and political non-interference. They were able to do so chiefly by demonstrating the economic advantage to the tax-payers of research for state needs. Where this implemented research has never been sufficiently emphasized, as in many of the Southern states, and in parts of the country, like New England, where private institutions have long been dominant, the single most convincing argument for support has been lacking and, as an inevitable result, the state universities have fallen short of greatness.

Neighboring Minnesota was faring less well in 1876 than Wisconsin. Although the state university existed on paper as early as 1851, seven years before Minnesota became a state, red tape and virtually nonexistent support delayed its effective opening until 1869, when the Board of Regents accepted Andrew D. White's recommendation of William Watts Folwell as president. Folwell's remark that he was interested in everything from Plato to hog cholera hardly endeared him to the "Bourbons," his term for the traditionalists on the faculty, but it was a good trait for the encouragement of the all-embracing character that the university eventually attained. Mindful that a course in agriculture was essential under the terms of the Land-Grant Act, Folwell prodded the Regents in 1873, and again in 1874, but without success. He was finally allowed to hire Charles Y. Lacy, a recent Cornell graduate, to manage the university farm and to give courses in agriculture. Lacy worked hard. He posted notices in every post office in the state. Once he sent out five hundred postcard announcements. He invited the Patrons of Husbandry to visit the farm. The net result of his diligence was the enrolling of three agricultural students in the fall of 1876—but all three of them failed out before the term was ended.[33]

Farmers were by and large a conservative lot in 1876, as representative of the "show me" tradition as any other element in the population. Since hardly any of them had been to college, it took a great deal of effort to convince them that professors could tell them anything worth their knowing, or that chemistry and other newfangled sciences could put money into their pockets. Their own wits and their fathers' techniques were all they thought they needed. The scientists they scorned, however, began to show research results—frost-resistant wheat; new strains of corn that fattened pigs faster; ways of minimizing various diseases that killed cattle and horses; better kinds of fertilizer; scientific drainage; and much, much more—all of it designed to increase the income of farmers and their families. The farmers, like other groups in the nation, did not realize their own most immediate needs until technological experts identified them and followed up with demonstrations of scientifically proven methods of meeting those needs. The academic revolution in progress in 1876 was in large part just this: the anticipation of public needs, the creation of a demand for university efforts to meet these needs, and a radical redirection of higher education for the public benefit. It was the academic mind that perceived the readiness of the culture for new techniques, and it was the academic mind that implemented the need by training the specialists and devising the research techniques.

Agricultural education was not an American innovation; it had begun in Europe about 1775. Nor were its American beginnings in the midwest, although it has reached its greatest development in that region. Massachusetts Agricultural College was by 1876 a thriving institution. The Commonwealth had acted swiftly to take advantage of the Morrill Act; M.I.T., founded a year before the Act was passed, was assigned the mechanic arts share of the proceeds from the 360,000 acres assigned to the state, and the share for agriculture, sought unsuccessfully by Harvard, went to a new institution in Amherst, chartered in 1863 and opened in 1867. E. H. Libby described the new college, in *Scribner's* for October, 1876, as "the exponent of a new departure in education, of a vital principle in the welfare of the race. . . . Professors in the classical college are not expected as part of their regular duties to advance science by original investigation; a fundamental principle in the organization of the Agricultural College is, that investigation and research shall be prominent features. . . . The object and result of the old education is Culture; of the new, Knowledge." [34]

These words, which could as well have been applied to the Johns Hopkins, put squarely on the line one of the major instruments used in the academic revolution—emphasis on research. But Massachusetts Agricultural College did not grow as the Western state universities did. Tight legislative control severely limited its development, starving it financially and forcing it for years to keep within its original narrow purpose; for another facet of the academic revolution was the combining in single institutions many and diverse purposes—"Plato to hog cholera." Simon Newcomb, reviewing abstract science in the nation's first century, offered several reasons for its underdevelopment: minimal federal support and public encouragement, lack of the continuity that colleges might have provided had they taught science, and the absence of "the mutual attrition of ideas, the competition of rival works, the zest gained by intercourse with kindred spirits" [35]—in short, the absence of intellectual cross-fertilization that is one of the glories of multiple-purpose universities.

To Southern educators in 1876, this brave new world of research, graduate study, and professional training for multiple purposes might have existed on Mars; most of the institutions of the region had not even regained their pre-war stability. In South Carolina, for example, the entire student body at the university ignored the advice of the faculty in 1861 and marched off to war; by 1869 the faculty itself was breaking up. In 1874 the Radical Republicans gained control of the governing board and converted the campus into a school for Negroes; but even this effort was short-lived, for Wade Hampton, as one of his first acts as governor, closed it in 1877 and it remained closed until 1880. The damage to Southern education caused by the Civil War and the post-war political struggles would be hard to exaggerate; what was true of South Carolina was true, in varying degrees, throughout all the former Confederacy.[36]

But war and post-war conflict cannot be blamed for the course the Southern university presidents followed when they got their chance to start rebuilding their institutions. The moment of resuming operations would have been an excellent one in the South for redirecting higher education toward some of the newer concepts. Instead, the characteristic Southern way of thinking—agrarian, aristocratic, tradition-centered—dictated the revival of the old educational patterns. To adopt the revolutionary ideas of higher education in the North might have seemed one more humiliating surrender of Southern principle. While Virginia and Alabama chartered and opened agricultural-mechanic arts institutions in 1872, their counterparts in Mississippi, North Carolina, and South Carolina did not open until 1880, 1889, and 1893. Even after several decades the South did not learn to put a high priority on the research-technology principle, to the dismay of educators who knew how much this principle might, if applied, have served to close the economic gap between the South and the rest of the nation. But apart from the general failure to grasp so golden an opportunity, the South did have its Centennial heroes in education, without whose efforts the subsequent progress might have been even slower.

The University of North Carolina at Chapel Hill, dating from 1789, is the nation's second oldest state university. But neither age nor prestige of the sort that it had come to enjoy could spare the institution once its support was removed. Not all the student body marched off to the Civil War; four men stayed to graduate in 1865. Two years later the disorganized state government, unable to supply any money for the university, persuaded the faculty to resign, and a new board of trustees, set up under the Reconstruction constitution of 1868, accepted their resignations as final. Even when federal soldiers closed the campus gates President Swain could not believe what had happened. He was injured in a buggy accident and died on August 24, 1868. With him died the university.

Resurrection was painful and slow as rival political factions used the university as a pawn. One effort in 1870 proved abortive; despite the presence of fifteen students, a lame-duck board of Radical Republicans, angered by the victory of their conservative opponents in the fall elections, again closed the university and abandoned the faculty. During 1873 and 1874 campus buildings were broken into, books and apparatus scattered. Finally, in 1875, a new board found the means of raising money—not much, but enough to resume operations. The night the news reached Chapel Hill, March 20, one Cornelia Spencer climbed into the belfry of South Hall and gained local immortality as "the woman who rang the bell," the first time it had been heard in five years. It galvanized her neighbors into painting the long rows of picket fencing, for the village of Chapel Hill existed, then as now, solely for the university. In September the reopening, this time for good, attracted fifty-five students. The first commencement after the opening, held in June 1876, was a gala occasion, with 750 people crowding the chapel. There were no graduates, but old-timers welcomed the revival of academic ceremony and lofty oratory.[37]

A month later the new term began, with 112 students, a heartening increase. But state finances were still precarious, and poverty plagued the university. A new president, Kemp Battle, drew a salary of $2,500; the top professonial salary was $2,000. Tuition fees, $60 a year, helped a little, and a sum of $18,000 collected and donated by a citizens' committee helped somewhat more. The closest thing to an endowment was the considerable acreage the university owned, but it was yielding no income. The standard faculty teaching load, fifteen recitations a week, left no room for such frills as research and elective courses. On the Fourth of July in 1876, President Battle went to Raleigh, the state capital, to deliver a Centennial address. Picture him returning in his buggy that evening. His tired horses have given out at the foot of the long grade up into Chapel Hill, and the weary president has no choice but to walk the last hard mile—peculiarly symbolic of the uphill struggle this president, and others in the South, had to face in 1876.[33]

But nowhere in the country could a presidency be considered a sinecure in 1876. One handicap of national scope was the paucity of students—only about 25,000, roughly a twentieth of 1 percent of the population and proportionally fewer than forty years earlier. Considering the reorientation of the entire economy, from aristocratic privilege to equalitarianism, from agriculture to industry, from village and farm to city, from family self-sufficiency to interdependence and delegated functions, it seems obvious, in retrospect, that traditional higher education was increasingly remote from actualities. But even the most radical curricular changes were rather limited in their social impact by the small number of candidates for trained leadership.

On the other hand, any significantly larger enrollments would have made the problem of financial support even more acute than it was. The much-publicized gifts of Johns Hopkins and Ezra Cornell were already proving inadequate; the Cornell faculty were vocally bitter about their low salaries, and the Hopkins hospital and medical school had to be deferred. Commodore Vanderbilt had given more than half a million dollars to the institution in Nashville that bears his name, and early in 1876 he gave an additional $100,000—not very much by later standards of giving or in relation to Vanderbilt's fortune, but enough to make Vanderbilt University the envy of the South. A second Nashville institution, ten-year-old Fisk University for Negroes, dedicated a fine new building on the Centennial New Year's Day; the money to erect it, $120,000, represented the receipts from concerts by the Fisk University Singers.[39] This may be the only college building in America ever financed by a student music group. The academic revolution was creating a need for much more money than had ever before been available for education, but the greatest single source of this money, other than taxes, was not quite ready to be tapped. Most of the great fortunes, especially those of Carnegie and Rockefeller, which would one day provide magnificent and enduring benefactions to higher education, were still in the process of being amassed.

The Depression of 1873 had its influence on education. Among other things, it persuaded many families that they could not afford to send their sons to college. The contemporary cost of higher education was extremely small, in modern terms, but even so it was prohibitive to a large proportion of the population. Harvard had the highest tuition rate in the country—$150 a year, with Yale a close second at $140, but at both these colleges the total annual cost to the student averaged $1,000. At Harvard the most frugal student could scrape by on about $450 a year; it was also possible, by joining select societies, attending the theatre often, and keeping servants, to spend as much as $4,000. New Haven was somewhat more austere. Country colleges in the East, such as Amherst, Dartmouth, and Hamilton, were much less expensive, with an average of about $700. The large Western institutions, such as Northwestern and Michigan, ran about the same as the Eastern country colleges; while the Western country colleges, such as Oberlin and Beloit, cost just about a quarter as much as the Eastern urban universities. But even a tuition fee of $36 a year and a total cost as low as $250 looked steep to families with annual incomes below $500, and such families were the great majority.[40]

With income from college fees so low, with so few students to pay them, with limited donations, and, especially in the South, with heavy war damage to faculties and facilities, a given president would have deserved enduring praise for keeping his institution alive—a sizable number of colleges never did reopen after the war—and for regaining lost ground. The great presidents, admittedly, were spared the most crippling handicaps, but this does not explain their greatness, for not all presidents who were spared the worst problems achieved academic immortality. It was a time for greatness, but a good many presidents took the cautious, easier course of merely administering, conducting a holding operation, siding with the conservatives on their faculties and their governing boards, stifling campus radicalism, 1876 brand, and thus making the work of the radicals that much harder—and their achievement that much greater.

All the advances of civilization are presumably due to superior intelligence, seizing the opportunities at hand, as Emerson suggested, or serving as agent of the progress the culture is ready for, as some anthropologists prefer to put the case. The Centennial challenge to greatness lay in identifying both the cultural readiness and the opportunities. Specifically, the great college and university presidents in 1876 set themselves to the tasks of loosening and modernizing the curriculum, prying control from religious bigots, improving the quality of instruction, introducing utilitarian subject matter, creating the new dimensions of research and graduate training, reducing academic chaos, building sound financial support, and educating the public to the needs and the changes.

The librarian as educator, and the library as an educational tool, also made significant progress in 1876. The A.L.A.— American Library Association—was founded that fall, and so was its very useful publication, the *Library Journal*. These were two results of an impulse shared by an articulate handful of librarians virtually badgered into action by a radical thinker— Melvil Dewey.

No doubt the beginnings would have come, soon enough, through group pressure, and Dewey could have done little without like-minded men who were willing to cooperate. The culture was ready for the professionalizing of librarians and for what they call library science, which is actually a systematized uniform methodology. European culture was presumably no less ready for these innovations; what brought them first to the United States was no doubt the characteristic American impatience with laborious detail, together with the equally characteristic propensity for standardization and organization. Like the leading university presidents, Melvil Dewey was a young man contemptuous of tradition for tradition's sake, and eloquent enough to convince older and more cautious men of the necessity for change. To the many who were not fond of him as a person, the word "brash" was a suitable adjective; and his eloquence often bordered on glibness—but it worked.

Dewey was just twenty-five in 1876. Before his graduation from Amherst College in the class of 1874, he taught shorthand to fellow students—Lindsley's Tachygraphy, as it was called. The college authorities made him stop charging fees but he kept on teaching anyway—he was a true enthusiast. He also worked in the library, and devised a scheme of classification that he published in 1876 as *A Classification and Subject Index for Cataloguing and Arranging the Books and Pamphlets of a Library*—a classic in the field and still being reissued in modified form. Upon graduation he had been named assistant librarian, but he was a young man on his way and Amherst could not hold him long.

Week after week Dewey read the remarks and proposals of R. R. Bowker in his editorial columns of *Publisher's Weekly*. One Bowker suggestion of special interest to Dewey was for a catalogue of all American books in print as of July 1, 1876, with annual supplements thereafter. The project was delayed for two years, but the idea was typical of Bowker and the *American Catalogue* eventually proved of tremendous utility. On April 22 Bowker reported a proposal made to the London Academy for an international congress of librarians; this tipped the scales for Dewey, who hurried to New York for his first meeting with Bowker.

Put two enthusiasts together and something is pretty certain to happen, especially if both can think of new ideas by the minute. Dewey had his close knowledge of library problems; Bowker had the facilities for publication. Both knew numerous librarians and wrote to them, so persuasively that more than a hundred journeyed to Philadelphia in the first week of October, wisely avoiding the torrid Centennial summer, to organize a national group. Justin Winsor of the Boston Public Library was elected the A.L.A.'s first president, and Dewey its secretary and managing editor of the *Library Journal*. With Bowker's help he had already printed its first issue, in September, and the delegates liked it well enough to adopt it as their official magazine. From the outset it was a financial liability but of great help to the profession—or rather to the occupation it helped to convert into a profession.[41]

Journal and association also served to stimulate the growth of public libraries, which in 1876 began to multiply at an astonishing rate. According to *Public Libraries in the United States*, issued in 1876 as the first systematic tabulation of library holdings, there were in the nation 3,647 libraries with three hundred or more books, and the number of volumes available in all libraries—excluding private collections—was twelve million, about one book for every four people.[42] The largest holding was that of the Library of Congress, with an 1876 book count of 293,500; its increase over 1875 was 19,350, about 7 percent.[43] Broadening education meant more literate people and a growing body of potential readers; public libraries had no choice but to grow. Library methods were also forced to change, and a major improvement was the instituting of card catalogues. These were originally of many different sizes and shapes, and they varied in legibility with the handwriting of the cataloguer—for the typewriter was still a novelty. But despite this initial difficulty, the use of cards was a necessary adjunct to Dewey's "decimal system."

Library growth accelerated most rapidly in the nation's colleges. Harvard had by far the largest collection in 1876, with 228,000 titles; Yale was second, with half that number, and the figures trailed off rapidly in other institutions. But the extension of the elective system, the proliferation of courses, the discarding of the traditional system of recitation from a few fixed textbooks, and the establishment of graduate programs, all put a sudden strain on college libraries. Until 1876, and for some time afterwards on many campuses, there were no separate library buildings; the libraries had to share structures with laboratories, offices, and classrooms, as *Scribner's* and *Harper's Monthly*, competitively describing American colleges month by month throughout 1876, clearly showed in the numerous sketches illustrating the articles.

When a library was small, it was usually put in charge of a faculty member as one of his responsibilities; only when it grew large enough to require the full time of at least one person could there be much thought of making librarians professional. Not until 1887, when Dewey opened the country's first library school, at Columbia University, could would-be librarians find the means of formal preparation—one more example of the practical emphasis in higher education; but by 1876 the larger college libraries, at least, had competent and forward-looking management. The limitations of earlier days, when librarianship was a sort of avocation, are reflected in what may be the most famous of librarians' anecdotes. It concerns John L. Sibley, Harvard's head librarian until Justin Winsor replaced him in 1877, who was seen crossing the Yard one day, all smiles. When a friend asked him why he was so happy, he is said to have replied, "All the books are in their places except two. Professor Agassiz has them, and I'm on my way to get them."

In the *Atlantic Monthly* for October, 1876, John Fiske described the mechanics of the Harvard library in "A Librarian's Work," chiefly, so he said, to correct the notion that his job as assistant librarian was a sinecure. The regular routine kept him and twenty assistants busy full time. Seventeen of the assistants spent most of their time cataloging. He traced the course of a given book from the moment it arrived. First an entry was written in the record-book, showing the particular fund it was charged against—for books at Harvard were not bought out of general university funds but from the income of specific gifts and bequests. Next came the collation, meaning a close examination of the volume to identify the edition. The book was then shelved and recorded in the shelf catalog of its particular alcove. The general Harvard catalogue, originally in cumbersome volumes like those still in use at the British Museum, was in the process of being converted to cards; Ezra Abbott had begun the conversion in 1861, and after fifteen years some 50,000 volumes were yet to be cataloged, and as many pamphlets. New books were cataloged on cards at once, but the back-log absorbed any time remaining after new books had been processed. Abbott had wisely planned both an alphabetical listing by author and a subject index, a procedure that Europeans shrank from as much too bold, and one that barely survived a strong effort for discontinuance in 1877. Abbott's twin card catalogue by author and subject was already fifty-one feet long in 1876, with a total of 336 drawers.

Fiske was hardly a man to be content with describing the present; he went on to consider the future of the university library. "What will its dimensions be a century hence, when our books will probably be numbered by millions instead of thousands?" What if a fire should destroy the catalog? He suggested that cataloging by cards, improvement though it undoubtedly was, would prove only a temporary expedient, giving way to a printed catalog every ten years, with cards accumulating only between the decennial printings.[44] This proposal was never adopted; but his worries about space were soon justified. Gore Hall, supposedly reminiscent of King's College Chapel at Cambridge but more closely resembling a North River steamboat, as James Lowell once remarked, had been built specifically as a library in 1841 but was already too small for the collection. Fiske wondered if it would be large enough in 1976 to house even the catalog. An addition in 1877 provided space for 235,000 more books, and added stacks made room for another 240,000 in 1893; but by 1900 the saturation point was reached again.[45]

Most college libraries in 1876 were so much smaller than Harvard's that Fiske's speculations about the future may have seemed to some of his readers rather absurd; but by 1965, thirty-six university libraries owned more than a million volumes each, while Harvard, still the leader, counted about seven million. Even the libraries in very small colleges today have so many books that card catalogs are practical necessities, along with the professional librarians that were considered a luxury, or were nonexistent, for some years after 1876. As long as education was limited to a few traditional subjects, there was slight need to multiply library holdings; the education "revolution" of 1876 virtually forced a change, and Dewey and his colleagues were ready to act at just that time to be agents of the change.

Educators abroad often echo Dom Pedro's opinion about our "educational palaces," and seem convinced that only a very rich country can afford so extensive an educational system. Some American educators, however, are far from satisfied; in their opinion what John Hoyt wrote for 1876 still seems a valid criticism of the generality of Americans, as "an over-confident, procrastinating people, less appreciative of education, notwith-standing their claims on this score, than of their material progress and power." They would, moreover, counter the European view by insisting that Americans do not have this education because they are a rich people, but are rich because they have this education. Less over-confidence and procrastination, and more appreciation in the years since 1876, might have created an even higher per capita income and standard of living; but even so, the contributions made by education, especially through ap-plied university research and professional training, have been almost too vast to measure. It is surely no mere coincidence that the great forward progress in material wealth has paralleled the educational developments that were being pioneered in 1876. No other investment has ever yielded such dividends.

Emerson said in "Self-Reliance" that "an institution is the lengthened shadow of one man." By "man" he meant a non-con-formist, a self-reliant individual, indifferent to prevailing opinion and unafraid of the popular denunciation that radical behavior always attracts. Long shadows were being cast in 1876, by a handful of academic individualists who shared a vision that is now, because they dared, our reality. Now, almost a century later, it is easy to see both the magnitude of the Centennial need and the magnitude of achievement of the few who saw it then.

Footnotes for Chapter Eleven
A GREAT YEAR FOR EDUCATION

1. Merle Curti and Roderick Nash, *Philanthropy in the Shaping of American Higher Education* (New Brunswick: Rutgers Univer-sity Press, 1965).
2. Lawrence Cremin, *The Transformation of the School: Progres-sivism in American Education, 1876–1955* (New York: Alfred A. Knopf, 1961).
3. *Historical Statistics of the United States.*
4. *Twenty-third Annual Report of the State Superintendent of Com-mon Schools* (Augusta: State of Maine, 1876).
5. *Reports and Awards,* Vol. 8 of *Centennial Reports.*
6. *Schedule for the Preparation of Students' Work for the Centennial Exhibition* (Washington: National Education Association, 1875),

and *Suggestions Respecting the Educational Exhibit at . . . Centennial Exhibition* (Washington: Government Printing Office, 1875).

7. Daniel Coit Gilman, *The Launching of a University and Other Papers. A Sheaf of Remembrances* (New York: Dodd, Mead & Co., 1906), pp. 22–23.

8. "In order, however, to have a reservoir of students ready for this graduate work the original plan also called for an undergraduate school and this we have had from the beginning." Josephine Cole, Alumni Records Office, Johns Hopkins University, to author, March 2, 1959.

9. *Autobiography of Andrew Dickson White*, 2 vols. (New York: Century Co., 1905).

10. White, *The Warfare of Science* (New York: D. Appleton, 1876), later reissued as *A History of the Warfare of Science with Theology in Christendom*, 2 vols. (New York: D. Appleton, 1896).

11. Carl Becker, *Cornell University: The Founders and the Founding* (Ithaca: Cornell University Press, 1943).

12. Earl D. Ross, *Democracy's Colleges: The Land-Grant Movement in the Formative Stage* (Ames: Iowa State College Press, 1942).

13. Andrew D. White Papers, Cornell University.

14. Olivia Howard Dunbar, *A House in Chicago* (Chicago: University of Chicago Press, 1947). Among other Cornell coeds in 1876 were Martha Carey Thomas, who in 1894 became Bryn Mawr's first woman president, and Florence Kelley, pioneer in the struggle to end child labor; see Dorothy Rose Blumberg, *Florence Kelley: The Making of a Social Pioneer* (New York: Augustus M. Kelley, 1966), 21–23.

15. The *Cornellian* was published by the secret societies at Cornell.

16. Elmira *Daily Advertiser*, January 5, 8, 14, 1876.

17. "The Late Intercollegiate Literary Contest," *Harper's Weekly*, February 5, 1876.

18. Martha Goddard to White, January 10, 1876, in Andrew D. White Papers. Some people apparently believed that attending college adversely affected the health of young women, for the Chief of the Bureau of Statistics of Labor in Massachusetts took the trouble, in 1885, to canvass the alumnae of eight institutions; he found "no marked difference in general health from the average . . . of women generally." Carroll D. Wright, *Health Statistics of Female College Graduates* (Boston: Wright & Potter Printing Co., 1885).

19. Robert Lincoln Straker, *Horace Mann and Others: Chapters from the History of Antioch College* (Yellow Springs: Antioch Press, 1963).

20. Henry James, *Charles W. Eliot, President of Harvard University*

1869–1909, 2 vols. (Boston: Houghton Mifflin, 1930); Samuel Eliot Morison, *Three Centuries of Harvard* (Cambridge: Harvard University Press, 1937).

21. "The Manufacture of Doctors," *Scribner's Monthly*, 12 (August, 1876), 590.

22. *Harvard Quidquennial Catalogue: the Officers and Graduates 1636–1925* (Cambridge: Harvard University, 1925).

23. Darwin's opinion cited, without indication of source, in W. B. Gallie, *Peirce and Pragmatism* (Harmondsworth: Penguin Books, 1952), p. 12.

24. St. Paul *Pioneer-Press*, January 11, 1876.

25. Jurgen Herbst, *The German Historical School in American Scholarship* (Ithaca: Cornell University Press, 1965).

26. *The Letters of John Fiske*, ed. Ethel F. Fiske (New York: Macmillan, 1940).

27. John C. French, *A History of the University Founded by Johns Hopkins* (Baltimore: Johns Hopkins Press, 1946).

28. "Herbert Baxter Adams," *American Masters of Social Science*, ed. Howard W. Odum (New York: Henry Holt, 1927).

29. Huxley, "Address on University Education," collected in *American Addresses* (New York: D. Appleton, 1877).

30. Elmira *Daily Advertiser*, April 22, 1876.

31. *Charters and Basic Laws of Selected American Universities and Colleges*, ed. Edward C. Elliott and M. M. Chambers (New York: Carnegie Foundation for the Advancement of Teaching, 1934.

32. Merle Curti and Vernon Carstensen, *The University of Wisconsin*, 2 vols. (Madison, University of Wisconsin Press, 1949).

33. James Gray, *History of the University of Minnesota* (Minneapolis: University of Minnesota Press, 1951).

34. E. H. Libby, "Massachusetts Agricultural College," *Scribner's Monthly*, 12 (October, 1876), 836–849.

35. Simon Newcomb, "Abstract Science in America, 1776–1876," *North American Review*, 122 (January–February, 1876), 88–123.

36. A general survey of higher education in the South after the Civil War is given in F. Merton Coulter, *The South during Reconstruction 1865–1877* (Baton Rouge: Louisiana State University Press, 1947). The South Carolina situation is reported in Hampton Jarrell, *Wade Hampton and the Negro: the Road Not Taken* (Columbia: University of South Carolina Press, 1949).

37. Phillips Russell, *The Woman Who Rang the Bell: the Story of Cornelia Phillips Spencer* (Chapel Hill: University of North Carolina Press, 1948).

38. Kemp P. Battle, *History of the University of North Carolina*, 2 vols.

(Raleigh: Edwards & Broughton, 1907–1912); and Memorabilia in the University of North Carolina Library.

39. *Harper's Weekly*, January 1, 1876.

40. Charles W. Thwing, "College Expenses," *Scribner's Monthly*, 13 (November, 1876), 83–85.

41. Fremont Rider, *Melvil Dewey* (Chicago: American Library Association, 1944), Volume 6 of *American Library Pioneers;* Edward McClurg Fleming, *R. R. Bowker, Militant Liberal* (Norman: University of Oklahoma Press, 1952). A detailed account of the planning for the A.L.A. organizational meeting in Edward G. Holley, *Raking the Historic Coals: The A.L.A. Scrapbook of 1876* (Chicago: Lakeside Press, 1967). Beta Phi Mu Chapbook, No. 8.

42. U. S. Department of the Interior, Bureau of Education, *Public Libraries in the United States; Their History, Condition, and Management* (Washington: Government Printing Office, 1876).

43. *Harper's Weekly*, January 29, 1876.

44. John Fiske, "A Librarian's Work," *Atlantic Monthly*, 38 (October, 1876), 480–491. Other details drawn from "Cambridge on the Charles," *Harper's Monthly*, 52 (January, 1876), 191–202.

45. *The Library of Harvard University*, 4th ed. (Cambridge: Harvard University, 1934).

12

A Mighty Fortress

"I DID NOT hear one dull or tedious sermon." So wrote John Leng after his return to Scotland. He was honest enough, however, to admit that he sought out the men with the biggest names —in Boston, Phillips Brooks at Trinity Church; in Brooklyn, Henry Ward Beecher (whom he described as "a broad set, florid, healthy man with bright eyes and white hair"); in Chicago, Dwight L. Moody at one of his weekday meetings in Fanevil Hall. One man Leng had never heard of, the Reverend Professor Jenkins of Amherst College, struck him as the finest of them all. He was equally well impressed by church singing in America, whether it was the great choir in the Mormon Tabernacle or the congregation at Beecher's Plymouth Church. "America," he concluded enthusiastically, "is a Christian Land." [1]

John Leng was hardly alone in this opinion. It was shared by most Centennial Protestants, especially the members of the major sects—Methodist, Baptist, Presbyterian, Episcopal. They might have been shocked to learn that only one American in five belonged to any church, even though this was a much better showing than a century before, when churches enrolled only one person in eight in New England, one in fifteen in the Middle Colonies, one in twenty in the South. If he noticed the Continental Sabbath in the middle western cities he visited, where Catholics were numerous, he was not aware of how much it disturbed the Protestants in the East, who viewed it as an example of the insidious Catholic threat; nor did he realize, when he listened raptly to the Tabernacle choir, that Mormonism was held in equal reprehension. He did notice the general Protestant aversion to the new scientific hypotheses; he quoted at length from one sermon that was sharply critical of Darwin, Tyndall, and Huxley. But he did not mention, and may not have known, how very few of the working class attended the Protestant churches, or how coolly they would have been welcomed if they did attend.

No visit of a few months, of course, could yield an expert knowledge of American religion, which has had a history at least as complex as that of the political or economic spheres. The dominant Protestants, may be supposed to have known little more than Leng discovered; knowledge of church history is seldom a condition of membership. Pious historians in the early 1800s had painted a picture that Protestants liked to believe was true but was full of obvious errors. For one thing, at no time were church members in the majority during the Colonial period. The Great Awakening of 1726, with George Whitefield the central figure, produced a momentary upswing in religious interest but, after prompting the founding of Dartmouth and Princeton, it soon subsided. The Great Revival sparked by the Wesley brothers in the late 1780s was more durable, yet in 1800 only 7 percent of the population belonged to churches, and the memoirs of such stalwart preachers as Peter Cartwright reveal the widespread antagonism to religion, especially in frontier regions. The notion of universal piety, and a Bible in every home, was a pious fraud. A more accurate picture would represent heroic itinerant preachers, uneducated but devoted, risking every peril including tar and feathers in their stubborn uphill campaign to convert an essentially irreligious people.[2]

One of the numerous reviews of the progress of American

religious institutions since 1776 prompted by the Centennial was a lengthy article on religion in the *North American Review*. Congregationalists, though confined to New England, were the country's largest religious denomination in 1776, with about seven hundred churches; Baptists were second, with three hundred; Episcopalians third; Presbyterians fourth; and then a number of smaller groups—Dutch Reformed, Roman Catholic, Lutheran, Moravian, Methodist, Jewish, Quaker, and Mennonite. There was one church for every 1,700 people. By 1876, when there was a church for every 500 people, the order was quite different: Methodists the most numerous, followed by Baptists, Presbyterians, Roman Catholics, Christians, Lutherans, Congregationalists, and Episcopalians. The Methodist priority symbolized by the choice of Bishop Simpson to give the prayer at the opening ceremonies at the Exhibition, was clearly the result of the proselyting zeal and appeal to the emotions adopted by the Wesley brothers and subsequent Methodist clergymen. In general, speculative theology had yielded to pulpit reliance on the Bible.[3] Orthodoxy had shifted its base, from the Calvinistic logic of the Puritans to the authority of the Bible. Doctrinal differences, meanwhile, had to be maintained to distinguish one Protestant church from another.

Some people in the Centennial year could well recall the Panic of 1857 and the revival that began, oddly enough, in Wall Street, where penitent bankrupt stockbrokers organized curbside prayer meetings. The revival spread, aided by a stirring hymn, "Stand up, stand up for Jesus!" By 1860 church membership had reached a peak far above anything ever known earlier—23 percent of the nation's people. But the Civil War distracted attention and the percentage gradually declined until 1890, when the Social Gospel, ignored or ridiculed by orthodox Protestants in 1876, broke down the middle-class exclusiveness and opened church doors to everyone.[4]

Dominant Protestantism, in 1876, accepted several notions as being so obviously true that they needed no arguments to support them. Calvinism was on the wane, but its stress on the individual conscience still served to smother the concept of brotherhood. Individual salvation was what really mattered. Emerson, unorthodox though he was in most respects, had expressed social orthodoxy when he asked, in his essay "Self-Reliance," "Are these my poor?" Individualism called for determined hard work that would make a man independent; poverty was a sign of weakness. In a land of unlimited resources and opportunity, failure could easily seem to be the result of inadequate virtue, if not of viciousness. Being poor, indeed, flouted what the orthodox considered divine intent, and to welcome the laboring classes to church membership would have meant weekly association with individuals who, by remaining poor, were flaunting their essential sinfulness. The opposite side of the coin was the general notion, in the Puritan Ethic of long standing, that success was proof of essential virtue.

The Emersonian position had more validity in the 1830s, perhaps, than forty years later, when the great majority of the population no longer lived on farms and in villages. The great majority of Protestants, however, still lived outside the cities in 1876, and considered the cities to be wicked and threats to the American way of life as they knew it. Rural self-sufficiency, vital to Emerson's golden rule of individualism, could not work under city conditions, where functions were delegated. But what Protestant America by and large was not ready to comprehend in 1876 was that the urban poor were poor not from lack of virtue but because, arriving as penniless immigrants, unable to speak English or to adapt at once to American patterns, and easily victimized by the owner classes, they were in no position to exhibit their virtue in success. Native-born Americans, in their migration from farm to city were hardly better off under unfamiliar city conditions. But, one author has expressed it, "Protestant Christianity, bound by doctrine and tradition to spiritual religion alone, . . . necessarily ignored the problem of human welfare in the great cities." [5]

The rapid urban growth, far from challenging rural Protestants to feel responsible, was rather a source of alarm. But in general the Protestant majority was complacent; long success had made it so. A few radicals questioned this success and came to believe that it was more material than spiritual; some even charged that the churches were being corrupted by their attraction to contemporary business practices. Theodore Parker, in 1858, boldly asserted that "no institution in America is more corrupt than her churches," and added that "no thirty thousand men and women are so bigoted and narrow as the thirty thousand ministers." It was scandalous talk, but easy to discount because Parker was well-known as a radical. But others had said much the same thing earlier—Stephen Colwell, for instance, whose book in 1851, *New Themes for the Protestant Churches*, detailed Presbyterianism's outright encouragement of greed and selfishness and accused Protestants in general of compromising with worldly men, and of assuming "many of the maxims and practices of business." People could forget Parker's outrageous sermon, but Colwell's book continued to be read, and to challenge complacency.[6] It never gained the wide currency, however, of a certain popular anecdote with the same theme: Storekeeper to his son, "John! Have you watered the milk? Have you sanded the sugar? Then come to prayers." [7]

Radicalism was whatever departed too far from the orthodox center, whether in extreme new theologies like Mormonism, Christian Science, or Ethical Culture, or in the efforts of a minority of "do-gooders" to tamper with the economic status-quo, or in the frontal attacks of such men as Parker and Colwell. New ideas from Europe were quickly dismissed as radical, and probably dangerous, because Europe was considered morally corrupt and the breeding-ground of pernicious notions—like the Continental Sabbath. In the rural Northeast, especially in New England, as we have seen, strict sabbatarianism prevailed. Were it not for the practice of eating cold on Sunday the beans and brown bread and Indian pudding that made up a traditional Saturday supper, Protestant housewives would otherwise have been hard pressed to prepare meals between the services—morning, afternoon, and evening—that occupied most of the Sabbath. It was a time-honored pattern that must have seemed to these people what God intended Sunday to be. But the opposite pattern, of early mass and the rest of Sunday free for relaxation and simple pleasure, was just as logical an interpretation of the Fourth Commandment. The two concepts collided at the Centennial Exhibition when the management decided to keep it closed on Sunday to the great bewilderment of many newer Americans. Then, when General Hawley, the president of the Centennial Commission (and a Connecticut Protestant), conducted the Emperor of Brazil and Sweden's Prince Oscar on a private tour of the grounds, one Sunday in July, the incident drew some very indignant comments.[8]

Most Catholic bishops counseled their people to refrain from open arguments with Protestants, and in fact discouraged Catholic participation in interfaith action of any sort—thus keeping the gulf wide between the two great branches of Christendom. There could not, in any case, be much interfaith activity, when most Protestants were middle-class and lived outside the big cities, while most Catholics were urban workingmen. Nativistic opposition before the Civil War had strengthened Catholic unity and had made Catholics wary of Protestants. With the steady increase in immigration, mostly from Catholic countries, Catholicism came to be thought of as "the Church of the Immigrant," a pejorative phrase in orthodox Protestant thinking, and one that for some Catholics suggested a lack of Church concern for certain other groups, notably the country's Negroes. Protestant leaders did not need to advise their congregations not to mix with Catholics; prejudice already existed, based in part on Catholic acknowledgement of the supremacy of the Pope, a foreigner, but also on the Catholic practice of engaging in the rescue of souls in city slums [9]—an activity that only the most radical of Protestant clergymen dreamed of undertaking.

Sermons in Protestant churches seldom attacked Catholicism outright, but their common theme of defending Protestant orthodoxy was a constant irritant to Catholics. A typical priest, making his rounds of the city's poorest people, meanly paid or unemployed, and doing his best to extend a little solace, could hardly be expected to applaud the familiar Protestant sermon with its aspersions on the undeserving poor, or to appreciate the newspaper custom of printing, on Mondays, generous extracts from such sermons. The common phrase "poor but honest" reflected a general orthodox notion that poverty and honesty did not usually occur together. It must have been easy for Catholics to believe that Protestant preachers were in league with the owners of factories, and were deliberately justifying the current starvation wages. Henry Ward Beecher was as often quoted as any other Protestant sermonizer. Again and again he professed good will toward the workingmen—as long as they kept their place. It was not God's will, he was positive, that they join labor unions. In one sermon in 1877 he announced a truism of Protestant orthodoxy: "God intended the great to be great and the little to be little." Labor unions were wicked because, he said, they destroyed liberty. But bad habits were also to be avoided: "I do not say that a dollar a day is enough to support a working man (who insists on) smoking and drinking beer. . . . But the man who cannot live on bread and water is not fit to live." [10] It is unlikely that any of his Plymouth Church audience would ever have to live on bread and water. Beecher's words were hardly welcome among the city poor for whom a dollar a day *was* common, and who knew, from newspaper reports, that his salary as pastor of Plymouth Church was $20,000, and his annual income from all sources was at least $45,000.[11]

Men who preached the laissez-faire, anti-labor doctrine, and the hundreds of thousands of church members who approved and paid the ministers' salaries, seemed unaware that the doctrine was in any way vulnerable. They would probably have laughed at anyone who predicted its overthrow within a quarter of a century. But Centennial orthodoxy contained one element that did much to cause eventual change—the Emersonian, Transcendental, heterodox belief in human perfectibility. Orthodoxy of an older variety, explicit in the writings of Emerson's friend and neighbor, Nathaniel Hawthorne, denied the possibility of real improvement. But the national faith in progress, supported by the rapid material advance made in the past two centuries, led people to think that God not only favored the American experiment but intended individuals—if they were Americans—to be better and better. The failures were a reproach to the whole society, and in time the Protestants swung around to the view that a better social environment would raise the less favored toward their highest potential of ethical, esthetic, and material aspirations. There would always be some poor people, as Jesus once said, but the number might be whittled down, leaving fewer to be tempted into vice and crime. Such thinking, however, was radical in the extreme in 1876, when any social action was condemned as interference with the gradual development of God's plan for America. Human tampering with that plan would only endanger its success.[12]

Catholic efforts to ameliorate slum conditions were one example of the tampering opposed by Centennial orthodoxy. Another was the planned society in Utah, where the Mormons, after long harassment by the "Gentiles" in the East, were free to build the theocratic state of Joseph Smith's inspiration. The success of the Catholics in the big cities, and the success of the Mormons in converting barren land into a garden, undermined the theory of laissez-faire—and heightened old-line Protestant resentment. In quite a different way, the orthodox notion of divine guidance was brought under attack in 1876 by the formation of the National Liberal League, which opposed a Constitutional amendment, first suggested in 1863, that would assert the supremacy of God and Revelation. Had this pious monstrosity succeeded, it might have perpetuated the dominance of orthodoxy. The same impulse later added the words "under God" to the national oath of allegiance; but an oath lacks the force of an amendment.

The notion of divine guidance and special favor, inspiring to Pilgrims and Puritans in the seventeenth century and reiterated by the historian George Bancroft in the early nineteenth, has not been one to die easily in a country of steady material progress. A parallel notion, that Protestant thinking has been a constant, consistent force in the shaping of American institutions, especially the political, has been no less durable, even though the record fails to support it. The Declaration of Independence and other documents of the Revolutionary period owe much more to the radical eighteenth-century Deism that Centennial Protestants prided themselves for having suppressed.[13] But dominant groups have a habit of assuming that their own ideas are alone right, and, indeed, have always been the sole, unchanging truth. A peculiar obtuseness is detectable in the high-riding Protestants of 1876—an almost total inability to read the past and to see that vast changes in religious thinking and behavior are among the best examples of the steady evolution of American life.

If there has been any notable continuity, it has been the continuity of radicals, courageous individuals forced to fight every inch of the way against defenders of entrenched tradition, and to wear the badge of ignominy that conservatives were only too eager to pin upon them. The struggle is never quite the same at different times. The Colonial pattern of locally established churches was repressive to whoever argued, then, for the radically-different pattern that was the norm after 1800, of churches free to enter any state and of no one church enjoying legal preference in any state. Anne Hutchinson's radicalism in the seventeenth century was entirely different from that of the radical Protestants in the nineteenth century; the fight she waged (and lost) was far removed from the religious battles of 1876.

One of the most interesting radical thinkers of the Centennial period was a mixture of quack, crank, and idealist named De Robigné Mortimer Bennett. At fourteen he joined the Shaker colony at New Lebanon, in upstate New York, and in time became the colony's physician. In 1846 he seceded from the colony, moved to Cincinnati, married, and began selling Dr. Bennett's Quick Cure, Golden Liniment, Worm Lozenges, Root and Plant Pills—with the same great success that many enterprising nostrum-vendors enjoyed in those gullible times. The money poured in, but he tired of the racket and in 1873 began publishing *Truthseeker*, combining freethinking notions "borrowed" from Thomas Paine's *Age of Reason* with lively sketches of prominent living clergymen; one victim sued him for libel, and Bennett was found guilty and sentenced to thirteen months in prison. There, following an old tradition, he began his autobiography, which he published in 1876 as *The World's Sages, Infidels, and Thinkers*. It was hardly one of the significant books of the year, but it was an effective exposition of liberal ideas in religion and ethics and a tangible proof that Deism, supposedly killed off by orthodoxy, was not yet in its grave.

Orthodoxy had also routed Transcendentalism—or rather, had never let it flourish. Octavius Brooks Frothingham brought out this movement's first comprehensive history in 1876, *Transcendentalism in New England*. The reviewer for the August *Scribner's* felt that Frothingham was too negative, giving the movement less than its due and belittling its influence, and too vague about his own positive teachings on God and human destiny. Nevertheless, the critic thought,

> he is clear enough in his rejection of the brutish and low-lived ethics and metaphysics which threaten to animalize

man and to turn his schools of science into mocking sepul-
chres of his decaying faiths and buried hopes.[14]

The arrogance of triumphant orthodoxy would be enough, one
might think, to make a one-time Transcendentalist feel something of an anachronism—like Emerson, who still had six years
to live, or Bronson Alcott, who still had twelve. But Frothingham was not one to lapse into dignified silence; he published
Religion of Humanity in 1872, biographies of Theodore Parker
and George Ripley in 1874 and 1882, and served, from 1867 to
1878, as president of the Free Religious Association.

This Association, which began its short life in Boston, drew
largely from Unitarians who felt that their church had lost the
drive that had made it a vital force in the early years of the
century. It was like history repeating, however, for Unitarianism
had always been a seed-bed for more aggressive action. Emerson,
to cite the most conspicuous example, had outgrown even its
extreme liberalism early in life. Almost as notable an example
was that of Orestes Brownson, who was a Presbyterian minister
before becoming a Unitarian but drifted into Catholicism, where
his criticism of Catholic conservatism, in his editorial columns of
Brownson's Quarterly Review, displeased many Catholics.
Brownson died in 1876, without many friends and without
much being said about him in the obituaries.

The Free Religious Association represented a continuity of
liberal Protestant involvement that Brownson once shared but
had deserted when he became a Catholic. The Association fused
the old Trandscendentalist principle of thinking that was entirely divorced from any established creed with an ethical, ideal-
ized version of Darwinism; its slogans were solidarity (suggesting Christian Union), progress (echoing the Emersonian faith in
human improvement), and the Golden Rule, which was notably
in abeyance in Centennial America.[15] But the Association had no
concrete program, nothing for members to turn their energies
to; ideas, alone, however interesting, can seldom maintain group
enthusiasm. Considerably more effective, because it did develop
a positive program, was one of the major products of 1876,
Ethical Culture. Its stated aim resembles that of the Free Religious Association: "to assert the supreme importance of the

ethical factor in all relations of life, personal, social, national, and international, apart from theological or metaphysical considerations." The concept of religion freed of historical precedent, dogma, and ritual, religion without the conditions that tend to reduce it to formalism and unthinking acceptance, was often enough expressed by individuals and organized groups, but Ethical Culture was distinctive for implementing such idealism. It held its followers, by the establishment of free kindergartens and adult education. The founder, Felix Adler, was a dynamic organizer with a contagious enthusiasm. One further ingredient of success was the urban setting; New York needed just such a movement far more than smaller cities did. The Ethical Culture Society welcomed individuals of all sects and did not insist that they break their other ties; it was a practical kind of Christian Union, one that could work without affecting any church's membership list.[16]

If it seems odd that Felix Adler, a Jew, is regarded as a pioneering practitioner in social Christianity, the oddity shrinks when we recall, first, that Hebraism is the oldest ethical religion and second, that world Jewry has survived by implementing its commitment to mutuality. Like other unfamiliar newcomers, Jews found in America the double stimulus of social hostility and economic discrimination; and their response to the stimulus is a stirring chapter in the great American story of group adaptation. Their chapter has a special quality, as Oscar Handlin has pointed out in *The Uprooted* and other books: these were mostly people from farms and small villages in Eastern Europe, accustomed to a traditional regimen and totally unaccustomed to self-determination; in America they had to make their adjustment in the most urban of environments, Manhattan Island, with no predetermined patterns to rely upon. The Protestants long dominant in the nation were also mostly a farm and village people, but unlike the Jewish immigrants they were not forced to face the urban problem, or even to be concerned about its existence. It can almost be said—if we can disregard, for the moment, what the Catholics were doing for the urban poor— that America's Protestants left to the Jews the invention of social Christianity.

One advantage which the Jewish community had over some

..e gradual migration from 1800 to 1870 that
. eight thousand persons to America, and the
..nost of these to become economically secure,
..hy, before the great Jewish migration began. A
..ic in 1868, a famine in Poland in 1869, a pogrom
.. region in 1871—these, as well as poverty, made the
..tern Europe extremely receptive to the low rates
..by German steamship companies that had been losing
..n Central Europe, with the result that some forty
.. Jews crossed the Atlantic in the 1870s. The rate con-
..to increase until by 1914 an estimated one third of Eu-
.. Jews had become Americans; but it was the great first
.., in the 1870s, that faced the greatest problems and de-
..es, no doubt, the greatest credit. New York was the "Prom-
..d City" but as a city it was hardly ready to accommodate so
..any of them all at once.

The synagogues, pre-eminent among them the fashionable
Temple Emanu-El, soon reached the limits of their ability to
help the newcomers. Nor could the wealthy older families—Alt-
mans and Strauses, Sterns and Bloomingdales—carry the rapidly
increasing burden, although without their help the situation
would have been much worse than it was. What the Jewish
community did, with its minority of "old-timers" and its majority "just off the boat," was to organize a large number of
lansmanschafts—group ventures of a wide variety, some merely
fraternal, some resembling modern credit unions, some offering
medical care, some providing vocational training. In 1874, when
the year-old depression deepened, several of these groups
merged to form the powerful United Hebrew Charities. To a
great extent, the Jews themselves *made* New York their "Promised City." [17]

Felix Adler had been expected to succeed his scholarly father,
Rabbi Samuel Adler, at Temple Emanu-El, but after study in
Europe he came to find formal Judaism and even Jewish-style
Unitarianism untenable. He was most at home among Protestant
intellectuals, especially college professors who, like himself, had
outgrown established orthodoxies. Yet when he conceived his
scheme for a Society for Ethical Culture, and set about organizing it, he leaned heavily on the aid and advice of the nation's

best-known Jew, Joseph Seligman, the president of Te
Emanu-El. From the outset, then, this society that firmly
claimed itself non-denominational, and enlisted mostly Pro
tants, had a solid grounding in Jewish tradition and principles.

The Protestants who joined the Society for Ethical Cultu
were obviously not orthodox. For the only human welfare tha
concerned most Protestants in the cities was their own vis-à-vi
the pressure from Catholics and Jews and other groups they
considered un-American. The course of action that some of
them adopted was to move en masse to outlying sections, away
from the undesirables, and to take their churches with them.
Others, where it was feasible, fortified themselves behind invisi-
ble walls, forming demographic enclaves from which they could
bar the unwelcome by the same methods they used to exclude
them from jobs other than menial ones. A particularly notable
method was the development of what were called "fashionable
churches," where impoverished Protestants were no more eligible for membership than Jews or Catholics. These were the
churches that so impressed John Leng, with their golden-
tongued preachers and their professional choirs. Such churches
deliberately sought to illustrate the divine approval of successful
Protestantism in a Protestant America. Nowhere in the hinter-
lands could there be such conspicuous examples—or so formidable a barrier to social action by Christians. Religion, in these
famous city churches, became social in quite another sense: at
their services young Protestants on the way up the economic
ladder could rub shoulders with those already on the upper
rungs, and not have to give a moment's thought to those who
had never attained even the lowest foot-hold.

The element of the fashionable existed in Catholicism, too, but
without any sense of possible cooperation with Protestants. The
Catholics could boast of James McCloskey, for example, the
Archbishop of New York who in 1875 became the first American cardinal, but the Protestants ignored him, pointing instead to
their own most eminent preachers, like Henry Ward Beecher
and arguing that they could be famous without the accolade of
Rome. Protestants could also ignore the *American Catholic Review*, founded in 1876, and *The Faith of Our Fathers*, published
the same year by James Gibbons, later a cardinal; it was the first

American exposition of the Catholic position, and over the years it sold more than two million copies.[18] It did little for the Catholic image among Protestants when, on June 2, 1875, James A. Healy was consecrated at the Cathedral in Portland, Maine, as the first Nego bishop in the United States.[19] There were Negro bishops in the Methodist ranks, but only in the Afro-American department; and in no Protestant denomination would it have been conceivable, in the 1870s, to elevate a Negro above white officials. Bishop Healy represented for orthodox Protestants just another of the alien, suspicious practices of Catholicism.

Not all Protestant thinking, however, was so stereotyped. In the decade before 1876 a small nucleus of Protestant radicals began to build the foundation of the movement that led to the triumph of the Social Gospel by the end of the century. Catholics and Jews were not quite alone in "applied Christianity."

Before 1865, the only socially active Protestant agencies were the Young Men's Christian Association and the Young Women's Christian Association, founded in 1851 and 1858 respectively. During the Civil War a nonsectarian United States Sanitary Commission was organized to alleviate hardship and physical suffering among the Union armies, and at the war's end it was renamed the American Christian Commission. War conditions permitted good working relations among the various churches, but with peace the old dissensions re-emerged, the notion in each denomination that it alone was the exclusive Church of Christ. Cornell's President Andrew White collided with this notion when he tried to implement the nonsectarian principle in Cornell's Chapel services. The American Christian Commission, after a survey, concluded that Protestant missionary enterprise was feeble, ineffective, and hampered by obsolete methods and minimal cooperation. The orthodox majority clung to a system of relief that humiliated the people needing help.

With the growing awareness that narrow sectarianism was the chief barrier to the progress of Christianity, several groups were formed to encourage unified effort. In 1867 the Evangelical Alliance of England formed an American branch, which had as its primary purpose the promotion of Christian Union. Five years later, the Christian Labor Union (the CLU) was established, with solid financial backing from T. Wharton Collens of

New Orleans, a "Utopian Catholic" who in 1876 published *The Eden of Labor; or The Christian Utopia.* The CLU was radical enough, in orthodox thinking, and realistic enough, by later standards, to realize that Protestantism would never measure up to true Christian standards until it abandoned its exclusionist policy toward working people. The CLU sponsored another group, the obviously pro-labor Eight Hour League Convention, in 1874, again, a direct challenge to status-quo Protestants.

The CLU effectively dramatized the plight of workingmen and the urban crisis. One CLU leader, E. H. Rogers, wrote a book in 1876, *Like Unto Me,* which described that plight and suggested ways it might be alleviated. In fact, a few clergymen had independently anticipated Rogers' proposals; others adopted them later. Thomas K. Beecher, the brother of Henry Ward Beecher and Harriet Beecher Stowe, and the brother-in-law of Mark Twain, was active in this respect in Elmira, New York, where for fifty years, 1850 to 1900, he was pastor of an independent Congregational church. In the 1870s he persuaded his congregation to raise the money for a new church building equipped for social service—including free baths for those of the members who had no bathing facilities at home.[20]

By 1876, the church building designed for worship services only was approaching obsolescence. The Sunday School movement that was barely half a century old had forced changes—a remodeling of the church basement, or an addition to the main building, or, in some cases, a separate new building for the use of the Sunday School. The Mormons in Utah had from the beginning erected next to their churches, separate buildings for recreation. Such plans avoided the violation of the sanctuary, for where space was at a premium, Bible classes, graded Sunday school classes, the organized church women, and other such groups had to invade the church proper, to the genuine distress of the devout. When it was proposed that further demands be put on the structure, the distress mounted, sometimes creating a split in an ordinarily harmonious congregation.

A good example of this was Edward Eggleston's non-denominational Church of the Christian Endeavor in Brooklyn, New York. Eggleston had earlier, in Minnesota, been a very successful Sunday School man, and in Brooklyn he soon built up one of the largest Sunday Schools in the city, with more than twelve hundred members. What attracted more attention, however, was his Endeavor Club, open to all men, whether members of the church or not, and offering various kinds of recreation (including a shooting gallery), a good library, and financial advice. When Eggleston was criticized in letters to the editors of local newspapers, he replied that if he thought opening a grocery store in the church would salvage some defeated souls, he would open one the next morning. But before five years were out he had to abandon his enterprise under mounting pressure from conservatives within the congregation; the 1870s were not congenial to either the non-denominational principle or to church programs for social welfare.[21]

Nor were mission churches, specifically serving the city's poor, any more certain of continued support, although one that did succeed was Holy Trinity Church in New York, ably managed by the Rev. Stephen H. Thyng, Jr. Any new departure roused the uneasy opposition of the orthodox. Even so, Bible classes steadily grew in number, along with such other phenomena as laymen's institutes and the use of lay helpers in church services; antiprostitution campaigns; the Women's Christian Temperance Union, founded in 1874; and the American branch of the Salvation Army, created in 1878. Some of these endeavors fell by the wayside; others, including the movement toward Christian Union, held on, albeit tenuously, until conditions were somewhat more favorable.

Proper Protestants, it seems safe to say, were generally unaware in 1876 of Felix Adler, or of the Christian Labor Union, or of the plight of working people in the big cities. They were somewhat more aware of non-denominational experiments, Bible classes, church clubs, and the growing numbers of Jews and Catholics in the population. But they were distinctly and uncomfortably aware of insidious alien ideas and their proponents. One of the feared names was that of the French writer Auguste Comte, known in the United States as early as 1853 through a condensed translation of his *Cours de philosophie positive*. By 1876, nineteen years after his death, a new English translation, *System of Positive Polity*,[22] was arousing deep concern. The cause of this concern was Comte's proposal for a new theology based on science, with humanity as its god. Comte, who incidentally was the coiner of the term "sociology," saw three stages in man's thinking: theological (or authoritarian), metaphysical (or speculative), and positivistic (or scientific). Only in the third and final stage, he believed, could man know his proper position in exact, demonstrable, predictable terms. American Protestantism in 1876, hostile to the implications of recent scientific thought and the infant social sciences, stood somewhere between the theological and the metaphysical in Comte's scale. Any new theology based on the disturbing scientific hypotheses was recognized as a threat to orthodoxy and to the entire Protestant system as it then existed in the United States.

Best known of the scientific hypotheses that Comte's positivistic theology was to lean on was of course Darwinism. This is not to say, however, that Darwin's ideas were well or widely understood, for the Civil War, beginning just two years after the publication of *Origin of Species*, deferred any such debate as the book touched off in England. The visit of T. H. Huxley in the summer of 1876 briefly brought the hypothesis into national prominence. In addition, the versatile John Fiske was doing his best to become the leading interpreter of the "new science." One of his books, *Outlines of Cosmic Philosophy (1874)*, earned him the reputation of infidelism. During 1876 he turned from the sciences themselves to their implications for religion. No real conflict, he tried to make his readers realize, existed between religion and science; instead, he recognized only a struggle between more-crude and less-crude opinions. Although the more crude were often defended in the name of religion, the eventual triumph of the less crude he considered inevitable. "The religious sense," he told his *Atlantic* audience in February, 1876, "is as yet too feebly developed in most of us; but certainly in no preceding age have men taken up the work of life with more earnestness or with more real faith in the unseen than at the present day, when so much of what was once deemed all-important knowledge has been consigned to the limbo of mythology." Now that science, especially geology and astronomy, had removed the need for seeking supra-natural causes for the working out of God's plan, men were free to develop their religious instincts in more constructive directions.[23]

Fiske was also the foremost American champion of Herbert Spencer, who interpreted evolution most optimistically. Every change, Spencer thought, took man a little nearer to eventual perfection; human society in the large was also evolving toward its perfect form. All that people needed to do was give divine law complete freedom to operate, for this was the one certain guarantee of social advance. Within a quarter of a century perceptive Americans were to realize the dismal results of such uncontrolled laissez-faire and, in their disillusion, to begin groping for other paths. What was really wrong with Spencerian logic was that a dominant minority could foist off on the entire economy its own interpretation of divine law. No absolute parallel is possible between biological and social processes, yet survival of the fittest, borrowed from Darwin and applied to economics, was generally accepted in 1876 as both scientific and divinely ordained. Some very eminent men openly defended the prevailing business anarchy: William Graham Sumner, a onetime Episcopal minister who in 1872 became professor of political and social science at Yale, persuasively argued the case for extreme laissez-faire and denounced all efforts to interfere with the status quo.[24] Christian ethics had no such academic spokesman, such notions being radical in the orthodox lexicon of 1876, wherein the one genuine sin was being poor.

Darwinism, however, produced a curious ambivalence: the same people who gladly adopted the notion of survival of the fittest to support their own cut-throat business competition rejected indignantly the theory that mankind had developed from lesser forms of life in a protracted struggle between more fit and less fit species. Huxley, in the last week of his American visit, gave three lectures at Chickering Hall in New York on the evidence for evolution. He drew heavily upon the fossil collections of Othniel Marsh, professor of paleontology at Yale. Marsh's most striking exhibit, showing the development of the horse, was the best evidence yet available anywhere in the world, of the orderly process of evolutionary change, and Huxley made the most of it. Newspaper reaction to his lecture series, however, centered on the term "Miltonic," which he used for the first of three theories of the origin of life. An editorial witticism was soon parroted in newspapers everywhere: "John

Milton and not Moses wrote the best book of Genesis—according to Huxley." The New York *Sun* accused him of evasion and suggested that "instead of attacking Moses over the shoulders of John Milton, he should strike at Moses face to face." The editors of *Scientific American,* who might have been expected to defend him, were no better satisfied; it was a waste of time, they wrote, and an insult to American intelligence, to attack the six-day theory of creation which "every American school boy knows to be inconsistent with the commonest facts of geology." [25]

A typical orthodox opinion appeared in an editorial, probably by Josiah Holland, in the December *Scribner's:* "It seems to us repugnant to human reason that a low form of life uninformed by a higher life, has the power to evolve a form of life higher than itself. . . . If this is all; if we are only animals; if we have no responsibility; if our destiny does not take hold of eternity . . . Life loses all its meaning." To suppose the earth began as scientists now say "is to suppose an absurdity which no healthy reason, healthily working, can possibly accept." [26]

It was this kind of black-and-white thinking, and the orthodox suspicion of all new scientific findings, that Andrew White sought to rout in his *Warfare of Science.* He felt so strongly that he italicized two sentences in his introductory chapter:

> *In all modern history, interference with science in the supposed interest of religion, no matter how conscientious such interference may have been, has resulted in the direst evils both to religion and to science—and invariably. And, on the other hand, all untrammeled scientific investigation, no matter how dangerous to religion some of its stages may have seemed, for the time, to be, has invariably resulted in the highest good of religion and of science.*

"But logic is not history," and science has been held back by well-meant ignorance. The terms "atheist" and "infidel" have, through the centuries, been applied to "almost every man who has done anything new for his fellow-men." White did not insist that the fault lay with religion, but rather with "the short-sighted views which narrow-minded, loud-voiced men are ever prone to mix in with religion, and to insist are religion." But all in vain, for no scientific theory based on scripture has ever endured. He concluded by urging religion and science to cooperate "for justice against injustice; for right against wrong; for the living kernel of religion rather than the dead and dried husks of sect and dogma." [27]

Huxley and other scientists had been saying the same thing, or implying it, for many years, but the impact of *Warfare of Science* was the greater because White was an historian and not a scientist, and was known for his solid conservatism on other issues. Intelligent people were divided on the relationship between science and religion; totally opposite viewpoints could be found to be expressed even within the same periodical. In the January 1876 issue of *Presbyterian Quarterly and Princeton Review*, a reviewer praised *Science and Revelation: a Series of Lectures in Reply to the Theories of Tyndall, Huxley, Darwin, and Spencer*. Citing in particular Tyndall's Belfast lectures in 1874, which had "excited the abhorrence and detestation of Christendom," the reviewer felt that "an antidote was needed in that city where the poison was sown." Three months later, in the April issue, the Rev. William A. Halliday discussed "Theories of Labor Reform and Social Improvement" and leaned hard on Darwin to make this point: society advances but, as Darwin had shown, not all its members advance equally, and "the survival of the fittest is nothing the unfit can cheer about." The *Quarterly* did not join in the mud-slinging at Huxley during his visit, but the majority of its contributors, and presumably its board of editors, showed a marked hostility toward foreign ideas. A note in the October issue, for example, attributed the prejudice against sociology to its "popular attraction . . . for infidel authors, such as Comte, Buckle, John Stuart Mill, and Herbert Spencer." [28]

Centennial orthodoxy ignored one piece of scientific writing that was potentially more dangerous than some it did attack. It appeared in installments from October, 1875, to May, 1876, but the obscurity of both the journal, *Transactions of the Connecticut Academy*, and the author, Willard Gibbs, saved it from the condemnation heaped on Comte and Huxley. Gibbs, professor of mathematical physics at Yale, was as little in the public eye as a professor could be, and his lengthy paper, the first part of what later would be hailed as his monumental work on thermodynam ics, did not stir even scientific interest in 1876. Accepting the dual concept of infinity and eternity, Gibbs carefully and convincingly proved the indestructibility of matter and showed the relatedness of physical and chemical forces. All materials of life, he held, are mixtures and capable, with proper effort, of being scientifically managed, not only in scientific fields but also in the social sciences and the humanities. The implications of Gibbs' thesis are staggering: one is that in theology no area of possible investigation is exempt from scientific management; another is that crime, povery, and vice can, with the "proper effort," be efficiently controlled. A third implication was the most significant of all, that advancing knowledge might and probably someday would probe deep into the operations of what was called divine law. But at the moment nobody saw these implications, or even realized the more immediate applications of Gibbs's thinking to scientific matters.[29]

Myopic toward the growing urban problem, conservative Protestants also wore blinders regarding the human issues called into question by the Civil War and its aftermath. Most Southern Protestants accepted without question the inferiority of Negroes as a race, and saw it as a manifestation of divine intent. At one time, Southern churches commonly had galleries for the slaves and free Negroes, but gradually the Negroes had formed their own churches, a change that both races liked. Abolitionist behavior before the war, and the efforts of Northern idealists after peace was restored to give Negroes rights and privileges equal to those of the whites, were viewed in the South as heretical. The feeling was often intense, and it widened the breach between Southern and Northern branches of the same churches. One Southerner, irritated by the aggressive behavior of Northern Methodist clergymen in the South, expressed what was no doubt a widespread attitude: "There is no use of a hell if such damn rascals are not sent to it." [30] A few Southerners were more magnanimous, and there is one story of a Negro, sometime during Reconstruction, entering a church and kneeling at the altar; it was a very tense moment until one man rose from his pew and knelt down beside him—the man being General Lee.[31]

Abolitionists had also been cordially disliked by conservative

Northerners, and the rank-and-file Protestant clergy had divided on the issue. But during the war, by simple band-wagon contagion, the majority of Northern clergymen claimed active participation in the pre-war movement to abolish slavery. Later, they almost universally hailed the Union victory as a victory of American Christianity over Southern infidelism and depravity, as spelled out not only in the South's defense of slavery but also in its resistance to the advance of industrialized economy, which God had willed. To a number of Northern Protestants, the post-war prostration of all classes in the South seemed a punishment richly deserved.

With opposing groups both firmly convinced that their ideas alone had divine approval, true Christian ideals of forgiveness and brotherhood had small chance. During and after the Civil War, the federal government had given specific help to the Northern churches, which, after all, were strong supporters of the federal position. The provision of military protection for Methodist bishops sent South during Reconstruction was a sure means of rousing great indignation among Southerners. So were the widely-publicized actions of the General Methodist Conference in Chicago, in 1868, to ensure the impeachment of Andrew Johnson; the delegates devoted half an hour of prayer to solicit God's help in the Congressional deliberation. In Washington, at the same time, a session of the African Methodists staged their own prayer-meeting tactics; but God, apparently, saw fit not to cooperate, for Johnson remained in office.

The separation of church and state has often enough in our history been ignored in practice. Active church support of a political party or clique, seems in retrospect, at least, venal and un-Christian; but churches in the South were no less loyal supporters of the Southern political view. It is a kind of consolation, perhaps, to learn that the same federal government that was highly partial to Northern Methodists was showing better wisdom in the matter of Christianizing the Indians. The Quakers in 1868 were given permission to deal with certain tribes, as a beginning of what has been called the "peace policy" which replaced military force with education under religious auspices and which described the Indians as wards of the nation. In 1869 Congress authorized the creation of a Board of Indian Commissioners to be nominated by the various churches. All the tribes were divided among twelve churches, for whatever educational work they might decide to do, on a contract basis with fixed remuneration from public funds. The Catholics felt they were assigned too few of the tribes and refused to cooperate, but in 1874 they established their own very effective Bureau of Catholic Missions. The drama of Custer's Last Stand is all too easily taken as a dominant symbol of Indian relations in 1876; but the quiet civilizing work of the churches extended to more fronts than the Army had to cope with.

This church work was, unfortunately, impeded by the opportunistic shenanigans of post traders abetted by agents in Washington, and advocates of Indian missions had to combat the stubborn myth, given fresh support by the great Sioux movement that crushed Custer, that Indians were savages without souls to redeem. J. Elliott Condit observed drily in the *Presbyterian Quarterly* that although the Presbyterians were administering in 1876 to thirty thousand Indians in eleven tribal missions, they were spending only a fifth as much money as spent in 1857, before the federal contracts were even thought of. More mission money, Condit noted, was being spent in the Orient than went to the Indians.[32] There were, of course, more Orientals, but another factor was the long-standing Protestant tradition favoring missionary work as far from home as possible. Heathens in the Far East, moreover, were posing no immediate threat to the expanding nation.

The Indians were not the only threat to the westward expansion of American institutions. To a great many orthodox Protestants, the Mormons in Utah were more dangerous. During 1876 the Supreme Court was considering what action, if any, to take in suppressing polygamy, which the Mormons practiced in their belief that it had been authorized through divine revelation. Radicals and conservatives alike, however, within the older churches, were united in their opposition to the very idea of plural marriage. Congress, goaded by general public outrage, had outlawed polygamy in 1862, but the Mormons had fought back. The Supreme Court, when the issue was finally forced upon its attention, took its time, and handed down its decision only in 1879, in *Reynolds* v. *United States*,[33] finding against polygamy. No other decision, probably, could have been made without the risk of a popular uprising. Other religious practices even stranger than polygamy, which at least had solid Biblical precedents, have gone undeterred by law, and it seems quite clear that the forced suppression of polygamy reflected the overwhelming opposition of the dominant orthodox. Public indignation, for example, was not similarly roused by the flagrant behavior of business entrepreneurs who had become laws unto themselves.

Part of the orthodox outrage stemmed, presumably, from the fact that the Mormons were becoming as successful, in material ways, as the pious members of conventional denominations. According to the Protestant Ethic, success was both the reward and the evidence for sufficient devotion to Christian principles. According to *The Elements of Political Economy* by the Rev. Francis Wayland, president of Brown University, hardly a new book but reprinted as late as 1875 and widely used as a college textbook, God had established the laws of economics and nobody should tamper with those laws. Wayland's support of free trade irritated the protectionists, who argued for high tariffs, but anybody who challenged his central thesis risked being branded as an infidel. If God did not approve of laissez-faire, why was He permitting its practitioners to be so prosperous? Even the law of supply and demand was thought, in this view, to be ordained by divine will.

Even Horace Bushnell supported laissez-faire, to the probable chagrin of Protestant radicals who did not realize that the New Theology, of which he was the first and most important advocate, prepared the way for the Social Gospel. Beginning with *Christian Nurture* in 1847, Bushnell wrote a number of influential books before he died in 1876, all of them whittling away at the tenets of Calvinism. His own Congregational Church came close to trying him for heresy, but ultimately, his careful, persuasive reasoning, especially in *Christ in Theology* (1851), persuaded the Congregationalists to abandon Calvin's stern logic. Bushnell's argument for the religious instruction of the young, in place of the long-standing reliance on conversion alone, was a giant step leading his followers in the direction of a belief in the innate *goodness* of man, rather than in his innate corruption.

Equally revolutionary was his view of the Atonement: that the sacrifice of Jesus was an expression of his essential *human* nature. Theology, gradually shifting to Bushnell's views, became increasingly humanistic—for that small member of the clergy, at least, who were trained in the respectable seminaries. God as an unyielding judge in the Calvinistic sense became instead a loving father, immanent and not transcendent.

People who did not close their minds to fresh ideas, such as the scientific hypotheses that were demolishing what remained of the medieval geocentric universe, were finding it ever harder to think of their planet, and their race, as all-important under God. In addition, the findings of Biblical scholarship in Europe challenged traditional interpretations of the Gospels and weakened the authority of the orthodox theology. One result of these trends was an effort to revive the idea of Christian brotherhood, long neglected in Protestant practice and in the Protestant emphasis on individuality that Calvin had urged as a way of undercutting Papal authority. Another result, equally slow to be recognized, was the abandonment of the notion of fixed social law. This New Theology did not directly produce the Social Gospel, but it did help provide the atmosphere in which the latter could develop. In 1876, however, the Social Gospel had as yet to wait until the newer generation of seminary-trained preachers replaced the old.

To the assorted critics of orthodoxy cited earlier may be added one more, the journalist Edward Bellamy. He came by his radicalism honestly: his father had been dismissed as too liberal by his Baptist congregation in Chicopee Falls, Massachusetts. The younger Bellamy, on the staff of the Springfield *Daily Union*, combined his father's idealism with his own skill as a reporter in attacking the conditions that kept social sores festering in New England mill towns. Bellamy was greatly attracted to both Emerson's concept of a friendly, harmonious universe and Comte's substitution of the human race for God. Living for others struck him as the highest goal. In reviewing Washington Gladden's *Working People and Their Employers*, on June 1, 1876, he stated his opinion that if the orthodox churches were to survive they would have to adopt both the New Theology and the Social Gospel—a prophecy more accurate, so far as can now be seen, than that of a totally socialized world envisioned in his famous novel *Looking Backward* (1888).[34]

In the decades since 1876, it is obvious, American Protestantism has not uniformly adopted either the New Theology or the Social Gospel, but both have widespread acceptance within the modern range of doctrine and practice. The growing acceptance, both inside and outside of the churches, of the doctrine that we *are* our brothers' keepers in a world increasingly interdependent, marks a vast change since 1876. The large number of Fundamentalists and the persistence of archaisms of dogma and ritual even in liberal congregations are proof that the New Theology has not won its struggle for complete acceptance. The Social Gospel, despite its later start, has had better success, although many of its implementations have been transferred by the churches to secular welfare agencies, both private and governmental. Few of these agencies existed in 1876; the prevailing Protestant opinion was not ready to admit the need for them. But it was almost ready to. In more ways than one, the Centennial Year was, if not the last stand of Protestant complacency, at least its high-water mark.

Too literal a reading of Genesis can never square with hypotheses of geological time, nebular space, and biological heritage; and as men become knowledgeable in science they commonly are brought face to face with a serious decision: whether to view Genesis as poetry or to abandon any church that enforces a literal interpretation. Yet no man can deny another man's right to believe what he wants to, so long as the belief leads to no behavior dangerous to the social peace. What the New Theology proposed on theoretical grounds, and the Social Gospel later sought to put into practice, was a kind of new literalness, or rather a shift of attention from the Old to the New Testament. Jesus Christ, a carpenter by trade, chose disciples from among the lowly and either rebuked the favored classes or declined to engage in their debates. His words, the great bulk of them, were directed toward the underprivileged and unsuccessful—encouraging words that Protestant orthodoxy in the 1870s seldom bothered to examine. The infinite worth of "even the lowliest of these, my brethren," squares with the democratic ideal of the rights and the dignity of each living individual.

Centennial Protestantism simply could not rise to this noble concept. In an age of unparalleled industrial growth and economic dislocation, churches filled with Christ's own compassion for the lowly might have done much to alleviate human misery. The record shows just the reverse.

AFTERWORD

It was not just another year; it was the Centennial. With the second centennial just ahead, we may expect that the nation will pause again to take stock, and we may wonder, how it will seem, those few years from now, not to a Centennial but to a Bicentennial American. Will there be new abuses of power, and will the people be divided? Will there still be a Southern Question? Will the arts be more integral a part of our living, religion a vital force for good, and education still in flux? Will we still seek the decent opinion of mankind?

The author is haunted by the words of T. H. Huxley, one day in Baltimore, and especially by the phrase which said that our sole safeguard "is the moral worth and intellectual clearness of the individual citizen." May this never sound archaic!

Footnotes for Chapter Twelve
A MIGHTY FORTRESS

1. Leng, *America in 1876.*

2. General studies of American religion include Anson Phelps Stokes, *Church and State in the United States,* 3 vols. (New York: Harpers, 1950); William Warren Sweet, *The Story of Religions in America* (New York: Harpers, 1930); and Henry F. May, *Protestant Churches and Industrial America* (New York: Octagon Books, 1949).

3. J. L. Diman, "Religion in America, 1776–1876," *North American Review,* 122 (Jan.–Apr., 1876), 1–47.

4. Archie Robertson, *That Old-Time Religion* (Boston: Houghton Mifflin, 1950).

5. Aaron Ignatius Abell, *The Urban Impact on American Protestantism, 1865–1900* (Cambridge: Harvard University Press, 1943).

6. *Ibid.*

7. Anecdote reported in Robertson, *That Old-Time Religion.*

8. Editorial exchanges in Elmira *Daily Advertiser*, Jul. 25, 1876; and John Lewis to his brother, Aug. 7, 1876, in Lewis Letters.

9. John Tracy Ellis, *American Catholicism* (Chicago: University of Chicago Press, 1956).

10. Beecher quoted in James Dombrowski, *The Early Days of Christian Socialism in America* (New York: Columbia University Press, 1936).

11. Beecher's income estimated in *Potter's American Magazine*, March 1876:

    Salary from Plymouth Church $20,000
    Salary as editor of Christian Union 10,000
    Lecture income 5,000
    Royalties from Life of Christ 10,000

    TOTAL $45,000

12. The Social Gospel has been amply reported in such books as Charles Howard Hopkins, *The Rise of the Social Gospel in American Protestantism 1865–1915* (New Haven: Yale University Press, 1940) and *The Social Gospel in America 1870–1920*, ed. Robert T. Handy (New York: Oxford University Press, 1966).

13. An exchange in 1958 illustrated these opposing notions: the case for unbroken Protestant enlightenment was asserted in Norman Cousins, *"In God We Trust," the Religous Beliefs and Ideas of the American Founding Fathers* (New York: Harpers, 1958), but was demolished in a review of that book by Perry Miller, New York *Times*, Apr. 6, 1958.

14. *Scribner's Monthly*, 12 (Aug., 1876), 600–601.

15. Stow Persons, *Free Religion: An American Faith* (New Haven: Yale University Press, 1947).

16. *The Fiftieth Anniversary of the Ethical Culture Movement* (New York: D. Appleton, 1926). Adler's breadth is suggested by an article he wrote about Buddhism, "A Prophet of the People," *Atlantic Monthly*, 37 (June, 1876), 674–89.

17. Moses Rischin, *The Promised City; New York's Jews, 1870–1914* (Cambridge: Harvard University Press, 1962).

18. Ellis, *American Catholicism*. Ellis calls Gibbons (p. 104) the "greatest single figure the Church in the United States has produced."

19. James A. Healy (1830–1900) was the son of an Irish immigrant,

owner of a prosperous Georgia plantation, and his mulatto wife, a former slave. Healy's brother Patrick was president of Georgetown, the nation's oldest Catholic university, from 1874 to 1882; three sisters became nuns. See Albert S. Foley, *Bishop Healy: Beloved Outcaste* (New York: Farrar, Straus and Young, 1954).

20. Abell, *The Urban Impact on American Protestantism.*

21. Randel, *Edward Eggleston: Author of the Hoosier School-Master* (New York: King's Crown Press, 1945), Chapter 12, "Creedless Church."

22. 4 vols., London: Longmans, Green and Co., 1875–77.

23. John Fiske, "The Unseen World," *Atlantic Monthly*, 37 (Feb., 1876), 170–181.

24. William Graham Sumner, "Politics in America, 1776–1876," *North American Review*, 122 (Jan.–Apr., 1876), 47–87.

25. Criticism of Huxley's lectures, quoted on various dates in Elmira *Daily Advertiser.*

26. "Mr. Huxley's Visit," *Scribner's Monthly*, 13 (Dec., 1876), 268–69.

27. Andrew D. White, *Warfare of Science* (New York: D. Appleton, 1876), pp. 8–10, 40, 63, 150–51.

28. "Contemporary Literature," *Presbyterian Quarterly and Princeton Review*, 5 (Jan., 1876), 173; Halliday's article, *ibid.*, 5 (Apr., 1876), pp. 425 ff.

29. Muriel Rukeyser, *Willard Gibbs* (Garden City: Doubleday, Doran, 1942).

30. Ralph E. Morrow, *Northern Methodism and Reconstruction* (East Lansing: Michigan State University Press, 1956), p. 237.

31. Robertson, *That Old-Time Religion*, p. 189.

32. J. Elliott Condit, "Our Indians and the Duty of the Presbyterian Church to Them," *Presbyterian Quarterly and Princeton Review*, 5 (Jan., 1876), 76–92.

33. Cited in Charles Warren, *The Supreme Court in American History*, rev. ed. (Boston: Little, Brown, 1926), p. 697, fn. 2. The Court maintained its position in several subsequent cases.

34. Joseph Schiffman, "Edward Bellamy's Religious Thought," *Publications of the Modern Language Association of America* (Sept., 1953), 716–32.

Bibliographical Note

SOURCES USED GENERALLY INCLUDE:

Statistical Abstract of the United States. First number, 1878. Prepared by the Chief of the Bureau of Statistics, Treasury Department. Washington: Government Printing Office, 1879.

Historical Statistics of the United States, Colonial Times to 1957; a Statistical Abstract Supplement. Prepared by the Unted States Bureau of the Census with the Cooperation of the Social Science Research Council. Washington: Government Printing Office, 1960.

Official Register of the United States, Containing a List of Officers and Employees in the Civil, Military and Naval Service, for 1877. (Issued biennially by the Department of the Interior.) Washington: Government Printing Office, 1877.

Adna Ferrin Weber, *The Growth of Cities in the Nineteenth Century: A Study of Statistics*. New York: Published for Columbia University by the Macmillan Company, 1899.

U. S. Centennial Commission, *International Exhibition, 1876. Reports*. 11 vols. Washington: Government Printing Office, 1880–84.

Appleton's Annual Cyclopedia and Register of Important Events of the Year 1876. (New Series: Vol. 1). New York: D. Appleton, 1877.

W. H. DePuy, *The People's Cyclopedia of Universal Knowledge.* 2 vols. New York: Phillips & Hunt, 1882.

The Encyclopedia of American Dates and Facts. Ed. Gorton Carruth and associates. New York: Crowell, 1956.

1876 issues of available magazines.

1876 files or microfilm of available newspapers.

PRIMARY SOURCES:

The John Lewis Papers, the Edward Eggleston Papers, the Andrew D. White Papers, the Ezra Cornell Papers, and other official records, at Cornell University; library records and Centennial Exhibition photographs and mementoes at Harvard University; the Folwell Papers at the Minnesota Historical Society; Memorabilia at the University of North Carolina; the Huxley Papers at the Imperial College, London; Brooks and Fiske Family Papers owned by Miss Margaret Fiske, Petersham, Massachusetts; family letters, diaries, and clippings owned by the author.

Index

Abbott, Ezra, 428
Abbott, Jacob, 350–51
Abilene, Kansas, 113
Adams, Charles Follen, 359
Adams, Charles Francis, Jr., 169–70, 215
Adams, Charles Kendall, 412–13
Adams, Henry, 236 *fn* 1, 314–15, 409, 411, 413, 415
Adams, Herbert Baxter, 414–15
Adams, President John, 5
Adams Express Company, 162
Adeler, Max, 359
Adler, Felix, 444–46, 449
Advertising, 30, 56, 57, 111, 189, 287, 382
Agassiz, Alexander, 63
Agassiz, Louis, 323, 411, 428
Agrarianism, 102, 123, 171
Agriculture, 48, 158, 419–20
Agriculture, Department of, 263
Alaska, 7, 122, 264
Alcott, Amos Bronson, 352, 369, 443
Alcott, Louisa May, 352
Aldrich, Thomas Bailey, 349, 354
Alger, Horatio, Jr., 185, 312–13, 359

Allegheny River, 42
American Association for the Advancement of Science, 64, 65, 66, 275, 401
American Book-Trade Association, 348
American Chemical Society, 413
American Christian Commission, 447
American Ephemeris and Nautical Almanac, 272
American Express Company, 162–63
American Historical Association, 415
American Journal of Medical Sciences, 5, 168, 326
American Library Association, 348, 425, 426
American literature, 17–18, 347, 348–62
American Medical Association, 325–26
Amherst College, 414, 415, 426
Amusements, 17, 51, 67–68, 328
Andersonville Prison, 242, 244, 245
Angell, James B., 415
Anglo-Americans, 11, 52, 84, 99, 137, 248
Anthony, Susan B., 315
Antioch College, 407

Anti-Saloon League, 311
Appalachian Mountain Club, 97
Appalachicola, Florida, 44
Appleton, William H., 61
Arbor Day, 275
Architecture, 33–34, 39, 50, 51, 52, 54, 91, 98, 138, 296–97, 337, 339, 364–74, 415–16
Arkansas, 110–11
Army Engineers, 262, 268–69, 271
Army posts and forts, 47, 48, 73, 74, 75, 127, 128, 129, 132, 211, 270
Art historians, 365 ff.
Arthur, Chester A., 279
Arthur, T. S., 314, 358
Astor, John Jacob, 18
Atlantic cable, 266
Atlantic City, N. J., 322–23
Atlantic Monthly, 98, 349–50
Avery, William, 203

Babcock, Col. Orville, 203 ff.
Baggage-checking, 50, 61
Baird, Henry C., 195
Baird, Spencer F., 265, 279
Baltimore, Maryland, 50, 101
Baltimore and Ohio Railroad, 164, 169
Bancroft, George, 10, 88, 441
Banks, 96
Barbed wire, 113, 140–41
Barnegat Bay, N. J., 41
Barnum, Phineas T., 327–28
Bascom, John, 415, 418
Baseball, 319–20
Battle, Kemp, 423
Battle Creek, Michigan, 318
Battle of the Little Big Horn, 129–34
Beale, Gen. Edward F., 144–45
Beecher, Rev. Charles, 45
Beecher, Rev. Henry Ward, 173, 434, 439–40, 446, 448, 461 fn 11
Belknap, William Worth, 207 ff., 270
Bell, Alexander Graham, 178–79, 186, 294, 402
Bellamy, Edward, 458–59
Belmont, August, 320, 321
Belmont, Perry, 135–36
Bennett, De Robigné Mortimer, 442
Bennett, James Gordon, 320
Bertie-Marriott, M., 328
Best-sellers, 76, 350, 390 fn 33
Beveridge, Albert J., 407
Bicycles, 79, 319
Bierstadt, Albert, 82, 384
Bigelow, John, 283

"Billy the Kid" (William H. Bonney), 145–46
Bishop, Nathaniel, 41–45, 87, 181
Bjornson, Bjornsterne, 406
Black Hills, 125, 126, 141
Blaine, James G., 217 ff., 242 ff., 253
Blue-laws; see Sabbatarianism.
Boat racing, 79, 302, 320–21
Bolles, Albert S., 175–76, 192, 345, 379
Boston, Mass., 39, 54, 63, 93, 389 fn 21
Boucicault, Dion, 314
Bowker, R. R., 346, 348, 426
Bowles, Samuel, 363
Bowling, 319
Boxing, 320
Boyton, Paul, 42
Bradley, Joseph P., 234
Brazos Bottom, Texas, 46, 144
Bridges, 330, 371
Bristow, Benjamin, 202 ff., 211, 220
British investors, 137–38
British universities, 411, 414
Brooklyn Bridge, 32, 70, 371
Brooks, Phillips, 434
Brownson, Orestes, 443
Bryant, William Cullen, 215, 216, 360–61, 363
Buchanan, President James, 405
Buck, Dudley, 291, 343, 353
Buffalo (bison), 71, 124
Buffalo, N. Y., 64
"Buffalo Bill" (William F. Cody), 132, 338
Bureau of Catholic Missions, 456
Bureau of Hydrography, 262
Burroughs, John, 370, 377, 378
Bushnell, Rev. Horace, 457–58
Business, 32, 35–36, 78, 96, 123, 137, 164, 170, 171, 175, 177, 186, 190–91, 302

"Calamity Jane" (Jane Canary), 147–48
Calhoun, John, 247
California, 38, 119–21, 264, 323–24, 401
Californios, 120
Cameron, J. Donald, 135, 253–54
Campbell, John L., 283–84
Canada, 57, 80, 122–23, 135–36, 158
Canal Ring, 206, 222
Canals, 161
Capital punishment, 97, 107, 114, 154 fn 1
Carnegie, Andrew, 198 fn 35, 424
Carpet sweeper, 316
Carpetbaggers, 55, 252, 255

Castle Garden, 329
Catholics, 435, 439, 441, 443, 444, 446–47, 449
Cattle, 46, 56, 121, 140–44
Cattle trails, 141
Census Bureau, 151
Centennial Commission (U. S.), 284–86, 300, 303, 400
Centennial Exhibition, 3–4, 6, 7, 10, 35, 70, 75, 82, 91–93, 102, 165–66, 186 ff., 228, 246, 261, 265, 275, 276, 283–304, 318, 327, 348, 351, 352, 353, 364 ff., 397, 399, 402, 438–39
Central Pacific Railroad, 117, 118, 164
Central Park, 21, 27, 28, 34, 53, 77, 87, 299, 380
Chamberlain, Daniel H., 227, 232, 253 ff., 259 fn 17
Chandler, William, 173–74, 227
Chandler, Zachariah, 150, 211, 224, 227–28
Chapel Hill, N. C., 101, 422
Chapman, A. W., 44
Charleston, W. Va., 101
Chase, Salmon P., 277
Chesapeake and Ohio Railroad, 55
Chicago, 33, 35–36, 41, 53, 57, 59, 77, 79, 81, 83–84, 100, 106–7, 109, 164, 169–70, 379–80
Chicago, Burlington and Quincy Railroad, 132
Child, Francis James, 410, 411
Chinese-Americans, 84
Chisolm, William Wallace, 255–56
Christian Labor Union, 447–48, 449
Christian Science, 438
Christian Union, 443, 447, 449
Christmas, 67 ff., 73–74, 76, 409
Churches, 21–22, 34, 36, 53, 71–72, 80, 81–82, 148–49; see Chapter 12.
Cincinnati, 2, 55–56, 105, 312
Cincinnati Southern Railroad, 371
City College of New York, 403, 416
Clemens, Samuel (Mark Twain), 15, 42–43, 59, 63, 89, 118, 161, 225–26, 228, 346, 347, 348–50, 351, 359, 360
Cleveland, 2, 105, 467
Clubs, 82, 137, 195
Clymer, Heister, 128, 210 ff., 234, 359
Coaching clubs, 78–79, 321–22
Coast Survey, 262, 264, 279
Coeducation, 20, 107, 406, 407
Cole, Timothy, 357
Collens, T. Wharton, 447
Colorado, 37, 115–16, 263–64
Colton, David, 174

Columbia River, 121
Columbia University, 428
Columbian Exposition (Chicago), 275
Columbus, Ohio, 105
Colwell, Stephen, 438
Comanche, 131, 132
Company towns, 138
Comstock, Anthony, 312–14
Comte, Auguste, 449–50, 453, 458
Condit, J. Elliott, 456
Coney Island, 68
Congress, 18, 123, 151, 174, 184, 195, 265, 267, 268, 284, 313, 347, 400, 455, 456
Conkling, Roscoe, 100, 217 ff.
Connecticut, 97, 310, 400
Connelly, Pierce Francis, 386
Conservation, 274–75
Constitution, 7–8, 246, 247–48, 263
Continental Sabbath, 435, 438
Cooper, Peter, 193, 195
Coordinate education, 407
Copyright, 346–47, 389 fn 28
Corliss engine, 293–94, 303–4, 374, 402
Cornell, Ezra, 404, 423
Cornell University, 72, 294, 319, 403–4, 405–8, 600, 617, 623
Courrier des États-Unis, 26
Cox, Samuel Sullivan ("Sunset"), 243–45
Cranch, Christopher, 63–64
Crawford, Capt. Jack, 132–33, 338
Cricket, 78, 137
Crime and criminals, 44, 110, 145, 162, 276, 302, 440
Croquet, 308, 319
Crystal Palace (London), 283, 372
Cummings, Rev. Dr., 6
Curtis, George W., 217, 220
Cushman, Charlotte, 354
Custer, Elizabeth (Mrs. George A.), 127
Custer, Lt.-Col. George A., 75, 89, 125–34, 147, 214, 253, 390 fn 36, 456
Custer City, Dakota Territory, 125, 132
Customs; see manners and customs.

Daly, Augustin, 314, 335–36
Dana, Charles A., 363
Dartmouth College, 453
Darwin, Charles, 411, 435, 451, 453
Darwinism, 59, 63, 443, 450 ff.
Daughters of the American Revolution, 10
Davidson, George, 264, 279

Davis, David, 233
Davis, Jefferson, 242–46
Davis, Rebecca Harding, 295
Deadwood, Dakota Territory, 141, 148, 149, 312, 338
Declaration of Independence, 3, 7–8, 301, 441
De Forest, John W., 348–49
Deism, 441, 442
Delaware, 101
Denominations, religious, 71–72, 90–91, 95, 436
Denver, 56, 87, 116
Detroit, 57
De Vinne, Theodore, 357
Dewey, John, 398, 429
Dewey, Melvil, 425–27, 428, 429
Dialect, 108
Dickens, Charles, 15
Dickinson, Emily, 355
Dime novels, 185, 312, 347–48
Dining cars, 56, 168, 317
Disasters, 26–27, 160–61, 168, 176, 267–68, 329–30, 372–73
Divorce, 314
Dobie, J. Frank, 143
Dodge, Mary Mapes, 357–58
Dodge City, Kansas, 143, 149–50, 312
Dom Pedro, Emperor of Brazil, 6, 31, 169, 291, 294–95, 301, 315, 416, 429, 437
Domestic life, 74, 75, 308–9
Draper, John W., 413
Drew, Daniel, 172–73, 186
Drink; see Food and Drink.
Drugs and medicine, 324–27
Duluth, Minnesota, 109

Eads Bridge, 37, 371
Eakins, Thomas B., 385
Earp, Wyatt, 149
Eastlake, Charles Locke, 368
Edison, Thomas Alva, 28, 178–79, 186
Education, elementary and secondary, 72–73, 95, 397–401
Education, higher, 20, 72, 95, 105, 106, 113, 114, 116, 120, 121, 401–25
Eggleston, Edward, ix–x, 23, 109, 348, 385, 448–49
Eight Hour League Convention, 448
El Paso, Texas, 45
Elevators, 295, 377
Eliot, Charles William, 401, 408–10
Elmira, New York, 164, 244, 245, 288, 337–38, 448
Elmira Prison Camp, 244–45

Elsie Dinsmore books, 359
Emerson, Ralph Waldo, 17, 306, 352, 355, 358, 366, 425, 430, 436–37, 440, 443, 458
Emma Mine, 138
Engineer Bureau; see Army Engineers.
Erie Railroad, 164, 172, 184
Ethical Culture, 438, 443–44
Evarts, William, 288, 301
Everett, Edward, 63

Fairmount Park, Philadelphia, 285, 287, 299; see also Centennial Exhibition
Faith in progress, 440
Farmers' markets, 316–17
Fashion and dress, 28, 29, 63, 74, 76, 106, 288, 308–9, 322
Faulkner, William, 46
Fernandina, Florida, 41
Ferrel, William, 272, 279
Ferry, Thomas W., 232, 315
Ferry boats, 34, 38, 50, 52, 70, 160
Field, Stephen, 278
Finance, 96, 171
Fire fighting, 35, 328–29
Fires, 175–76, 297, 302, 329–30
Fireworks, 3, 26, 302, 328
Fish, Hamilton, 205–6, 211, 213
Fisk University, 423–24
Fiske, John, 60, 63, 428–29, 450–51
FitzGerald, Emily (Mrs. Jenkins), 73–77, 87, 134, 194
Fitzgerald, F. Scott, 112, 377
Flagg, Wilson, 369–70
Florida, 44–45, 226 ff., 250–51, 257, 310, 322
Flour, 107, 161
Fogerty, William, 376
Folwell, William Watts, 395, 415, 419
Food and drink, 37, 43, 48, 52, 56, 57, 67, 68 ff., 82, 168, 288–89, 298–99, 316–19, 375, 438
Football, 319–20
Forestry, 274–75
Fort Lapwai, Idaho Territory, 75 ff.
Fort Lincoln, Dakota Territory, 127, 128–29, 132
Fort Smith, Arkansas, 115
Fort Stockton, Texas, 48
Fourth of July, 6–8, 26, 116, 187, 253, 315, 299–301, 423
Franklin, Benjamin, 294, 317
Free Religious Association, 443
French, Daniel Chester, 386

Frontier, 89 ff., 111–12
Frothingham, Octavius Brooks, 442–43
Fulton, Robert, 396

Gardiner Lyceum (Maine), 404–5
Garfield, James A., 195
Gelletti, Gen. Bartolomeo, 315
Geological Survey, 263
German universities, 411–13
German-Americans, 47, 70, 85 fn 7, 105, 109, 266, 340
Gibbons, James Cardinal, 446
Gibbs, Willard, 453–54
Gibbs, Wolcott, 411
Giedion, Siegfried, 365, 370
Gilman, Daniel Coit, 60, 101, 354, 400–3, 414, 418
Gladden, Washington, 19–20, 192–93, 458
Goddard, Martha, 407
Godkin, Edwin, 218
Goodyear, Charles, 182
Goshorn, Alfred, 188–89, 285, 303
Gould, Jay, 171–72, 177, 186, 327
Government organization, 262 ff.
Government Printing Office, 263
Graham, Sylvestre, 317
Grange (Patrons of Husbandry), 106, 277, 287, 419
Granger Cases, 106, 277–78
Grant, President Ulysses S., 2, 6, 10, 54, 116, 128, 169, 201 ff., 207 ff., 253–54, 257, 260, 261, 280, 290, 291, 296, 301, 303, 456
Grantism, 7, 40, 214, 215, 225, 227, 349
Gray, Asa, 63, 411
Gray, Elisha, 178–79
Great Atlantic and Pacific Tea Company, 316–17
Greeley, Horace, 123, 215
Greenbacks and Greenback Party, 75, 193, 194–95
Gulf Coast, 44 ff.

Halliday, Rev. William A., 453
Hammerstein, Oscar, 340
Hampden-Sydney College, 401
Hampton, Wade, 232, 251–54, 421
Handlin, Oscar, 91, 444
Harper's Magazine, 355–56
Harper's Weekly, 134, 189, 295, 298, 406–7
Harris, Joel Chandler, 363
Harris, William T., 395, 398, 413
Harrisburg, Pennsylvania, 100

Harte, Bret, 89, 349
Hartranft, Governor John F., 220, 290
Harvard, John, 396
Harvard University, 407, 408–11, 420, 424, 427–29
Hatton, Joseph, 77–84, 180, 337
Hauk, Minnie, 342
Hawaii, 123, 157–58, 210
Hawley, Gen. Joseph, 225, 285, 291, 301, 303, 315, 363, 438–39
Hawthorne, Nathaniel, 64, 356, 368, 440
Hay, John, 216–27, 357
Hayden, Ferdinand V., 263–64, 279
Hayden's Survey, 116, 263, 400
Hayes, Rutherford B., 36, 105, 220–36, 253, 302
Hayne, Paul Hamilton, 354
Healy, Bishop James A., 447, 461–62 fn 19
Hearn, Lafcadio, 357
Helen's Babies, 76, 78, 350, 360
Hell Gate, 70, 268–70
Hemingway, Ernest, 377
Hendricks, Thomas A., 221
Henry, Joseph, 265–267
Herne, James A., 336
Hewitt, Abram S., 182, 186, 192, 223
Hickok, James Butler ("Wild Bill"), 133, 146–47
Hill, Benjamin, 243–44
Hippodrome, 24, 70, 327, 340
Historiography, 10, 88
History, the teaching of, 10–11, 88
Holbrook, Stewart, 9
Holland, Josiah, 16–23, 26, 28, 32, 40, 50, 87, 313, 347, 355, 357–58, 360, 400, 452
Holly, H. Hudson, 369
Holly, Marietta, 360
Holmes, Oliver Wendell, 95, 411
Home Insurance Building, 371
Homer, Winslow, 386
Homestead Act (1862), 123
Hopkins, Johns, 423
Horse racing, 79–80, 321
Horses, 47, 48, 52, 80, 129, 150, 161, 169, 299, 302
Hot Springs Arkansas, 323
Hotels, 25–26, 33, 38, 51, 56, 58, 75, 119, 120, 292, 322–23
Hough, Franklin B., 274–75, 281 fn 21
House furnishings, 67, 74, 129, 309, 375, 377 ff.
House of Representatives, 127, 130, 209, 210, 219, 233, 241

Housing, 28, 50, 67, 74, 377–78
Houston, Texas, 45–47
Howells, William Dean, 6, 15, 92, 104, 225, 228, 290, 292, 293–94, 295, 296, 298, 314, 346, 349, 350, 355, 360, 362, 374, 375, 382, 400
Hoyt, John W., 399–400, 429
Hudson River, 61, 82
Hudson River School, 82, 384
Hunt, Richard M., 376–77
Hunting, 79, 124–25
Huntington, Collis, 174–75
Huntington, West Virginia, 55–56
Hutchinson, Anne, 442
Huxley, Nellie (Mrs. T. H.), 59–66, 87
Huxley, Thomas Henry, 21, 33, 59–66, 87, 97, 98, 104, 125, 266, 372, 402, 414, 415–16, 435, 450–52, 453, 460

"Ik Marvel"; see Donald Grant Mitchell.
Illinois, 36, 106–7
Illinois Industrial University, 401, 418
Immigrants, 11–12, 52, 91, 96, 192, 248, 437, 439, 444
Implements, 35, 38
Independence Hall, 300
Indian Territory (Oklahoma), 115, 153
Indiana, 106, 401
Indians, 31, 47, 48, 70–71, 74–76, 114, 125–26, 130–32, 263, 270–71, 354, 455–56
Ingersoll, Robert, 80–82, 218
Ingram, John S., 291
Insurance, 175–78
Intercollegiate academic contest, 406
Interior, Department of the, 126, 162
Interstate oratorical contest, 407
Inventions, 178–80
Iowa, 39, 401
Irish-Americans, 71, 96, 105, 109, 194

Jackson, Helen Hunt, 354–55
Jackson, Dr. James, 317
Jackson, William Henry, 279, 387
James, Henry, 349, 356–57
James, Jesse, 110, 111, 162
James, William, 411
Japanese, 287, 294, 299
Jefferson, Thomas, 5, 122
Jenney, William Le Baron, 371
Jerome, Leonard, 320, 321, 342
Jerome Park, 28, 79–80, 320
Jewell, Marshall, 211, 220, 226, 276

Jewett, Sarah Orne, 353
Jews, 26, 99, 444–46, 449
Johns Hopkins University, 60, 65, 121, 169, 395, 402–3, 422

Kane Arctic expedition, 262, 296
Kansas, 37, 113–14
Kansas City, Missouri, 56, 113
Kansas Pacific Railroad, 140, 164
Kellogg, Clara Louise, 341–42
Kellogg, John Harvey, 317–18
Kemper County, Mississippi, 255–56
Kent, Laura Ann, 407
Kentucky, 157–58, 401
Kimball, Fiske, 367
Kiowa Comanche Agency, 124
Kitchens, 315–16
Knott, Proctor, 219
Knoxville, Tennessee, 104
Kouwenhoven, John, 374
Ku Klux Klan, 102, 194, 229, 247 ff., 359–60

Labor, 19, 39–40, 96, 123, 175, 180, 181, 191–94, 308, 440, 448
Lacy, Charles, 419
La Follette, Robert M., 407
La Follette, Suzanne, 365
Laissez-faire, 7, 158, 193, 196, 273–74, 277, 278, 440, 441, 451, 457
Lamar, L. Q. C., 243–44, 246, 255, 258 ff.
Lampoon, 408
Land sales, 46, 97, 110, 112, 114, 120, 138, 257
Lanier, Sidney, 291, 353–54, 390–91 fn 43
Lansmanschafts, 445
Larkin, Oliver, 365
Lathrop, George Parsons, 356
Lathrop, Rose (Hawthorne), 63
Law and order, 40, 75–76, 97, 110, 120, 141, 145, 150
Leadville, Colorado, 77
Leclercq, Jules, 49–57, 337
Lee, Richard Henry, 301
Lee, Gen. Robert E., 454
Leng, John, 32–41, 42, 49, 53, 97, 99, 191, 434, 435, 446
Levin, David, 10
Lewis, Dr. Dioclesian, 311
Lewis, Ed, 70, 87
Lewis, John, 2, 66–73, 286–87, 289, 295, 297, 298
Liberal Republicans, 209, 215, 261
Libraries, 425–29
Library Journal, 425, 426–27

Library of Congress, 427
Lick, James, 264
Light-House Board, 262, 266
Lightning, 30, 63, 182–83, 337
Lilly, Col. Eli, 325
Lincoln, Abraham, 36, 106, 224, 225, 240, 247, 290, 405
Little Rock, Arkansas, 111
Lobbying, 173–75
Locke, David Ross ("Petroleum Vesuvius Nasby"), 359
Lodge, Henry Cabot, 236 *fn* 1, 411
Long Branch, New Jersey, 323
Longfellow, Edith, 63
Longfellow, Henry Wadsworth, 18, 351, 352, 355, 411
Louisiana, 122, 230–32
Lowell, James Russell, 241, 257, 258 *fn* 1, 349, 355, 411, 429
Lumbering, 109, 274

Machinery, 106, 172, 294, 374–75
Macleish, Archibald, 45
Magazines, 82, 346, 353, 362
Maine, 68, 97, 108, 399
Manifest Destiny, 90, 123
Mann, Horace, 398, 407
Manners and customs, 27, 40, 54, 56, 57, 78, 64, 67 *ff.*, 83, 308–10
Manufacturing, 70, 103
Mark Twain; *see* Samuel Clemens
Marriage behavior, 57–58
Marsh, Caleb, 210
Marsh, George P., 274, 278
Marsh, Othniel, 61–62, 125, 402, 451
Martin, Henry Newell, 414
Maryland, 101
Massachusetts, 92, 95–97, 401
Massachusetts Agricultural College, 420
Massachusetts Institute of Technology, 397, 417, 420
Masterson, Bat, 149
McCabe, James, 293, 301
McCloskey, James Cardinal, 446
McDonald, Gen. John, 203 *ff.*
McDowell, Tremaine, ix
McGuffey readers, 88
McKee, William, 206
Meat-packing, 35–36, 55–56, 139
Mechanic arts, 395, 397, 421
Melville, Herman, 16, 273, 352, 356
Memphis, Tennessee, 104
Men, 27, 39, 51, 57, 87, 399
Merrimack River, 95
Mexico, 122–23, 158

Michigan, 106
Michigan State University, 418
Mining, 106, 117, 119, 125, 137–39, 161, 181–82
Minnesota, 3, 108–110, 381
Minority groups, 12, 52, 56
Minstrel shows, 337–39
Mission churches, 449
Mississippi, 296
Mississippi River, 42–43, 45, 46, 161
Missouri, 36, 107, 441
Mitchell, Donald Grant ("Ik Marvel"), 15, 295, 298
Mitchell, Dr. S. Weir, 326
Mollie Maguires, 193–94
Money, 38, 53, 75, 102, 194–95, 221, 289, 335, 388 *fn* 1
Montana, 142
Moody, Rev. Dwight L., 21, 434
Moody and Sankey, 1–2, 24, 36, 70
Moore, Julia A., 358–59
More, Thomas, *Utopia*, 181
Moran, Thomas, 264–65, 384
Morgan, Lewis Henry, 135
Mormons, 38, 58, 117–18, 338, 350, 434, 435, 441, 448, 456–57
Morrill, Justin, 213, 405
Morrill Land-Grant Act (1862), 213, 395, 404 *ff.*, 418, 419
Morris, Charles D., 414
Morris, Clara, 83, 336
Morse, Samuel F. B., 385, 396
Morton, Oliver P., 220, 235
Mulligan, James, 219
Mumford, Lewis, 365, 378–79, 387
Munn v. *Illinois*, 277–78, 281 *fn* 23
Museums, 383–84
Music, 24, 82, 291, 294, 298, 300, 303, 304, 305 *fn* 8, 339–46, 353, 424, 434, 436
Musical instruments, 345–46
Myers, Gustavus, 9

Nashville, Tennessee, 65
National Academy of Art and Design, 384, 385, 394 *fn* 104
National Commission of Education, 400
National Education Association, 400
National Labor League of America, 193
National Liberal League, 441
National Museum, 265–66
National Woman Suffrage Association, 315
Nautical Almanac Office, 272

Naval Observatory, 272
Navy, 159, 271–72, 296
Navy Department, 262, 271–73
Nebraska, 38–39, 113
Negroes, 11–12, 26, 48, 50, 54, 71, 101–2, 103, 136–37, 229, 250 ff., 257, 294, 382, 399, 421, 423, 439, 447, 454
Nevada, 118–19
Nevins, Allan, 9, 159, 185, 214
New England, 94–99, 102–3, 108, 109
New Hampshire, 96
New Haven, Connecticut, 61–63
New Jersey, 148, 167
New Orleans, 43, 55
New Theology, 457–59
New Year's, 1–3, 67–68, 200, 424
New York, 99–100
New York Central Railroad, 99, 165, 184
New York City, 2, 21, 25, 27 ff., 34, 51 ff., 68 ff., 71, 81, 82, 93, 100, 445
New York Custom House, 2, 273
New York *Herald*, 3, 27, 33, 267, 294
New York Philharmonic Orchestra, 343
New York *Tribune*, 52, 61, 267, 372
New York University, 413
New York *World*, 62
Newcomb, Simon, 262, 272, 279, 420–21
Newspapers, 11, 362–64
Newton, Lt.-Col. John, 268–69
Niagara Falls, 24, 26, 30, 31, 57, 58, 65, 348
Noble Savage, 31, 126
Non-denominational churches, 403–4, 449
North American Review, 236–37 *fn* 1, 436
North Carolina, 101
Northern Pacific Railroad, 125, 164
Northfield, Minnesota, 110, 111
Norton, Gen. Charles B., 283–85
Norwich Academy, 405
Nursing, 326

Offenbach, Jacques, 24–32, 34, 50, 59, 290, 298, 340–42, 343
Ohio, 105
Ohio River, 42
Oklahoma; *see* Indian Territory
Old Blue, 143
Olmsted, Frederick Law, 380–81
Omaha, Nebraska, 113
Oneida Community, 58, 72
Opera, 119, 340–42

Oregon, 38, 115, 121, 232, 364, 401
Oscar, Prince of Sweden, 301, 439

Pacific Mills, 39, 97, 191
Paine, John Knowles, 63–64, 291, 343
Paine, Thomas, 442
Painting and paintings, 82, 134, 382–86
Palladio, Andrea, 368
Paris Exposition (1867), 181, 283
Parker, Judge Isaac, 115, 145
Parker, Theodore, 437–38, 443
Parkman, Francis, 411
Parrington, Vernon Louis, 275
Patrons of Husbandry; *see* Grange
Paxton, Joseph, 372
Pecos River, 48
Peirce, Benjamin, 279, 411
Peirce, Charles Sanders, 411
Peirce, James Mills, 411
Penn, William, 51
Pennsylvania, 100, 284, 310
Pennsylvania Railroad, 160, 165, 184
Petersham, Massachusetts, 63
Petroleum, 182–85
Pettit & Wilson, 365, 372
Phi Beta Kappa Society, 401, 405
Philadelphia, 1–2, 4, 39, 50–51, 66 ff., 87, 93, 100, 160, 284, 287, 290, 311–12, 376, 381
Philadelphia and Reading Railroad, 165–66, 194
Philanthropy, 312, 314, 396, 416
Photography, 387
Pierrepont, Edwards, 205
Pinchot, Gifford, 275
Pinkerton Agency, 194, 331
Pinkham, Lydia E., 324–25
Pittsburgh, 39, 42, 100
Poe, Edgar Allan, 17–18, 361
Polo, 320
Pomeroy, Jesse ("the Boston Boy Fiend"), 348
Poor Whites, 11
Popular music, 41, 60, 63, 129, 134, 255, 311, 325, 331, 343, 345–46
Population, 93–94, 100, 151–52
Portland, Maine, 41
Portland, Oregon, 38, 74, 75
Post Office Department, 266, 273, 276, 296, 313
Powers, Hiram, 386
Presidential campaign, 36, 116, 214–26
Preventive medicine, 327
Princeton University, 435
Progressive education, 395, 398
Prohibition, 97, 114, 136, 310–11

Public health, 312
Publisher's Weekly, 346, 426
Publishing, 98, 346 *ff.*
Pulitzer, Joseph, 363
Pullman, George M., 168–69, 327
Puritan Ethic (Protestant Ethic), 18, 40, 357, 396, 416, 437, 457

Quakers, 118, 402, 455
Quarterly Review, 8

Railroads, 46, 56, 96–97, 107, 113, 115, 118, 121, 124, 159–63, 171, 267, 295, 322, 370–71
Railroads, elevated, 327
Randall, Samuel, 234, 235, 241–42, 245
Reconstruction, 12, 101–2, 223, 224, 229, 240–42, 247 *ff.*, 259 *fn* 20, 422, 455
Regionalism, 102–4
Rehan, Ada, 83
Reid, John C., 227
Reid, Whitelaw, 351, 357, 363
Religion, 21, 76, 80–82, 148, 173; *see also* Chapter 12.
Religious radicalism, 442 *ff.*
Remsen, Ira, 414
Resorts, 109, 322–24
Restaurants, 22–23, 25–26, 34, 69, 168, 298
Revenue Cutter Service, 273
Revivals, 435, 436
Richardson, H. H., 367
Ripley, George, 443
River boats, 161, 162, 183, 345
Roads and streets, 21, 27, 38, 103, 171, 286, 287, 290, 300, 304, 327
Robert's Rules of Order, 271
Roberts, Howard, 386
Robeson, George, 205, 211
Rockefeller, John D., 165, 184–86, 377, 396, 424
Roe, Rev. Edward Payson, 358
Rogers, E. H., 448
Rogers Groups, 129, 386–87
Ross, Charles, 330–31, 335, 340
Rowing, 319
Rowland, Henry Augustus, 414
Rubber, 182
Rural life, 308, 437
Ruskin, John, 77, 366
Russian Orthodox Church, 74

Sabbatarianism, 25–26, 52–53, 69, 81, 103, 166, 288, 308, 438
Saint-Gaudens, Augustus, 385, 386
St. Lawrence River, 41

St. Louis, Missouri, 36, 56, 107, 113, 203–5
St. Paul, Minnesota, 3–4, 160
St. Paul *Pioneer Press*, 1, 2–3, 109
Salt Lake City, Utah, 38, 58, 117
Saltonstall, Leverett, 300
Salvation Army, 449
Samantha books, 360
San Francisco, 33, 34, 38, 120–21, 160, 264, 339
Sankey, Ira D., 346; *see also* Moody and Sankey.
Saratoga, New York, 33, 63, 87, 321, 322
Scalawag, 255
Schurz, Carl, 206, 208, 210, 215–16, 224–25, 275
Schwarzmann, Herman J., 365, 372
Scott, Tom, 174, 184–85
Scribner's Monthly, 16
Scully, Vincent J., Jr., 367
Sculpture, 129, 382, 386–87
Seattle, 122
Secret Service, 276
Seelye, Julius H., 134, 415
Seligman, Joseph, 446
Senate, United States, 212–13, 232
Sennett, Mack, 312
Seward, William H., 123
Shakers, 58, 72, 379, 442
Shaler, Nathaniel Southgate, 411
Sheep, 121, 142, 144–45
Sheridan, Gen. Philip H., 126, 128, 134, 135, 278
Sherman, Gen. William Tecumseh, 124, 126, 128, 228, 254, 270, 278, 301
Shingle style, 367
Shipping, 158–61, 173, 267
Shoes, 182
Shorthand, 426
Sibley, John L., 428
Signal Bureau (or Signal Service), 262, 267, 271, 296
Simpson, Bishop Matthew, 291, 436
Sioux Indians, 124 *ff.*
Sitka, Alaska, 73–74
Sitting Bull, 71, 126, 127
Skating, 319
Sleeping and parlor cars, 31, 37, 50, 61, 111, 168–69, 294
Smalley, George W., 61
Smith, Joseph, 441
Smith, Walter, 374
Smith College, 407
Smithsonian Institution, 263, 265–67, 276, 284, 400

Sneak-box, 41 *ff*.
Social Gospel, 436, 447, 457–59
Society of American Artists, 385
Sousa, John Philip, 340
South, The, 11, 12, 55, 91–93, 101–4, 137, 171, 209, 224, 246, 353, 399, 421–23
South Carolina, 101–2, 231–32, 251–52, 253
Southern Homestead Act (1866), 257
Southern Pacific Railroad, 64, 120, 164, 174
Southern Railroad and Steamship Co., 170–71
Southern universities, 421–24
Southworth, Mrs. E. D. E. N., 358
Spencer, Cornelia, 422
Spencer, Herbert, 21, 158, 414, 451, 453
Spiritualism, 173
Spoils System, 40
Sports, 78–80, 308–9, 319–22
Spreckels, Claus, 157–58
Springfield, Illinois, 36, 106
Squibb, Dr. Edward Robinson, 325
Standard time, 409
Stanton, Elizabeth Cady, 315
Steamboats, 37, 43, 115, 129, 159–61, 292
Stedman, Edmund Clarence, 132, 355
Steel and iron, 167, 181, 370 *ff*.
Stewart, A. T., 99
Stockton, Frank R., 359
Stockyards, 35–36, 57
Stoddard, Richard Henry, 361
Story, William Wetmore, 386
Stowe, Harriet Beecher, 322, 448
Strauss, Johann, 389 *fn* 21
Streetcars, 27, 30, 83, 292
Streets; *see* Roads and Streets.
Sullivan, Louis, 373
Sumner, Charles, 243
Sumner, William Graham, 451
Sunday schools, 448–49
Supreme Court, 100, 114, 276–78, 456
Sylvester, James Joseph, 414
Swinburne, Algernon, 355
Symphony orchestras, 340, 343

Taft, Alphonso, 217
Taft, William Howard, 217
Taine, Hippolyte, 385
Tallahassee, Florida, 227
Tallmadge, Thomas E., 365, 366–67, 368

Taylor, Bayard, 17, 288, 301, 351, 353, 354, 390–91 *fn* 43
Taylor, Col. Nathaniel Alston, 45–49, 87, 136
Technical institutes, 396
Telegraph, 70, 179
Telephone, 178–80, 294–95
Temperance, 20–21, 40, 133
Tennessee, 104, 266
Tennis, 308, 319
Territories, 150–52
Terry, Gen. Alfred H., 127, 128, 130, 131
Texas, 45–49, 70, 87, 114–15, 120, 377–78
Texas and Pacific Railroad, 174
Texas Western Railroad, 46
Theatrical productions, 29–30, 59, 82–83, 314, 335–40
Theatres, 24, 29–30, 51, 58–59, 82–83, 330, 335, 337–41
Thomas, Julia, 406–7
Thomas, Theodore, 290, 298, 342–43
Thomasville, Georgia, 322
Thoreau, Henry David, 109, 188–89, 274
Thyng, Rev. Stephen H., Jr., 449
Tiffany, Louis, 337, 385
Tilden, Harriet, 379–80, 406
Tilden, Samuel Jones, 36, 100, 221–36
Tobacco and smoking, 288–89, 309–10
Tocqueville, Alexis de, 15
Toledo, Ohio, 167
Tourgée, Albion, 102, 360
Toutain, Paul, 57–59
Track, 319
Trains, 31, 37, 38, 50, 55, 61, 110–11, 116–17, 295, 375
Transcendentalism, 442–43
Treasury Department, 262
Trollope, Mrs. Frances, 15
Tunnels, 70, 97
Turner, Frederick Jackson, 139
Tweed Ring, 18, 206, 222
Tyndall, John, 21, 414, 435, 453
Typewriter, 180, 294

Union Pacific Railroad, 113, 117, 138, 140, 141, 164, 172, 173–75, 219
Unitarians, 443
U. S. Coast Guard Academy, 273
U. S. Military Academy, 272–73, 284
U. S. Naval Academy, 272–73
University of California, 120, 417–18
University of Cincinnati, 416
University of Florida, 250

University of Georgia, 418
University of Kansas, 132
University of Michigan, 404, 413, 418
University of Minnesota, 395, 419–20
University of North Carolina, 101, 422–23
University of South Carolina, 421
University of Wisconsin, 418–19
Upton, Emory, 270
Utah, 117–18, 151
Utensils, 35, 42, 68

Vanderbilt, Commodore Cornelius, 18, 99, 169, 170, 172–73, 423
Vanderbilt University, 423
Vaux, Calvert, 368, 380
Vehicles, 27, 28, 38, 79, 117, 129, 293–94, 312, 383
Velocipedes, 319
Veterinary medicine, 327
Vice, 84, 110, 121, 139, 140, 148–50, 297, 311–12, 339, 440
Vicksburg, Mississippi, 16
Violence, 40, 194, 232–33, 284 ff.
Viollet-le-Duc, Eugene, 369
Virginia, 101
Virginia and Truckee Railroad, 118
Virginia City, Nevada, 38, 118–19, 133
"Virginius" affair, 272

Wabash College, 284
Wagner, Richard, 24, 29, 288, 291, 341, 343
Wagon freighting, 161–63, 183
Waite, Morrison, Chief Justice, 205, 220, 236, 277–78
Walker, Francis A., 19, 189–90, 191–92
Walking, 41–42, 79, 81
War Department, 126 ff., 209, 262, 270–71
Warner, Charles Dudley, 349, 389–90 fn 30
Washington, George, 5, 91, 288, 296, 382
Washington Territory, 38, 122
Washington, D. C., 2, 39, 54

Water supply, 35, 170, 312, 326
Wayland, Rev. Francis, 457
Weather, 52, 54, 57, 107, 109, 144, 187, 218, 226, 267–68, 289, 290, 299, 300, 303, 337, 372
Wellesley College, 407
Wells Fargo, 161–62
Welsh, John, 190, 285, 291, 305
West Virginia, 101
Western Union, 61, 179, 371–72, 377, 404
Weston, Edward, 41–42
Wheeler, William A., 36
Whipple, Edwin P., 356
Whiskey Ring, 22 ff.
White, Andrew D., 195, 400, 401, 403–5, 414, 418, 419, 447, 452–53
Whitman, Walt, 14, 16, 17, 132, 185–86, 342, 351–52, 356, 357–58, 361, 387, 390 fn 36
Whitney, Josiah, 411
Whittier, John Greenleaf, 291, 307
Wild animals, 44, 48–49, 124, 129, 144
Wilson, Bluford, 205–6, 226
Winsor, Justin, 426, 428
Wirz, Capt. Henry, 242–44
Wisconsin, 107, 310
Woman suffrage, 20
Women, 27, 28, 50, 51, 57, 58, 79, 107, 147–48, 150, 314–16, 399, 431 fns 14 and 16
Women's Christian Temperance Union, 311, 449
Women's Centennial Union, 288
Wood engraving, 387
Workingmen's Party, 193
Wyoming, 37, 141–42

Yale University, 400, 424, 427
Yellow fever, 326–27
Yellowstone National Park, 263
Youmans, Edward L., 60
Young, Brigham, 38, 85, 117, 338
Young Men's Christian Association, 313, 447
Young Women's Christian Association, 447

THE AUTHOR

William Peirce Randel, director of English graduate study at the University of Maine, has also taught
at Minnesota, Missouri, Florida State, Duke, Wyoming, and on foreign assignment in Helsinki, Athens, Jamaica, and Bologna. New York born, with a
Columbia doctorate, Randel is an authority on the
Hoosier realist Edward Eggleston. His most recent
book is *Ku Klux Klan: A Century of Infamy*,
which has appeared in six foreign editions. He
maintains a homestead at Waterboro Old Corner
in the heart of Maine's York County, where he
experiments in naturalistic landscaping and the suppression of woodchucks.